CHRISTIAN GLOBALISM AT HOME

Christian Globalism at Home

CHILD SPONSORSHIP IN THE UNITED STATES

Hillary Kaell

PRINCETON UNIVERSITY PRESS
PRINCETON AND OXFORD

Published by Princeton University Press
41 William Street, Princeton, New Jersey 08540
6 Oxford Street, Woodstock, Oxfordshire OX20 1TR

press.princeton.edu

Library of Congress Cataloging-in-Publication Data

Names: Kaell, Hillary, author.
Title: Christian globalism at home : child sponsorship in the United States / Hillary Kaell.
Description: Princeton : Princeton University Press, [2020] | Includes bibliographical
    references and index.
Identifiers: LCCN 2020001403 (print) | LCCN 2020001404 (ebook) | ISBN 9780691201450
    (hardback ; alk. paper) | ISBN 9780691201467 (paperback) | ISBN 9780691201474 (ebook)
Subjects: LCSH: Poor children—Services for—Developing countries. | Church charities—
    United States. | Public welfare—Religious aspects—Christianity. | Church work with poor
    children—Developing countries. | Globalization—Religious aspects—Christianity.
Classification: LCC HV804 K34 2020 (print) | LCC HV804 (ebook) | DDC 362.7/7569091724—dc23
LC record available at https://lccn.loc.gov/2020001403
LC ebook record available at https://lccn.loc.gov/2020001404

British Library Cataloging-in-Publication Data is available

Editorial: Fred Appel and Jenny Tan
Production Editorial: Leslie Grundfest
Production: Brigid Ackerman
Publicity: Kate Hensley; Kathryn Stevens, UK
Copyeditor: Karen Verde

Jacket art: Handprint, Michael Burrell / Alamy Stock Photo; Silhouette of United States,
Ted Grajeda / Noun Project

The author expresses appreciation to the Schoff Fund at the University Seminars
at Columbia University for their help in publication. The ideas presented have benefited
from discussions in the University Seminar on Religion in America

This book has been composed in Adobe Text and Gotham

Printed on acid-free paper. ∞

Printed in the United States of America

10 9 8 7 6 5 4 3 2 1

CONTENTS

ABBREVIATIONS

All other publication titles and organization names are written in full.

ARCHIVES

ABCFM	American Board of Commissioners for Foreign Missions Archives, 1810–1961 ABC 1–91, Houghton Library, Harvard University, Cambridge, MA
BAA	Boston Athenæum Archives, Boston, MA
BGCA	Billy Graham Center Archives, Wheaton, IL
CFA	ChildFund Archives, Richmond, VA
CIA	Compassion International Archives (unprocessed), Colorado Springs, CO
GCAH	General Commission on Archives and History, United Methodist Archives Center, Madison, NJ
HIA	Hoover Institution Archives, Stanford University, Palo Alto, CA
HUA	Harvard University Archives, Cambridge, MA
LEC	Papers of Mrs. Leland E. Cofer, Hoover Institution Archives, Stanford University, Palo Alto, CA
NER MRL 2	Near East Relief Committee Records, The Burke Library Archives, Columbia University Libraries, at Union Theological Seminary, New York, NY
UA	Unbound Archives (unprocessed), Kansas City, MO
UNDA	University of Notre Dame Archives, South Bend, IN
UVL	Special Collections, University of Virginia Library, Charlottesville, VA
WBMR MRL 12	Women's Board of Missions Records, The Burke Library Archives (Columbia University Libraries) at Union Theological Seminary, New York, NY
WDG	Records of the Women's Division of the General Board of Global Ministries, United Methodist Archives Center, Madison, NJ
WVIA	World Vision International Archives, Monrovia, CA

ORGANIZATIONS

ABCFM	American Board of Commissioners for Foreign Missions
CCF	Christian Children's Fund
FCF	Fatherless Children of France
NER	Near East Relief
OCC	Operation Christmas Child
WFMS	Woman's Foreign Missionary Society (Methodist Episcopal Church)
WV	World Vision

PUBLICATIONS

CC	*Christian Century*
CEM	*Child Evangelism Magazine*
CT	*Christianity Today*
HWF	*Heathen Woman's Friend*
MH	*Missionary Herald*
NYT	*New York Times*
WVM	*World Vision Magazine*

BRIEF NOTE ABOUT LANGUAGE

When discussing nineteenth-century sources, I use emic terms for mission stations and colonies (e.g., Foochow or Ceylon), as well as their English transliterations of foreign names. When discussing organizations, I refer to CCF by its mid-century initials, unless I am talking about ChildFund today. By contrast, I call Unbound by its current name, rather than the Christian Foundation for Children (1981–1987) or the Christian Foundation for Children and Aging (1988–2014), because I worked more closely with contemporary sponsors. The same applies to Compassion, which was the Everett Swanson Evangelistic Association until 1963.

Although the terminology is clunky, I use "conservative" and "liberal" to refer to U.S. Christians' ideological (and often political) commitments. I use these terms sparingly and only in particular contexts. Likewise, the terms "evangelical" and "mainline" are complicated; they are historically imprecise, and relatively few U.S. Christians use these words in everyday speech to refer to themselves. They are further complicated in the United States today by a deeply divisive two-party political system and because many Americans "church switch" over their lifetimes and consume religious media from multiple sources at once. I identify individual sponsors by church affiliation when possible and by the organizations they choose to support. When I refer to people as "evangelical," I do so based on these and other markers, such as being born-again. I also thought quite a bit about the word "America," which residents of the United States often use to refer to their country, although it more accurately encompasses North and South America as a whole. I use "U.S." most often, but for readability I sometimes use "American" as an adjective, including in reference to U.S. people.

Last, I have chosen not to correct orthography or insert [*sic*] in the letters and conversations I quote, unless the meaning is obscured. Otherwise, I prefer to let people speak for themselves.

CHRISTIAN GLOBALISM AT HOME

INTRODUCTION

How shall we dare to speak of distance, near or far,
To Him who swung the spheres to roll in rhythmic grace . . .
His thoughts are not as ours,—our narrow thoughts of space.
And, looking down from heaven, "Home" and "Foreign" are one.

—Mrs. M'Vean-Adams, Methodist laywoman,
   Mound City, Kansas, 1892

The earth is the Lord's, and everything in it,
the world, and all who live in it.

—Psalm 24

The United States looms large in studies of globalization. Scholars have coined terms like "McWorld" or "Fundamentalist Americanism" to describe its influence, including the spread of its Christianity.[1] America—its promise and its problems—has loomed so large, in fact, that comparatively few studies have closely examined how U.S. Christians themselves make and imagine global forms. And those that do generally converge around people who travel—missionaries, statesmen, pastors, migrants, or (in my own earlier work) tourists and pilgrims.[2] Yet here is the thing: most Americans do not fall into those categories, at least not most of the time. Statistically speaking, about 40% of U.S. people have a passport and perhaps two-thirds have left the country at some point, but this travel is irregular and mainly within North America, the Caribbean, and Western Europe.[3] So if we want to know something about how globalization works *within* U.S. Christianity, we are left with a question: how do Christians imagine and experience the world in conditions of relative immobility?

   This book responds by tracing how "Christian globalism" is made. The term is shorthand for a cluster of ideas, cultural forms, structures of feeling, and social connections that at a very basic level emerge from the understanding that the Christian God encompasses all human beings as their creator and eventual judge. All forms of globalism, Christian or otherwise, take shape within specific societal frameworks and institutional structures.[4] With that in mind, I focus on one site in particular: child sponsorship programs in the United States. This fund-raising model, which began in Protestant missions two centuries ago and then spread to NGOs, is familiar in North America and Europe. It requests a defined yearly or monthly amount to aid a foreign child, with some promise of communication between donors and recipients. Today, most sponsorships cost about $40 a month, and an estimated 9 million children are supported worldwide.

Sponsorship is a good vantage point from which to address the "immobile global" since less than 1% of U.S. sponsors actually meet the child they support.[5] It nurtures a kind of globalism that happens here and there, at odd times and at home. At the same time, sponsors participate in an enterprise that is arguably the most profitable private Christian fund-raising tool today, circulating billions of dollars and millions of letters and photos around the globe every year. It expresses and champions some of Christianity's "biggest world-making dreams and schemes."[6] This world-making—its hopes and limitations—is the subject of my study.

*   *   *

When U.S. Christians engage globally, they aspire to universalism.[7] This vision understands all people as created by a single God who became immanent in the form of Jesus, an anointed teacher whose death and resurrection has worldwide relevance. It usually implies a Christian teleology, although not always; the most liberal of those with whom I worked described a "Force" that unites human beings and spoke only vaguely of a divine plan for the world. Regardless, at root it insists there is some sort of oneness—or potential oneness—in the human condition. Christian aspirations in this regard are not unique: Muslims may interpret *tawhid* as a form of unity that extends from Allah to all human life; Hindu nationalists promote *sanatana dharma* as a universal truth, while elites may view *Brahman* as all-encompassing reality. Oneness ideologies buoy many other endeavors from humanitarianism to Communism, international law to advertising to ecological activism.[8] Such "totality concepts" have no indexical relation to what they signify. In other words, one cannot unambiguously point to Christian globalism or display it, and this plasticity is highly effective since "abstraction and generality can capture and digest . . . unanticipated ideas and actions."[9] However, abstraction also poses a major challenge to the practical reality of human lives.

This book tracks globalism in living rooms, church lobbies, and shopping malls. It argues that Christians come to understand themselves as global people with a global God by cultivating particular forms of discourse, aesthetics, sensations, and embodied exercises. In terms of sponsorship, one thinks immediately of photography (the sad-eyed orphan) and its associated slogans ("For just pennies a day, *you* can save her!"). I do not ignore these well-studied media, but I contextualize them within a much broader spectrum of what I call participatory techniques. These multisensory activities include how nineteenth-century Americans impersonated "heathen" by wearing their clothes and imitating their speech. Or how, in the twentieth century, they ate "orphan fare" and endured "30-hour famines" to viscerally feel a foreign child's deprivation. Today U.S. Christians experience displays of global poverty in church parking lots. And throughout, sponsors have engaged in the everyday labor of penning letters to a child, pinning up his photos, and praying on his behalf. In short, "being global" is an ongoing and flexible process that reaffirms physical and spiritual connections. In Christian terms, it is "to *manifest* love toward [others] as being one with us in the bonds of Christ."[10] Not surprisingly, to feel enmeshed in this totality is a demanding task with fleeting results. Globalism's techniques must be honed and repeated.

A second point follows from this one. In order to make globalism a visceral (if momentary) reality, Christians mobilize a dialogical relationship between *immensity* and *particularity*. In this regard, I am inspired by the classic theme in studies of globalization that asks how global and local scales interact.[11] However, I want to rethink the general assumption that immensity is a negative quality when it comes to local engagement with global issues: the avalanche of numbers related to global "poverty, profit, and predation" writes anthropologist Arjun Appadurai in a typical assessment, "threaten to kill all street-level optimism about life and the world."[12] My contention is that sensations related to immensity are in fact productive and even necessary for Christians to make real God's global reach. As a result, many U.S. Christians try to reproduce them, for example through the use of world maps, aggregated statistics, and hymns about universal salvation. As I use it, "immensity" also includes what might be thought of as a middle-global scale, such as frameworks for imagining relations between nations or photos that crowd hundreds of people into one frame. All of these forms are meant to evoke awe—a "pleasurable swept-up-ness"[13] or even an awe-ful dread—when one is confronted with the immensity of God's creation. The goal is to reify God's presence and power.

If one is a Christian intent on co-laboring with God, these techniques and attitudes exist together with those that operate on a human scale, which promise intimate connections across vast distances. One might engage in mutual prayers with an individual overseas or meditate on the photo of a single child in need. Through such actions, sponsorship purports to change the inner being— the soul in Christian terms—for donors and the children they support. As I elaborate below, bodies are fundamental in this process. The type of globalism under study promises to shatter differences by emphasizing what are assumed to be common human experiences, such as hunger, sadness, or hope, along with common human aspirations, such as education and financial security. While this idea could describe humanitarianism writ large, in this case it arises from the particular assumption that all humans are the product of a single divine creative act, which translates into the further assumption that all bodies share basic emotional cues and somatic reflexes.[14] It leads U.S. Christians to cultivate global intimacy by engaging in embodied facsimiles of other people's experiences. Thus, immensity and particularity are both affective and often bodily forms of globalism, but the former lifts one up and outside humanness while the latter seems to deepen it to connect with people far away.

The globalism I study has specific attributes born of Christianity's social location in the United States and the country's place in the world. Throughout the book, I identify four major tendencies in this respect. The first tracks how "love" came to offer U.S. people (and especially white middle-class women) conceptual space to frame their intimate actions and emotions as moving a global God to make impacts elsewhere. The second concerns how U.S. Christians came to trust their bodies as sites of deep knowledge about God and about others, as noted briefly above. The third explores the hope that unity can arise out of human diversity. I argue that this hope is, in fact, dependent on the continued existence of historically specific assumptions about binaries between Christian/other, white/black, and rich/poor. The people I discuss in this book do not think such divisions are a good thing, but they also generally assume they are natural to humanity in its earthly state. As a result, when global projects do succeed in creating deeply felt empathy and unity, it can be credited as evidence of a higher power. Fourth, and last, I examine a broad tendency that encompasses love, bodies, and unity-in-diversity within its scope: globalism's inseparability from vexing questions about power and inequality. While the country's relative global power has changed over sponsorship's two centuries, U.S. Christians have always viewed themselves as givers and not recipients of global charity. This assumption is characteristic of Western missions and humanitarianism, but it is especially resonant in a country built on the mythos that anyone can, and should, prosper economically. It is further entangled within sponsorship's promise that, to some degree at least, global unity can be achieved through the loving actions of individual givers.

Sponsorship is a call for human action, and more specifically a call for action by those who have been "blessed" by resources—that is, U.S. sponsors themselves. It therefore widens Americans' global perspective, while also continually re-centering them as the axis through which God's resources flow.

As a result, sponsors often grapple with how material inequality troubles the Christian imperative to view the world as a communion of equally valued "brothers and sisters." Why does God's "abundance" seem to favor certain places over others? What role do Americans have in circulating God's "love" to elsewheres near and far? As these kinds of questions show, being global isn't easy. Globalization, and its variant "global Christianity," have never flowed unencumbered across the world, and (even) U.S. Christians—though "Western," American, and often evangelically minded—do not effortlessly occupy global subjectivities. They make and remake their commitments to a global God.

*   *   *

The American Board of Commissioners for Foreign Missions (ABCFM) started sponsorship plans in Bombay and Ceylon in 1816, shortly after sending the first North American missionaries abroad. These initial programs, and the others I define as sponsorship, have a few distinguishing characteristics: they raise funds by *systematic giving* (a defined amount donated on a regular schedule), they seek to produce *sustained commitment* over an extended period, they benefit *individual children* who are not relations or neighbors, and they provide *regular news* about the child during the period of support. At no point was sponsorship viewed as a "free gift" in the anthropological sense of an unrequited act of charity. It has always been understood as a method to cement relational ties—hence the use of the terms "protégé," "adoption," or "godparenting" in its earlier iterations. In the nineteenth century, this relation was usually between a child and a small group of donors. Since World War I, it has generally been conceived as a one-to-one (1:1) relation with a single donor or donor family. In either case, sponsorship's success owes a lot to the type of fund-raising it popularized: small, regular payments over a sustained period of time. This system appealed to Americans and Europeans on the inside margins of economic power—women, children, and the petty bourgeois. It declared that all givers were of equal value; through penny donations, millions of people came to see themselves as charitable givers on a global scale.

Sponsorship developed through transatlantic dialogue. The ABCFM picked up the idea from models in German-Danish missions supported by English churches. When nascent NGOs started permanent plans after World War I, it was Europeans who first introduced them to the United States.[15] Today, of the approximately 200 substantial child sponsorship organizations in the world, all are based in Western Europe and North America. Anglo-Protestant places provide an especially favorable ecology for their spread: 61 organizations are based in the United States and 43 in the UK.[16] Throughout its history, sponsorship has widened the "external footprint" of these nations by sustaining networks of people, technologies, and techniques alongside the formal institutions of industry, government, military, and diplomacy.[17] It is no accident that U.S. sponsorship plans began in India (where British imperialism opened the way for missionary presence), then moved to France and Belgium (where U.S. troops fought a war), and later flourished in Korea (where they fought another one).

For more than a century after 1816, Protestant missionary societies and then wartime relief organizations started such plans to raise funds quickly and curtailed them once they became too onerous to maintain. But the experience of war inspired Save the Children, an English organization founded in 1919, to successfully transition sponsorship into a permanent fund-raising tool, ushering the way for a new phase in its history. China's Children Fund, later renamed Christian Children's Fund (CCF), was the first major permanent organization founded in North America. It began in 1938 through a partnership between a Southern Baptist missionary in China and Presbyterian pastor J. Calvitt Clarke in Virginia, who knew sponsorship well from his work for Near East Relief in the early 1920s and Save the Children Fund (USA) in the early 1930s.[18] In the 1940s, Clarke expanded his operations considerably—and attracted Christian competitors. Evangelical pastor Bob Pierce founded World Vision (WV) in 1950 and conservative Baptist pastor Everett Swanson started what became Compassion International in 1952. Far outstripping previous sponsorship plans, by 1960 CCF supported 36,000 children and World Vision had 21,000; by 1964, Compassion had another 22,000 in its care.[19]

These organizations scaled up quickly through partnerships with established missionary-run orphanages. Initially based in Asia, until the 1970s their approach to global coverage was largely ad hoc, depending on which missionaries accepted their offers of partnership and which governments allowed their presence. In this formative period, CCF, WV, and Compassion competed for charity dollars and sometimes bickered over who supported which missionary, but they were also closely connected. They hired (or poached) each other's personnel and ran joint training sessions. Pierce showed Swanson around Korea before the latter began operations; CCF and WV learned from each other as they transitioned to computers in the mid-1960s.[20] A few years later, first WV and then Compassion initiated meetings with CCF and Save the Children to discuss best practices. In the mid-1970s, they collaborated on a fund-raising code of ethics.[21] They also developed institutional structures that remain the norm today. Each organization has a U.S.-based headquarters, support offices in other donor countries (for example, Germany or Canada), national offices in recipient countries or regions, and local projects that interface directly with children and their families (see appendix B).

As sponsorship expanded in the 1970s, it attracted the attention of U.S. Catholics. Sponsorship had not been completely absent in Catholic circles. In 1866, for example, the Spiritans promoted it to secure European support for slave children in Zanzibar. In 1868, the Archbishop of Algiers used it to appeal to French donors after a famine left hundreds of orphans in his care.[22] Yet sponsorship was never widespread, perhaps because Catholic missionary orders did not compete on the same voluntary basis as Protestants and felt less need for popular, cross-denominational programs. Whatever the case, individual U.S. Catholics did sign on. At least some contributed to Protestant plans in the late nineteenth century and many more did so by the 1960s and 1970s; the Franciscans promoted Compassion, female religious joined World Vision's intercessory prayer team, parish schools incorporated WV activities for Lent, and CCF advertised in Catholic magazines.[23] By 1980, almost 20% of World Vision's U.S. donors were Roman Catholics.[24]

Bob Hentzen and Jerry Tolle, former missionary priests in Latin America who had left their orders and returned to Kansas City in the 1970s, encountered sponsorship as it expanded on two fronts. At the time, World Vision and Compassion were moving into Latin America and Hentzen and Tolle realized that U.S. Catholics who wanted to help Catholic-majority countries often unwittingly funded evangelical outreach.[25] Closer to home, they encountered sponsorship in their work for the Holy Land Christian Mission (today Children International), a nonprofit in Kansas City that piloted the model in Latin America in 1980. The following year, Hentzen and Tolle struck out on their own and created the Christian Foundation for Children, which is now called Unbound. As liberals who were strongly influenced by Catholic social teachings, Hentzen and Tolle built an organization that differed in ethos from its Protestant and non-religious counterparts, while reiterating the same basic fund-raising plan; in fact, they toured Compassion's headquarters to establish an initial framework.[26] Following the Protestant model, Unbound also began by supporting established (Catholic) missionaries and expanded its networks through personal connections. By 1998, it supported more than 135,000 children, about 90% of whom were in Latin America and the Philippines.[27]

The Protestant organizations I studied underwent a major shift in the late 1970s, which was echoed at Unbound in the late 1990s. They abandoned the system of transferring direct payments to established missionary orphanages and schools in favor of programs that supported children's families. They created their own legal entities to administer these programs, usually called project or field offices, which were generally staffed by middle-class "national" Christians who liaised between local workers and the U.S.-based headquarters. For CCF and WV, this system offered more control over programming and the flexibility to support local church or government programs as needed. For Unbound, it underlined its independence from institutional Roman Catholic structures, which appealed to its liberal Catholic base. For Compassion, it provided a method to strengthen local evangelical and Pentecostal churches that administered its programs, with the twin goals of serving the poor and augmenting these churches' social capital.

Today, WV and Compassion have about a million U.S. sponsors each, and CCF (now ChildFund) has 450,000. Unbound, the largest organization for the U.S. Catholic market, has close to 300,000. When I started writing this book in 2015, estimates put the number of sponsored children at about 9 million globally, with more than $3 billion in support each year.[28]

NEW THEORIES OF GLOBAL PRACTICE

Studies of globalization began in earnest in the mid-1970s as sociologists, political scientists, and philosophers sought to understand the connections between modernization, nation-states, and capitalism. These early studies largely ignored religion or assumed it was a reactionary type of anti-modernism.[29] By the late 1990s, however, so many scholars of religion had begun to address globalization that its faddishness, wryly noted the authors of a 2001 volume, made some of their colleagues "apoplectic with ire and others giddy with excitement."[30]

A key text from this period, familiar to many anthropologists, religionists, and historians, is Arjun Appadurai's *Modernity at Large* (1996). Revising historian Benedict Anderson's famous thesis about the nation-state as an imagined community, he argued that global "scapes" had surpassed this older order to form new "imagined worlds."[31] The idea was highly productive, not least in how it stimulated critique. Four years later, in his study of globalization among Swedish charismatic Christians, anthropologist Simon Coleman argued that Appadurai's model wrongfully implied that the "globe" was imagined and accessed in equivalent ways regardless of social location. The same year, anthropologist Anna Tsing voiced a growing concern that metaphors of flows and scapes obscured the frictions that accompany globalization.[32] More recently, studies have called attention to how inequalities and power differentials not only inhibit certain people from traveling but also promote certain ideas over others, even within the framework of a supposedly global church.[33]

For my purposes, Coleman's study of Swedish charismatics is seminal in how it emphasizes the construction of global identities that result in "new ways to experience and orientate the self towards the world in physical as well as aesthetic and broadly material terms." For example, Coleman shows how congregants favored images of Jesus striding or moving. They used televisual media to project their message to the world, through which they came to experience themselves as people whose words had no bounds.[34] His observations concur with trends in non-religious spaces, too. In Karen Ho's study of Wall Street, for example, investment bankers are socialized into global subjecthood by repeating their companies' hyperbolic claims about continual expansion.[35] Like Coleman, Ho underlines the process of making globalization, rather than only tracing its effects. This book sets out to do the same, though with more sustained attention to material, sensory, and performative aspects.

In this respect, I turn to studies that take up Mauss, Bourdieu, and Foucault to explore the bodily disciplines that produce religious subjects. Saba Mahmood's work with Egyptian Muslims is well known for articulating the idea that contra Bourdieu (and to some degree Mauss), actions may be self-consciously undertaken in order to cultivate changed attitudes. This turn to self-making in studies of religion is well suited to sponsorship as a form of non-denominational, voluntary, and intentional engagement and, in many ways, I interpret the actions of U.S. sponsors along the same lines.[36] However, unlike the Muslims in Mahmood's study who practice religious habits on a daily basis, most sponsors engage in globalism sporadically, triggered by receiving a letter from the child they support or seeing something in the news.

As I began this project, my thinking was also buoyed by ecotheorist Timothy Morton's work on hyperobjects. At first, the connection may seem tenuous. Morton's interest in Christianity is minimal and my work diverges from his in a number of ways.[37] What is helpful, however, is his careful discussion of the affective quality of immensity. Writing of global warming, Morton describes hyperobjects as "viscous": they are so pervasive that we already live within them, though we only experience them in brief flashes as they seem to "phase" in and out of our spatiotemporal world. Thus, we are already "within" a changing climate, for example, but only experience it when global warming results in a sunburn or heats up a thermometer. For Morton, the sheer scale of a hyperobject disturbs our sense of being in the world; it "humiliates" humans by displacing us from the center of things. Morton associates the resulting ontological threats with feelings of weakness, lameness, and terror. At one point, though, he offers a synopsis that corresponds better with how I characterize Christian globalism: "These entities cause us to reflect on our very place on Earth and in the cosmos."[38]

Globalism may create anxieties, and even a sense of hopelessness, among U.S. Christians. But my contention is that it also creates a "quake in being," paraphrasing Morton, that makes possible the awe, euphoria, and humiliation (in a theological sense) that for Christians holds the potential to supersede the merely human scale and glimpse the massive work of God. Put differently, when U.S. Christians engage globalism, they reify what for them is a tangible manifestation of God's wholeness and power. Thus, whereas Morton focuses on how the hyperobject oppresses humans uninvited, the Christians about whom I write usually seek out such engagements. This brings us back to the work on embodiment and materiality noted above: I track techniques and modalities by which U.S. Christians render globalism usable for short periods—harnessing its "phasing," as it were.

Morton's work underscores a "knotty relationship" between immensity and intimacy. This is important because sponsors often describe what they do in terms of intimacy, rather than in the triumphalist strain of continual expansion found in Coleman's megachurch or Ho's investment banks. On this note, I return throughout the book to historians and critical theorists of U.S. culture whose work demonstrates how domestic intimacies and affective sensations are entwined in larger political processes. I also explore the trust required to invest in global projects; people must come to feel intimately engaged with, and dependent upon, faraway people—those pictured in need and those charged with disbursing one's money abroad. I am certainly not the first to raise this issue. Since Georg Simmel's pioneering sociological work a century ago, studies of capitalism have asked how people come to trust unknown networks and commit their money without seeing immediate results. The gap between the immediate and the projected yawns especially wide in global projects, with their time lags and spatial distance. Sponsors must trust that things go places and make impacts. If they are Christians, they must trust that other humans are similar enough to themselves to respond to care and ultimately advance God's project. Emotional engagements and participatory techniques are crucial because they lend specific sensory and material dimensions to these spatiotemporal projections.[39] The experiences they provoke make Christianity's global projects seem natural and effective—at least for a time.

A GLOSS ON TERMS

Over the course of the book, I use a few terms to flesh out the discussion above. The most important ones are the following.

Globalism. I use this term to mean a world characterized by interconnections, as well as "how *the idea of the global* has worked to excite and inspire."[40] Globalism is not a modern phenomenon but it is intensified at different times, which social scientists often call "thinner" or "thicker" periods.[41] Globalism's rate of increase—the "thickening"—is globalization. I use globalism also to signal that this project is oriented differently from those on "Global Christian-ity" (or World Christianity) that track various forms of Christianity and the interactions between them.

Absent/present. The collapse of absence and presence through technology or travel is a classic theme in studies of globalization.[42] I bring a religious sen-sibility to bear on this discussion, since my use of "absent/present" refers to a variety of physically absent beings that are rendered present in some capacity through imaginative and sensory practices. Sponsored children are a potent example of living human beings who may fall into this category. It also en-compasses other-than-human beings, such as the dead or the divine, which in various ways all Christians understand as sometimes present with believers de-spite bodily absence. Absent/present beings—human and divine—exert claims on believers as they waver between distance and proximity.[43] That wavering quality is important: globalism is not only about better communications and deeper experiences of knowing. It is equally characterized by the frustrated possibilities of what is partially grasped.

Engaged empathy. Global objects may call forth conflicting feelings of "over-stimulation and numbness, alarm and anaesthesia."[44] U.S. sponsors most often describe anxiety, frustration, wonder, compassion, "thrills," and joy. I explore these feelings as affects and emotions. Following general scholarly use, I tend to use "affect" for broadly circulating sensibilities or moods and "emotion" for more personal feelings, bearing in mind that even the most visceral of these are richly social phenomena.[45] Globalism may be conscious or inadvertent but, as the word *engaged* suggests, the focus on sponsorship leads me to privilege the former: sponsors choose to be engaged although they cannot, of course, anticipate all the results. In brief, then, engaged empathy refers to emotional and affective attachments from afar, which in sponsorship are expected to yield sustained spiritual concern and financial giving.

Participatory techniques. Engaged empathy arises through visual stimuli and embodied experiences that I call "participatory techniques." The term "technique" is a nod to anthropologists, such as Mauss, who have used it to discuss the embodied *habitus* that frames subjective experiences of the world. The techniques I discuss include writing letters, taking photos, and looking at images, along with eating or walking through multisensory displays. They are legible to participants within authorized social forms and are often explicitly promoted by authoritative institutions, such as sponsorship organizations. At a fundamental level, they also raise questions about the possibility of empathy; Michel de Certeau insisted that embodied actions are opaque—one is always within one's own body, not in another's—and thus they necessarily organize a familiar here in relation to a foreign there.[46] From sponsors' perspective, the assumption that all bodies share certain fundamental qualities—feeling hunger is painful, seeing a smile makes one happy, reading encouraging words creates hope—means that participatory techniques often seem to shatter barriers and even produce a type of visceral participation in another's experience.[47] Because this engaged empathy is fleeting, participatory techniques are repeated. It is helpful to think of events of varying scales: the prolonged intensity of fasting for 30 hours differs from saying a prayer on a child's behalf. Yet both actions have engaged empathy as their goal and Christian globalism as their impetus.

Mirroring. I use "engagement" and "empathy" in part because of their positive connotations in the United States. The contemporary organizations I studied use "engaged" to describe their most committed sponsors. Yet the paradoxical nature of deep engagement, as critics of sponsorship and humanitarianism note, is that givers become so enmeshed that they fail to distinguish self from other.[48] This idea is amplified through Christian globalism's ontological substructure, which assumes that bringing people into contact, or awareness of each other, can make them into something new ("one new man" in Christian parlance). What I call "mirroring" contributes to this project by evoking difference—often demarcated by accent, dress, and skin color—to portray members of a diverse global public performing actions that are legible to Americans as godly.[49] For example, sponsorship organizations often circulate photos of foreign children in a typical American prayer pose—hands together, head down, eyes squeezed shut (figure 4.4). They also feature foreign children singing familiar hymns in accented English. By participating in forms that mirror what they already know, U.S. Christians experience a sense of their God's global reach. It is a key mechanism through which sponsors reproduce unity-in-diversity. The larger point is that to understand "the politics of felt difference"[50]—the charged divides between rich/poor, Christian/other, white/ black, West/rest that orient U.S. Christians' actions in the world—one must attend closely to the politics of sameness too. American exceptionalism and Christian universalism have always depended on the existence of others. There is no "center" without a "periphery."

MRS. JANE Q. SPONSOR: ON SUBJECT AND METHOD

I am often asked whether sponsorship works. The question implies something to the effect of how many cents on the dollar go to children in need and whether the poor become less poor as a result. While the organizations under study do differ somewhat in their budgets and programming, critics (going back at least to the 1940s) have condemned the one-to-one (1:1) approach for creating "little enclaves of privilege" within communities and failing to redress the underlying causes of poverty.[51] Development industry experts also criticize sponsorship's comparatively high overhead—the cost of translations, photos, postage, and extra staff to manage relations with sponsors. Such analyses treat the 1:1 aspect as a fund-raising gimmick rather than part of the "real" work that occurs in the field.[52] By contrast, sponsorship organizations, and most sponsors, perceive it as *integral* to combating poverty. In their view, 1:1 communication creates a channel for divine Love and, in more secular terms, fosters self-esteem for children who have experienced little encouragement to dream of a different future.

Many of the sponsorship professionals with whom I spoke, and the scholars whose work informs mine, also weigh differences between charity and philanthropy, sympathy and compassion, or mission and mutual solidarity. While I explore such issues as they came up during my research, I do not offer prescriptive suggestions for best practices or track what happens in the places where U.S. money ends up. I limit my discussion of organizations' inner workings to what is needed for clarity and insofar as it affects U.S. donors' experience. These topics are covered elsewhere in a number of excellent studies and dissertations.[53] On that note, sponsors and I sometimes discussed my role as a scholar in shaping the analysis. They were right to point it out. This book tries to do justice to their experiences, but it does so framed within my ultimate goal of tracing the contours of Christian globalism. By the same token, the fact that I have chosen sponsorship as a (semi) coherent site for this study shapes particular points of focus. It means that Protestants feature more prominently than Catholics, and Asia more than Africa. It means that certain contemporary forms of Christian global engagements, such as "End Times" prophecy and spiritual warfare, appear only in endnotes; evangelical organizations avoid beliefs they feel could alienate any segment of their audience. It means that the places where globalism "happens" tend to be at home, online, or at church-related events, rather than in streets, government offices, or courthouses.

This book also emphasizes female donors—"Mrs. Jane Q. Sponsor," as one Compassion executive termed it when we spoke. Women have always been sponsorship's most reliable target market. Indeed, when the ABCFM started the first sponsorship plan in 1816 it did so explicitly for women and youth who, it believed, needed concrete connections to fully comprehend the abstract concept of global responsibility.[54] (As many historians have shown, women were actually some of the earliest and staunchest supporters of foreign missions.) During the nineteenth century, sponsorship was yoked to sentimentalism, a growing trend in Christianity that seemed to secure a role for maternal influence within republican politics and industrial capitalism. At the time, groups of women typically pooled their resources to support a child overseas. By the mid-twentieth century, women often initiated sponsorship on behalf of their families. Throughout, mothers and female Sunday school teachers have used the plans as a pedagogical tool for children in their care.

A 1977 WV survey identified the typical sponsor as a middle-aged married Christian woman with a lower or fixed income.[55] She was also white. Although mid-century organizations showed some interest in courting the "economically rising Negro population," they largely failed to do so.[56] In 1974, Compassion's team likely summed up the issue correctly: African Americans were concerned about domestic poverty and distrusted white-run organizations with no ties to black communities.[57] Today, sponsorship continues to appeal mainly—though not exclusively—to white women. I worked most closely with contemporary sponsors at Compassion and Unbound. At Compassion, 70% of sponsors are female, 74% are married, about 88% are white, and 99% are self-described Christians of the evangelical variety (the two largest groups are 34.7% non-denominational and 17.8% Baptist). The average sponsor is 46 years old and roughly 60% do not have children at home, which Compassion's team attributes to a significant number of college students and retirees. At Unbound, the demographic is virtually identical (swap 99% evangelical for Catholic), but the average sponsor is a decade older.[58] My sample of 118 interviewees was quite consistent with these estimates. Rounding the numbers up or down, 87% of them were married or recently widowed; 90% had children (many grown); 75% were female; all self-identified as Christian and most went to church. My interviewees were more likely than organizational estimates to self-identify as white—all of my Protestant interviewees did so, along with 95% of Catholics. Their ages ranged from 30 to 87, but they were also older than organizational estimates; among my Catholic interviewees the average age was 65 and among evangelicals it was 55. In other words, this book should be taken for what it is: a glimpse at some, albeit rather typical, U.S. Christian sponsors. It leaves ample room for subsequent studies to compare across more social groups.

Sponsorship subtly stitches together moral communities. At one of my field sites, a Presbyterian church in New Hampshire, the Sunday school class sponsored a child and a bulletin board in the foyer displayed photos of the children supported by individual members. A few events during the year brought sponsors together, such as a Christmas card writing session (figure 7.5) and a Compassion Sunday event. Whether or not they could name other sponsors, my interlocutors had a collective sense that their church "does" sponsorship and thus contributes to God's global work. While this may be a motivation for participating, the actual tasks related to sponsorship happen sporadically in people's homes. It made research slow going at times and led me to adopt a pragmatic, interdisciplinary approach that combined archival work, participatory fieldwork, and surveys, as detailed in appendix A.

The book's first two chapters focus on missionary boards that used sponsorship in the nineteenth century—the ABCFM and two women's foreign missionary societies. Chapter 3 draws on archives from World War I relief organizations, especially Near East Relief and the Fatherless Children of France. The remaining chapters mix archival and ethnographic fieldwork related to the four post-war organizations mentioned above: CCF (mainline Protestant in the mid-twentieth century), World Vision (neo-evangelical) and Compassion (initially conservative Baptist), and Unbound (Roman Catholic). Today, WV and Compassion are both evangelical, but the former also draws many liberal Protestant and "secular" donors. Appendix B clarifies some basic details about these organizations as a quick guide for readers.

As the project progressed, I realized that the Protestant organizations cultivated self-definitions and affiliations that were much more fluid than I expected. In part, this reflects the pragmatics of creating overseas networks. For example, CCF's founder, J. Calvitt Clarke, tried to keep his staff free of "fundamentalists," but he made an exception for his longtime overseas director Verent Mills, a Pentecostal formerly with China Inland Mission. In the field, CCF partnered with everyone from the Assemblies of God to the Russian Orthodox Church. In South Korea in the mid-1960s, the conservative evangelicals at Compassion supported orphanages in partnership with Church World Service, an arm of the liberal National Council of Churches.[59] Mid-century Protestant organizations (and "secular" ones like Save the Children) also used flexible advertising strategies that included Christian symbolism, especially during the lucrative Christmas season. Audiences drew their own conclusions, which meant that an organization like CCF attracted liberal Unitarian Universalists alongside Moody Bible Institute–trained fundamentalists. World Vision and Compassion drew evangelicals alongside Catholics and Jews. In a gem from the archives, Compassion received its first major publicity boost from the Jewish advice columnist Esther Friedman Lederer, better known as Ann Landers, who endorsed it with the proviso that Compassion remove the word "Christ" from any mailings with her photo; a few years later, her twin sister and rival, Pauline Esther Phillips of Dear Abby fame, signed on as spokesperson for Compassion's evangelical competitor, World Vision.[60]

This book begins in the early nineteenth century, in part to correct the common misconception that twentieth-century humanitarians invented sponsorship.[61] Tracing the trajectory of a single fund-raising technique demonstrates how foreign missionary bodies were connected to nascent relief and humanitarian circles, both of which then bolstered the transition to faith-based NGOs after the 1940s. This point is of evident importance for readers interested in the rise of humanitarianism or missions, but it is worth noting for others as well. Excavating this history underscores globalization in the making, then and now, and emphasizes continuities between the modern and late modern period within which sponsorship has flourished. Of course, that does not imply an absence of diachronic change. Sometimes I point out such shifts explicitly; other times, careful readers will discern them in the chapters. Each one is structured around techniques, objects, or ideas that developed or were reinterpreted during the period in question. For example, chapter 3 centers on new visual media technologies in the late nineteenth century and the concomitant rise of global relief campaigns. Chapter 5 focuses on new interpretations of materialism in the 1970s, which diverged from how this issue was discussed a century before, as described in chapter 1.

On that note, I should clarify two significant shifts that molded sponsorship today. One was already mentioned: in the 1970s, the organizations under study went from supporting missionaries through transfer payments to creating their own legal entities to support children at home. At the same time, they began courting a broader market through slick advertisements and infomercials featuring those now infamously graphic portrayals of destitute children. The strategy produced a serious crisis of representation, which many organizational staff members recognized: their new media campaigns promoted the orphan model just as they were discarding it in the field. In the 1990s, programming and advertising became better integrated. Today, the organizations under study generally focus on children's joy and optimism and rarely feature images of destitution.

The second shift of note was much broader in scope. In the 1960s and 1970s, more U.S. Christians began to grapple with the liberatory politics that accompanied the end of formal colonialism. Over the next decade, they also became aware of the comparative growth of Christianity in the global south. Among Catholics, the Second Vatican Council, the ecumenical movement, and Liberation Theology contributed to an emphasis on local cultures and the need for mutual support across the global Church. Although liberal Protestants employed different language—"contextualization" instead of the predominantly Catholic term "inculturation"—they also reworked their interpretation of mission to argue that the Gospel was uniquely embodied in each local culture. They spearheaded what they began to call "partnerships" with global south churches, hoping to emphasize self-determination rather than paternalism.[62] Evangelicals picked up on these trends in the 1980s and 1990s. Today, all the organizations under study embrace these principles in a basic sense, including those on the more conservative end of the spectrum (Compassion explicitly refers to its ministry as "contextual"). In the world of child sponsorship, evangelicals have moved closer to Catholics and liberal Protestants in their emphasis on global partnerships and mutual solidarity; Catholics and hierarchically organized mainline Protestants have moved closer to evangelicals in their focus on local churches and community sovereignty.

OUTLINE OF THE BOOK

The first two chapters mine missionary archives to explore the development of sponsorship as one facet of the rise of systematic giving and child-centered charities. Chapter 1 discusses informal evangelical theologies that fused the circulation of human love and Divine Love into a basis for U.S. Christian globalism. Chapter 2 examines an equally important set of building blocks: how the statistical science of "large numbers" worked dialogically with the penny donations of systematic giving and the individual recipients associated with "special objects" charity. Both chapters emphasize the participatory techniques that encouraged a vast economy of missionary giving. They also refute the assumption in earlier studies that the nineteenth-century turn to sentimental Christian "love" replaced an earlier emphasis on the glory of a "distant and majestic" God.[63] In Christian globalism, both aspects worked together.

Chapter 3 turns to World War I, when relief organizations introduced sponsorship to a wider public. At a basic level, it offers a corrective to how histories of nineteenth-century U.S. women's missionary work often end in the interwar period with the dissolution of separate female boards. Instead, this chapter traces the link to non-sectarian relief organizations, in which many men and women from missionary circles were involved. Thematically, it focuses on new visual media, especially photography, that bolstered U.S. Christians' ability to incorporate absent/present children into the intimate spaces of family life, while honing a god's eye view of the world. It considers this visual media together with visceral (embodied) techniques as collaborative tools in emergency relief. I rely on a few guides, including cultural theorists Lauren Berlant and Susan Sontag, each of whom has asked how other people's suffering may make moral demands on our minds as well as our bodies—our "hearts and tears," as Berlant puts it.[64]

Chapter 4 explores the mid-century archives of CCF and WV to tackle what is in a sense the crux of 1:1 sponsorship: the promise of transglobal relationship. Taking up themes from chapter 1, it examines the tensions inherent in globalism's attenuated forms of knowing—and the mediation it requires and conceals. It situates the discussion amid key trends at the time, including the formation of the United Nations and transnational adoptions from Asia. Along with chapter 3, it shows how Protestants positioned sponsorship as a type of intimate "heart conversion" that could repair the massive failures of mid-century diplomacy. This chapter most clearly introduces the role of mirroring in building a Christian ideal of racialized unity-in-diversity.

Chapters 5 and 6 incorporate archival materials from the 1960s to the 1980s alongside contemporary interviews and fieldnotes. Both chapters build on the discussion in chapter 4 about global forms of relationality. Along with chapter 1, these chapters also most closely examine capitalism and the futures it projects. Chapter 5 takes up morally freighted questions about materialism and some common coping tactics. Chapter 6 traces how Christian sponsorship organizations adapt secular audit culture. More broadly, it tackles what Appadurai calls "the capacity to aspire," asking how U.S. Christians envision futures for themselves, the children they support, and the world as a whole. And finally, chapter 7 covers the broadest chronological period and revisits a classic theme in globalization theory related to spatiotemporal collapse. It builds on previous chapters' discussions of intimacy, a god's eye view, and unity-in-diversity, by examining three forms of participatory technique: vocal arrangements, mapping techniques, and the virtual space of social media.

Writing an interdisciplinary book is challenging and liberating. Since I did not set out to produce a history of child sponsorship, I felt free to opt for a loosely chronological structure set within a thematic approach. It leads me to interrupt the chronological narrative at times; for instance, I include "postscripts" at the end of some chapters to clarify how a particular theme resurfaced in another period. I sometimes insert a brief remark about contemporary trends. The final chapter, which includes both historical and contemporary objects, is meant to disrupt any impression that early chapters were merely a historical prelude to the ethnography that follows. Another considered choice is the inclusion of two "interludes" about sponsor-child duos in the 1840s and 2000s. I have inserted them, first, to suggest the usefulness of experimental approaches to writing when globally dispersed sources are inaccessible or incomplete. I also hope that the prose will allow readers to gain a better sense of the temporality of sponsorship, which is shaped by sporadic letters over many years. Most important, I use the interludes to evoke the gaps in sponsorship's intimate relations. This theme appears in the chapters, but to some extent my authorial voice overwrites it by filling in explanations and clarifications. Though highly curated, the interludes re-center the absences, misunderstandings, and differing expectations that inevitably constitute global projects.

Christian Globalism at Home moves between private prayer closets and family dinner tables to moments that evoke some of humankind's biggest aspirations and concerns. For U.S. Christians at home, a perpetual challenge is how to harness globalism's wavering intensity so that, for a moment at least, absent becomes present and one feels the flash of God's expansive power.

CHAPTER 1

Love and Sin

Sense and Sentimentalism in Christian Globalism

People and realms of every tongue
dwell on his love with sweetest song;
and infant voices shall proclaim
their early blessings on his Name.

—Isaac Watts, "Jesus Shall Reign Where'er the Sun" (1719).
   As sung at WFMS branch meetings, 1870s–1890s

For we must share if we would keep that good thing from Above,
ceasing to share we'd cease to have. Such is the law of love.

—Rev. R. C. French's *Law of Love*. Reprinted in WFMS auxiliary
   minutes, November 3, 1910, Methodist Church, Pasadena[1]

On May 24, 1815, Samuel Newell, Samuel Nott, and Gordon Hall penned a letter to the ABCFM's Prudential Committee in Salem, Massachusetts. The young nation's first foreign missionaries, they had settled in British-controlled Bombay in 1812, treading lightly as their country and England waged war at home. Besides being in a politically precarious position, the missionaries found their new surroundings challenging to say the least. Bombay was a vibrant, dirty, diverse port city of nearly 2 million people: Persians, Arabs, Parsis, Goan Portuguese, Jews, and Africans joined locals and immigrants from the neighboring areas of Karnataka and the Deccan. English, German, and Danish settlers were also drawn to the colonial heart of British India, through which tons of raw materials passed each day for shipment across the world. In short, Bombay was nothing like the provincial New England towns in which the missionaries had been raised. Even their country's largest cities paled in comparison; New York City had fewer than 100,000 inhabitants and Boston one-third of that.[2]

Newell, Nott, and Hall's letter was printed in the ABCFM's *Panoplist* periodical in January 1816 and it candidly enumerated for U.S. readers some of the dispiriting realities they faced. The ABCFM and its (male) missionaries had initially envisioned their role as akin to a pastor at home.[3] But there were no orderly New England audiences that gathered at church to hear one preach. In India, the Americans had to attract impromptu crowds along roadways or in markets where people were generally too busy to decipher a foreigner's halting speech. Observing the better-established English and Danish missions, the young missionaries lit upon a potential solution: the "indirect dissemination" of Christianity through day schools or by taking children into their homes. They assured *Panoplist* readers that "heathen children might be obtained [in Bombay] in greater numbers, and with greater facility, than almost any other part of India" since poor families streamed into the city during times of famine or disease and the parents "not infrequently" died. In fact, they had an example in mind. The year before, Mr. M—a friend of the young Americans in Bombay—had happened upon one such child, nearly dead from exposure in the street, and kept him for a year. Since Mr. M was heading home, he bequeathed the boy to the Americans, who estimated his age at between 12 and 14 years old. By this point, he spoke English well and showed signs of conversion. Such rewards cost "a mere trifle" since a child's upkeep was only about $2 a month. "Here is a way in which *so great good* can be done at *so little expense*," the missionaries enthused.[4]

The response was electric. Over the ensuing months, the ABCFM committee reminded the missionaries in nearly every letter that "the plan for educating poor heathen children in the families of missionaries is very captivating" and "contributions and communal subscriptions for this object exceed our most sanguine expectations . . . we hope you will prosecute the design with enlarged views & with various and well devoted exertions."[5] By 1817, the ABCFM annual report devoted eight pages to listing donations, and in 1819, almost $11,000 was contributed to the cause. Even in the U.S. South, the project sparked interest and individuals gave enough money to establish schools in Bombay named after donors' native cities: Charleston, Savannah, and Augusta.[6] "The publick will not let your object fail. Moreover, the women will not," ABCFM secretary Samuel Worcester assured the missionaries. In fact, he had personally witnessed their excitement. At the monthly prayer meeting he attended in Salem, a recent letter from the missionaries was read aloud and "the effect was instantaneous." The next morning, the women organized a society whose members would each contribute 25 cents a year "for the support of heathen children in Missionary families."

The Salem group was typical of those that formed throughout the nineteenth century. While some individuals could afford to pay the subscription, most donors pooled their pennies. Each group was assigned a child to be supported by it alone—exclusivity has always been fundamental to the 1:1 model—and donors expected their pennies would be devoted to that child's upkeep and instruction at the mission. The Salem society decided to start with a child from Tillipally, Ceylon (Sri Lanka) who they wanted to rename Samuel Worcester out of "affectionate respect" for the ABCFM secretary himself.[7] They requested that the Ceylon station find such a child without delay. "This is a beginning," Worcester wrote euphorically, "The spirit shall spread. Hundreds more may be supported."[8]

By participating in the ABCFM sponsorship plan, U.S. people contributed to a broader missionary project that evaluated the world's inhabitants according to an Enlightenment metric that ran from savage to civilized—in which Anglo-Protestants always found themselves at the top. Such judgments were universalizing and exclusionary.[9] They were also structured around the assumption that universalism was the ethically superior position. Drawing on an older trope that juxtaposed Judaism and Christianity, missionary supporters viewed "heathen" religions as inadequate for the human condition since they seemed unable to progress beyond inward-looking tribalism. This seeming failure to express a sense of global responsibility was interpreted as a clear sign that Christianity was needed, and would soon be adopted.[10] To that end, sponsorship circulated money and objects around the world, along with what nineteenth-century donors understood as Christian emotions (pity, love, and humility) and what we, from our vantage point today, might identify as not so Christian ones, such as disgust and aversion.

All sentiments have a history. In a sense, this chapter tells the back story to what critical theorist Lauren Berlant notes about women's "intimate publics" in the contemporary United States: this form of public views society as an affective space "where people ought to be legitimated because they have feelings and because there is an intelligence in what they feel that *knows* something about the world that if it were listened to, could make things better."[11] Historians have tracked aspects of the development of this "knowing" felt-life in earlier periods too. Sociologist Colin Campbell's pathbreaking study of the nineteenth-century Anglo-Protestant middle class refined the link between this subjectivity and emerging capitalism. Rejecting Weber's austere Protestant ethic, Campbell shows how Calvinism and Pietism both championed a type of individualism that viewed emotions as the ultimate indicators of a person's moral worth.[12] To this we can add the eighteenth-century development of humanitarian moral philosophies, which taught nineteenth-century Americans that by examining one's conscience, a Christian could intuit natural laws that governed the self and, extrapolating further, humanity as a whole. This "science of subjectivity" was based on the assumption that inherent regularities in human nature reflected the work of a single Creator.[13] For child sponsors caught up in the pietism, romanticism, and sentimentalism of their day, one intuited such laws less through a conscious, philosophical examination than by nurturing Christian feelings to spur moral action.

The means by which U.S. Protestants learned to isolate and recognize those feelings led them to view states related to love and sin as transhistorical and universal. Doing so, they cultivated an all-encompassing reality that was central to the production of globalism—a world where all people by dint of their assumed relationship to the Christian Creator had certain traits in common. One might think of it as "viscous" in Timothy Morton's sense: the more Christians "discovered" this worldview (such as when a heathen converted or an American was born again), the more they became convinced that they already lived within it.[14] In short, Christian sponsors were at the forefront of trends that entwined intimacy and immensity by making it seem self-evident that the felt-life of human love was one aspect of a globally circulating Divine Love. This point is important since at first glance nineteenth-century Americans described "heathens" in such a way that only seemed to emphasize difference. To understand how globalism becomes real, we need to recognize how the opprobrium heaped upon "heathens" was *also* a way to subsume all humans into one family of sinners ("The heart of man is the same in all nations," missionary magazines reminded them). Of course, it generated the potential of universal redemption too.

The chapter begins by clarifying how nineteenth-century Christians came to understand childhood innocence as a shared attribute of humankind; without this revolutionary shift, sponsorship would likely never have come about. It asks how this idea was implicated in a sentimental turn that forged Christian globalism as we know it today by insisting that U.S. women could "enlarge" their hearts based on their own experiences of human love and Divine Love. It then turns to how the rising middle classes grappled with vexed questions about adult sin among heathens and in their own communities. Ultimately, a productive tension between a growing theology of love and earlier ideas about sin became the engine driving thousands of nineteenth-century Americans to band together, announce their sins, make objects, save pennies, and adopt a child abroad.

CHILDREN AND COLONIAL CHRISTIANITY

Before the nineteenth century, most Christians viewed original sin as imputed to every human from birth, which left infants in a state of moral ambivalence. Some churches softened this doctrine by arguing that the sacrament of infant baptism washed away one's sins for a time. In the early modern period, Catholics assigned children's souls to a more neutral limbo. By contrast, Calvinists were at times emphatic about infant damnation. John Calvin thought "the whole nature of children is the seed of sin," an idea reiterated by America's best-known eighteenth-century pastor Jonathan Edwards, who compared children to "corrupt young vipers." His comment was so out of step just a generation after his death that his followers quietly expunged it from his published works.[15]

As Edwards's example demonstrates, such ideas were in flux in the eighteenth and early nineteenth centuries. Influential European thinkers had suggested that childhood was less as a time of unruly sin and more one of high plasticity during which lasting moral dispositions could be molded. In England, John Locke convincingly argued that early education could produce disciplined citizens. His contemporary, German Lutheran pastor August Hermann Francke, argued that it did the same for evangelical Christians. In 1695, he founded his highly influential "orphan-house" at Halle based on the Pietist principle that each person was converted to Christ by their own will; for Francke, even the youngest and poorest child needed the religious education to prepare for personal salvation. Pietistic strands of Protestantism also championed the idea that the very young could consciously accept Christ. Hymn writer Isaac Watts claimed children as young as three understood his popular *Divine Songs Attempted in Easy Language for the Use of Children* (1715). Jonathan Edwards, along with Methodist founder John Wesley, recorded children between four and seven years of age converting in revivals. By the 1830s, children between ages six and eight were being saved in American Sunday schools and American-run missionary schools, though they may have come "right out of heathenism" just months before.[16]

Although humanists like Locke and Pietists like Francke had different ends in mind, they concurred that poor and non-Protestant children needed disciplining institutions (a workhouse in Locke's estimation, a well-ordered orphan house in Francke's). In this enlightenment view of sin, environment and heredity worked together. If an individual or class of individuals habitually sinned, it was believed these tendencies would alter their makeup and be transmitted to their offspring. Change these behaviors and one could break the cycle of inherited sinfulness. It was a profoundly optimistic vision about human nature and its ability to change, which depended on highly coercive instruments of religious and social control.

Early in the eighteenth century, Anglo-Protestants adapted the model at Halle into a system of charity schools across England, which were then exported to the colonies. English evangelist George Whitefield founded a school along these lines in Georgia in 1740. Three years later, Eleazer Wheelock also cited Halle when he started his Indian orphan school, which today is Dartmouth College.[17] Observers of childhood in this period noted that children were susceptible to corruption by the adults around them and seemed to "harden" in sin as they aged. This belief justified their removal from environments deemed deficient. In 1735, English reformers first suggested removing Irish Catholic children far from their parents and priests, a plan that became more practicable after the crippling famine of 1741. The system was replicated in residential missionary schools in North America, India, and China. The ABCFM schools that first used sponsorship exemplified this model and they tried to limit enrollment to children younger than age nine, the age at which missionaries deemed them still sufficiently pliable.[18]

Tracing the roots of child sponsorship, the most notable transplant to the colonies was the mission school at Tranquebar, a Danish colony in Tamil Nadu. Two of Francke's protégés settled there in 1706 at the behest of the Danish crown and, employing what they had learned at Halle, gathered together 18 pupils, including "charity" children.[19] The newly formed English missionary organization, the Society for Promoting Christian Knowledge (SPCK), was intrigued by the possibilities. It began a subscription campaign on their behalf and then supported the Tranquebar missionaries to open another school at Madras in British East India Company territory. Both experiments were short-lived. Converts were not forthcoming and the relationship between colonial governments, local elites, and missionaries was often strained.[20]

The turn of the nineteenth century saw a more congenial atmosphere for missionary expansion and for the Tranquebar schools.[21] It was this model that Newell, Nott, and Hall called "peculiarly encouraging" in their letter from Bombay in May 1815. In the correspondence that followed, Worcester repeatedly recommended that they read Rev. Dr. John's report on the topic in the *Missionary Register*, the organ of the London-based Church Missionary Society (CMS).[22] He even enclosed the piece in a letter to make sure they perused it closely. The man in question was Christoph Samuel John, a Halle-affiliated Lutheran at Tranquebar who died suddenly in 1813, leaving the CMS in charge of his network of schools. The article that so intrigued Worcester told how, when the Anglo-Danish war (1801–1813) had plunged the Tranquebar mission into debt as donations from Germany and Copenhagen dried up, John decided "to make an experiment, trusting in God."[23] He expanded the preexisting school system, reduced its costs, and developed a reading curriculum using the Bible.

The fledgling ABCFM mission also faced pecuniary and political precarity, partly because of the British colonial government's still ambivalent attitude about missionaries and partly because the United States had just waged war on the English colonies (1812–1815).[24] Creating schools potentially justified the presence of missionaries in British territory, including American ones, and created a comparably captive audience who they expected would become "native Christian" translators and teachers. Perhaps most important, it was cheap; heathen teachers were plentiful and could be paid a pittance. John's 1813 CMS report did not mention fund-raising with 1:1 "adoption plans" or the costs per pupil, but Newell, Nott, and Hall made it explicit. Based on their study of Tranquebar and the recent experience of their friend Mr. M., they estimated that they could educate a heathen child in a boarding school for $12 a month and in a missionary home for just $2. These sums formed the basis for their proposed "adoption" plan.[25]

The Bombay missionaries seemed blindsided by the excitement the idea generated among home audiences fired up in the revivals sweeping New England. Just a year and a half after launching the scheme, they admitted it was impossible to secure enough children to fill demand. Jeremiah Evarts, ABCFM Treasurer and *Panoplist* editor, wrote angrily from Boston. "We are under some little embarrassment . . . A considerable number of such children have been provided for, as you have been informed; & the benefactors will be quite disheartened & discouraged to be told, that no children can be found." He ended with a thinly veiled threat: "I hope Providence will enable you to find suitable recipients for these charities; if not, the money will probably be diverted to Ceylon or some other promising field."[26] Ceylon was indeed promising in this respect, and the ABCFM ended up expanding its adoption plan most steadily in that location in the 1820s and 1830s.

The children enrolled in Ceylon, and anywhere else the fund-raising model spread, were called variously orphans, heathens, scholars, and protégés. They hailed from a wide range of backgrounds. Many well-off parents were willing to pay for a Western education to enhance their sons' career chances (and sometimes their daughters' marriage prospects). According to the missionaries at Ceylon, the young boy renamed Samuel Worcester, one of the first to be sponsored, was from a middle-high caste and came to the mission with five companions because their parents were "anxious" that they learn English to secure government posts. Young Worcester proved a success, from the missionaries' perspective at least: he stayed at the school for a decade, converted, and became a tutor at their new seminary.[27] Other times, missionaries acquired foundlings or the victims of failed infanticides. Poor parents also left children, only to retrieve them when times improved, much to missionaries' frustration; as the century wore on, many missionaries devised contracts that parents signed to ensure the child would stay for a stipulated period of time. Other parents viewed it as a clean exchange, once they were given the money for a bride price or, for the really desperate, "a little rice."[28]

The children who grew up at missionary schools—a longevity that made them good candidates for sponsorship—often had very personal stories of trauma or loss. Fast-forward to the 1850s and we can trace an example: a girl from Moradabad, India, who was renamed Fanny Garretson Hyde. She was born into a shepherd caste family of at least four children. When she was very young, her father assaulted her mother during an argument, which prompted the woman to pack up her two youngest children and escape to the nearby town of Tanda. A few days later, Fanny's brother and mother both fell sick and quickly died. Local police found the girl wandering alone and sent her to the Methodist orphanage, where she stayed for a decade. In 1864, about four years after her arrival, she converted to Christianity. In 1870, she married a native Christian pastor and shortly after finally returned to visit her natal village. "Her father and [other] brother [were] still living; and were delighted to see her," noted a missionary. "The people in the village all remembered her and thought it a very strange thing that they saw her again. They all said such a thing had never happened in their village before," in which a child presumed dead had returned.[29] Fanny's story is a reminder that even kin who may have wanted to find children often could not, especially if they were poor. Nor could children necessarily return, even if they knew the names of their villages. At other times, parents did complain to colonial authorities, especially when missionaries gathered up large numbers of children at once. Thus, when famed Methodist missionary William Butler acquired a number of orphans in the chaos following the Indian Sepoy Rebellion of 1857, he assured his worried Board back home that he had settled it all legally, having asked a local magistrate to issue "deeds" for each one.[30]

Violence and colonial governance enabled missionaries like Butler to "acquire" foreign children for missionary stations. Stateside, another factor enabled such projects by making them legible and important to U.S. Christians who provided the necessary capital: a rising theo-cultural stream of thought, often called Christian romanticism. Building on Locke and Francke's theories of childhood development, Romantics argued that children were actually more *intuitively religious* than adults, if they were sheltered from vice. In the United States, this idea is most closely associated with Calvinist pastor Horace Bushnell (1802–1876). He rejected revivalism's emphasis on crisis conversions in which an individual was often dramatically born again. He associated this means of grace with a rampant individualism promoted by theologies of predestination and emerging U.S. capitalism. Instead, Bushnell sought to distribute spiritual responsibility beyond the individual by arguing that the circulation of affective Christian sentiments created "secret foundations of life and society" that bonded people into a regenerate whole. When a person "insensibly" poured out Christian feeling into the world, others would be changed by it. While Bushnell believed this process operated at a national level, he is best known for his writings about the family. It was within this basic societal building block that he saw a truly "organic" link between parent and child: by nurturing a young child's "plastic, passive soul," the parent opened a channel for God's grace. Based on his own New England mother, Bushnell viewed women as most embodying the "passive virtues" of Christ: gentle, sacrificial suffering that exerted a power so persuasive as to retain a hold deeper than consciousness itself. For Bushnell, maternal and divine nurture were virtually indistinguishable: when mother-love was cut off after the death of the parent, God's perfect love continued to grow from the seeds it had planted.[31]

Among the white middle classes of Europe and North America, women came to be seen as guardians of societal virtue encased in the "innocence" of domestic interiors, while their menfolk navigated the heady changes of political and industrial revolutions. As Bushnell's thought suggests, sentimentalism can be viewed as a form of "sensorial discipline" in which all civilized people, but especially women, were required to master their impulses in order to circulate and regulate Christian feeling within the family and thus secure moral authority in society at large.[32] This process was structured through "reciprocal sentiments" where unequal parties (men-women, parents-children) created a sense of "mutual responsibility and exchange within a culture of emotion." In the family, the mother nurtured her child in faith, while her own heart was also "enlarged" by observing childhood—its spontaneity, simplicity, responsiveness—to renew her love for God. And yet these affective relations were never stable: women noted that their children seemed both innocent and sinful at the same time, since the young succumbed especially frequently to vices such as dishonesty, greed, and selfishness.[33]

This ambivalence spilled over into missionary portrayals of heathen children, who were viewed as both innocent (because they were young) and damned (because they were susceptible to child-sin and lacked Christian nurture). As a result, perhaps, periodicals such as *Heathen Woman's Friend* (HWF), the official organ of the Methodist WFMS, skirted the issue of what exactly happened to foreign children who died unredeemed, as U.S. readers were assured they did by the millions every day. A good illustration is Emily C.

Pearson's poem "The Little Hindu," which was first issued by the ABCFM and popular enough to be reprinted by the WFMS in 1870. It begins in a child's voice: "I am a little Hindu girl/Of Jesus never heard/O! Pity me, dear Christian child/And send to me His word." The second stanza responds as a chorus of American children: "Here's our money, little girl/To buy God's word for you." The last stanzas continue in the aggregate plural, describing a union in Heaven: "And if at last we reach the shore/Where sorrow is unknown,/We hope to greet thee, Hindu girl,/Safe, safe before the throne."[34] It is clear that the girl is not being nurtured at home in the Bushnellian sense, nor has she had a personal conversion experience. The U.S. children are told to pity her unregenerate state, and the implication is that if heaven is a possibility so, too, must be hell. Yet there is no suggestion that the girl will be damned necessarily, since death and judgment are pushed into the unspecified future ("if at last . . .").

Sentimentalism—with its rejection of original sin and its vague optimism about child innocence—was a middle way that produced the conditions for U.S. women to labor on heathen children's behalf. If they had believed in the unredeemable nature of childhood, they would have been unlikely to support child sponsorship; if they had eliminated all fear of damnation, they would have been unlikely to support overseas evangelism. The twin engines of love and sin drove their investments in children far away.

FEELING ADULT SIN AND THE CYCLE OF CHRISTIAN LOVE

Mrs. Esther Baldwin, a missionary at Foochow, wrote a series of reports for *Heathen Woman's Friend* in 1870. She began by warning her readers that China's rampant infanticide would "reach every mother's heart," but she softened the blow with the reassuring reminder that, "safe from every taint of sin, from the degradation of heathenism, these little [infants] go straight to heaven, and are saved from Satan." She easily extended this safety net to older children too; it was adults who proved problematic. Not wanting to dissuade a potential convert, Mrs. Baldwin balked when a Chinese woman asked point blank if her beloved, deceased husband—who had drowned their baby girls in a culturally acceptable infanticide—would also greet her in heaven. Mrs. Baldwin reluctantly replied that perhaps even he retained some innocence since he had never heard of Christ. But as she penned the report for her U.S. readers, she could not quite exonerate him. "Yet I feared that he had not done as well as he knew, even by nature," she concluded rather ominously for his eternal soul.[35]

While the possibility of child sin was muted and even denied in WFMS literature, adult sin was everywhere, especially in descriptions of non-white people. Yet recall that in Christian terms, the correlation between race and civility was never static. The Enlightenment view of sin understood vice as transmitted through heredity and social context.[36] This understanding helped missionaries explain why sin seemed to be more entrenched in the "lower" races at home and abroad, while retaining the universalizing claim that all people could rupture this cycle through conversion and progress into Christian civility. Nineteenth-century missionary periodicals were filled with proof texts for this theory. They provided their audiences with a continual stream of stories about regenerate heathens—including sponsored children—who showed themselves able to think, talk, and even look like U.S. Christians. Within these many individual examples of change, however, there loomed questions about "heathen" society at large. In the Bushnellian vision and others like it, the "national or family spirit" that exerted an insensible influence upon a child's development seemed at once a highly effective way to spread Christian feeling in largely Christian environments and a highly destructive way in which sin could taint an entire national "race" unawares (Bushnell himself focused on Catholic Europe: France was infected by a spirit of infidelity, he wrote, and Spain by a spirit of bigotry).[37]

Along the same lines, mission-minded U.S. Protestants often portrayed heathen sin as so immense as to elude definite form, a kind of darkness obscuring whole peoples and places. "We are pioneers for Jesus in the dense forests of sin and superstition," declared the secretary of Cincinnati's WFMS branch in 1872.[38] These vague, poetical metaphors worked alongside precise anecdotes meant to provoke sensory experiences of fascination and disgust. In the first issue of *HWF* in 1869, Jennie F. Willing, secretary for the Northwest branch and the magazine's most prolific early contributor, noted that "the depth of [heathen] degradation is, as we are often assured, altogether beyond our realization." And yet, she told her readers that U.S. women had a duty not only to digest "the hard, ugly facts about the lying, thieving, and women-flogging, the licentiousness and infanticide of all pagandom," but to actually "sicken at their rottenness." Because detailed information was viewed as a prerequisite for emotional investments in faraway places, U.S. Christian women were treated to what today reads as a jarring mix of sensationalist accounts of heathen sin next to rather neutral ethnographic descriptions of (even religious) events. Jennie Willing concluded bluntly, "Get people to feel these things, and there will be no trouble about the collections."[39]

In his study of mid-nineteenth-century revivals in New England, historian John Corrigan traces how emotion began to be essentialized as an object that could be circulated, traded, given, or withheld. He points out that in the 1740s, proponents of Scottish Common Sense, a theo-philosophical stream with broad influence in Anglo-America, broke the barrier between metaphysics and physiology by arguing that moral emotions produced physical vibrations in the brain. The opposite was understood to be true as well, as argued by Jennie Willing more than a century later: by stimulating physical sensations, one could produce moral feelings. Just as important, Common Sense popularized the idea that by examining one's conscience individuals could come to "natural" conclusions about the moral self that could be extrapolated into larger conclusions (even "laws") about the nature of human existence. In the sentimental Christianity that infused sponsorship, the truths of felt-life came to be viewed as a thing that could be cultivated and circulated through revivals, but also among family members, at deathbeds, and even by reading the vivid anecdotes in missionary periodicals.[40]

Christians prized feelings such as love, sympathy, and awe,[41] even as missionary reports also sought to provoke "ugly feelings" that included irritation, anxiety, or disgust. Such feelings have a temporality—literary theorist Sianne Ngai calls it "flatness or ongoingness"—that contrasts with the sudden power and cathartic release associated with major emotions, such as rage or terror. For this reason, many philosophers and psychologists have ignored ugly emotions as largely without political or social consequence.[42] Yet adverse emotions, such as disgust, are actually important and flexible strategies for delineating boundaries between self and other because, unlike animals that may be repelled momentarily by a strong odor or sensation, humans cast whole *categories of things* as disgusting by virtue of their relatedness, whether or not they actually come into contact with them. Although most frequently associated with tastes or odors, disgust is also prompted by noxious vices, such as cruelty or hypocrisy.[43]

Missionaries and their supporters linked moral and physical disgust to reinforce the line between Christians and others by subsuming foreign habits, foods, built environments, rituals, timbres of voice, and domestic relations into a broad category called "heathendom." The affective, temporally "flat," and unannounced power of disgust was socially and culturally productive precisely because its embodied aspect did seem instinctual (the churning of one's stomach, the frisson down one's spine, the lump in one's throat). As Jennie Willing hoped, U.S. women came to view the disgust provoked by heathen sin as both natural and deeply personal since it was embodied. Thus, when a returned missionary offered examples of sin in India, it "chilled the blood in our veins," one New England Branch secretary recalled. Or, as a woman in Michigan reported, each time she read her monthly copy of *HWF* it stirred such strong feelings that she retreated with "tear-bedimmed eyes to my [prayer] closet to again ask for the abolishing of all idols, and the hastening of the coming of that kingdom."

These embodied engagements could be challenging. In 1874, just three years after her first *HWF* missives from Foochow, Mrs. Baldwin told her readers that she had become so sickened by heathendom that she felt *"indescribably hopeless"* and even doubted her capacity to love Chinese souls at all.[44] Early theorists of sentiment acknowledged this possibility. Disgust could stymy the "impartial spectator" of refined sensibilities who recoiled from excessive displays of emotion, according to Scottish Common Sense philosopher Adam Smith in *The Theory of Moral Sentiments*. Yet Smith also believed that disgust, once transmuted into loving contempt (or pity), could unite "a world of impartial spectators into a moral community, as cosharers of the same sentiments, as guardians of propriety and purity."[45] Members of this moral community tried to experience others' feelings vicariously, but always insofar as they judged how the other *should* feel; disgust and indignation could be felt on behalf of another whether or not she felt that way herself, which she very well might not. For sponsors, aversion to heathen sin was thus viewed as a natural and productive Christian feeling, first, because it protected U.S. women from degradation and, second, because it motivated the circulation and "enlargement" of Christian love through charitable action. Thus, love bore a complex but necessary relation to disgust.

This vision relied on Christian globalism's central conviction that all people had souls and were therefore susceptible to the same sins and eligible for redemption. In its humanitarian form, this universalism assumed that whatever Western people suffered when deprived of Christianity was reproduced in facsimile—or exacerbated—among people without access to Christianity. In her call to sicken at heathen sin in order to become bound up in God's chain of obligation, Jennie Willing makes this point by quoting from *The Present Crisis*, James Russell Lowell's 1845 poem about U.S. slavery (although she does not identify it as such):

> One in spirit, and an instinct bears along,
> Round the earth's electric circle, the swift flash of right or wrong;
> Whether conscious or unconscious, yet Humanity's vast frame
> Through its ocean-sundered fibres feels the gush of joy or shame;—
> In the gain or loss of one race all the rest have equal claim.

In Willing's hands, the poem transmutes the money she is asking Americans to give into a globally circulating set of shared emotions—gushes of joy and shame that course throughout a shared Body ("Humanity's vast frame") in swift flashes of moral recognition evoking the newest technologies of the day. Fundamental to this universalizing humanitarian theology was the idea, self-evident to Western Christians, that (to use emic language) heathen people were *already Christ's inheritance.* Because Jesus had "paid" for the sins of humanity, he inherited a responsibility for every single soul. It was up to Americans to recognize how they themselves were also already implicated in this corporate human story. Activities like sponsorship provided key frameworks through which they could put their love into action, even without the imperial institutions and rhetoric of obligation familiar to their Protestant counterparts in Britain.

As noted in the discussion of Bushnell's writings about his mother, sentimentalists viewed human love as productive, true, and Christian (words that meant largely the same thing for them) when it was tightly bound to, and dependent upon, God's Love. So, even when missionary magazines acknowledged that Chinese families, for example, might think they loved each other they were in fact mistaken, since "the *motive power* is absent." Without Divine Love, and the constraining power of Christ, human love was an impossibility since "the paramount questions in all hearts are self and gain."[46] It was in this sense that other religions, such as "Hindooism," were understood as having "no thought of human helpfulness," to quote the secretary of a WFMS auxiliary in Pasadena, regardless of Hindus' own understanding or actions. Over the course of their monthly meetings, the women in that auxiliary supported 19 foreign children, and the record they left demonstrates how sponsors deployed love/ Love in ways that amplified missionary magazines' use of these terms: in their reports, "love" indicated their own missionary exertions and aspirations to "gird" the earth for Christ; "Love" (which I mark with a capital L) indicated an extra-human spiritual force that "uses" people as needed in order to further God's Kingdom.[47] The (weaker) love must be enlarged by the (infinitely stronger) Love in order to reach faraway places. The best illustrations of this principle focused on the "weakest" form of human love—that of a baby who is not even cognizant of why she contributes to the collection plate, as in this sentimental poem: "I am but a penny/From a baby hand;/Can I bear glad tidings/Over all the lands?/Baby's love goes with me/So her penny's blest:/ *God's love joined with baby's/Will do all the rest.*"[48]

Given this framework, U.S. women generally viewed their heathen counterparts as deficient on two major grounds: they were unable to circulate moral (Christian) emotion *to* their children and to absorb moral inspiration *from* their children. Without this circuit of human emotion, God's Love could find no entry point. Even if a heathen mother seemed to love her offspring, it was understood as useless at best and perverted at worst. (Missionaries reported on monstrous mother-love where heathen women lavished such affection on their sons that even as adults these men would not risk offending her by converting.)

A HEATHEN GODDESS DEVOURING CHILDREN OFFERED BY
THEIR MOTHERS.

FIG 1.1A AND 1.1B. Monstrous heathen motherhood depicted in 1833 in the *MH* and idealized Christian motherhood depicted in *HWF* in 1894. The latter reproduces visual tropes often associated with Anglo-Protestant mothers at the time, while also recalling images of the Madonna and Child.

Christian motherhood of the kind replicated in portraits of the Madonna and Child, the American mother and child, and the redeemed Heathen mother and child was, to quote an 1894 article in *HWF*, "the most beautiful form of truth in the world" (figures 1.1a and 1.1b). Once this ideal of white, middle-class motherhood was made into truth—the universal channel for God's universal Love—it projected backward across the centuries to the holiness of Jesus's incarnation on earth and forward to "Christian centuries yet to be, giving us faint shadowings of the future Holy Family, 'Toward which the whole creation moves.'"[49] It was this image of an eternal, globally circulating, pre-cultural love that American women came to view as "natural."

SINS AT HOME: A CHAIN OF OBLIGATION IN THE CAPITALIST AGE

Drawing on Marx, who declared that the value of good conscience grows in proportion to exploitation, we might well ask how charitable impulses take shape within unequal forms of capitalism.[50] Some studies suggest that this relationship contributed to the very rise of capitalism since notions of brotherly love initially enhanced "the legitimacy of proto-capitalists."[51] While nineteenth-century sponsors by no means thought of themselves as proto-capitalists per se, they were certainly enmeshed in the complex ethics of a time marked by massive political and economic change. U.S. sponsorship plans developed in the charged atmosphere of the new Republic. Religious volunteerism was replacing church establishment. Cash-based mercantilism and industrialization were sweeping society. Many Protestant pastors accommodated these changes by arguing that God had blessed the United States more abundantly than other nations, making it incumbent upon Americans to give back by voluntarily supporting God's churches.[52] Capitalist inequity and democracy unfolded alongside moral ideas about obligation and sacrifice.[53]

In response, sponsorship reiterated older covenantal theologies that saw God's blessings as tied to obligations.[54] However, these messages were newly contextualized: the women and men who responded to the ABCFM sponsorship plan were part of the first U.S. Protestant generation that could compare their own material and spiritual wealth with detailed observations about non-European places. Whether middling or poor, sponsorship's supporters agreed that Western Protestants had inherited the lion's share of God's global blessings. The question was why.

Two subtly different responses emerged. The first relied on the stewardship model from the Parable of the Talents (Matthew 25:14–30), which pictured God as the benevolent sovereign "who sits over against the treasury, notes with deepest interest all the gifts, and where there is the most sacrifice gives his richest blessing." This God missed nothing related to the circulation of his abundance on earth: when an American gave charitably, "every cent will be registered in Heaven."[55] A second iteration viewed the nation more corporately as the agent of Christ bound to advance his earthly Kingdom or forfeit its own prosperity. ABCFM General Secretary Rufus Anderson embodied this approach when he refused to close mission fields, even as his organization spiraled into debt and the country plunged into civil war. Writing in November 1861, he emphasized that humans must seek the Kingdom of God as "the *condition* of receiving and retaining their temporal blessings." To withdraw even a dollar, argued Anderson, would spell calamity for the U.S. nation and for God's work; it would be "a violence upon the kingdom, upon the church, upon the body, of our Lord and Savior."[56]

Both visions balanced freedom and constraint. While missionary materials viewed God's Love as freeing heathen women from spiritual and bodily "bondage," in the U.S. context it was also expected to bring welcome restrictions: "the Love of Christ Constraineth me," as it says in Corinthians. This principle lay behind Jennie Willing's comment that U.S. women must "sicken at the rottenness" of heathen sin, since her interpretation of the Bible was that all God's creatures were soldered into "a chain of obligation" that undergirds the Creator's model of moral governance. The chain, according to Willing, linked the neediest and the most blessed. American women were the latter, and their indebtedness to God increased proportionally to the suffering of the world's least favored—heathen women and children. The intensity of connection meant that all should sicken when sin corrupted one part of the whole. It also enjoined constraint upon those who had been given so much that they could succumb to greed and forget that their relative prosperity compared to other human beings actually signaled an ever-mounting *debt* to the Creator.

More pragmatically, counseling constraint justified the system of regular, systematic tithing upon which sponsorship depended. As WFMS agents raised funds, they not infrequently faced a theologically inflected argument that could be hard to refute: God's law of Eternal Love had replaced the Jewish law, with its constrained and specific religious injunctions. They responded (more or less successfully) by framing controlled, systematic giving as one aspect of God's immense, creative force, as expressed in a *HWF* article from 1888:

> [I]n view of *debt*, and duty, and privilege, and opportunities; in view of God, of humanity in its vastness, with its multiplied wants, and suffering, and sorrows, and sins; of eternity . . . let us intelligently, conscientiously seek to determine how *much*, not how *little*, we may do and give. Then let us do it as we are taught—regularly, continually, cheerfully; thus bringing glory to God in the carrying out of his purposes, unspeakable blessing to our own souls in thus allying ourselves to him as co-workers, and salvation to a sinning, perishing world.[57]

To be co-workers with God also meant sharing in Jesus's personal sacrifice for "humanity in its vastness." WFMS women debated if the money given for God's purposes should therefore also arise from a personal sacrifice and, if so, what that meant. In general, nineteenth-century Anglo-Protestant women often bore the burden of sacrificial giving in their society, which "cleansed" the money that men made (this is still capitalism's moral order, argues anthropologist Daniel Miller).[58] Middle-class women were expected to purchase an increasing number of luxury goods considered necessary for inclusion in "polite" company without succumbing to the vainglory of caring too much about things or appearances (a sin to which women were viewed as prone). They were expected to refrain from small pleasures and put away their pennies for charity since, quoting well-heeled New Englander educator Mary Lyon, "economy and self-denial are the two great springs which feed the fountains of benevolence."[59] They were expected to monitor and regulate their own

Christian sentiments and those of their children since, as Bushnell noted darkly, in well-off American families "sometimes you will almost fancy that you see the shapes of money in the eyes of the children."[60]

The resulting message was paradoxical. On the one hand, middle-class women were told that giving pennies to support an orphan was easy, the emotions engendered joyful, because the amounts were so small; they were merely asked to give up "loose nickels" or "cheerfully sacrifice superfluous expense in dress or equipage."[61] On the other hand, they were reminded that they should feel the pinch of sacrifice. "The planting of Christ's kingdom, whether in the individual heart or in a heathen nation, always means sacrifice" wrote a Philadelphia Branch secretary, "the first steps are taken in hardness and affliction."[62] Yet "few of us know the meaning of the word 'sacrifice,' in the Lord's work," admonished Jennie Willing from Chicago. "Some do: they prick out their two cents a week [for WFMS membership] at the needle's point, or they earn it by hard rubbing upon a washboard. [But] it is hardly worth the name of sacrifice to wear last winter's hat, or two-button instead of four-button kids [gloves], a cheaper trimming or plainer style of dress."[63] Middle-class women were therefore encouraged to give just a little *more* than made them comfortable; the goal was to momentarily grasp the emotional power of precarity—dread, anxiety, and even "morbid fear" of poverty—through which a middle-class woman might share in the immensity of Jesus's sacrifice for others.

Because subscription charity required such small amounts, it also drew thousands of nameless givers who likely did feel "hardness and affliction" on a regular basis. These women sometimes addressed the middle-class WFMS leadership directly. During the 1878 depression, women in the Pennsylvania coal and iron districts reported that it was "simply impossible" to give when they struggled even for "bread itself." Women in the Midwest wrote pointedly: "[We] are not women of leisure, with both money and time at our command: [we] . . . sacrifice almost as much as the missionaries for whom [we] work and pray; and often it happens that the names Jesus knows best, because of the patient toiling for his dear sake, are not the ones found in the annals of the societies."[64] The poorest givers wrote nothing at all, but their traces remain in the archives. They walked from their rural farmsteads to local WFMS offices to bring their donations in kind—handmade clothes, quilts, and produce. Others told WFMS collectors that they saved pennies from their and their children's labor at piecework, in factories, and in middle-class homes.

It is impossible to assess the attachments and anxieties these poorer donors may have felt, but it is clear that the middle-class women who circulated their stories used them as a foil for talking about money-sacrifice in the Christian terms above. "Surely such offerings will more rapidly usher in Christ's kingdom than the thousands given with less faith and loving sacrifice," opined Jennie Willing.[65] They circulated these stories along with those about another group of pecuniary unfortunates—their own children. Middle-class children gave up candy money and the like, but they also agonizingly agreed to part with beloved dolls, pet rabbits, and other important objects. For their mothers, such struggles modeled an ideal of "child-like" confidence: when told to give, they did so at great (emotional) cost without questioning whether an immense God truly needed such a comparatively small sacrifice.[66] Poor women were lauded for similar reasons. WFMS writers called them women "who live on promises" because their actions flew in the face of capitalist accumulation by giving as much as they had and placing their entire trust in God. By contrast, middle-class women chastised each other for so often being "haunted with the ghost of a *future* poverty."[67] They remarked wonderingly how poor givers seemed impervious to material fears. Their economic recklessness distanced them from this world—and pulled them closer to God.

Capitalist hauntings indicate a particular temporality, a future orientation characteristic of what philosopher Ernst Bloch calls "expectation emotions." Ngai adds to his assessment by noting how such feelings are often spatial too, in the sense that one's anxieties can be projected onto another.[68] Perhaps it is not surprising, then, that middle-class women like Jennie Willing so explicitly presented the actions of materially poor givers—lower classes, their own children—to come to terms with the fear of future poverty that stalked many middle-class households, especially during capitalism's bewildering cycles of confidence and panic. Writing on the heels of the 1880s recession and the Panic of 1884, a *HWF* contributor wrestled with this issue. "Perhaps there is no country more subject to business fluctuations than our own," she wrote: "Its countless departments of manufacture, trade, and speculation afford a constantly widening marketplace, where fortunes are made and lost with astonishing rapidity . . . [Even] Christians,—the most earnest, and active, and useful,—are often reduced to poverty." The proper, that is to say Christian, response to this disastrous loss of wealth was never to grieve for oneself but for God's causes, to which one could no longer contribute.[69]

In this context, Christians sometimes referred to investments in God's "savings bank" as the only prospect that never failed. Even if one lost everything in a market crash, whatever was stored in God's bank would continue to accrue interest in one's favor in Heaven. Thus, the worst possible outcome of capitalist anxiety and competition was to withdraw inward and cease to circulate God's money: "Indulgence in a morbid fear of possible future want is one of the surest ways to bring [a total loss] about; while as a rule, a cheerful and grateful use of present means is the sure way to even larger possibilities [in Heaven]."[70] This was not the prosperity gospel of later periods—where "seed" money reaps riches here on earth; rather, the stewardship system was meant to reiterate that all personal wealth in fact belonged to God and would only be properly fruitful if (some of) it returned to the source.

Whether poor or middle-class, Christian givers at home reminded each other that it was missionaries who *truly* sacrificed, no matter how much one gave and at what personal cost. In 1876, Mrs. W.W. Fink attended the Western Branch's annual meeting in Des Moines, Iowa, and was struck with the conflicting emotions that could result. "There is something wonderful in the thought that we, working quietly and modestly, as becometh women, are yet bridging the oceans and continents with influences of love, and planting the banner of the cross in the lands of Confucius, Tamerline, and Monteczuma," she wrote in praise of the small sacrifices women in her district made. And yet, "those who represent us in foreign lands are giving *their lives,*" she concluded.[71] It was Jesus's bodily sacrifice that redeemed humanity; missionaries, like the ancient martyrs, came closest to repaying that debt by assuming bodily risk.

Home audiences mediated this issue somewhat by engaging in techniques that made money sacrifices into embodied events. For well-off women, one method of doing so was through "practical Christianity" that required one's physical labor. This kind of sacrifice meant choosing to do with one's hands that which poor women did out of economic necessity. For example, in 1881 Mrs. Caroline Wright, a wealthy New York widow and president of her WFMS Branch, decided to build a mission school at Hakodate, Japan. The required amount was $1,800, more than five times an average annual salary at the time.[72] Although Mrs. Wright could have raised the sum outright, she refused to "offer unto the Lord that which cost her nothing." Instead, she made embroidery with "her own hands" and sold it in her Manhattan home. She named her school the Caroline R. Wright Memorial School, as a "precious memorial" to her recently deceased daughter of that name. She also sponsored Yoshi San, an orphan girl, and renamed her Caroline R. Wright (figure 1.2). Thus, sacrificial love was embodied in hands that labored for the coins they gathered; it was also expressed by re-materializing absent loved ones in the buildings and heathen bodies that bore their names.[73]

The relation between money and bodies also produced the evocative custom of putting "bodies" onto the collection plate. In a rather literal substitution, a mother could write her child's name on a scrap of paper and contribute it to the church collection plate in lieu of money. Individuals sometimes did the same. Ann Wilkins, the first single female missionary in Africa, is

FIG 1.2. Girls at the Methodist school in Hakodate, Japan, reprinted in *HWF* in November 1884. The one on the far right is Yoshi San, who was renamed Caroline R. Wright.

probably the most famous example. When she was a schoolteacher in Sing Sing, New York, Wilkins "literally put herself on the plate" at a missionary talk by contributing her name and a note to the collection that read, "A sister who has but little money at her command gives that little cheerfully and is willing to give her life as a female teacher if she is wanted."[74] The story was repeated by Methodist women for a generation and then printed on Wilkins's tombstone.

A SENTIMENTAL VANGUARD

Through sponsorship, nineteenth-century U.S. Christians honed the idea that the shared humanity of all people crystallized in the soul—and that these souls provided a universal mechanism through which God's Love traveled. Yet, according to missionary literature, the sheer monstrosity of (adult) heathen sin could seem to foreclose commonality. Other times, it was U.S. Christians' own sins that seemed stumbling blocks to connection as they confronted middle-class greed and fears of future poverty.

Globally minded Christians never resolved these ambivalences when they wrote about love and sin, but they did address them in a way. Sponsors were the vanguard of a new trend in U.S. Christianity—sentimentalism—that suggested religious feeling passed organically through families and societies. As a result, many U.S. women (and some men) came to view themselves as catalysts for Christian change: their own hearts were "enlarged" through personal experiences, resulting in their own loving actions and feelings, which then provided an entry point for God's Love to impact others. Once it was scaled up, this model of love/Love became an indispensable ideational building block for contemporary Christian globalism since it cleared a path for U.S. people at home to impact the world as whole. It also helped define a Christian parent's emotions as sacred—even when they pertained to a child she had never met—and a heathen parent's emotions as always stunted, and even perverted, since they denied the ultimate goal of circulating God's Love. Sentimentalists conceived of the proliferation of Christian feeling in the world as akin to sensations traveling along a body's nervous system.[75] And this metaphor—along with those about electrical currents, scattering seeds, and infusing light into darkness—made the spread of Christianity seem natural and organic. Like the "flow" metaphors later used by theorists of globalization, it rhetorically denied friction and failure (though in fact Anglo-Protestants *did* fail to evangelize "the world" since they made relatively few converts during this period). What all these metaphors did, however, was provide a way for U.S. Christians to speak to each other about God's immensity.

Nineteenth-century Christian globalism also reiterated older covenantal theologies that saw God's blessings as tied to obligations but set them within a new reality in which Americans could compare their own wealth with comparatively detailed descriptions of non-European places. Their conclusion was that Western Protestants were definitely more blessed than others. The resulting model of moral governance linked the most and least blessed through their shared relation to a common Creator; thus, American women's indebtedness to God increased proportionally with what was understood to be the suffering of heathen women and children. It enjoined constraint upon globally minded U.S. Christians, and especially women, so that they could recirculate God's monetary and emotional resources to those in need.

Sponsors often signaled these ideas with a phrase from Matthew 25:40 that said, "Inasmuch as ye have done it unto the least of these, Ye have done it unto Me." So ubiquitous was this phrase in the last half of the nineteenth century that it became a kind of unofficial slogan of sponsorship. Many women simply jotted "Inasmuch" at the end of the notes they penned. Although it did not originally refer to children or to foreigners, for sponsors it came to mean that foreign children—now viewed as innocent—were so closely associated with the divine whole that to send resources to them was in fact to channel resources to God. Thus, the pennies that sustained an individual child's growth also grew God's global "body" and secured one's place within it. The task of U.S. Christians, and women in particular, was to stoke personal emotions, ranging from love to pity to disgust to fear, in order to circulate the Love that God had set in motion.

Belinda Coles (Cortlandt, New York) and Belinda Coles (Millsburgh, Liberia)

This interlude imagines a sponsor-child connection through an elaboration of historical sources. Belinda Coles was a woman in upstate New York and "Belinda" was a girl she renamed after herself at Ann Wilkins's Methodist school in the 1840s. I draw on extant letters that Wilkins sent to Coles and to Mary Garrettson (also in upstate New York) about two other girls at the school. While all the events discussed took place where the girls lived, I have imagined how they may have felt. I also make an educated guess that "Belinda" was from the Queah tribe and I call her Donyen, which means beautiful in Kru languages, a variant of which was likely her mother tongue. I hesitated about imagining a name for her, but ultimately I decided it was important to signal how her life exceeded the sponsor-donor relationship and the name conferred upon her in that context. My hope is that this interlude will spur readers' thinking in a few respects. From a methodological perspective, it raises the possibility of experimental approaches to writing when globally dispersed sources are incomplete. From a narrative perspective, it offers a sense of the rhythm of child-sponsor relations forged through sporadic communication. In either case, the larger point is to foreground how absences constitute even the most intimate global projects—for scholars and for the people we study.

MILLSBURGH, LIBERIA, FEBRUARY 1845

Donyen tapped the windowpane again. It was hot to the touch because of the sun, but she knew from experience that it would cool at night. It was an odd thing, she thought, to make windows that let in so much heat but block the sun everywhere else. In her mother's hut, slivers of light peeped through between the ceiling beams and palm fronds, under the cracks in the walls and the door.[1] This schoolhouse where she lived now was very large and square, much bigger than any in Robertsville. She liked its simple furnishings, with mats for the beds. She smoothed her hands on her skirts happily. True, so much cloth made her hot, but it was worth it: only the wives of King Zoda Quee had enough material for clothes this fine.[2]

Things had changed for her people. That was why her mother sent her with the King's stranger over the river to the whiteman's school in Millsburgh.[3] She could not remember ever having traveled so far, though she had often heard about the time when she was very little and Zoda Quee went to Heddington for such a God-palaver[4] that he decided the people would be Christians and the Queah traveled to make the new town, Robertsville.[5] Her first memories were of the days and nights when the people called out to God together and burned their gris-gris, which pleased the American God-man Taylor. Then the wars at Heddington came quickly. Many people left, but her family stayed.[6] The real problem, she knew, was that her mother was a third wife and the new God only allowed one wife for each man. Now she had no status as her father's child, no suitors, and her mother had no dash.[7] The head God-man came and asked mothers to give him their girls. "White and black men are the same and made by God," he told them in the palaver-house, "We heard in America that men here make and serve gree-gree so we came to teach them to read books and serve God. Women who learn these things can help the men. They will make the best Christian wives."[8] Her mother listened closely. That night, she told Donyen that she must go and become a marriageable woman.

So here she was, along with four other girls from the Pessah and Vey and American colonists from the towns.[9] She ran her hand over her cropped hair. Before she left, her mother said, "Your name means beautiful" and she cut her hair short except for one beautiful long braid on the left side. Why did it make the colonist children laugh and Ma'am Ann Wilkins angry? She cut their hair the day they arrived. She told Donyen, "You are lucky to have such coarse and straight hair. It is of much better quality than negro people in America."[10] Some of the girls cried when they lost their braids, but she didn't mind because of her new dress. Besides, Ma'am Ann Wilkins promised to find a lady from her home across the ocean to send dash. That was a mystery, thought Donyen. Did this lady need a young wife for her husband? Why would she give dash to a girl and not her parents? It was one more thing to learn once school began.

CORTLANDT, NEW YORK, JANUARY 1846

Belinda stared at the snow, thinking how it was a pleasant contrast with the dried leaves of the shrubs and oaks. Her hand rested on the letter in front of her, dated November 1845.[11] She did a quick calculation: Ann Wilkins had been in Liberia for eight years.[12] It was hard to believe. She remembered her from camp meetings in Westchester County, although they had not been close. Belinda had been so busy helping her husband pastor the new church, managing her two servants, and starting a family, while Ann had little means in those days after her husband had left; a distasteful affair.[13] Her conviction for God had to be admired though. What else could induce a decent woman to go alone to Africa? Belinda herself had never been more than a few hours' ride from her childhood home in South Salem. Now she was 44 and they lived at Cortlandt, just 20 miles away.

She turned back to the letter. When George's friend John Seys had been to dinner, he had regaled them with stories of the Liberian mission he supervised and the heathens Ann proposed to educate. It had been three years since the school was established at Millsburgh, but Ann had failed to enroll a single native girl. Belinda had read disturbing reports of the heathen in India and China who left their infant girls to die without a thought. The Africans did not, Mr. Seys assured them, but they sold them to the highest bidder for marriage. It was shocking, but she had not thought of it since. Now here was a child that Ann proposed would be hers to adopt! There was little information. The girl had been acquired in Robertsville and was about nine years old—the same age as her own Electa and Phebe.[14] She knew of such adoptions through Mary Mason and the women in New York. They sometimes named the heathen children for their babies who had passed away, for their pastors, and even for themselves. It tickled her to think of christening the child Belinda Coles. Mary Mason had done just that with a child in Ann's care.[15] Belinda had never known someone who was truly ignorant of God's word. All the Christians she knew had been raised in god-fearing families, even if they were Quakers or Presbyterians. Even her Negro servants came to her as Christians. Here was a chance to be a true apostle.

She started a bit at the sound of her husband's footsteps, home from his ride. "I heard from Ann Wilkins today about a protégée in Liberia," she began. "She begs us to be God's instruments for her instruction." As she expected, George was enthused: "In my days on the circuit, I always regretted the maxim I adopted as a young man, 'Let all the foreign tongues alone, Till you can speak and write your own.' It was expedient in those days but it limited the reach of my words."[16] He took one of his diaries off the shelf and skimmed through its pages. "Have I read you this passage? I wrote it in 1819 when I happened upon the great carriage of the Van Cortlandts. At first, I was in misery, imagining what we might do with wealth such as theirs." He looked down and read his words: "While some are blest with houses and lands . . . others there are to whom this grace is given, that they should 'preach among the Gentiles the unsearchable riches of Christ.'" He paused: "I have thought of that often. Who is the greatest philanthropist? The rich man who gives charity? What the rich man gives is not strictly speaking his own, since men are but stewards at best. But the ambassador of Christ gives in obedience to God so rather than diminishing his stock in giving, he increases it. He makes a multitude of friends who will welcome him in heaven."[17]

George paused as the sound of music drifted into the room; Electa was practicing piano in the parlor.[18] "Now that we are comfortably situated," he continued, "how can we deny this opportunity to increase our treasure in heaven?" Belinda nodded, suddenly feeling rather overcome with Christian pity for the Negro girl who was her daughter's age but had never played a piano nor heard the word of God. "I agree, George. Please tell Ann that we accept the privilege she affords us."

MILLSBURGH, LIBERIA, JUNE 1846

She had a new name—Belinda Coles. It pleased her since it proved that someone in America cared for her and was her patron, the English word for a lady who gives dash to girls. Ma'am Ann said, "She is your patron in America who will provide for you. Now that you bear her name you will always know someone cares for you and wants you to be a good Christian woman."[19] Her cousin Nyonweh, who had come with her from Robertsville, received a name from across the ocean too: Suzy-Ann Pitman.[20] These names were fun to say, with sounds that made one's tongue curl or twist, as they called out to each other.

Soon she liked her patron even more. Belinda Coles sent a cotton cloth called calico that was much softer than what she had before. A colonist woman from Millsburgh arrived and measured her for a dress. Ma'am Ann wrote down what the woman said: "Three feet ten inches tall, and measures round the waist about half a yard & half a quarter." Is that good? Donyen asked her and she replied, laughing, "You are straight and well formed."[21] The dash she liked best was a hymnbook and *Musical Repository*. She was so fond of singing. She liked the sound of drums around the fires at home but she liked the Christian songs much more, because even the youngest girls were allowed to join in. On Sundays, they sat in the schoolroom to sing until it was time to go to church.[22] It reminded her of the nights when her family walked to Heddington and stood outside Brown's school to join the students in Christian songs.[23]

She had no trouble remembering the words of hymns but was hopeless with sewing and gardening.[24] She did try her best. She and Nyonweh sometimes followed Ann Wilkins to watch closely as she touched and moved the objects to clean the house. When she did something they had never seen before, they were very happy and told her in English, "Tank ma'am!"[25]

Last week, the mothers from her village came to see how their daughters were improving. Her mother was very pleased with their new clothes, which rivaled those of the King's first wife. Upon hearing Donyen read out loud, she told her in Queah language to master this skill for it would be of great use to a husband. Ma'am Ann spoke no Queah, but said in English, "Belinda will teach the word of God to the bush heathen." She translated for her mother, who replied to Ma'am Wilkins, "She will not leave you until she learns all you can teach her."[26]

CORTLANDT, NEW YORK, OCTOBER 1846

"Ring for Caroline!" Phebe called breathlessly from the parlor. The servant girl brought in the letter and the children ran their fingers over the stamps.[27] "From Africa!" James said to his sister excitedly. George looked pleased. He had hoped that adopting the heathen girl would foster a greater interest in missions by giving the children an object upon which to pin their affections.[28]

"Shall we open it?" Belinda said as she carefully slit the envelope. She took out a watch guard, rather clumsily made, with a note that said it was the first one knit by the girl Belinda.[29] The girls excitedly clamored to touch it. She handed the envelope to James, who clutched the precious stamps to his chest. And then she asked George to read the letter aloud, "Did Ann answer my questions about Belinda? How old is she and of what size?" Electa chimed in, "Did she like the hymnbook we sent? Does she still like to sing? Can she play piano?" George looked it over: Ann had answered these questions and more, adding details about native styles of dress and hair. Phebe and Electa looked a little shocked: they shear the heads of *girls*? Perhaps it was better that way— Negros had such funny hair! Their servant, Caroline, sniffed a little, "Well, they are heathens, not *Christians*," she said. This began a lively discussion about the African Belinda and her mother, who Ann said was a Christian. Why did they shear their hair or go around in heathenish nakedness if they were Christians? Belinda and her daughters busied themselves with what they could send their protégée next. Ann had suggested summer clothes suitable for an American girl.[30] Phebe helped her mother find a pattern and Electa chose another songbook to include.

George allowed them to go on, aware that such womanly concerns were their way of caring for the child, as when they agonized over gifts to make for a neighbor or the items in their trousseaux. But he could not help weighing in, suddenly the preacher again, "Let us consider why we wished for so favorite a name to be perpetuated on a pupil in that dark continent. We wanted to feel a greater interest for Africa's children, as fellow beings possessing immortal souls bound to the same destinies as other human beings."[31] His children looked at him with serious countenances, he noted with satisfaction.

MILLSBURGH, LIBERIA, MARCH 1847

Donyen heard the praise singing she loved so well. She and the other girls in the dormitory clattered downstairs to see a knot of Congo and colonist children shouting and hugging their Bibles. A cry went up as a Congo they called Davis W. Clark shook his body and fell to the floor: "I grow warm! My soul is bound for the Kingdom!" Donyen looked in surprise. She had heard Ma'am Ann say that these slave "Congoes" who were found in a great ship were the most heathenish of heathens, without any notion of decency. They were common thieves who took anything they desired to eat from the gardens and kitchen. She had said this very thing! Even slave Congoes must be shown Christian charity, Donyen knew, since God was also the God of the Congoes, even if they called their god Toaumba.[32] But now God seemed to have found them. Davis Clark's cries rang out and they were so powerful that the Queah and Pessah girls joined in. Now more of the Congoes shouted about their new faith: Mary Mason, Thomas E. Bond, John Cornish, and Martha Elizabeth. Ma'am Ann was shaking with excitement: "I am more than paid now for all the years spent in Africa!"[33]

The next morning, Ma'am Ann called Donyen to her with more dash from her patron. "Belinda Coles has sent you these books and she has written to you personally, with her expression of many good wishes. She asks about you and tells you to be a good Christian woman when you return to your people so you can bring the Word of God to them." Donyen's way was different from some of the others, who always shouted with joy at each small thing. But she looked pleased and said quietly, "I mean to be a good girl." She turned the books over in her hands, touching the hard covers and the light pages. She was slower than the other girls, but with her teacher's help, she was finally nearly even with them in reading; she could read in a primer and make out words tolerably in the Bible. And now she had a Bible of her very own—the book revered above all others![34]

Ma'am Ann spoke very seriously. "Belinda, soon you will be a Queah woman. You know, my foremost aim in all my teaching is to lead you to know your great Creator and to worship him, that you may become a true Christian.

It is the only reason I left my friends and home, and all the enjoyments of civilization in my country. I rely on you to aid me to accomplish, by the help of Grace, such a work as shall extend the benefits you have to all the immortal souls in Africa."[35] She paused. "Will you marry Charles Pitman? As his help-mate you can bring hope to your people." Donyen's eyes widened but she made her face calm. Ma'am Ann still knew very little! Charles Pitman? That Queah nobody orphan who went to school with girls and didn't even know how to hunt? The Americans said he was no longer an orphan since he belonged to God, and they said he would be a great God-man one day. But he had no kin to give dash, knew no headmen, and had no name except the American one.[36] What a disgrace to be his wife!

ZODA TOWN, LIBERIA, JANUARY 1850

"Donyen, a gift!" She looked up in surprise and settled her infant on his mat in the sun to sleep.[37] Her mother sat with her in the doorway and they looked at the package curiously. English words. Donyen sounded them out slowly for lack of practice: M-I-L-L-S . . . from her teacher! But she had left Millsburgh nearly two years before—and now a gift? It was unexpected, too, because Ma'am Ann had been very sad when they parted.

Donyen left quite suddenly when King Zoda Quee broke ties with the Christians. The Negro colonists were expanding their farms around Mills-burgh, just as the new head God-man from America stopped giving dash to the kings. Zoda Quee reminded him of his proper share, since the colo-nists were given so many gifts of land and food. The God-man replied that the government gave land, not the Methodist Church. It was a grave insult nonetheless, and the King told his people that if this god was too weak to give dash then they would no longer be Christians.[38] The people took down their houses at Robertsville and Donyen's mother fetched the Queah girls after the rains subsided and the rivers were passable. Now that they were no longer Christians, her mother explained, Donyen's father accepted her and arranged her engagement to a worthy man. Her mother was very pleased and in gratitude she presented Ma'am Ann fine gifts of cassava flour and a gourd for water, decorated in the style the Americans liked so much. But her teacher was not happy, and Donyen knew why: she feared that Donyen's soul would not rest in the Eternal Mansion with her American friends and her patron, Belinda Coles. "You must remember God loves you and you must not touch the heathen idols," Ann Wilkins warned her as she left. Donyen nodded and pressed her hand in farewell.[39]

It was a long time before she felt at ease with her people. When she and Nyonweh arrived, the headmen's first wives made them give up their American dresses, which were too fine for their status.[40] They had to learn many things they should have known: how to cook cassava, grow arrowroot, and replace palm thatch on a roof—skills they needed before they could be married.[41] But in time, they had learned and now she looked at her child. He was peaceful still. "Shall we open it?" her mother asked. Donyen undid the string and slid out a book, which she knew was a Bible. She slid her hands over the leather cover and touched the paper with its black and white markings. She sounded out the inscription. It was from Belinda Coles! She said she had not forgotten her protégée and expected to see her in Heaven, if the girl did not forget to pray.

Donyen was pleased with the gift. She and her mother carefully removed its pages and pasted them onto the walls, next to the sheets from her hymnbook and the *Musical Repository*.[42] Her house was one of the most beautiful in the town. Sometimes colonist traders came with her husband just to see it. She fixed the page with her patron's inscription above the doorframe, next to the wooden talisman that protected against evil spirits—together they would be very powerful. She liked to see the American markings and the hymns she loved so well, which she remembered and sometimes sang to her son as he slept.

CHAPTER 2

Systems and Statistics

Aggregate Numbers and Particular Objects

Hark! The wail of heathen nations / . . . Ye who dwell in Christian
lands / Read ye not we're dying, dying / More in number than the sands!

—Maria A. West, "The Great Famine Cry."
    As read at WFMS meetings, 1880s

How wonderful that a private man should have such an influence on
the temporal and eternal happiness of millions literally, millions on
millions yet unborn!

—Samuel and Robert Wilberforce, *The Life of William Wilberforce*,
    v. 4 (London 1838), 115–16

In 1885, four women met in a village in Dauphin County, Pennsylvania. Encouraged by the Methodist minister, they had initiated a Wednesday meeting
to pray for foreign missions. As the first gathering approached, nervous-
ness set in: how would they hold their listeners' attention? One of the four,
Miss N., said, "I have just been reading last year's [missionary] report, and
think I can sum up the statistics in a few words, so as not to be wearisome."
One of the others offered to read a letter from a missionary, another to make
the pitch for donations. Then "something a little unusual happened," they
later recalled. A quiet, sweet-faced woman who had taken little part in the
discussion, said: "I can't talk, but I can pray." And at the meeting that evening, she poured forth such a powerful prayer that even "the statistics were
read in such a way as to make us wish for more." The women of Dauphin
County cried and laughed with emotion. Time seemed to stand still. Those
who normally objected "to a prayer-meeting of five minutes over the hour
stayed an hour and fifty minutes, and thought the clock must be wrong when
they got home."[1]

As classic work by Adorno, Horkheimer, and Foucault clarified, emerging nation-states in Europe developed statistics and taxonomies as controlling mechanisms to govern domestic and colonial populations. But these tools were never limited to the upper echelons; they were also "social technologies" that everyday people used and adapted, including the women in Dauphin County.[2] The record of their meeting suggests a few important things in this regard. First, statistics were often assumed to be wearisome, as Miss N. says, yet they were also ubiquitous in mid- to late nineteenth-century constructions of Christian globalism. Further, and importantly, statistics were incorporated into participatory techniques that combined prayers, hymns, readings, and fund-raising to produce at times remarkably affective moments. The women cried, laughed, and even felt time stop.

Child sponsorship began as the "first great Statistical enthusiasm" swept England and America in the 1820s and 1830s,[3] and forms of quantification were essential to its development in a number of ways. The first part of this chapter builds on the previous chapter's mention of systematic giving—the regular contribution of predetermined amounts from middling or poor people.[4] This "shareholding" was modeled on the strategies of early joint-stock companies. It enjoined citizens to carefully tabulate and save even the smallest amounts to contribute at set times during the month and it democratized charity by insisting that each one of their pennies was of equal value. It was a pragmatic way to adapt to newly disestablished, voluntary forms of Christian giving, which also appealed at an ideological level in the early U.S. Republic. In 1821, ABCFM secretary Samuel Worcester rather poetically claimed that systematic giving could unite "the whole nation . . . from the North to the South, in one common and glorious cause . . . No person on earth is in a condition too high to take part in this work—none in a condition too low."[5] Sponsorship made a striking contribution to this charitable culture through its promotion of "special objects"—that is, the opportunity to designate one's money to support a particular child. It, too, was pitched as a type of democratization: by designating the object, each donor could track the outcome of her charity.

Whereas the previous chapter explored how sponsors made money moral through sacrifice and redemption, here I focus on the conditions of its collection. Designated giving was enormously successful yet morally ambiguous for sponsorship promoters since it transferred significant power to grassroots donors. By contrast, both sponsors and sponsorship promoters viewed the systematic side of giving—with its regular and careful tabulations—as an eminently modern and moral form of charity. This chapter examines each of these two essential components in turn. Designated and systematic giving proved a powerful combination that encouraged those on the margins of power with new access to small amounts of ready cash—white U.S. women, children, and petty bourgeois men—to see themselves as Christian citizens with a personal responsibility for global projects of moral uplift.

The second part of this chapter turns to another form of quantification: the tabulation of "big numbers," notably population statistics. I am especially interested in what I call *statistical aesthetics* and *linguistic gigantism*, where missionary audiences were treated to display after display of numbers, graphs, and maps that portrayed global immensities. These aesthetic forms shared a common message with designated and systematic giving: they reiterated the "burdensome calculus"[6] of millions upon millions of perishing heathen souls and the millions upon millions it would cost to convert them. In this respect, charts and statistical reports did not simply transmit large data in a more compact form: it was "the naming of excess and the making of astonishment."[7] It brings us back to what I noted in the introduction: analysts often suggest that global statistics crush humans under their numerical weight as they project into uncountable futures and pasts.[8] But for U.S. Christians, big numbers did not crush to kill. Instead, they were meant to uplift and enliven moral action in service of global projects. For example, famed future missionary Hudson Taylor felt the burden of China's "perishing millions" so intensely that his health completely broke down; but out of the darkness he was born again and founded the China Inland Mission.[9]

Of course, Hudson Taylor was not your average guy. The vastness of heathenism—Americans were told to imagine hundreds of outstretched hands grasping at them—could seem an "appalling responsibility" that was incommensurate with their "hopelessly small and inadequate" efforts.[10] Even promoters who used big numbers worried about their stagnating effect: what if immensity provoked frustration and inertia? It was a dire problem for charitable schemes based on voluntary giving. One solution was to juxtapose big numbers with particularity—the single pennies that accumulated to form a mighty pile of coins for God; the foreign child for whom one could pray "intelligently" and directly. The last section of this chapter moves away from tabulations—whether in designated/systematic giving or statistical aesthetics—to explore participatory techniques that nineteenth-century sponsors used to make foreign people more distinct, such as reading letters aloud, praying, and personating "heathen." These activities were inseparable from the "statistical enthusiasm" of the age.

This point bears commenting since missionary literature often portrayed these aspects as at odds: "One live Hindoo baby, on its way to the bloody Ganges, would move [donors] more than the new Mission House full of statistics," noted one of the very first issues of *Heathen Woman's Friend* in 1869.[11]

The fact that missionary publications continued to use statistics, even as they regularly bemoaned their inclusion as wearisome or dull, has led historians to suggest that U.S. women's missions were split between those at the top who drove scientific professionalization (the Mission House full of statistics) and the majority who wanted personal sentimentality (the wee Hindoo baby). This internal struggle so weakened the movement, goes the argument, that it collapsed after World War I.[12] By contrast, I foreground the "knotty relationships between gigantic and intimate scales."[13] The aggregate and the individual (or immensity and particularity) were held in productive tension to awe Americans with the vastness of their God's global projects, while assuring them that even one Christian at home could contribute in meaningful ways.

MORAL MONEY I: THE LURE OF SPECIAL OBJECTS

Early nineteenth-century sponsorship plans were the product of a remarkable revolution in market capitalism and charity. Until the late seventeenth century, the most common form of charity in Europe was the bequest. Wealthy donors named an established institution, such as a church, hospital, or monastery, as executor of their estates after their death.[14] However, in the humanitarian temper of the modern period, Anglo-Protestants began to reinterpret poverty as a social problem rather than a divinely appointed order. And donors began to give during their own lifetimes and request an accounting of how their money was used. They wanted to see results. To that end, they formed private corporations to deal exclusively with raising and administering charitable funds, which sought a steady flow of income to offset the previous dependence on large gifts or bequests that arrived on an irregular basis. Nascent market capitalism provided a solution: by promoting small investments, joint-stock companies had successfully "tapped new sources of capital, hidden hitherto in the stockings of maiden ladies and country clergy."[15] Charities followed suit and issued their own kind of stock—a "subscription" that would appeal to "middling" people and produce a regular ("systematic") source of donations.[16]

The challenge of subscriptions was that one had to capture and retain people's interest year after year. Charities also had to cater to donors' increased demands for control over their donations. To address these issues, certain charities innovated by tailoring giving differently: they began to promote "special objects" where donors could designate their funds for a particular purpose. Charity schools adopted this system early, notably in the Society for Promoting Christian Knowledge that was founded in England in 1698, and as the eighteenth century progressed, donors could specify that they wanted to only support girls, for example, or one worthy student.[17]

In the early 1800s, many newly formed U.S. missionary societies adopted the model. In the post-Revolutionary zeitgeist, they emphasized subscription charity as a collective endeavor uniting people of every station. Of course, this inclusivity had major limits, as the role of women attests. Like market capitalism in general, Anglo-Protestant charitable giving incorporated enlightenment assumptions about the close association between male homosociality, Christian civility, and economic function.[18] Women were not viewed as the primary audience for major charitable projects, and once female missionary societies did form they had to assiduously avoid competing with the male-run parent boards for resources. Across denominations, women responded with a shared strategy: they proclaimed themselves "gleaners" who only collected the monetary "fragments" left behind. Ironically perhaps, this strategy fit especially well with subscription charity—the very model that grew out of early capitalism. When the first U.S. foreign missionaries set out in 1812, women's newly formed "cent societies" contributed immediately.[19]

Child sponsorship programs—called special objects or designated funds in this early period—grew out of these trends: each person gave a small amount and could specify where the donation should go, either to a particular orphan or mission station abroad. Givers were then able to track results through updates in missionary periodicals or direct letters. Donors responded readily to special objects, but such programs also provoked controversy about who would control these grassroots contributions. As early as 1835, ABCFM head Rufus Anderson wrote to his missionaries in the field, "I feel concerned and even alarmed when I see the growing disposition . . . [of] each auxiliary want[ing] its particular mission or missionary." He was especially bothered by women who chose their own "special objects" based on personal networks and then insisted on them, regardless of whether the male-run Board approved.[20]

The ABCFM phased out child sponsorship in 1853, but the system found fertile ground in the women's missionary societies that denominations began to organize in the late 1860s. To get a sense of how it spread, we can turn to the women in Anderson's proverbial backyard—ABCFM-affiliated Congregationalists in Connecticut. In April 1870, missionary Amelia Leonard addressed a group of ladies in New Haven, Connecticut, about her work in Marsovan, Turkey. The group responded by organizing a circle to "adopt" two of the pupils at her school through subscription giving. Then they officially formed the New Haven branch of the Women's Foreign Missions Board (ABCFM). Among the missionaries who spoke at their first annual meeting in April 1871 was Clementina Butler, the Methodist missionary to India and Mexico who, along with her husband William, was perhaps the most influential promoter of child sponsorship at the time. The New Haven ladies enthusiastically expanded their scope: they asked Amelia Leonard if they could support *all* the girls in the Marsovan school.[21]

Much of this growth was fueled from below. In May and June 1871, women formed local groups across Connecticut to support "their" adopted girls, as they had already begun to call them: Grace Hall Mission Circle provided $50 for a girl younger than 10 years of age; five well off ladies each promised to support a pupil; the Infant Club of Third Church Sunday School sent money for a "little beneficiary" in India whom they were "very anxious" be renamed Lizzie Wilcox.[22] All of this activity occurred just a month or so after the New Haven branch's first annual meeting, before there was even any clarity about how much it cost to support a child. Over the next four years, the branch created or incorporated nearly 150 local groups across the state, which supported 46 children in what today encompasses Turkey, Indonesia, China, Sri Lanka, India, and South Africa.[23] They requested—often demanded—regular letters about the children, which were read aloud at meetings and passed from parlor to parlor. Even after the Board's program solidified, individuals and mission bands continued to initiate adoptions, whether or not they knew exactly what it entailed. The Branch regularly received sums of $10 to support a child for a year, though they had set the cost at $25.[24]

As Anderson might have predicted, it was difficult to maintain centralized control. The auxiliaries nurtured their own connections with missionaries and set up adoptions of children, regardless of whether these missionaries were officially sanctioned by the ABCFM.[25] Branch secretary Hannah O. Hume urged Board officials to acquiesce to local demands, since it was clear that the auxiliaries would do as they pleased either way.[26] Sometimes she managed to secure a compromise, such as in the spring of 1876 when the ABCFM refused the request of a new auxiliary formed at Ansonia, Connecticut to support a child in Miss Payson's Foochow orphanage on the (rather reasonable) grounds that there were no available children at that site. Hume was not dissuaded. She located another auxiliary that supported Golden, a girl in Miss Payson's care, and asked them to switch their "little protégé" for one in India or Ceylon, where there were children to spare and at a slightly lower cost. They agreed and forwarded their letters about Golden to the Ansonia women so they could pick up the adoption.[27] Hume's efforts were not always so successful. In the autumn of 1884, a group of young ladies was enchanted by a visiting missionary's description of Chinnapulli, a girl at her Ceylonese school. Shortly after, Hume wrote to the Board for official approval for the sponsorship. Months passed and there was no reply, despite the group's single-minded interest in the child and Hume's repeated attempts to put Chinnapulli on the rolls. For more than a year, the group pressed the issue until finally Hume dropped her inquiries to the Board—but only after reiterating the depth of the young ladies' "special interest" in the girl and their wish to (at the very least) be assured that she was adopted by another group.[28]

By the 1880s and 1890s, the women's boards also began to phase out adoption plans.[29] A heated exchange in *HWF* laid bare some of the issues. In June 1884, Mrs. Annie Gracey, a respected missionary to India, penned a short article titled, "An Orphan It Must Be." She began by acknowledging that

> There is no phase of work connected with the Woman's Foreign Missionary Society so popular as the support of orphans . . . The members [of a local group] conclude that it will be just the work for their Society to support this orphan, and get letters from her; and they at once settle upon some name, and announce their arrangement to the Conference or Branch secretary. I have received letter after letter [to this effect].

But women must "look at the facts," she chided. It was impossible to supply more than 3,000 societies with their own orphan. Sniffing at U.S. women's need for sentimental stimulus, Gracey listed some unpopular but essential needs—building repairs, furniture, rent—concluding:

> Give your money, by an act of the most spiritual worship, directly to the Lord, and drop it quietly and unquestioningly, laden with prayer, into the treasury, having confidence (you must have that) in those who disburse it for you, and let them send it wherever needed most. And if the Master wants twine, string, wrapping paper, and pine boxes, so practical and so unromantic, let your funds go for these.[30]

The WFMS Board liked the article so much that it was reprinted as a stand-alone tract. But the women Mrs. Gracey addressed were less enthused. In September, a response was printed from Luthera Whitney, a member of a small auxiliary in Springfield, Vermont. While she agreed that charitable giving was an act of worship, she refused the implication that longing for a special object indicated spiritual weakness. "Perhaps Mrs. Gracey does not fully recognize the wide space which separates her, with her extensive knowledge of both the home and foreign work of our Society, from the average member of our inland auxiliaries," she wrote. Most members had never spoken to a foreign missionary, let alone traveled to the places Mrs. Gracey had been. Thus "it must be presented to us in tangible shape . . . [especially when] head and heart and hand are too full of the pressing daily burdens of life. But when the food and raiment and religious instruction of an orphan is derived directly from us, the work assumes such a practical character that we gladly make the sacrifice necessary to meet the demand." Further, she justly noted that the Board was at fault since "when the orphanages were established, the orphans were *urged* upon the auxiliaries as special work."[31] In her eloquent rebuttal, Luthera Whitney implied that globally mobile, and thus highly privileged, women like Mrs. Gracey were just as ignorant of certain facts. Perhaps they did not need a special object, but women at home did.

MORAL MONEY II: SYSTEMATIC GIVING

Systematic giving courted none of the controversy of special objects. Nearly all women's missionary boards agreed that having a system made their charitable model supremely, even relentlessly, moral. "The great defect in all money-raising for charitable purposes is lack of system," admonished the New England Branch secretary of the Methodist WFMS, "Giving is largely from impulse: it should be from principle."[32] WFMS women continually measured themselves against others in this regard. They compared new cities like Chicago with "the steady principle of mature communities" in the northeast. They compared U.S. missionary societies to European ones. They compared Protestants to Roman Catholics, pictured as devotedly setting aside pennies for the Pope. They also (sometimes gloatingly) compared their own systematic efficiency with the male-run "parent" boards of their denominations, which drew large donations and had big budgets but could not stay out of debt.[33]

As historian John Modern notes, among nineteenth-century evangelicals the moral nature of systematic organization began with the self, where piety was seen to rely on careful self-mastery; a Christian should exude a pleasant atmosphere of efficiency, self-control, and kindness, and encourage the same qualities in others.[34] For WFMS women, the moral nature of systemization thus rested in part on its capacity to organize human relationships. Specifically, they found it disagreeable in the extreme to ask money of neighbors and friends who were in arrears of promised payments to church charities. For the same reason, they bemoaned the fact that traveling missionaries had to embark on "begging" tours.[35] While systematic giving never eliminated these issues, in theory individuals became responsible for their own monthly payments and recognized that giving (without being asked) was part of the moral lesson. Being systematic also meant giving the right proportion of one's wealth; God's share should increase along with one's earnings. Advocates went so far as to argue that scriptures confirmed it was God's preferred method of fund-raising. In 1885, Mrs. Esther Tuttle Pritchard, a Quaker from Chicago, wrote a popular tract in which she offered numerous examples of systematic giving in the "law prescribed for the Israelites," which she averred was then refined by the early churches in response to Paul's counsel that "upon the first day of the week let every one of you lay by him in store as God hath prospered him."[36]

Pritchard advised individuals to compile a personal chart over the course of the year in three columns: Income / Tithes / Freewill Offerings. "By making use of this plan you will readily see at the end of the year how much you have given, and how it corresponds with the degree of prosperity God has given you."[37] Women also made specific promises related to shorter-term systemization. For example, a Methodist woman in Cincinnati had a serious accident in the winter of 1881 when her horse bolted. She survived and thanked God with a vow: she would donate every piece of gold that came into her hands for a full year. As she told the story to her church sisters, she noted how God had tested her. When she was shopping, she was continually given her change *in gold*, each piece of which was therefore earmarked. Sometimes she had to end her errands early, not having any more non-gold coins in her purse. True to her promise, she deposited every piece. She spread out the full $45 in coins in front of her friends.[38]

All missionary spokespeople (and likely most supporters) believed that the money in missionary coffers should grow exponentially. To some degree, this expectation speaks to a capitalist ethic that defines growth as the highest good, both for individual investors and for capitalism itself as it spreads globally by opening "new markets."[39] Weber famously proposed a link between political economy and Christian morality that undergirded this system: Calvinist Protestants viewed disciplined accumulation as a moral way to live out one's God-given vocation on earth. Significant recent work in anthropology and history of religion has complicated and refined this idea, showing that monied exchanges may be seen in a variety of ways, as corrupting, morally benign, and honorable.[40] In the context that interests us here, my sense is that when U.S. Protestant missionary supporters were thinking in global terms, their God was no longer the immanent Jesus who ingathers his lambs. Instead, it was an immense Deity with a world vision, and Christians needed to find ways to knit themselves into his plans. Perpetual growth was one way to do so.

Well-known missionaries, like Methodist Bishop James M. Thoburn of India, repeatedly expressed this idea. He exhorted U.S. audiences to "expect victory . . . and widen your vision in anticipation of it. If you are faithful to your trust, our thousands of [dollars] to-day will become our hundreds of thousands in the early future . . . How long it takes us to comprehend that Jesus Christ is in earnest in his efforts to save our race!" Such ideas circulated at the local level too. At a meeting of the WFMS branch in New York, a woman named Mrs. Easter declared to her sisters, "The word 'world' . . . to some it means only their home and friends, to others more; but when we understand God's definition, we shall help give light to the millions out of Christ."[41] While these ideas view accumulation as a moral good, they do not simply reiterate Weber's idea about individualistic vocations. Instead, they point to accumulation within sociality: Christians are individually responsible, perhaps, but always in order to pool their resources (thousands of dollars, millions of pennies) to create a never-ceasing stream that approximates, and thus participates in, God's global projects.

THINGS THAT HOLD: STATISTICAL AESTHETICS

The immensity of God's plans took shape in other ways too, specifically in how nineteenth-century Christian globalism was shot through with statistical aesthetics and linguistic gigantism. I use the first of these terms to refer to how the prose in missionary literature was peppered with statistical tables, tabular views, and row after row of aggregate numbers. The second term, which I draw from literary theorist Susan Stewart's essays on exaggeration and tall tales, refers to often-hyperbolic references to big numbers ("millions and millions!") to describe other people and places, generally with very little explanation or overtly moralizing content. For example, an 1895 issue of *Heathen Woman's Friend* announced, "the human family living on earth to-day consists of 1,450,000,000 souls." And it continued,

> In Asia . . . there are now about 800,000,000 people, densely crowded, on an average of about 120 to every square mile. In Europe there are 320,000,000 . . . In Africa there are, approximately, 210,000,000, and in the Americas . . . 100,000,000 . . . On the islands, large and small, there are probably 10,000,000 more. The extremes of the blacks and the whites are as 5 to 3, the remaining 700,000,000 intermediate, brown, yellow and tawny in color. Of the entire race 500,000,000 are well clothed . . . 230,000,000 habitually go naked, and 700,000,000 only cover the middle parts of the body; 500,000,000 live in houses, 700,000,000 in huts and caves, the remaining 250,000,000 virtually having no place to lay their heads.[42]

This patterned model, characterized by densely clustered zeros that arrest the attention and draw the eye, can be considered a form of aesthetics if we follow anthropologists Birgit Meyer and Jojada Verrips in defining the category more capaciously than the high arts favored by neo-Kantians.[43] Yet I do not want to lose Kant's interest in how aesthetic contemplation may provoke feelings of the sublime. As Meyer notes elsewhere, sublime awe is fundamental to the "sacred surplus" or emotional excess that scholars have long understood as central to religion.[44] This link between statistics and sublime excess (although not religion per se) also finds precedent in subaltern studies, where historians have argued that the colonial Indian government often circulated statistics not in "the sober register of . . . careful collection of data," but as affective constructions. Their magnitude evoked both excess and specificity, stoking fear or excitement.[45]

Statistical aesthetics in this period rested on rather recent claims to legitimacy. Early statistical science developed from the mid-seventeenth to mid-eighteenth centuries in two major forms, both of which are evident in the paragraph above. The first emerged out of the English school of "political arithmetic" and consisted of innovative techniques for calculating large numbers based on taking representative samples and extrapolating for larger territories. By the late eighteenth century, this method made it possible to estimate world populations.[46] A complementary form of reasoning was taxonomic: the enumeration of simple elements in a progressive ordering. Foucault viewed taxonomies as an insidious form of knowledge production. The taxonomy announced itself as exhaustive while it restricted a field of experience to what could be categorized; it transformed random items that were a priori incommensurate into determined and stable aggregates ("heathens" or "population" or "livestock") and in so doing promised to reveal the very *order of nature*.[47] To quote a popular nineteenth-century book about U.S. missions, statistics were thought to reveal "the true inwardness and unclothed outwardness of the subject."[48]

Statistics and taxonomies "made things that hold" because the objects they produced could to some extent be mastered by human beings in order to manage their social worlds.[49] As Timothy Morton writes, the scientific process of plotting, charting, and graphing data allows humans (partial) mastery over a hyperobject like global warming, insofar as it renders a small slice usable to us. Thus he views arithmetic as a "warm and fuzzy thing"—not the humanities, as one might assume—because we process large numbers in order to domesticate what is beyond our capacity for knowing.[50] Likewise, new tools for calculating aggregate populations reified universalized abstractions like sin, progress, governance, and Providence. A major way they did so was by ordering God's world according to religious and racial taxonomies. In the paragraph above from *HWF*, U.S. audiences could gaze at neatly printed round numbers that delineated black, white, and intermediate races ("brown, yellow and tawny"). Another such abstraction was religion itself. Older Christian theology held that religion fell into four classificatory branches: Christianity, Judaism, Islam, and Heathenism (or Paganism). Based on these categories, late eighteenth-century statisticians estimated the number of heathens at "600 millions" in a global population of "800 millions." These numbers were then translated into another powerful aesthetic form: global maps that color-coded areas occupied by heathens, Catholics, Muslims, and Protestants.[51]

Historians of missions have paid little attention to statistical aesthetics and linguistic gigantism, perhaps because of their ubiquity. Famed Baptist missionary William Carey incorporated the "appalling" global population of heathens into his famous 1792 manifesto that inspired the first major Anglo-Protestant foreign missions. In 1818, just as the ABCFM launched its child adoption plan, its Bombay missionaries Gordon Hall and Samuel Newell published "The Conversion of the World: or, The Claims of Six Hundred Millions," an enormously popular tract based on "accurate computing."[52] Big numbers were also integrated into initial decisions about where to send missionaries as Americans gauged supposed levels of civilization, existing educational infrastructure, and population density in order to evaluate where their efforts could make the greatest impact.[53] At the level of linguistic gigantism, Western Christians used big numbers so often in reference to "China's millions" in particular that it began to seem like an inherent characteristic of the Chinese people. "Millions" bound together a series of abstracted enormities: the literal bodies of heathens, the size of their territory, the economic might they commanded, and the ancestral gods they worshipped. In missionary periodicals, "millions" also projected forward to the awe-inspiring possibility of uniting this mass of humanity under one God—when people listed in separate columns (Christian/Pagan) would merge into a coherent whole. Statistical aesthetics sought to create moral coherence out of the new intensities of global interrelations.[54]

A series of pedagogical exercises were developed to train U.S. Christians to read big numbers in this light. For example, the Methodist WFMS issued a set of instructions in September 1886 detailing one such exercise recommended for their local auxiliary groups. The appointed leader was counseled to begin with a communal hymn. She was then to stand before her peers and carefully write the following numbers on one side of a blackboard:

Population of the United States.

2d, underneath, population of India.
3d, population of China.

4th, population of Japan.
5th, population of Corea.
6th, estimated population of Africa.

The audience was left staring at a column filled with zeros, where the numbers for China and India jutted out past the rest. Then the leader was told to add the last five numbers to tally global heathendom and print the aggregate number in the space directly below the U.S. population. Now the zeros were overwhelming in comparison. She was to face her audience (with a flourish?) and name the religion of each heathen nation and its objects of worship. She ended forcefully with two rhetorical questions: *Why send missionaries to them? Has Christianity any benefits adequately to atone for their innocent ignorance of Christ?* Then she was instructed to turn back to the board and begin again, this time with the smaller and newer WFMS missions:

Population of Bulgaria.
Population of Italy.
Population of Mexico.
Populations of the States of South America.

She repeated the pattern of listing their religions—in this case, Catholicism and Orthodoxy—and ended by prompting her audience again: *Why send missionaries to these countries?* To aid in preparing the discussion portions of the exercise, the instructions included expert statements by "one in a position to know" to the effect that "the Methodist Church expended $16,000,000 in the year 1885, in its various enterprises for saving men in the domain of the United States!" It was followed by another rhetorical question: "[W]hat is our duty toward the hundreds of millions who will never hear of Christ except [through what] we send?" The exercise concluded with a communal hymn of thanks.[55]

It seems that pedagogy associated with statistical aesthetics did have a strong effect on its intended audience. We might cast a glance into the comfortable parlor room of First United Methodist Church in Pasadena, California where 30 ladies assembled on a July evening in 1904 for their WFMS auxiliary meeting. Miss Crum, a member of the Branch's "literature department," came from Los Angeles for a special presentation. She heaped an impressive number of leaflets, calendars, maps, books, and song sheets produced by an array of Protestant denominations in multiple languages. As the women contemplated the pile of objects, Miss Crum recited statistics regarding their global spread. "The total circulation of this missionary matter is now World-wide," was the core of her message. The recording secretary noted, "the marked increase [during] her statistical report of increasing wonder, by reason of this rapid growth. Many remained [afterwards] to look over her splendid sample supply and spoke of the help of such reading in promoting their interest in the cause of missions." As during this event, physical objects and statistics often functioned together to create the impression of immensity, which was then transmuted into theological terms as an increase in *wonder*. Although the recording secretary's phrasing is not completely clear, one assumes she was thinking of wonder on two counts: the feeling such objects might provoke in their intended audience overseas, as well as the feeling these big numbers and piles of circulating objects provoked in homebound U.S. audiences.[56]

U.S. Christians also recognized that statistical aesthetics fell short in many ways. Even after carefully tabulating and displaying money given and souls saved, WFMS members noted the impossibility of computing the hundreds of prayers they offered up—an important consideration for individuals and auxiliaries with fewer monetary resources. "The report from these [prayers] will be given when the books above shall be opened," one secretary from northwest Iowa comforted her church sisters.[57] Another issue went even deeper. Faced with repeated reminders of the millions upon millions in "pagan lands," some U.S. Christians questioned how a just God could damn so many for being born in the wrong region of the globe. And yet, judging from the reports that auxiliaries sent to the Methodist WFMS Board, most of their members did appreciate statistical aesthetics. Big numbers portrayed reality in ways that were "stimulating" and "inspiring" because seemingly objective mathematical calculations made visible what could not be seen with the human eye—God's immense work in the world.[58]

PARTICULARS OF PRAYER AND PERSONATING

Statistical aesthestics found a necessary counterpart in the particular. This dialogical relationship was crucial for reasons already mentioned: immensity could bring one closer to a god's eye view, but it also risked inducing pessimism if the work seemed too impenetrably vast. Another problem was more mundane but potentially ruinous for voluntary systematic giving: statistics and abstractions could become boring (or "wearisome," as Miss N. in Dauphin County put it). Writing from New Haven in 1875, ABCFM branch secretary Hannah Hume discerned a palpable difference in Congregationalist women's modes of attention: "I notice in reading [missionary] letters to an audience a quickened interest . . . as I read a name, or describe an individual case after having given generalities."[59] The name of a single child changed the physical nature of listening; women shifted, sat up straighter, their eyes widened. It was enough to let Hume know that the details mattered—deeply.

Throughout its history, sponsorship has been characterized by U.S. donors' constant demands for specific information about the children and their lives. Promoters like Hume or (a generation earlier) ABCFM secretary Samuel Worcester pestered missionaries accordingly. Based on his experience in his own Salem church prayer circle, Worcester regularly reminded the missionaries to supply "somewhat particular [details] respecting [the children]—their numbers, their ages, their conditions, their dispositions, their manners, their capacities, their proficiency."[60] These particulars were not meant to provide detailed contextual knowledge or clarify accurate facts about people's lives in foreign places, as post-colonial scholars later tried to do. Rather, they revealed truth *in a Christian sense* that fed into global forms of affective prayer. In 1816, Worcester clarified this intent in a letter to his friend, Reverend Edward Payson (soon to sponsor a Ceylonese child): "To pray with understanding, feelings, and fervor, people must have . . . knowledge of the state of the world, or the deplorable condition of a great portion of the human family. . . . This cannot be too strongly represented & impressed."[61] Worcester's prayer "with understanding" draws on I Corinthians 14:15 ("I will pray with the spirit, and I will pray with understanding also"). Since the 1970s, U.S. Protestant sponsors have tended to use the term "intelligent prayer" for this laser-like focus on particular needs. It remains crucial to Christian globalism, especially in the evangelical idiom.

Writing about the influential ministry of Worcester's friend and child sponsor, Edward Payson, historian Richard Rabinowitz notes the link between intelligent prayers and the sentimental Christianity discussed in chapter 1. Whereas earlier Calvinists focused on formalized, abstract prayers precisely because their abstraction clarified the enormous distance between God and man, "sentimentalists" like Payson sought to reveal the inner workings of the human heart by enjoining congregants to pray aloud for specific, human-scale needs. Rabinowitz argues that these deeply personal prayers ushered in new modes of worship that sought to produce affective states and humanize God. Because these specific prayers were often for others, they also made intensely real the needs of human beings apart from oneself.[62] An innovation in Payson's and Worcester's time, this type of prayer has become a hallmark of contemporary U.S. Christianity and crucial for how Americans at home make absent people present, including the children they sponsor.[63]

As demonstrated in Hannah Hume's records from New Haven in the 1870s and 1880s, U.S. sponsors wanted to know four main things about the children they supported: ages, proficiency in school, spiritual state, and, most important, their names. "You know a name makes up much of the individuality of an individual," Hume wrote about the six Dakota Indian girls the Connecticut women sponsored. "We can think of a girl whose name & characteristics are known, and so pray for them as we never can for one of a group . . . We talk about 'our Indian girls' and the [sponsors] who have seen their photos just long to 'know how they turn out.'"[64] Even when Hume acknowledged that missionaries likely found burdensome the many requests for details, she emphasized that, "To pray for you and your pupils in faith and earnestness, we must more than imagine who and what we are to pray for."[65] What constituted this more-than-imagined sphere was subjective and Hume seems to have defined it as a combination of "warm sympathy, intelligent prayer, and a loving cheerful support."[66] It was a manifestation of nineteenth-century ideals of Christian love and systematization.

The ultimate goal was to bring Americans and their foreign interlocutors into mutual recognition of a shared humanity under the Christian God. Hume wrote Miss Payson in Foochow in 1874, "Do not count us strangers because we have not met face to face, but remember we are all children of Our Father." She ended as she typically did, by insisting that Payson tell the sponsored Chinese girls about the U.S. Christians who sacrificed for them and felt such a "peculiar and tender interest" in them.[67] Hume also reminded missionaries not to sanitize their reports: U.S. Christians wanted the good and the bad. To her correspondent in Manissa, Turkey, Hume wrote, underlining as usual for emphasis: "Your success shall be our joy, and in all your disappointments we participate . . . and then we know what to ask our Dear Lord to do for [you]." Global mutuality depended on the details. For foreign missions to truly be "the work of the Lord's people," as Hume insisted it should, Christians across the world needed to be able to feel the same affective highs and lows; they needed to be able to distinguish needs to know what to ask of God.[68]

None of this work was accomplished through letters alone. Participatory techniques were also highly valued tools in this regard, notably through the display and production of "heathen" bodies. Non-Europeans were brought before European and Euro-American audiences as entertainment during the nineteenth century in traveling exhibits and world's fairs; in Christian circles, it was especially edifying to view a recent convert. But only centrally located sponsors had access to such events, which at any rate were a rarity. U.S. Christians had to innovate proximity to heathens. Thus, in Connecticut in 1880, for example, a large crowd watched an ABCFM performance in which white children from the nearby orphan asylum "personated" their heathen orphan counterparts by donning their national costumes and pleading for the Gospel. A few years later, Methodist circles in Philadelphia experimented with "foreign

native testimony given by proxy" where U.S. women and children read translated statements of conversion aloud; a "novel and most interesting exercise,"
the local recording secretary reported. In 1882, at Ocean Grove, New Jersey,
the annual camp meeting closed with a collection for the group's sponsored
children in Foochow during which two children stepped on to the stage: an
American girl dressed in Chinese costume and a "native Chinese" in American costume (who was almost certainly U.S.-born). They stood together as
a silent testimony while the crowd sang the Methodist Doxology: "Praise
God from whom all blessings flow. . . ."[69] The following year, 800 guests were
treated to an even more elaborate spectacle in Minneapolis. Each of the four
local Methodist churches constructed loose facsimiles of the architecture,
color schemes, and objects they associated with India, China, Japan, and
Africa. Young ladies dressed in "native" costume and, circulating through
the crowd, "made it seem as if the millions in the thraldom of idolatrous
superstition had sent their representatives to ask the knowledge of the truth
as it is in Christ." Frank Wagner, a local layman, gave a sense of its impact on
participants: "The sight was an inspiration and a prophecy; an inspiration
to send the life-giving word to all lands, and a prophecy that the kingdoms
of the world will yet be redeemed unto God, and become the loyal subjects
of our royal King."[70]

When adults participated in such "personating," it normally implied a foreign subject who was already or almost a Christian. By contrast, child players
were much more likely to "become" unregenerate heathen for (adult) audiences, perhaps because their own assumed innocence made the role-play less
dangerous. We cannot know what these children felt as they donned foreign
dress (and especially interesting, how U.S. orphans felt as they were remade
into heathen orphans, or how a Chinese American child felt as she stood beside
her white counterpart in "Chinese" costume). From the audience's perspective,
however, children's personifications were supposed to make absent/present
foreign bodies more real—an embodied version of the specific details they
demanded in letters and that missionary literature juxtaposed with statistical
immensity.

These Christian techniques are lesser-known examples of a cultural form
then flourishing, in which white Americans play-acted as racial others. Middle-
class whites "played Indian" (or biblical Jew or Turk) as they performed rituals
in fraternal clubs, secret societies and, later, summer camps.[71] Working-class
whites developed minstrelsy shows, which became popular across the northern United States. In the wake of post-colonial studies, scholars have underlined the inherent power dynamics in these mimetic acts, which sought to
reinforce often unstable gendered and racial hierarchies.[72] More recent studies

emphasize how such performances constituted and constructed white privilege.[73] The activities we have been discussing did reinscribe a seemingly natural dichotomy between the white bodies that brought God's Word and the brown ones that received it. Just as important, they relied on mimetic comparisons that ultimately reconfirmed Christian universalism: the goal was to viscerally *feel* how all human beings were fundamentally the same, once one stripped away local clothing, customs, or (false) beliefs. All people were children of the God from whom blessings flowed (paraphrasing the Methodist doxology) and their personated voices—viewed as their "true" inner selves perhaps—mirrored Americans' own global aspirations. Such performances remained popular among Christians into the mid-twentieth century. Most poignantly perhaps, in 1930, Hwal-lan (Helen) Kim, a young Methodist laywoman from Korea, became the first non-American to compose a service for the ecumenical World Day of Prayer. Steeped in the missionary culture exported to Korea, she wrote a script that called on (mainly) white congregants in churches around the United States to personate Japanese and Chinese Buddhists, a "Latin American skeptic," and even "Ghandi (*sic*) of India" in order to plead their need for Jesus.[74]

Scaling up again, these multiple "non-Christian" voices found an echo in imaginative exercises that encouraged donors to hear the sound of thousands of prayers and the clink of millions of pennies that constituted the subscription model. Missionary materials emphasized how these prayer-laden pennies united women across America and then traveled together across the world or heavenward where God listened to the hum of "twenty-six thousand [fervent prayers that] ascend every day [as a] mighty voice that will be heard in the courts of heaven as the sound of many waters."[75] In conjuring up the mighty sound of prayers and pennies, individual givers could step away from their own auditory field for a moment to imagine how the world "hummed" for God. The ultimate goal was well put by the Methodist WFMS in its October 1888 study lesson for its auxiliary circles. "It is a supreme *privilege* and highest *glory*" to contribute money to God's cause, the WFMS told its supporters.

> And until we have mounted up to this standpoint [of God's], and seen from this altitude, we shall probably fail in the measure . . . Just so truly as health in the body depends not so much upon the amount of blood therein, as its circulation through the system . . . so true riches is not simply accumulation, and aggregation, and possession . . . In our thus giving unselfishly, unsparingly, we are likest unto God. By it we become both associated with, and akin to him, and humanity reaches its high-water mark when it thus touches the divine.[76]

POSTSCRIPT: BIG NUMBERS A CENTURY AFTER

"We live in a world of statistics, of bigness," country star Pat Boone told U.S. television viewers in 1974. "With so many people in the world and so much need, it's very hard to know what to do. Who to help." The Compassion commercial then cut away to an "extreme high long shot" of the zoo in which Boone was standing, where hundreds of people moved along walkways in what the TV script called "a confused, indistinguishable mass of humanity." Then Boone's voice again: "A lot of people like this are a crowd. You can't relate to a crowd." The camera slowly zoomed toward one group of children as Boone's monologue continued, "And when you think . . . [about] this huge planet spinning in space, carrying a cargo of over three billion human beings. It's just too much. But when you narrow down your focus—" The camera inched closer. "When you can see one human being then you can handle it." The camera moved in for an "extreme close-up" of one child in the group as Boone delivered the final punch: "It's no longer abstract. . . . *It's that one person.*"[77]

Tracing sponsorship over two centuries reveals the dialogical relation between statistical aesthetics and particularity over different periods. By the 1970s, neo-evangelicals had embraced the big numbers that mainline missions had honed for more than a century. As an aesthetic form, it was especially prominent in coverage about China. The country had been the "crown jewel" of the mainline Protestant movement until Mao Zedong's communist party tightened restrictions on foreign missionaries—including child sponsorship organizations—leading to their mass exodus in the early 1950s.[78] Although China remained inaccessible to U.S. Christians, it retained an outsized importance in their conceptions of global space. *World Vision* magazine covers in the early 1970s read, "One quarter of the world's people, 800 million, in search of an answer!" "Asia: Where 57 percent of the world's people are crowded into one continent." The illustration showed a collage of faces, one on top of another, squeezed into the frame.[79] According to the magazine's editor, China was "the greatest mystifying and stupefying fact in the modern world."[80] Of course, if one was Chinese it was likely neither mystifying nor stupefying. If one was a WV supporter, however, the mystery lay in how, as "God's most multitudinous people," the Chinese seemed both utterly central to world history in Christian terms and yet so curiously remote. "History haunts them. Destiny quivers before them," wrote World Vision VP Paul Rees in 1971.[81] In fact, it was U.S. Christians who saw their own view of destiny quiver. For, without the Chinese, how could Christians be convinced their God was global? To convert China often seemed tantamount to converting the world.

Even top evangelical leaders admitted to feeling overwhelmed by the immensities of Asia.[82] As in decades past, WV urged Christians to harness the power of particular prayer: they led sponsors in an effort to focus on a different Chinese surname every few weeks—Chang, Chao, Chen—until all its people had been "covered" with U.S. prayers. Echoing missionary optimism at the century's start, it confidently predicted that "the world's millions . . . could be won to faith in Jesus Christ in a generation."[83] Given the abiding interest in big numbers, perhaps it is unsurprising that World Vision also collaborated with missiologists at Fuller Seminary who championed the Church Growth Movement that measured success in big numbers and mega-churches. Together, they developed a massive computer database of 16,750 "unreached people groups."[84] The project provoked debate when it was first presented at the 1974 International Congress on World Evangelization in Lausanne. Was consolidating population, GDP, and degree of "reachedness" an exercise in mere "statistical Christianity"?[85] Or did it reveal particulars that could stimulate the focused prayers God desired?

Of course, big numbers were never either/or, at least not in Western Christianity's global projects—as nineteenth-century child sponsorship plans attest. The larger point concerns what historians have long noted, namely that mid-nineteenth century U.S. Protestants of an evangelical bent developed an individualist, personal kind of religion where God became a loving Son and Friend and an intimate Spirit that filled up human hearts, rather than the more abstract Sovereign Father of yore. While there is truth in this characterization, overemphasizing it may also obscure how certain kinds of abstractions remained emotionally gripping and in fact central to the production of globalism: the "quivering destiny" that big numbers seemed to reveal, the limitless "Love" that encircled the earth; the Providential projects that encompassed the whole world at once. Child sponsorship, and Christian humanitarianism more broadly, has succeeded in part precisely because of its ability to bring such forms of immensity into dialogical relation with the particular—the focused prayer, the "heart" for a single cause, the 1:1 connection with a child far away.

CHAPTER 3

Food and Famine

The Visual / Visceral Production of Humanitarianism

Eat your dinner. There are starving children in China/Armenia/Africa.

—Twentieth-century American adage

I always found an excuse for why I couldn't sponsor a child. But then
I had a nightmare/revelation. I was one of those [starving] children
on the news . . . I could feel the nothingness in my stomach. It was so
real! I've woken up and I want to sponsor a child.

—Letter from Russell Baum (Allendale, New Jersey) in *Compassion
  Magazine*, July–August 1986: 3

It is a "peculiarly modern" fact, writes theorist Lauren Berlant, that everyday
Americans witness suffering in "elsewheres brought home and made intimate
by sensationalist media." Many other commentators have said the same. "Being
a spectator of calamities taking place in another country is a quintessential
modern experience," Susan Sontag noted in 1977 and again in 2004. "With our
communications technologies we have extended our senses and sensibilities in
making the scope of our eyes and ears conterminous with the inhabited earth,"
wrote U.S. theologian Richard R. Niebuhr in 1972. He worried about how "such
unremitting and extensive emotional sharing" might affect American viewers.
Would they become hopeful, empathetic Christians? Or would the culture of
spectatorship neutralize moral possibilities?[1]

New forms of visual media prompted these questions in the 1970s, notably
the 24-hour news cycle with its brutal images of death and violence. Sponsorship organizations contributed to the trend; CCF, WV, and Compassion all
developed high-value, gut-wrenching infomercials for mainstream television,
showing emaciated (brown or black) children often with a (white) celebrity
pleading for "just pennies a day" (figure 3.1). The prominence of these racialized

LENGTH: 60 SECONDS

COMM'L NO.: QCDW 2662

SALLY STRUTHERS: I wish you could be here with me.

Not because this is a nice place,

but because if you were here you could see for yourself how much a third world child needs your help.

You can't touch and hold these beautiful children like I am

but through the Christian Children's Fund you can reach out to one of them by sharing just a little of your good fortune.

Sponsorship is only $18.00 a month. And in a developing country that small amount can work wonders.

Schoolbooks, nutritious food, medical care, clothing or whatever your sponsored child might need most.

Being here I can really feel their hopes of living happier, healthier lives.

And if you were with me I'm sure you'd feel the same.

That's why I'm asking you to call this toll free number right now and find out about becoming a CCF sponsor.

There's no more personal caring way to send your love to a hungry child.

Please call. It'll take only a minute but it can improve a child's life more than you'll ever know.

FIG 3.1. Television stills of actress Sally Struthers. The most famous celebrity face of child sponsorship, Struthers signed on as CCF's spokesperson in 1976. Courtesy of ChildFund International.

shock images generated a flood of media and scholarly criticism, which argued that systemic injustice was buried beneath a veneer of sentimental compassion that, as Hannah Arendt once famously remarked, was "politically speaking, irrelevant and without consequence."[2] At their most biting, critics accused sponsorship of using emotional manipulation to become "one of the most powerful and seductive philanthropic devices ever conceived."[3]

While this trend is nearly always associated with the late twentieth century, its roots actually lie a hundred years earlier in the 1870s to 1920s, as emergency relief came to occupy a prime place in nascent humanitarianism. Sponsorship is an important and unexplored part of that history.

Humanitarian fund-raisers first introduced shock photography to spur donations during the Russian famines of the mid-1890s. Shortly after, Christian missionaries used the same technique during the Indian famine of 1896 to 1898. Although Berlant was not likely thinking of modernity in its *longue durée*, shock imagery is so "peculiarly modern," as she puts it, because of its link to the affordances of new communications technologies and the production of an absent/present: showing brutalized bodies in the late nineteenth century was justified as a way for humans distant from an event to be assured of its veracity and gripped by its reality.[4] It was akin to what Morton calls phase time: those brief but intense flashes when humans feel the affective reality of a hyperobject (in this case, "the human condition" or "global sin") as it intersects momentarily with our lives.

This chapter explores shock imagery in late nineteenth-century missions and the First World War. When war struck, relief organizations proliferated on a scale that far outstripped previous humanitarian interventions. Among the tools they mobilized was sponsorship. Although Save the Children, founded in England in 1919, is the best known such organization to have emerged from the war (eventually transitioning into the first permanent sponsorship plan), it was one of dozens and even hundreds at the time. Some were religious, but many were "non-sectarian." Most were limited and short-lived, such as an American Red Cross program in 1918 through which U.S. soldiers could sponsor a French child with their choice of sex, region, and "complexion" (the most popular request was a boy with brown hair and a "mischievous disposition").[5]

Two longer term programs were Near East Relief (NER) and Fatherless Children of France (FCF), both of which I discuss below. Like many equivalent organizations, they operated out of New York City, were non-sectarian, and championed by elite donors. Former ABCFM missionaries to the Middle East and their supporters were instrumental in founding NER in 1915, which garnered support from Christian philanthropists, including the Rockefellers. NER offered sponsorships of Armenian orphans for $60 a year from 1917 to the late 1920s.[6] A wealthy industrialist in Paris started FCF to supplement the meager French government allowance for war widows, asking $36.50 a year to support a fatherless "half orphan" living at home. In 1915, FCF representatives came to the United States and partnered with well-connected socialites to set up regional branches, which grew into the largest sponsorship plan at the time. When its appeals ended in 1920, FCF had raised more than $10 million and supported more than 286,000 French children, of whom two-thirds had individual patrons in the United States.[7]

Exploring the visual archive from this period, I make two major points. The first rereads shock imagery as part of a larger visual schema that juxtaposed the immensities of famine, war, and future aspirations for peace with intimate portraits of the individuals Americans supported. At a larger level, all of this imagery was "peculiarly modern" in the way it constructed universality. It stripped away local culture and contingency to reveal an assumed core human experience built on embodied qualities such as hunger and terror, which the (often Christian) advocates of nascent humanitarianism and the League of Nations argued required a universal response. I explore some of these discussions, focusing on World War I–era orphans who became metonyms for a unified, non-sectarian (but effectively Protestant) Pax Americana.[8] Although the political implications of sponsorship are important in any period, they are especially salient around World War I since it was the first time that sponsorship was pitched to a broad, and potentially non-Christian, audience in terms of global politics. Although many sponsors took up the call through a sense of Christian duty, war-era plans were generally divorced from the explicit missionary intent of earlier models, especially when children were Europeans.

The notion that universal experiences are embodied—we all suffer the same, we all love and hope the same—leads to my second point: "To see is not simply to be exposed to sensory data; it involves embodied interaction with the world."[9] Studies of sponsorship have thus far concentrated on cataloguing visual media, but in fact organizations embedded images within multisensory modes of engagement where sponsors were encouraged to viscerally grasp human sameness through bodily intensities. The last half of the chapter puts shock images of famine and war into context with practices in which sponsors ate or abstained from eating in an effort to cultivate the deepest possible engagement with another.

FIG 3.2. Florence Bird's postcard from Kollegal (Karnataka), India, 1890s. From Special Collections, Yale Divinity School Library.

GROUP OF FAMINE ORPHANS, KOLLEGAL, INDIA.
" Jesus, our own Lord Jesus, will be there, and we shall see Him, and He will smile upon us, and that will make Heaven's sunshine. And God will stroke our faces—so—to take away all the marks of crying from our faces. And nobody will have fever, and we shall not have to go to bed ; and there is a beautiful river." —Description of Heaven as told to other little ones by a rescued Indian Child.
Overweights of Joy.
Would you like to adopt one such little child at a cost of £3 per year? ❧ Matt. 18 : 5 and 10 to 14.
" God make our hearts tender, and give it to us to care so that we shall not be able to bear that the children are perishing."
Missionary Helps Depot, 13 Croxton Street, Liverpool. 4d. *per doz, India No. 3.*

LOOPHOLES OF SOUL ESCAPE: VARIETIES OF PHOTOGRAPHY

Florence Bird, a 23-year-old missionary with the English Brethren, arrived at Kollegal (Karnataka) in southern India in the mid-1880s. Shortly after, famine struck the northern state of Gujarat, and Florence traveled more than 3,000 kilometers by bullock cart and train to gather 150 starving girls. It was a hazardous trek and 50 of her charges died on the return trip. Nevertheless, she arrived with enough students to start a Christian school. As an independent faith missionary, Bird depended on free-will offerings and an orphanage was a good draw. Once back in Kollegal, she produced the first photographic promotional campaign for child sponsorship that I have been able to locate (figure 3.2). In the postcards she circulated in England and North America, Bird sits among some of her "famine orphans." The caption eavesdrops on a heart-warming conversation between the rescued children:

"Jesus our own lord Jesus, will be there, and we shall see Him, and . . . nobody will have fever and we shall not have to go to bed; and there is a beautiful river."–Description of Heaven as told to other little ones by a rescued Indian Child. . . . **Would you like to adopt one such little child at a cost of 3 pounds per year? Matt. 18: 5 and 10 to 14.**[10]

While Florence Bird's photographs were an innovation, her method of seeking out famine orphans and soliciting patrons was not. Sponsorship had always thrived in times of famine and war, when desperate parents brought their children to the missions, state officials dropped off growing numbers of orphans, and missionaries could "acquire" and "gather up" waifs as they drove through the countryside (at times, they simply absconded with those they deemed "friendless"). During the late nineteenth-century Indian famine alone, ABCFM missionaries estimated that 22,000 orphans had come into Protestant care.[11] While missionaries acknowledged the usefulness of such disasters as early as the first sponsorship plan in 1816, it was not until much later that they heavily publicized them to shore up donations. The Indian famine of 1876, which raged for two years and claimed 5–6 million victims, was arguably the first truly mediatized global disaster. In the United States, home audiences heard of a 14-year-old who was so traumatized that she could not speak for two days. Of a seven-year-old who was likely to die after days of eating clay. Of the "forty million of people in India who live *on one meal a day all their lives* [and the] eighty million who go to sleep hungry *every night*."[12] There were shocking stories of children sold into slavery for food, bands of roving thieves, and corpses in the streets. "The sights I saw last week held my eyes waking and almost made me sick," wrote an ABCFM correspondent in the *Missionary Herald.*[13]

Missionaries pinned their hopes on these disasters. The vast majority of children in missionary schools, and even orphanages, did have families, and they rarely converted to Christianity. By contrast, reporting exuberantly from India in 1901, Henry Fairbank of the ABCFM noted how famine orphans who had been traumatically separated from all they knew and nursed back to health in the missions "seem to receive Christian truth with positive avidity . . . And our missionaries look upon this rescue work in which they are engaged heart and soul as promising large results for the future prosperity of Christian work in India."[14] Despite sponsorship's acknowledged drawbacks in terms of efficiency and flexibility, it was helpful for this work; it raised money quickly during media coverage of disasters and provided sustainable long-term support after the initial surge of donations dried up.

However, the marriage of sponsorship and relief created serious difficulties too. The sponsorship ideal, which assumed a prolonged period during which children were thoroughly converted, benefited from *some* orphans but fell apart at times of extreme privation when thousands—even millions—of people needed immediate aid. In such emergencies, the Protestants who promoted sponsorship asked whether it was worth sheltering and assigning a patron to a child so sick she would certainly die before understanding the Gospel. (By way of comparison, Catholic missionaries in this period viewed caring for a dying child as accomplishing its own end, which was to perform a baptism *in articulo mortis* and thereby save a soul.) Sponsorship promoters also worried that donors would tire of the "multiplicity of new calls" in U.S. media (called "compassion fatigue" in the 1980s, after military jargon) and they chafed at how funds designated for a particular child could not be diverted for other uses as emergencies wore on.[15] And yet sponsorship remained yoked to relief, likely because the message proved so compelling for home audiences. The immensity of disasters produced overwhelming feelings of horror and awe, which sponsorship seemed to address with its targeted, human-scale response.

In the 1870s, sponsorship enlisted the new technology of photography. Like the statistics provided in chapter 2, photography was understood to reveal the "true" state of affairs with technological precision, even when conditions were so shocking that they seemed to stymy verbal or written description. The adoption of photography in nascent humanitarianism was the logical outcome of Enlightenment-era philosophy, and Scottish Common Sense in particular, which promoted the idea that sympathy was most thoroughly aroused by observing the distress of another (Adam Smith, whose work on sentiment was mentioned in chapter 1, belonged to this philosophical school). By the 1880s and 1890s, despite growing splits between social gospelers and evangelicals, most U.S. Christians agreed that sympathy was a "sentiment tuned primarily through sight."[16]

In sponsorship, the portrait was the first and most lasting type of photography used to cultivate sympathy (or what I call "engaged empathy"); snapshot portraits are still the primary visual aids traded between sponsors and children today. The advent of portraits was a product of the time. In the 1860s, carte-de-visite portraits became an "immensely popular social currency" in the United States, traded between friends and family and pasted into albums.[17] Soon after, missionary societies began to sell likenesses of missionaries and native Bible women, and occasionally sponsored children too. One of the earliest examples, from 1870, was the portrait of Frances Coryell, a six-year-old foundling at Bareilly orphanage who was supported by Mary Palmer from Nichols, New York.

Her shocking story was recounted in *HWF*—including speculation that she had been left to die as a sacrifice for the goddess Kali—and her photograph was distributed as a prize to children who raised $5 or more for the WFMS.[18] Shortly after, U.S. sponsors began to regularly request photos of "their" child directly from the field, although these images could still only rarely be procured.[19]

Portraiture exemplifies what Berlant might call fantasies of intimate possession. Susan Stewart remarks more specifically on the role of souvenir objects and photographs to privatize that which is public; the Eiffel Tower photo hanging in one's living room becomes "my Eiffel Tower."[20] In Stewart's terms, the portraits of sponsored children can be viewed as one way to make a "public" person (the freely circulating individual in India) into a private belonging, incorporated into U.S. homes as "my child" or "my adoptee." While we do not know whether nineteenth-century sponsors displayed such portraits at home as many sponsors do today, they did make them "theirs" through particular modes of consumption: the viewer was expected to gaze at the image closely to see a reflection of the sitter's moral qualities. This visual exercise had its basis in the biblical story of Adam's two-step creation: God fashioned a corporeal frame (clay) and then animated it with a soul (Divine breath). Exteriority and interiority were distinguishable yet irreducible. Late eighteenth-century Christian thinkers extrapolated that the soul was impressed upon the body in one's physiognomy or the expression in one's eyes, and this notion spread rapidly in the nineteenth-century United States.[21]

By the last decades of the century, home audiences expected they could contemplate the "clear-cut, placid countenance" in missionary portraits and study how the expressions on sponsored children's faces "show many times the impress that the Holy Spirit has left upon them."[22] In 1872, for example, a group in Pittsburgh received a photo of Mary Belle, the Indian girl they had renamed and sponsored, and pronounced her "dusky" face highly "appealing." In particular, they examined her large plaintive eyes and felt sure they expressed "considerable intellectual capability."[23] The portraits were expected to provide stimuli for the cultivation of similar virtues in U.S. women. Gazing at a missionary's placid face (especially if she had died for the cause) should transmit some of her assuredness and strength to the viewer; a child's "intelligent" or "sweet" face was meant to remind viewers that just as the child learned and sacrificed so much for Jesus, they must too.

This narrative of sacrifice rested on assumptions about racialized heathenness, whether or not U.S. Christians explicitly noted a child's "dusky" countenance. Emerging social theories about race in this period said that sin and civility derived from environmental factors and family heredity.[24] The child's sacrifice—her separation from natal kin—was seen as a first step in rupturing "heathenness" in both respects; if she learned morals and civility at the mission station and eventually married a fellow "native'" Christian, she could create a new hereditary line. In this regard, although the fact that sponsored children were alone in their portraits (or with other children) was not surprising per se—indeed, American children were often posed without adults in the frame—it is notable that these portraits circulated apart from *other* family portraits. By contrast, an American child's portrait would almost certainly have been incorporated into a family album or Bible, portrait wall or mantel. These aesthetic groupings made Christian families, while sponsored children's portraits seemed to indicate a rupture that incorporated them into the story of Christian globalism instead. "Firmly positioned within the charged chronography of sacred time," these racialized portraits documented a selective present, signaled a break from an imagined past, and seemed to presage the Christian future Americans believed could be built one convert at a time.[25]

Women used these portraits in techniques to create sentiment by arranging and pasting them into albums for regular use. Mollie Pilcher, the secretary of a WFMS auxiliary in Jackson, Michigan, described an example in 1880: one woman "who owns a missionary album [of portraits] often takes it with her into a consecrated spot, where she holds communion with her Saviour, and as she turns the pages, she remembers . . . all the waste places in heathen lands; while for the army of workers she weeps and prays, into her own heart there comes such an overpowering sense of the fulness [*sic*] and richness of Jesus' love, that she is enabled to go forth rejoicing and ready for work."[26] For the group in Pittsburgh, gazing at Mary Belle's face produced the kinds of imagined projections that undergirded engaged empathy; they felt assured that God (and they) would succeed in making this "intelligent" girl comprehend the Gospel. They were also "glad in looking forward to the time the rescued ones, and the patrons who have held out helping hands to them shall be set face to face among the risen saints, singing the 'new song' and the harping of the hosts of angels!" The joy of mutual recognition in heaven could not be adequately described, they concluded, but looking at her portrait assured them of its reality. Some converted orphans also used photos to reify and prepare for a next life. "I should be very glad to see you; but as that may not be in this world, will you kindly send me your photograph," wrote an Indian girl renamed Fanny Garretson Hyde to her patron in 1871.[27] For Christians, such as the Pittsburgh women or Fanny, who had converted at the mission after her mother's death, these photos gave comfort in this life because they projected the imagination into a future and secured one's place within it. In other words, when Christians used portraits to imagine the foreign people they expected to meet in Heaven, they affirmed that they would be there as well.

FATHERLESS·CHILDREN·OF·FRANCE, INC.

AVEZ VOUS PLACE DANS VOTRE COEUR POUR NOUS ?

IN YOUR NAME I AM GIVING HAPPINESS TO
A FRENCH SOLDIER'S ORPHAN FOR ONE YEAR
·IT IS MY CHRISTMAS GIFT TO YOU·

FIG 3.3A AND 3.3B. Compare a popular Fatherless Children of France postcard from Christmas 1918 with the portrait of six-year-old Jean Roy and his sister Suzanne, arranged by his mother and grandmother to send to C. H. Moran, his FCF sponsor in Tennessee in October 1918. Postcard in Hoover Institution Archives, Stanford University; Roy photograph courtesy of Nathan K. and Mary Moran, http://moranfamilytn.blogspot.com/.

By World War I, snapshot photography was more commonplace. At its inception, the FCF committee in Paris tasked a young lady volunteer with motoring around the French countryside to take pictures of sponsored children, using a portable camera; these images were used by local U.S. committees to reenergize interest if donors dropped off.[28] Many American patrons also asked the mothers of their adoptees to send snapshots and mailed the required funds (89 cents for the photographer, 95 cents for printing, 20 cents for postage).[29] The resulting images—thousands of French and Belgian children posed stiffly in their best clothing—speak volumes about how the objects of emergency relief could also sometimes use photography to make certain claims, in this case as respectable and patriotic. Take for example the photo of six-year-old Jean Roy and his sister Suzanne, arranged by his mother and grandmother for his FCF sponsor in Tennessee (figure 3.3a). The children are calm, serious, and carefully dressed. The boy wears a military uniform made by his grandmother with the number of his deceased father's regiment. It contrasted sharply with the distress imagery that circulated in FCF media (figure 3.3b). Like the photos in missionary circles, these portraits embodied a vision of the future. For the French women who composed them, it was a future built on a pride in their local histories, their self-reliant respectability, and the heroism of their fallen menfolk.

Between the time that Fanny Garretson Hyde lost her mother in the chaos surrounding the Sepoy Rebellion and Jean and Suzanne Roy lost their father on the French front, a new photographic idiom entered humanitarian fund-raising: the brutalized child. Early images of "famine orphans" generally followed the conventions of portraiture with the children shown clean, dressed, and posed for the camera, as in Florence Bird's postcard. Around 1900, missionary magazines began to print a different kind of portrait that showed children often stripped naked and in severe bodily distress. Such images were controversial. "It is not expedient to reproduce here some of the pictures of wasted forms that have been sent us from India, the result of the famine, but we will give one picture, the least trying of those received," acquiesced the *Missionary Herald* in 1900. The portrait shows a mother with her two children; they are emaciated but with the parent, and their bodies are partially covered.[30] White children were shown in distress too, but rarely brutalized and naked. As many scholars have shown, this discrepancy built upon and encouraged racist constructions of (white Christian) giver and (racially and religiously other) recipient.[31]

Distress images were circulated alongside another photographic innovation—the before/after portrait. This type of image, which likely first emerged in domestic child-saving campaigns in London in the 1870s before spreading to missionary fund-raising, juxtaposed two images to show the rapid changes that Christian conversion or humanitarian relief had wrought. By World War I, such images had become enough of a staple in U.S. fund-raising that sponsorship organizations noted the public's "repeated demands" for them, despite the practical impossibility in wartime of securing "before" photos.[32] Sometimes organizations responded by juxtaposing "similar" individuals, such as placing an image of a "heathen" in her "unregenerate" state next to one of a convert with the "sweet, modest, intelligent face" of a Christian.[33] World War I organizations sometimes used American children as stand-ins, which recalls how missionary circles engaged orphaned or immigrant children to performatively embody foreign ones (chapter 2). In November 1917, for example, NER organized a parade in New York City where the healthy bodies of Armenian American children provided an imagined "before" in contrast to the "after" images circulating in the press, and by NER, since the Turkish massacre. Dressed in national costumes, the children held signs aloft as they marched through the streets: "This was our past/Help us to be so in the future" or "Babies/400,000 Now Starving/They were like us before/Will you let them die?" (see figure 3.4).

FIG 3.4. "Help Now or Never," pamphlet by American Committee for Armenian and Syrian Relief, c. December 1917. From Burke Library Archives, New York.

NER honed another type of imagery in this period: the landscape photo-graph. I use this term to distinguish such images from portraits (a nod to how we still print documents in either portrait or landscape formats). Landscape photos were often framed horizontally and they were shot from above to dis-play hundreds of bodies grouped together in a unified image or message. The technique was almost certainly inspired by the new aerial photography of World War I, but its purpose was hardly novel. Almost from their inception, English charity schools had promoted their work by displaying hundreds of children grouped together in parades and choral performances. Sharp-eyed critics like Bernard Mandeville, author of *The Fable of the Bees* (1714), noted of these charity school events, "There is a natural Beauty in Uniformity, which most People delight in. It is diverting to the Eye to see the Children well match'd . . . two by two in good order."[34] This aesthetic principle also defined landscape photographs: the delight in seeing thousands of bodies perform an ordered task, such as NER photos where children's bodies spelled out "AMER-ICA WE THANK YOU," "GOLDEN RULE," or simply "SAVED" (figure 3.5 and figure 3.6). As with statistical aesthetics in chapter 2, landscape photos mobilized the power of immensity, this time by displaying the rewarding result

TWO THOUSAND CHILDREN AT THE NEAR EAST RELIEF ORPHANAGE AT ALEXANDROPOL, ARMENIA FORMED THIS DRAMATIC ONE WORD MESSAGE OF GRATITUDE TO AMERICA.

56 WASHINGTON STREET, PROVIDENCE, R. I.

FIG 3.5. Landscape photo of Armenian children spelling the word "SAVED" with their bodies produced by Near East Relief for circulation in the United States, c. 1920. From Burke Library Archives, New York.

of American giving: thousands of foreign bodies spelling out their gratitude and their regeneration through the "Golden Rule" derived from Matthew 7:12—"Whatsoever ye would that men should do to you, do ye even so to them."

These photos underline how most World War I–era sponsorship programs positioned their global projects as significantly larger than saving individual children or even providing disaster relief. NER claimed its "ultimate objective [was] . . . nothing less than a new Near East and a new era of love, goodwill and unselfish service in the old world."[35] The same message was cast as triumphalist manifest destiny in Anna Granniss's popular poem "America, Great Mother" (1924), which NER reprinted regularly: "America, lead on, lead on!/ Creation waits for thee/To prove to nations militant/That Love is victory . . . Join hands all races of mankind!/One Lord is ours above/Not war, but love His law fulfills/His law of laws is Love."[36] The poem linked Christ's new "law of Love," which Christian hermeneutics interpreted as the fulfillment of the old Israelite covenant of law, to America's role as God's new instrument to secure global harmony in the wake of war in the "old world."

NER reports were careful not to malign Orthodox Christianity, but they also portrayed Orthodox people and churches as mired in the past. This view overlapped with liberal assessments of other groups, such as Hindus and Muslims, and it was so common at the time that it would have seemed self-evident to most U.S. sponsors. A typical assessment from an ABCFM missionary writing during the Indian famine in 1900 was that, "one of the earliest manifestations of a new life, begotten in [new converts] by Christ, [is] the birth of ambition, a desire to shake off the old slavery to 'destiny.' Freedom to make the very best use of his powers and opportunities marks the [Protestant] Christian all

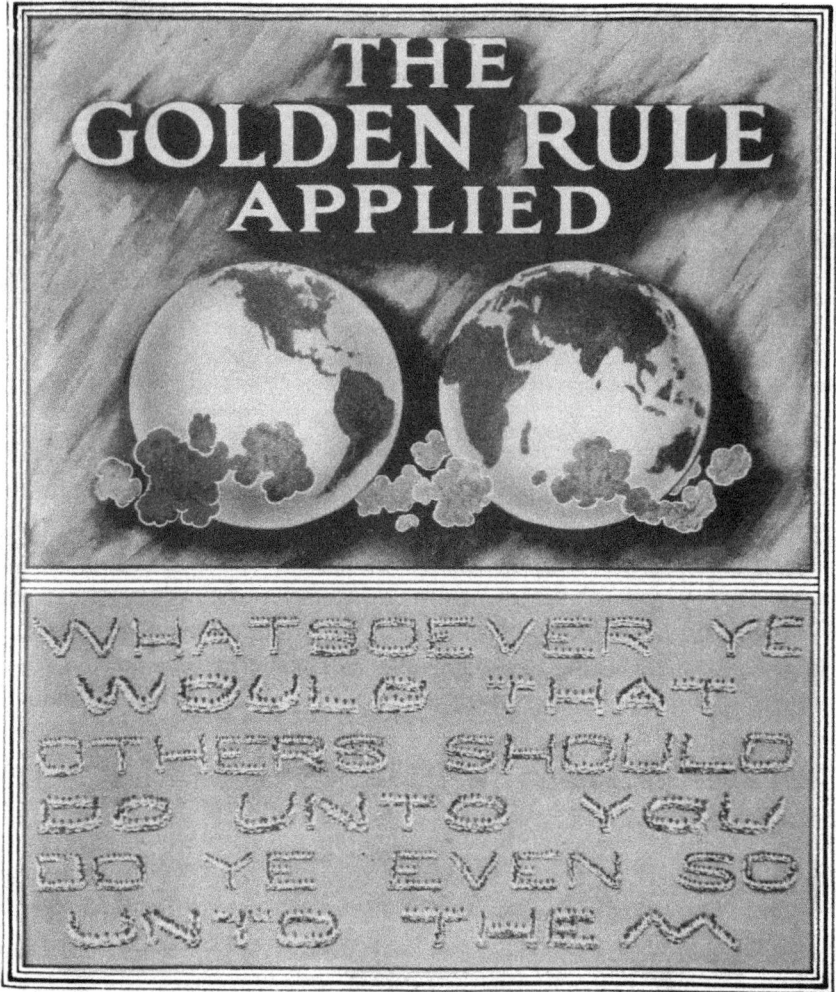

THE LETTERS ABOVE ARE FORMED BY ORPHANED CHILDREN

FIG 3.6. In another landscape photo, Armenian children use their bodies to spell out the Golden Rule for a publicity pamphlet, c.1926. For NER, the word "applied" signaled that its work was "practical religion" that created tangible outcomes, measurable here in the robust and ordered moral bodies of sponsored children. From Burke Library Archives, New York.

over the world."[37] For NER, liberal Protestant morality was interwoven with modern American qualities such as vigor, generosity, honesty, and international brotherhood. Thus could Harold McAfee, NER's managing director in Palestine and Syria, declare that the supreme achievement of his avowedly non-religious organization was its success in training children as a "moral and spiritual force" that would spread "God-honoring, altruistic-minded, and self-respecting" Americanism to their communities.[38]

In landscape photos taken from above, the magnitude of this project was manifested in the bodies of children that attested to the order and efficacy of U.S. charity. Such photos were printed alongside disaster imagery that showed the massive and chaotic upheaval of war. NER itself also produced many pamphlets that showed photos with hundreds of desperate people crowded into one frame—a staple of Western media by the late twentieth century, especially in coverage of war and famine.[39] Such imagery obliterated a horizon point and combined the intimacy of the portrait with the immensity of the landscape to produce a profoundly disruptive clash of scale. Donors were exposed to these images alongside landscape photos from above, sometimes in the same pamphlet. In juxtaposition, landscape photos became a prophetic vision of regeneration in which the miserable, disordered masses of the world came to embody a perfected Pax Americana.

Portraits and landscape group photos both constrained human subjects, albeit in different ways: the portrait constrained through proximity, cutting the subject off from her larger context; the landscape photo constrained through distance by effacing each individual as bodies were aggregated for effect. These constraints allowed viewers to arrange foreign bodies to best induce feelings of horror or soothing visions of (Western-led) improvement. For globally minded Christian sponsors and humanitarians, shock images thrilled not only because of their graphic nature (although that certainly may have been part of it) but because they were read in relation to aspirations for the world to come.

EATING LIKE AN ORPHAN TO SPREAD THE GOLDEN RULE

On Easter Sunday 1925, a man sat with his wife and two children around the supper table. He had been feeling restless for some time. Raised a liberal Protestant, he had repeated the Golden Rule from childhood: Whatsoever ye would that men should do to you, do ye even so to them. His generation had been the first to grow up with this gospel passage reproduced widely in Christian materials.[40] As his family grew more comfortable, it seemed hollow. He and his wife craved the best for their children, yet they still remembered how wartime relief campaigns had shocked them into recognizing dire needs abroad. He wanted his children, now five and seven, to develop "a world outlook and [be] lifted above the provincialisms of our modern American life." He was shaken by NER publicity that addressed him personally. "I was told that . . . the child must starve if I, or some one, did not accept the responsibility and privilege of saving its life."

That Easter, he and his wife seized upon a teachable moment. After naming their blessings, they steered the children toward thinking about those who had no homes, churches, or even food. To make the point, they borrowed a portable stereopticon with 50 pictures of orphans in the Near East. These children may be descended of the earliest Christians, they said. Pressed to make a decision, the children responded as their parents hoped, by offering to share their food with those in need. But how could it be done? The father made a suggestion: they would "literally share" their abundance by altering what they ingested. Thus began their weekly Golden Rule Dinner.

Following NER instructions, they began each meal with the international Golden Rule hymn—as NER renamed Anna Granniss's poem, "America, Great Mother"—to the tune of *America the Beautiful*:

> America, lead on, lead on! . . .
> Join hands all races of mankind!
> One Lord is ours above;
> Not war, but love His law fulfills . . .
> Around these hungry orphaned ones
> Unite, for World-Wide Peace!

Then they recited a blessing by Presbyterian pastor Henry Van Dyke, written for NER:

> Bless the great multitude of homeless children,
> The little ones far away in the Near East,
> Whom we greet in spirit at our table today. . . .
> [That] our hearts may hear the benediction
> Of our Lord and Saviour Jesus Christ:
> Inasmuch as ye have done it unto the least of these,
> Ye have done it unto Me. AMEN.

Then the mother passed around the dishes she had prepared following NER recipes, adapted from the Near East orphans' diet: Armenian rice pilaf, stewed beans, baked prunes, and olives. Their sponsored child's photograph was on the table with them—"the absent member of our family circle," the parents told their children. The five-year-old took this so much to heart that she sometimes propped the photo on an extra chair so the Armenian boy could sit among them. The parents focused the conversation on news about the place their orphan lived, gleaned from magazines and newspapers. At least twice a year, they read from NER's personal letter telling of his progress. As each meal ended, they turned to the box on the table and deposited $2, the money saved from eating the sparse Golden Rule menu. Later, the father wrote a list of his hoped-for results. He printed (1) and beside it, "one life saved." Perhaps his family was saving a future Saint Paul or Saint Helen, he mused. Then he continued: (2) The impact on my children's view of the world; (3) A permanent bond of friendship established between East and West; (4) Better health for our family due to plain, substantial food shared joyfully with others; (5) A weekly check on our stewardship of time and money.[41]

NER developed these Golden Rule dinners in 1923 as a way to promote "practical religion" and to garner wider support for extended child sponsorship plans—a necessity as their debts grew and donations dropped off after the war. The campaign was enormously successful. In 1924 alone, the female volunteers at Denver's NER office fielded more than 8,335 separate requests for information, and the New York office received 1,000 to 2,500 separate pieces of mail a day, an astonishing 87% of which were from new contributors. During December, 10,000 checks per day poured in from across the country, raising more than $1 million mostly in increments of less than $5.[42] Family dinners were the program's mainstay. Although some families held them every week, at minimum they were promoted at one symbolic time of year—the halfway point between Thanksgiving and Christmas when one could contemplate America's blessings as well as the (wasteful) abundance of upcoming seasonal gift giving (chapter 5).[43]

Canny about publicity, NER organized high-profile dinners for hundreds of distinguished guests who arrived in fancy dress to eat orphan fare in the ballrooms of the country's best hotels: La Salle Hotel in Chicago, Hotel Roosevelt in New York, Hotel Statler in St. Louis. In Washington, President Coolidge attended a Golden Rule dinner, and his speech was widely broadcast. Smaller and often innovative dinners also took place in churches and homes across the country. In 1925, for example, a group in Lemmon, South Dakota, held an orphan meal that included a scene in the next room where a woman and child play-acted at an elaborately set table. Playing a "pampered American girl," the child complained incessantly about the food her mother served. They acted it out loudly enough to repeatedly interrupt the sparse orphan dinner, creating a "very strong sentiment" among the diners.[44]

NER attributed the campaign's success to Americans' wish to support international causes that combined "practical idealism" with "spiritual significance."[45] NER, along with FCF and others, defined spiritual significance as *not* religious. The distinction they drew was that they did not explicitly seek to convert children in the field and they raised money on a non-sectarian basis. NER, for example, garnered support from a wide swath of Protestant bodies from the Southern Baptist Convention to the Federal Council of Churches to fundamentalist supporters of Billy Sunday, who collected for the cause at his tabernacle meetings. Catholic archbishops and fraternal groups lent their support, as did Reform rabbi Stephen S. Wise. NER eliminated religious messages when expedient and included as many stakeholders as possible in public events: a jam-packed 30-minute ceremony in New York in 1916 included speeches by local politicians, a performance by a Syrian choir, statements by Jewish and Catholic representatives, and a prayer by a pastor from the Presbyterian USA Board of Foreign Missions.[46]

At the grassroots, however, donors familiar with missionary sponsorship likely identified significant continuities. After all, NER arose out of ABCFM networks and distributed its funds through ABCFM missionaries—thus effectively supporting Christian missions. It fund-raised largely in local churches since, as its executive noted, "those who give to missions will be those who will feel responsibility for relief of Oriental sufferers."[47] Its messages often included biblical allusions and it prepared thousands of sermon helps, tithing cards, prayer sheets, and Christian educational supplements. FCF was not started by Christians, but many of its key fund-raisers worked for the YMCA at the same time and women's church circles were its most avid supporters; they held fund-raisers, formed sewing circles, and created Christmas boxes for FCF just as they did for foreign missions.[48] Promotional materials waxed poetic: "It seems that a great current of love has been set moving between these two republics [America and France] . . . [It] will wash away the dark stains of conflict and will give us faith to believe in the high destiny of humanity . . . It will again be true, as has happened all through the ages, that a little child shall lead us."[49] Love was no longer the constraining or liberating love of Christ per se, but the seemingly natural link between republics. Yet it remained couched in familiar Christian imagery—an allusion to Isaiah 11:6 (a "little child shall lead")—which could refer to FCF children, of course, but also to the Christ child. So it is no surprise that Luisita Leland, the New York socialite who oversaw FCF, would receive notes like this one, scrawled in poor handwriting and dated November 1917: "Dear Miss Leland, I my self give freely to my sisters support of three little [orphan] girls . . . I try to be a servant of Jesus Christ. I am sure there will be a star in your crown for your good. May God help us."[50]

Being "not religious" meant that World War I sponsorship organizations could appeal to "a servant of Jesus Christ" while also positioning their actions, and the moral ideology behind them, as universal—a global solution to the global problem of war. It was the globalization of what some contemporary scholars of U.S. Christianity have called "unmarked Protestantism," in this case of the liberal variety. By the late nineteenth century, certain thinkers in this camp had come to espouse a *consensus gentium*: it was believed that by contrasting different religions one could find a core similarity and thereby uncover a universal moral law.[51] The liberals at NER were not especially interested in actual comparisons, but they remade the "Golden Rule" gospel passage from Matthew 7:12 into a universal by purporting to discover its essence everywhere. It was, claimed NER, "a common denominator of all religions . . . Eternal and universal and an abiding constructive principle leading all people and nations forward."[52] To drive the point home, NER even changed the name of its yearly Golden Rule Sunday to the *International* Golden Rule Sunday. These ideas were by no means limited to NER at the time; they represented a broader political theology shared across the Christian spectrum, evoked by figures from William Jennings Bryan to Harry S. Truman.[53]

A concurrent and related trend viewed Americans as creating international "friendships," and sponsorship organizations promised that grateful children would remake their nations into "friendly neighbors" of the United States. Friendship seemed to distinguish the politics of a Pax Americana from the corrupt colonial powers that had plunged Europe into war; it was a key implement in twentieth-century Americans' rhetorical toolkit for securing "the foundations for an anti-imperial form of empire."[54] It also did rhetorical work specifically for liberal Protestants, who sought to reposition their missions as a dialogue between equals rather than an imperial imposition. In 1926, the Federal Council of Churches sponsored a Committee on World Friendship Among Children. The newly formed International Missionary Council called their children's groups World Friendship Circles. By styling such activities— including sponsorship—as friendships, U.S. adults positioned them as a natural form of connection between their children and foreign ones. Although such projects were orchestrated and kept up by adults, FCF was typical in how it recounted its foundation as when "the children of free America had the touching thought of extending a fraternal hand to their little comrades in France."[55] (No matter that FCF was actually the brainchild of a French industrialist.)

Promoting child-to-child friendships was thus mainly a message to and from adults who abstracted children into symbols of the future and metonyms for their respective nations. Further, and importantly in this context, sponsored children were also positioned as symbolic of a class of humanity that was the responsibility of all. "The world's wards," wrote NER, must be supported by the world's charity.[56] Decades later, anthropologist Sharon Stephens used nearly the same words—"the world's children"—in a 1995 essay that censured

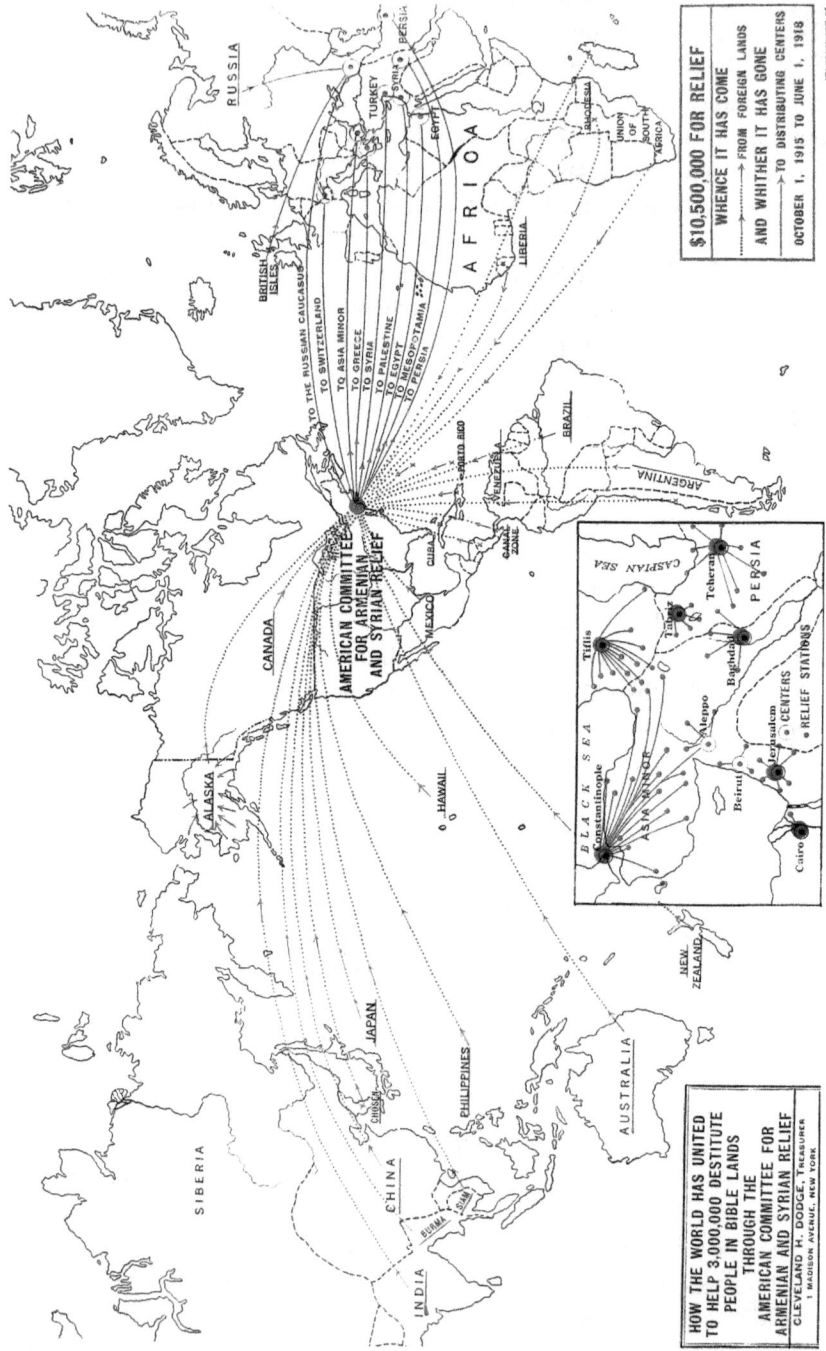

FIG 3.7. "How the World Has United," in Edwin Bulkley, Henry Morgenthau, and Charles R. Crane, *Report of Auditing Committee,* NER Pamphlet, June 4, 1918. From Burke Library Archives, New York.

U.S. media for portraying foreign children as symbols of a generic human family. As a result, she wrote, children seemed to provide a solution to cycles of global conflict, regardless of each child's biography.[57] When organizations like NER declared sponsored orphans were the "world's wards," they did this and something else too: they made U.S. donors into symbols of the world itself, with a responsibility to circulate love and friendship throughout.

War-era sponsorship plans made a world where money, food, love, and unmarked Gospel truths seemed to progress unimpeded across the globe. Media coverage of the Golden Rule dinners highlighted how they were being celebrated conterminously in 52 countries. NER printed or noted the many cablegrams sent to their New York office, claiming that they "revealed a spirituality abroad in the world that is frequently overlooked in this practical age. Not only in America but throughout Europe, and in countries as remote as China, Japan, Korea and Australasia."[58] On a number of occasions, it also reprinted photos of the Golden Rule Tea held in Jerusalem in August 1924, which evoked a small-scale Parliament of the World's Religions by bringing together members of 18 distinct nationalities and religions (Islam, Orthodoxy, Catholicism, Protestantism, and Judaism). They "differ widely in their ancient creeds," one caption read, "but all united in the universal creed of the Golden Rule, which, after all, is the law and the prophets (*sic*)." As the representatives broke bread together, it continued, they agreed that only by extending the Golden Rule could strife end in Jerusalem.[59] The solution to their divisive parochialism was the Rule that Americans brought to the world's people, while assuring them it had always been theirs.

In iconographic terms, NER maps illustrated this principle (figure 3.7). The metaphor of "global flows" is apt in this case, since these maps portrayed the unencumbered passage of things. Yet these flows by no means moved everywhere at random. They operated in a circulatory pattern that made New York into the spiritual and financial center of the world, nudging out Europe to become the axis around which people in the Near and Far East interacted with each other. The only exceptions were two arrows running from Britain and Russia to the Near East, a nod to how these countries had their own connections in the area. The ideological work of such maps becomes evident if we note some of what they leave out. Imagine if it included lines that traced the history of colonial wars between Persians and Russians, Ottomans, Germans, and English. Lines that showed how the USSR spent much larger sums among the Armenians than the United States and how after 1920 much of NER's work proceeded only with its permission. Lines that exposed how the "international" tributes praising the Golden Rule were largely—indeed almost exclusively—from U.S. ex-patriots. Lines that revealed how the religious representatives came to Jerusalem for tea only at the behest of U.S. and U.K. diplomats and missionaries.

NER promoters excised these messy details in large part because, just as they saw their project as not religious, so did they see it as "not political." They understood their interpretation of a gospel passage as a shared moral sentiment that could rupture old political paradigms, while remaining separate from politics itself. This view aligned with popular U.S. isolationism of the interwar period, which rejected further involvement in European politics and called for a uniquely American strategy for securing its peace and prosperity in the world. The Golden Rule, as a supposedly non-political form of foreign engagement, seemed to offer an alternative to European colonialism and the wars it spawned. Importantly, it was pitched as the everyday morality of friendship and fair play that was each American's birthright. By exporting it, even those people who were peripheral geographically and politically in the United States (at least compared to the elite New Yorkers running NER) could imagine themselves as globally central. Take, for example, the opening speech at a Golden Rule dinner in Topeka in 1924, when the state governor declared that Kansas had now joined "with this great humanitarian effort, in which . . . millions of citizens in all the participating nations will be seated, figuratively, at the same table, partaking of the same food, thinking the same thoughts, thus entering into a new realization of the brotherhood of mankind." Thus did (even) Topekans "make a substantial contribution towards world peace and a better understanding between the people of the world."[60]

GOLDEN RULE DINNERS AS PARTICIPATORY TECHNIQUE

Golden Rule dinners successfully tapped into the zeitgeist of mainline Protestant missionary work, nascent ecumenicism, and humanitarianism. As one might expect, then, the father in the initial account described the dinner as saving a foreign child and creating a "bond of friendship" between east and west. The dinners were also a ritualized performance and, on that note, his fourth point is especially interesting: "Better health for our family due to plain, substantial food shared joyfully with others." Golden Rule dinners exemplify a class of participatory techniques that made the absent present by ingesting or abstaining from food. These performances operated alongside and often incorporated the visual imagery discussed above.

The popular Oriental tea or coffee party can be viewed as a nineteenth-century antecedent. Young women usually hosted these events and charged small entry fees to raise money for foreign missions, not infrequently including the group's sponsored child. A typical "Hindoo party," such as the one held in 1882 by the young ladies of Hanson Place Church in Brooklyn, took place in a church parlor decorated with pan-Asian artifacts (in this case, "Japanese screens, banners, lanterns, parasols, and fans"). The hostesses donned versions of silk kimonos or Indian saris, modeled on photos from the mission field. Then these "natives" circulated among their guests with cakes and tea.[61] Nearly a hundred years later, in 1973, Sunday school classes still orchestrated events to embody the mission field (as some continue to do today). One class of girls spent a year "saturated" in Japan: they wore kimonos, examined Buddhist statues, used a rice cooker, and created Japanese floral arrangements. The culmination was a dinner where they sat on the floor and used chopsticks to eat sticky rice, seaweed, and rice crackers. They found sitting awkward, they fumbled with chopsticks, and felt new foods on their tongues. Pleasant or not, such experiences seemed a visceral connection to people in the mission field. "It's easier to pray for familiar things," one participant remarked.[62] Such exoticism is rife with inaccuracies, of course, but studies of sensory cognition argue that it is also integral to how humans often experience what is foreign. In fact, historians note that people in Asia also took pleasure in sensory experiences of exotic Americanness in the mid-twentieth century—albeit without evangelicalism's prayerful aims.[63]

Studies in new materialism offer another, and I believe helpful, way to think about such techniques, especially as they connect comestibles, bodies, and engaged empathy. For political theorist Jane Bennett, eating constitutes "a series of mutual transformations between human and non-human materials." To one degree, Bennett refers to transformation at a metabolic level: our bodies' digestive liquids and microorganisms transform edibles as we consume them, which transform us by producing physiological effects. What we eat may make us hyperactive, dull-witted, or focused. Yet she also relies on two nineteenth-century thinkers—Nietzsche and Thoreau—to suggest that food acts "inside and alongside intention-forming, morality-(dis)obeying, language-using, reflexivity-wielding, and culture-making human beings." For Nietzsche, German anti-Semitism grew through a multisensory experience of consuming certain foodstuffs (coffee and beer), reading certain newspapers, listening to Wagner, and cultivating military aesthetics. For Thoreau, vegetarianism not only produced bodily effects ("greater wakefulness") but also produced resistance against what he viewed to be harmful social conventions. For Bennett, both thinkers underline how food co-acts with "intensities often described as perception, belief, memory" in ways that may coarsen or refine the political (we might add, ethical) imagination.[64]

Golden Rule dinners operated on the same principle: organizers expected that the consumption of particular foods ("orphan fare"), combined with reading NER newsletters, reciting prayers and hymns, and gazing at the orphan's photo, would stimulate emotions such as pity, love, and euphoric connectedness. Ultimately, these intensities were expected to excite the imagination such that the absent child became momentarily present for U.S. families. The foods served at Golden Rule dinners were therefore important and they were detailed in recipe books. They were meant to taste like the Near East—stewed prunes and olives, for example—but they were also meant to be "plain," which NER seemed to define as a minimal number of ingredients, little or no meat, and no rich dessert. Plainness extended to the place settings and to one's frame of mind during the event. Ideally, plain food transposed the feeling of destitute, foreign orphanhood as one carefully chewed it. As noted earlier, from sponsors' perspective, the fact that all human bodies shared certain fundamental qualities—hunger is painful, plain food produces feelings of destitution and/ or simple gratitude—meant that the dinners seemed to allow one to viscerally participate in another's experience. The resulting sensations could repel or intrigue (so said the Sunday school class about their Japanese dinner of sticky rice and slippery noodles). Regardless, for a moment at least, food transformed the strange into something (quite literally) digestible—"familiar things," to quote one of the Sunday school students. While not precisely what I later call mirroring, such techniques worked to a similar end in how they bodied forth an idealized future in which all people—whether they ate olives or rice noodles—became intimately knowable to Americans at home.

As Bennett implies, food is powerful because it is digested into the very stuff that makes up our bodies, which is why rituals employ it to produce a mingling of bodies. For Christians, communion is the preeminent example: by eating blessed bread, a believer takes divinity into himself. He also mystically connects his body to others both proximate and far away in "the body of Christ." Even those Protestants who reject the doctrine of transubstantiation still generally view passing bread from person to person and ingesting it together as a powerful experience of unity. While NER never called Golden Rule dinners a communion, the similarities are unmistakable. Like communion, the dinners centered on plain food, which through its simplicity produced a surplus of signification. Like communion, they were meant to stimulate sensory connections to physically absent beings. One of NER's slogans was "Enlarge, enrich your family circle. Invite one of these little children as an invisible guest to our family table for the coming year."[65]

An advertisement from 1940 slightly postdates our period but offers a useful illustration of what the dinners were designed to achieve (figure 3.8). It

Our UNSEEN GUESTS

OH, little far-off unseen guests, today
We feel your spirit presence as we lay
The cloth, the plates, to hold this ample meal,
Almost your little fingers we can feel
Stretched out in pleading love, and blest indeed
Are we whose bread this day can help your need
But who, oh who is this with shining face
Who deigns to be our Guest and takes his place
With noiseless step about our humble board?
Ah, is it, can it be our Risen Lord?
Yea, it is He, with blessing in His touch,
What is it that He whispers? — 'Inasmuch!'
—By Bertha Gerneaux Woods.

There are millions of unseen guests awaiting our invitation. We may save their lives and they will enrich our lives. A great multitude of many nationalities, races, and religions. Take your choice — a boy, or a girl, or both. Enlarge and enrich your family circle. The children of your home will be happier, more unselfish, more radiant and more inspiring, with broader outlook. They will become better citizens of the community, of the nation and of this world neighborhood in which they must learn to live and serve.

IN GRATITUDE — that we live in a land of peace — that our homes have not been bombed — that our soldier boys are not on the battle fields, in hospitals, or unknown graves — that our families are not refugees — that our property is not seized for military purposes — that our food is not rationed or restricted — that our freedoms of speech, press, ballot and assembly are unchallenged — that we may be on the giving rather than the receiving end of the Golden Rule — **we dedicate this Coin-A-Meal Globe to OUR UNSEEN GUESTS.**

FIG 3.8. "Our Unseen Guests," from the back cover of the *International Golden Rule Fellowship* magazine, 1940. Courtesy of ChildFund International.

portrays a family enjoying an ample supper with a globe-shaped coin collection box at the head of the table. It reiterates familiar messages about American gratitude for blessings and training children to be unselfish. More pertinent, however, are the multiple presences at the table. The box is accorded human-like qualities: it sits next to a chair seemingly reserved for it and the family smiles at it solicitously. It enfolds humans within it as the faces of thousands of absent/present children burst forth and hover over the table.[66] The image is framed with a poem by Bertha Gerneaux Woods, first published in 1926, reading in part:

Oh, little far-off unseen guests, today
We feel your spirit presence as we lay
The cloth, the plates, to hold this ample meal
Almost your little fingers we can feel
Stretching out in pleading love

Preparing to serve the dinner, laying the cloth and plates—but presumably also the smell of the food, soon its taste in their mouths, the sound of clinking silverware—all compel the almost physical sensation of being touched by distant fingers in an emotional request for love and pity. Woods then adds one more layer to the encounter with unseen guests: the appearance of Jesus Christ. With "shining face and noiseless tread," he joins the family at their "humble board," arriving "with blessing in His touch." However much the family has compared with other people globally, their meal is but "humble board" compared to the spiritual riches of Heaven.

In this image, humility and engaged empathy are entwined with the power and security that characterizes U.S. Christians enjoying a lavish meal at home. The tension between these poles was nowhere more evident than in the response of a fair minority of mothers who, though tasked with the moral labor of creating a Golden Rule meal, refused to serve an orphan diet to their own children even for a night. NER attempted to address these concerns with new health indicators that quantified food in terms of calories. It showed how the orphans ate the requisite number of calories per day. It repeated that the plain fare was "consistent with considerations of health" and approved by the Good Housekeeping Institute. But in the end, it had to compromise: U.S. mothers could provide larger portions, more varied menus, and include meat *if* they told their children that it was not a faithful recreation.[67] Not wanting to dissuade participation, organizers concluded rather lamely that the details were perhaps less important than how the dinners "aid in directing our thoughts to our higher obligations."[68]

POSTSCRIPT: FAMINE REDUX

In 1969, Mary Bowers MacKorrell, a schoolteacher from Charlotte, North Carolina, had been dieting for months without success. One day, she was eating lunch in front of a television cooking show when she idly picked up a pamphlet that had come in the mail. Its cover showed a skeletal boy in Haiti, and she was stunned by the contrast with the sumptuous food on TV. "And then God gave me an idea," she wrote:

> It was one of those inspirations that I believe occasionally come to our minds directly from His Holy Spirit. Couldn't I take the pounds off myself and transfer them to the body of a starving child? Physicians are now transplanting hearts from one person to another. Could not the Great Physician enable me to "transplant" my extra pounds to a body which needed them?

"Under God's guidance," Mary skipped lunch for ten days and instead sipped a sugar-free drink while looking at the photo of the boy in Haiti. For each lunch omitted, she set aside a dollar saved. She successfully shed five pounds and gained ten dollars, but was still unsure how to transplant her pounds to the child. Then God spoke again through the U.S. post. She received another leaflet in the mail, asking for $10 to support a starving child in India. She immediately enclosed the money with "a prayer that those bowls of rice be used by God to 'transplant' the five pounds that I had lost to the emaciated body of some child."[69]

At turns touching and disturbing, Mary's story testifies to the continued links between emergency relief, shock imagery, and embodied techniques forged two generations before. But times had also changed. Mary was writing during a wave of new attention to world hunger then sweeping U.S. Christianity, in which sponsorship organizations played a key role. World Vision was especially engaged, using horrifying images of children in distress in its print campaigns and primetime documentaries with titles like *Children: Between Life and Death*. A hundred years after Florence Bird gathered up famine orphans in India, it ran sensationalized "baby airlifts" to evacuate war orphans from Korea, Cambodia, and Vietnam and place them with adoptive Christian families. In 1975, it recruited Senator Mark O. Hatfield, the famed evangelical anti-hunger advocate from Oregon, to chair its Year for a Hungry World campaign and join its Board of Directors.[70]

Hunger relief in this period was welded to "population explosion," a term that entered the public lexicon from scientific and humanitarian circles. It referred to the fear that the human population would grow until, to quote CCF director J. Calvitt Clarke at his prophetic best, "future generations will drink the rivers dry and, like a plague of locusts, eat the farms barren and shove against each other to find even standing room." "We are on the brink of global suicide," exclaimed Hatfield to WV sponsors.[71] These dark predictions were fueled by the new availability of UN global population statistics and rooted in Americans' long-standing anxiety about the "teeming millions" of India and China. Now it was "billions" and by the early 1980s, images of children with hollow eyes and distended bellies who were living in Uganda, Niger, and Ethiopia had taken center stage. The hunger associated with "population explosion" seemed to exceed faraway emergency relief; starving children presaged a nightmare that awaited humanity as a whole. Many mainline missionaries, including Clarke, strongly advocated birth control. "Are we rabbits or intelligent creatures?" he demanded in a letter to President Lyndon Johnson. CCF's *ChildWorld* magazine also told its readers that their demand for cheap food and luxuries was eating up the world's arable land.[72] Speaking to evangelicals, Hatfield and WV President Stanley Mooneyham framed it as a spiritual failure to adequately steward God's resources (chapter 5).[73]

Whether or not they agreed with these diagnoses, most sponsors in this period did view starving children as the world's top priority.[74] And many of them continued to hone engaged empathy through participatory feasting and fasting. Individuals in the late 1960s and 1970s innovated, as Mary MacKorrell's story makes clear. Others retained a weekly "sacrificial meal" of plain food.[75] And in the mid-1970s, sponsorship organizations resurrected group dinners that echoed NER's campaigns. Hatfield and Mooneyham hosted a 1974 luncheon for the U.S. Congress that consisted of a few ounces of rice, declaring, "until Americans willingly experience hunger . . . they cannot begin to comprehend the condition [of famine]."[76] The following year, CCF held dinners of watery soup in elegant hotels to underscore "what it feels like to be desperately hungry every day of your life." Compassion began "starve-ins" for teens and "Rich Man, Poor Man" dinners where one-third of the guests were served an ample meal and two-thirds given a small bowl of rice, making the U.S. Christians around the table into a microcosm of the world's people.[77]

The most widespread of these activities was World Vision's Planned Famine, today called 30 Hour Famine and still popular across North America. It was pitched in the 1970s as a group activity for Christian teens who would fast during a weekend retreat to raise money for famine relief. Though most groups that undertook it were evangelical, mainline Protestants and Catholics also participated (in at least one case, donating the proceeds to support a sponsorship at Unbound, rather than World Vision!). By coming "closer to *starvation*," quoting WV publicity, participants were expected to come "closer to a starving world. And closer to God."[78] Les Wagner, a man who helped facilitate a Famine for the youth group at his Lutheran church in Maryland in 1984, detailed its effects:

> Eventually I drifted off to sleep, trying not to think of hunger. That's like trying to ignore a throbbing toothache. No matter how hard you pretend, the feeling is still there . . . [L]ying there on the hard floor that chilly November night with my stomach growling and a dull ache in my head brought home the stark realization . . . [W]hat if there's nothing to eat? That question, so easy to pose in the abstract, became much clearer and sharper as my stomach contracted. Our fast was scheduled to end in 30 hours, but—I reminded myself—for many in the world, their fast will never end.[79]

Wagner's experience was precisely what WV hoped to achieve. Guided by the biblical texts his group studied that weekend, Wagner translated the sharpness of hunger pangs into the sharpness of fear during famine: *What if there's nothing to eat?* Gnawing hunger was sharp, but also a dull throbbing. At those moments, Wagner sensed what he felt to be the everyday grind of poverty. The aim was to viscerally share other people's hunger pain while also, as WV's materials put it, come closer to God. The euphoria of global connectedness, intermingled with the pain of hunger, created a performative link to a Deity who, in the U.S. evangelical imagination, has a heart that overflows with love for humankind even while it is also "broken" by human sin and sorrow.

Many scholars argue that shock imagery inevitably stifles empathy since it mobilizes universal categories such as "human sin," "world hunger," or "natural disaster" to occlude local contexts.[80] From the perspective of Christian globalism, however, such universals actually prompt empathy by acknowledging that people are fundamentally alike *despite* the particularities of local distress or cultural difference (which are therefore, in a sense, distractions if they fail to direct attention back to the real story of human sameness). Bodies are key to this universality since our common functions—we all need food, we all feel the same pangs when deprived of it—seem to attest to a common Creator. Read through this lens, a story like Mary MacKorrell's does evoke communion. As she transposed skipped meals into money that became meals abroad, she metaphorically passed the Eucharistic bread to the person next to her—the child in need—and forged bodily links within the global body of Christ.[81] Sponsorship is optimistic about what such interventions achieve. It has always suggested that the generosity of individual Americans, co-laboring with God, can provide an antidote to the systemic failures of armies and governments.

CHAPTER 4

Family and Friendship

Kin-like Relations and Racialized Universalism

All the children of the world
Red, brown, yellow
Black and white
They are precious in His sight.

—"Jesus Loves the Little Children," popular American hymn

Actually close observation dissolves the concept of foreignness and brings into sharper focus the reality of our oneness under God.

—Verbon E. Kemp, CCF Director, personal letter to Miss Genevieve Altman, a sponsor from Brooklyn, 1964

Situated just east of the White House in Washington DC, Calvary Baptist Church was the founding church of the American Baptist Convention and nearly a century old in 1951. Among its many members at the time, some had friends and family serving in the Korean war, while others volunteered at the church's weekly canteen for the nearby army base. These commitments led congregants to seek "practical expressions of Christian concern" for their "destitute Korean friends"—referring to South Korean civilians. To that end, they invited CCF Director J. Calvitt Clarke to speak at a Sunday service just before Thanksgiving.

Clarke obliged them with his typical fund-raising speech, in which he positioned sponsorship as a key tool in securing Protestant morality and American-style democracy abroad. He followed up with a letter, reprinted in the church newsletter, that shared his "cherished dream . . . that some church might start a sort of international club and adopt children in a dozen or so countries—one in each [where CCF operates], perhaps—and that somewhere in the church they would have the framed photographs of the children adopted and perhaps a bulletin board on which letters and reports from the adopted children would be posted."[1] This dream of Clarke's—rather specific and didactic in nature—resonated at Calvary Baptist. Within a few weeks, the congregation raised more than $6,000 to fund 48 sponsorships. Treasurer H. Loren Fassett requested at least one orphan in each CCF country, linking church members to children in places such as Japan, India, Malaya, Finland, and of course Korea. Fassett congratulated his co-congregants that their response "reveals once again the thrilling way in which Calvary's members respond to the needs of the whole world." Church member Mrs. Frances F. Nickels wrote directly to Clarke to underline the point: "Our church folks responded to your visit enthusiastically and many folks who hitherto had not known the joy of helping anyone specifically as the Orphan Fund provides are having a real thrill."[2]

Elsewhere, Clarke's pitch was less welcome. Writing in the *Michigan Christian Advocate* in 1954, a layman named Clark H. Phillips counseled his fellow Methodists to reject the sponsorship model hawked so effectively by new non-denominational organizations like CCF. "As humans, we want the thrill of the personal touch but we also want to know that our money was efficiently used to help the most people possible. Doing both is impossible." Methodists must choose, he wrote curtly: they could opt for a quick thrill or give to their own denomination with the more lasting satisfaction of knowing the money was well spent.[3] Other Protestant missionary boards echoed this complaint, viewing organizations like CCF with ambivalence and even classifying them as "secular" because they had "no connection with any Church group and over which no control is possible."[4]

Although Fassett, Nickels, and Phillips differed in their conclusions, they all agreed that sponsorship was "thrilling" for Christians at home. A thrill stimulates, exhilarates, and fires the imagination; it is often associated with surges of excitement and pleasure. The word, which is found throughout sponsor letters and organizational publicity in this period, was associated specifically with the promise of 1:1 connection. Sponsorship had been built on this idea, of course, but it was only after World War II that organizations like CCF successfully systematized communications between tens of thousands of children and sponsors through field reports, monthly magazines, Christmas cards, personal letters, and yearly photos. For the first time, they guaranteed that sponsors would hear *directly* from the child they supported, instead of from missionaries or parents, and, more than their predecessors, they employed terms of the closest kinship to describe these "adoptions," as it was called at the time. Not insignificantly, sponsorship grew at a meteoric rate in the 1950s alongside a wave of interest in the legal adoption of children from Korea, Japan, and Vietnam—the very places in which sponsorship also operated. Whether or not sponsors actually adopted (and very few did), it fueled conditions to imagine parenting a foreign child. In short, mid-century sponsorship was more thrilling than ever before.

This chapter interrogates the promise of intimacy by exploring the intersection of kin-like relations and racial ideologies in the 1950s and 1960s. It focuses on mainline Protestant CCF, founded in 1938 and the largest organization of its type at the time, along with two of its evangelical competitors, World Vision and Compassion, founded in 1950 and 1952, respectively. These organizations are exemplary of a major shift in twentieth-century sponsorship from emergency relief into a form of permanent fund-raising. Each one grew rapidly by partnering with established foreign missionaries and "native" Christian workers who ran orphanages and schools. Americans gave $10–12 a month, of which $4–8 was transferred for each sponsored child in the institution. Sponsorship was linked to the general proliferation of U.S. voluntary organizations working overseas (more than 200 were established in the four years after World War II alone).[5] It also fit snugly within the Cold War politics playing out in Asia, notably in how U.S. Christians, bemoaning the "loss" of China to communists in 1951 (when foreign missionaries were expelled), were galvanized by the Korean War. Dubbed the first "hot" war of the Cold War, it left 3 million Koreans dead. It also opened a door for evangelists like Bob Pierce (World Vision) and Everett Swanson (Compassion), who both arrived following U.S. troops. After leaving China in 1951, Clarke moved CCF there too. All three founders were stridently anti-communist (especially Clarke) and actively opposed any actions—including by their own foreign employees—construed as threatening their assets and power abroad.[6]

Sponsors were rarely privy to these, or any, details about field operations since there were few formal auditing or reporting measures at the time (chapter 6). Instead, their experience of Cold War sponsorship was defined by the intimate configurations of home and family. To explore this theme, I take my cue from two bodies of intersecting literature: the first focuses on kinship and transnational adoption, the second on how ideologies of race and domesticity impacted U.S. foreign politics.[7] However, my aim differs somewhat from this work and is more in keeping with my overarching emphasis on the dialogical relation between particularity and immensity at the heart of Christian globalism. In this respect, two main points emerge. The first concerns mid-century sponsorship's claims to be thrillingly "kin-like"—which, in emic terms, was often signaled by the word "love." Chapter 1 traced how nineteenth-century theologies of love universalized broadly white, feminine, middle-class values. By the mid-twentieth century, this type of love was so embedded in sponsorship that it rarely evoked comment. For that reason, it bears repeating: love is a foundational concept in modern Christian globalism. Although the word appears in the singular, it implies a confluence of Divine Love and human-scale love. Christians would never say that Love is *dependent* on love but that it is comprised of it: in God's relationship with his creatures, intimate and immense scales blend. The circulation of human love nourishes God's Love projects and attests to their reality. This idea animates domestic U.S. Christian activism,[8] but it has a special place in global projects where people seek to extend love and action worldwide.

The chapter's second major point concerns the role of race in sponsorship's promise of kin-like relations. Unlike their First World War antecedents, which principally focused on white children in need of wartime relief, mid-century sponsorship organizations solidified a pattern that continues today: the presumed white sponsor of the non-white child.[9] As these organizations moved from relief work to NGOs and from war zones to the world, they replicated the vision of an active, rich (white) "north" and a dependent, poor (non-white) "south." Mid-century sponsors rarely questioned this formulation, at least in their letters to the organizations they supported, likely because it had long been normalized within the binaries that structured nineteenth-century slavery, imperialism, and scientific racism. Of course, it is hardly novel to point out that racial categorizations were (and are) central to a U.S. worldview. The links between nation, universalism, and race are strong and well documented.[10]

What is less often discussed is how these factors relate to a *Christian* subjectivity. Mid-century sponsors incorporated the supposed particularity of one child's race or nation into a framework for an intimate form of immensity—that is, the human "family." Within Christian globalism, this hope was often phrased as becoming "brothers and sisters in Christ." It also often relied on mirroring, the mediated forms that showed racialized others engaging in activities that U.S. audiences recognized as familiarly Christian, which reinforced for them that there was indeed a prayer life/church life/Christian sentiment like their own in distant places (for example, CCF's Christmas cards in figures 4.3a and 4.3b). In discussing these dynamics, I follow other theorists in my use of the word "racialize" as a variant of racism. Distinguishing this terminology is useful because globalism often rhetorically and visually evokes difference— demarcated by skin color, clothes, and accent—to celebrate human diversity. Christians of all backgrounds who employ such forms rarely, if ever, view them as "racist" because they associate this word with antagonism and assertions of white superiority. "Racialize" acknowledges this perspective, while signaling the racist logic still at play: these forms order the world into seemingly natural (usually national) categories in which phenotype indexes human difference.[11] Thus, mirroring is always a cruel form of optimism.[12] Its affective power to bridge depends upon—is impossible without—structurally reinforced binaries between Christian/heathen, white/black, West/rest that U.S. sponsors treat as a natural (if lamentable) condition of humankind. Without difference, there can be no miracle of sameness under God.

The chapter begins with two sections that focus on sponsors' rather complicated yearnings for kinship and racialized unity, respectively. Taken together, these sections clarify how intimacy operated at two overlapping scales, both of which used family tropes—the 1:1 "adoption" of a child into one's family and the inclusion of an abstracted child within the "human family." The consumption and production of these tropes occurred within the literal spaces of mid-century U.S. homes, fueled by what was perhaps sponsorship's most important technology of intimacy at the time—personal letters. The second half of the chapter turns to how organizations shaped children's letter-writing and the dynamics of U.S. family life in which the letters played a part. It ends with a postscript that explores Christian conversion and the promise of kin-like relations today.

CONSTITUTING KIN-LIKE RELATIONS

Mid-century sponsors often employed terms of the closest kinship to describe the children they supported. In 1961, Mrs. Samuel Etchings from El Cajon, California wrote that Hwang In Sook and Jang Bak Soon "have joined our family circle . . . not as adopted daughters but as our very own." After Larry Ward and his wife failed to conceive a second child, they turned to sponsorship. "Now [our six-year-old] Sheri has a sister," he wrote, "and quite often Sheri, helping Mommie set the table, places an extra plate there for her little Korean sister." Dorothy Greiser, a widow in her seventies, reflected on what it was like when the children she sponsored left the program and communication ceased: "I felt like I have actually lost a child."[13] The Mortimer family created perhaps the most eloquent statement of all: pasting a photo of "their" Korean orphan into a family portrait (figure 4.1).

These professions of intimacy obscure as much as they reveal. Dorothy Greiser, who was so close to her only daughter that she still felt pangs of loneliness years after the young woman had moved out, likely recognized that even the abrupt termination of a sponsorship was not in fact equivalent to losing a child. Mrs. Etchings did correspond with In Sook into adulthood, but never met her and almost certainly did not view her as part of the "family circle" quite like her own daughter, Carole. In Ward's case, it turned out that Jung Hi had never been the orphan he assumed; after three years of searching, her mother

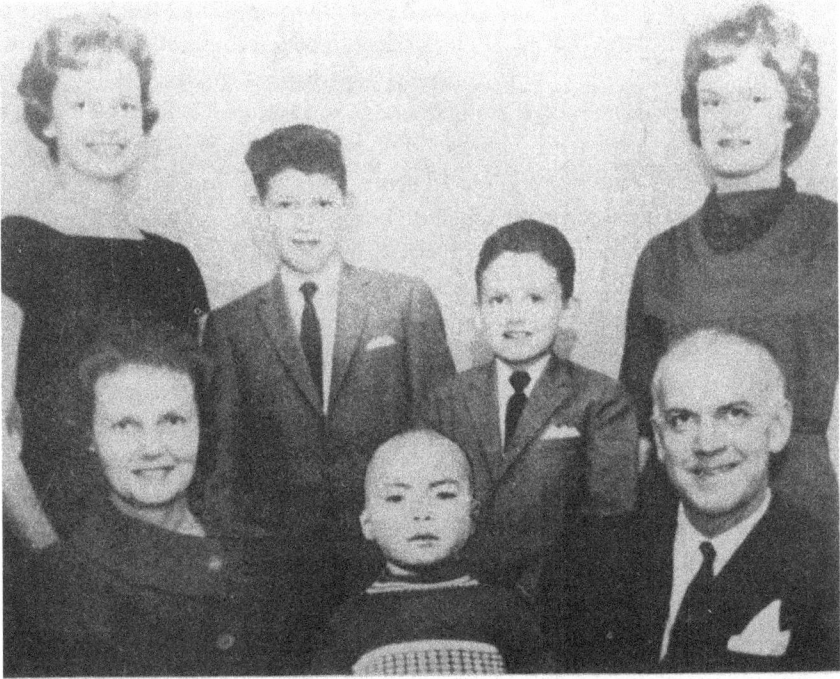

The W. Ross Mortimer family, Ontario, Canada.

FIG 4.1. W. Ross Mortimer and family with "their" orphan, 1962. They posed the portrait especially for this purpose, pasted in the image of the sponsored child, and then sent a copy to Korea for the boy to keep. Courtesy of World Vision International Archives.

located her and removed her from the orphanage. Ward, who was then working for World Vision, modeled the ideal response: he wrote the girl to say, rather limply, that he hoped her life turned out well and then immediately penned a letter to the new child WV assigned.[14] Over time, undoubtedly even little Sheri realized there is a difference between the loss of a sister and a sponsored "sister."

So then, what kind of relationship did sponsorship constitute? Recent anthropologies of kinship offer a helpful framework by focusing on the practical realities of making "relatedness." To this discussion, anthropologist James Faubion adds Foucault's distinction between morals (rules about behavior) and ethics (techniques of self-transformation). He argues that kinship operates beyond its obvious association with moral obligations to biological family members to also encompass ethics that are bound up in "the reception, negotiation, and revision of stories about the self and an 'elect' group of others, some living, some dead."[15] This idea resonates with the Christian model of "transcendent kinship" in which an individual is encouraged to forge new relations that reflect his or her cosmological commitments. Most obviously, Jesus tells his disciples to leave their families and form a community of saints. When mid-century Americans sponsored a child abroad, most of them hoped the child would become "theirs," not least through conversion to Christ. While we cannot know how many children did become Christians, their letters were peppered with Christian sentiments that seemed a very hopeful sign to those who supported them. In this sense, sponsorship was (and is) a form of ethical self-transformation, for the sponsor and perhaps for the child, that was expected to strengthen global ties between "brothers and sisters in Christ." Yet, as Faubion notes, even forms of kinship that are unmoored from biology, still interact with local understandings of genealogical continuity. Thus, sponsorship is "kin-like" in how it produces relatedness based on transcendent Christian categories that are also grounded in American assumptions about biological family life.[16]

One evocative way that mid-century sponsors created these intimate connections concerned the dead. As I discuss elsewhere, for 100 years U.S. Christians extended their families by renaming sponsored children after themselves or their deceased loved ones. Whole families could be reconstituted on foreign soil, joining living and dead members through the children who bore their names.[17] By the mid-twentieth century, sponsors had ceased this practice, but they retained the idea that sponsored children could reconstitute U.S. family relations ruptured by death or loss. Some older widows like Dorothy Greiser used sponsorship when their own children left home as a way to lift their spirits and combat loneliness. For others, it was a way to mourn. A number of stories are preserved in the archive showing how Americans initiated sponsorships following a child's death or a miscarriage. In a harrowing case from 1953, for example, a mother promised God that she would use the compensation she received after her three-year-old was killed in a car accident to support an orphan of the same sex and age. "In exchange for this beautiful life, the amount of money is being used to support a Korean baby boy through World Vision, Inc.," read subsequent publicity material.[18] When the courts valued her son's life at a certain amount and thereby in a sense converted a life into money, she translated life into life: the loss of her boy would sustain another boy abroad. In a variant of this pattern, a number of mothers of soldiers killed in Korea and Vietnam chose to sponsor a boy from the same place, thereby extending their son's "life" abroad.[19]

These trends are important, but I do not want to overstate the case. Most sponsors probably had feelings similar to those of an elderly man I interviewed in 2015 whose closest friend, with whom he had grown up as a brother, died while serving in Korea. He began supporting a Korean boy through CCF soon after and did not recall drawing a connection between the two events. Extrapolating from my work with contemporary sponsors, it is also likely that death and loss are overrepresented in the archives. For example, I did not encounter any such stories in my 52 interviews with Unbound sponsors in 2015, whereas the year before, among 93 letters sent to Unbound in response to their call for sponsor stories, 7.5% of respondents said they initiated sponsorship while mourning a recent death, another 3.2% did so as a memorial to a child who had died, and 6.4% to fill a void when their children left home.[20] Unbound explicitly asked for stories with "power to inspire," and it is not hard to imagine that mid-century sponsors were also more likely to send in personal stories that they felt represented inspiring circumstances, which organizations then preserved for possible use in publicity materials.

Contemporary research also sheds light on how sponsored children may have perceived kin-like ties. Anthropologists have shown that the recipients of global charity often mobilize their own understandings of kin and patronage as strategies for survival within Western-initiated humanitarian projects.[21] Compassion's recent surveys of selected field sites also suggest that children understand kin-like relatedness differently depending on their cultural context: many Peruvian children depicted the sponsor as close kin (perhaps because the Spanish word for sponsor is "godparent," noted Compassion's research director when we spoke), while Thai and Rwandan children generally did not if their own families were intact.[22] Based on extant archives, children in mid-century war zones did sometimes use sponsorship to reconstitute ruptured family ties. A Korean orphan named Kim Jun Ya is one example. Cecelia Costello, from California, sponsored her through Compassion between 1961 and 1965 (see figure 5.2 in the next chapter). Cecelia already supported two older girls, Myung Soon and In Sook, in the same orphanage in Seoul, and it was they who first told eight-year-old Jun Ya the news. "One day Oh In Sook told me she and Kim Myung Soon became sisters together with me. Many thanks, dear Mother," Jun Ya wrote right away. The girls cultivated this sisterhood, symbolized by their decision to wear matching carnations on Mother's Day as a mark of their shared bond with Cecelia. "Now Myung Soon, In Sook and I have become three sisters completely, even if we have different mothers who gave birth to us, but now we have only one mother who raises us—you," Jun Ya wrote in 1962. "So, Mother, please give us new names which are similar to your own name." Two years later, she still sometimes signed her letters "Jeannie Yun Ja," the American name that Cecelia had conferred at her request.[23]

The most profound way of (re)constituting family relations was through legal adoption. Although a negligible number of sponsors actually adopted, the rhetoric of possibility fuelled fantasies of transnational and transracial kinship in the mid-century United States. Sponsorship organizations received the first wave of requests to adopt during World War I. A second and much larger wave swelled when the Korean War ended in 1953 and the first legal adoptions from South Korea made headlines.[24] Mrs. Scotty Mitchell, a 22-year-old newlywed from Dos Palos, California, penned a typical letter to Compassion's director in 1966:

> I can't begin to express my feelings of joy when the picture of Le Jo arrived. I feel that God has answered my prayers. Although I'm only 22, I have wanted to adopt a Korean child for many years, and now I can hardly believe it is true. I would like to ask at this time if it would ever be possible to have Le Jo brought to this country. Although I know we probably cannot do this, I thought I would chance asking, for if it is at all possible I would bring him here to be with us. Please let me know.[25]

At the time, the South Korean government was promoting transnational adoption. With 40% of its budget devoted to defense and only 2% to social welfare, it compensated by privatizing social services through Western NGOs—encouraging sponsorship and adoption was part of this strategy.[26] In the United States, however, these adoptions had been hampered by a racist quota system that severely restricted immigration from Asia. One way around these rules was for individuals to lobby for a special act of Congress. If permission was granted, adoptions were often done "by proxy" where an agent went on behalf of many prospective parents to sign for the children and bring them back. Henry and Bertha Holt, a born-again couple in Oregon, ran the largest private agency of this type, which placed 2,587 Korean children with evangelical families between 1956 and 1961 (accounting for about 70% of the total children adopted from Korea at the time).[27]

At first, sponsorship organizations dabbled in legal adoption. In the early 1950s, CCF's overseas director organized them privately, with his wife serving as proxy. CCF trained prospective adoptees for U.S. life at one of its orphanages and, at the Korean embassy's behest, ran advertisements to recruit adoptive parents among "church people." Compassion also organized a limited number of adoptions for "active born-again people." The most extensive collaboration was between the Holts and World Vision. The Holts began their work after seeing the WV film *The Lost Sheep* and sponsoring a Korean child.[28] WV provided much of their initial publicity, including the film *Mercy's Child* (figure 4.2). But legal adoptions began to occupy too much time and money and sponsorship organizations soon pulled back from such commitments. Just three years after supporting the Holts's work, WV stopped promoting adoption. CCF and Compassion kept stacks of pre-typed letters to discourage such inquiries. The standard reply noted the bureaucratic difficulties and emphasized that

FIG 4.2. Bob Pierce and Henry Holt promoting sponsorship and adoption of "G.I. babies" from WV-supported orphanages in South Korea. Still from "*Mercy's Child: Holt Children*" Film, 1956. Courtesy of Billy Graham Center Archives.

sponsored children were expected to impact their communities from within: "We are training Christians to be useful in their own countries. You're creating a Christian witness in another country."[29]

Mrs. Scotty Mitchell, like so many others who wrote at the time, missed this distinction. But her note was also too good to pass up for future publicity. A Compassion employee put it aside, making an important change in pencil: quotation marks around the word adopt. Later that year, an excerpt appeared in a widely distributed brochure: "I feel that God has answered my prayers. Although I am only 22, I have wanted to 'adopt' a Korean child for many years and now I can hardly believe it is true."[30] Eliminating the letter's final sentences and changing adopt to "adopt" fundamentally altered Mrs. Mitchell's intent. Her words now echoed Compassion's policy of redirecting U.S. Christian fantasies of legal adoption into sponsorship instead.

While there is no record of Mrs. Mitchell's response to Compassion's presumably discouraging reply, other exchanges reveal the seriousness of such requests. Mrs. R. D. Mullins was typical of a class of inquirers who were older and lacked the ready cash necessary for sponsorship. A widow living alone in a large home in rural Virginia, Mrs. Mullins wrote to CCF in the winter of 1950 after reading that millions of Chinese children were starving to death. She had done careful calculations; she raised her own food and had "a fine Christian home" that could accommodate at least ten Chinese children, if CCF would send them. Clarke gently refused. A few months later she tried again. She was so haunted by the images in CCF's *China News* that she developed a lump in her throat each time she tried to eat—visions of underfed children were etched in her mind. Her letter was prompted by what she took as a sign: "Only last night I dreamed that I was holding a tiny, hungry, pitiful little baby to my breast, and this is only one instance that God has revealed to me that He wants to use me in this work." Although she acknowledged what Clarke had told her about the political and legal roadblocks to adoption, she had already begun to ready her house for the children she believed God had shown her.[31]

Mid-century fantasies of adoption were often stoked by stories of "GI babies," infants born of Korean or Japanese mothers and fathered by U.S. soldiers. The actual number of such babies was debated, but no one disputed that they faced significant discrimination. Korea and Japan required that all persons be registered in a male-headed household to enroll in school, find employment, or apply for a passport. Abandoned by their fathers and often rejected by their grandfathers, many GI babies were non-entities, socially and legally.[32] Their plight initially drove the adoption work of individuals like Henry and Bertha Holt who could see the impossibility in such cases of the evangelical dream that these children, if sponsored, would bring Christianity to their communities from within. In the segregated United States, word of their existence raised another issue: it was proof of miscegenation perpetrated by the soldiers fêted as moral exemplars and the nation's friendly face abroad. CCF's overseas director Verent Mills blamed soldiers who were not born-again Christians, but at a broader institutional level he held the U.S. Army responsible for its lack of supervision—a failing that required U.S. society to atone as a whole. For Larry Ward at WV, atonement was even more narrowly defined in terms of Christian sponsors. In a devastating letter to "an Unknown G.I." in *WV* magazine, Ward wrote: "[W]e—World Vision and its praying, giving friends—try to fill in the void you have caused [by leaving], to tell [her] that, above and beyond the painful realities of life, there is One Who loved her."[33] Sponsors could pay the soldiers' sinful debts.

As transnational adoptions increased in the mid-1970s, even the rhetorical use of adoption fell out of sponsorship (signaled most clearly when organizations swapped the word "adoption" for "sponsorship" in their materials). Nevertheless, the confluence of adoption fantasies and sponsorship realities during the 1950s and 1960s is crucial because it highlights how sponsorship was implicated in what theorist Jasbir Puar has called "the capacity for capacity" at the heart of biopolitical constructions of whiteness. Discussions about biopolitics often focus on heterosexual reproduction, but Puar argues that the development of "whiteness" encompassed a much larger set of assumptions about the "capacity to give life, sustain life, and promote life" within "forward-looking, regenerative bodies." Whiteness comprised the ability to prosper economically, generate innovation, construct a civilization and, in this case, create and sustain a charitable network.[34] It is an important point because previous studies suggest that sponsorship appealed especially to childless Americans as a substitute for gestational reproduction,[35] even though records show that the vast majority of sponsors (and transnational adopters) actually had their own children. Rather, sponsors cultivated kin-like relations to make themselves into people who regenerated and sustained others—into subjects who fully exercised their capacity for capacity on a global scale. It was the essence of their privileged position as (usually white) U.S. Christians. And from their perspective, this privilege was the direct result of their relationship to a Deity that was the only truly life-giving and life-sustaining force.

The GI baby craze faded in the 1960s. These children entered the sponsorship literature just once more, when the Amerasian Immigration and Homecoming Acts of 1982 and 1987 allowed the Vietnamese children of U.S. soldiers to qualify as refugees. These young adults' "mixed race" still bore remarking, but now the symbolism had shifted to reflect a newer multicultural ethic and the more liberal neo-evangelical outlook of organizations like World Vision. "I see this particular group of refugees as a living bridge of reconciliation between the United States and Vietnam," declared WV president Robert Seiple. "Vietnamese and American blood exist together in these people. Our two countries are inextricably linked and, as we reconcile the Amerasian issue, perhaps we have a chance at a larger reconciliation between people and before God."[36] The bodies of mixed-race children bore the symbolic brunt of reconciling U.S. Christians to what their nation had wrought overseas. Seiple's words are useful to keep in mind, along with Puar's notion of the capacity of whiteness, as we turn to the ubiquitous iconography I call racialized universalism.

THE "HAPPY DIVERSITY" OF RACIALIZED UNIVERSALISM

Over the long modern era, Western Christians crafted "chromatic identities" for themselves and others in which "the quality and intensity of racism" varied enormously in different contexts.[37] In mid-twentieth century sponsorship, this quality was not a pretension to race-blindness, as some previous studies have asserted, but a form of racialization yoked to universalism. One of its primary tools was what theorist Sara Ahmed has called "happy diversity documents"— images and literature in which the proximity of differently raced bodies is imagined as the force that unifies a group.[38] For Christians, this imagery indexed God's capacity to create and contain immensity. As such, it served as a cornerstone of their post war globalism.

This mid-century project was a long time in the making. Scholars trace the genesis of a more formal Christian theology of world order to early modern Europe when Catholic thinkers came to view all people as subjects of the same Creator and thus fully human, in the sense that they shared the same basic nature as Europeans. Christians still fostered racism, for example when nineteenth-century Americans interpreted the Bible as saying that people of African descent were inherently servile, or when some missionaries blamed failed evangelism on other people's inborn heathenishness.[39] Nevertheless, in general missionaries rejected the fixity of biologized racism. At least in theory, anyone had the potential to become humane, modern, and moral by accepting Christ.[40]

In part because race was not a rigidly exclusionary measure, nineteenth-century Christians waged an ongoing debate about the relationship between Christianity and culture. Were certain "civilizational" (cultural) forms also universal and a prerequisite to conversion? A related question concerned religious diversity: what were the rituals that Christians encountered abroad? One response was that they were false forms that arose from humanity's natural propensity to sin. Another answer was equally universalizing but with different results: as early as the sixteenth century, voices within the Catholic Church suggested that people's varied rituals were ways of worshipping one God, a notion that later gained popularity in a subset of late nineteenth-century liberal Protestants.[41] These ideas reverberated in the mid-twentieth century, where evangelicals often stressed the universality of sin while liberals stressed the universality of a God worshipped in different but equally valid ways. While historians and sociologists of missions often emphasize the split between these factions, both sides reinforced the same essential logic of Christian globalism.

Influential nineteenth-century American thinkers—including writers Catharine Beecher and John L. Sullivan (who coined the term "manifest destiny")—imagined a particular place for their nation in bringing about the unity-in-diversity that eluded the older, more homogenous European nations. As the only "nation of many nations," quoting Sullivan, the United States was "destined to manifest to mankind the excellence of [such] divine principles." He envisioned an American-led world as a boundless temple with a congregation "comprising hundreds of happy millions, calling, owing no man master, but governed by God's natural and moral law of equality." This kind of Christian universalism, envisioned through the prism of U.S. culture, was both deeply inclusive and exclusionary, since ultimately it could only imagine "free" personhood within the boundaries it created.[42] Not surprisingly, perhaps, these characterizations of national exceptionalism proved popular, especially in the wake of the World Wars. Compared to Europe, the United States seemed to exemplify happy coexistence.[43]

Americans were thus well placed, economically and ideologically, to play a major role in the twentieth-century turn to "universal" declarations and "international" gatherings.[44] While the role of mid-century U.S. evangelicals has recently garnered a lot of scholarly attention,[45] it was actually mainline Protestants and Catholics in the United Nations, World Council of Churches, and other bodies that defined this bold post-war era for their compatriots as they grappled with the impacts of the Holocaust, post-colonial movements, and Civil Rights.[46] In the process, they re-envisioned a capacious thing called "culture"—which included racial and religious differences—as a valued form of personal and societal identity deserving of protection. In Christian globalism, to make culture matter on the human scale was to universalize the divine scale: God saw beyond all those local particularities. Once neutralized as a man-made thing, culture no longer seemed to threaten a core level of belonging. It could be celebrated as strengthening Christianity instead.

The American/Christian spirit of universalism was powerfully communicated and critiqued. After a 1956 visit to the Paris showing of a famous American-sponsored photography exhibition called "The Family of Man," Roland Barthes wrote a disgruntled essay. The large-scale photos juxtaposed humans from around the world engaged in the same quotidian tasks. Its lofty goal was to promote global peace by showing how everyone shared the same basic needs and desires—the subtext was the assumption of a common Creator. The French captions at the Paris exhibit told visitors that the photos resembled "God's benevolent gaze on our absurd and sublime anthill." Barthes responded with emphatic italics: someone should ask the parents of Emmett Till, the African American boy murdered in 1955, what *they* thought of *the great family of man*.[47] To view racial difference in the photos as secondary to the "real" universal soul of humanity was a privilege afforded only those who did not actually suffer the effects of violent racism. To view the United States as a model of coexistence was a chimera as well.

Barthes's point is justified, and it has been reiterated many times. His reference to the segregated U.S. South is a good segue back to sponsorship and more specifically to the question of how closely sponsors and the organizations they supported linked domestic racism and internationalism in this period. It is difficult to gauge sponsors' views precisely, yet they clearly represented a broad spectrum. And because sponsorship organizations sought to appeal to the widest possible audience, they largely avoided domestic issues as a result. When *World Vision Magazine* did publish a pro–Civil Rights article in 1965, readers' reactions were mixed and the subject was dropped. When an anti-segregation sponsor wrote to CCF to inquire about its stance on the matter, the director hedged by replying that they supported children of all races, including U.S. orphanages for "Indians and negroes," omitting that these were in fact segregated institutions.[48] Like other child-centered charities before and since, they skirted racist politics at home by promoting racialized depictions of children as a metonym for global friendship and a prophetic vision of peace.

Happy diversity imagery was most developed at CCF in this period, undoubtedly because of its mainline Protestant orientation. Its yearly Christmas greeting cards were typical. They depicted children as the nations in harmonious friendships, pointing toward a unified peace under Christ (figures 4.3a and 4.3b). The imagery recalled a long lineage of allegorical paintings depicting people with different skin tones and styles of dress grouped around Jesus to illustrate the transcendent kinship of a global family of believers. It also overlapped significantly with exhibits like The Family of Man and UN promotional materials (which, for example, included photos of differently raced children reading the Declaration of Human Rights together). Such symbols of global harmony were replicated in many other mid-century contexts too—among Soviet communists, anti-colonial movements, corporations like Coca-Cola, and humanitarian NGOs.[49]

Yet the happy diversity in sponsorship materials had a more precise goal: to construct Christian globalism for its U.S. audience. It did so not just by depicting diverse children or people grouped together, but through forms of mirroring in which children's skin tones and cultural attributes (keyed as exotic) were juxtaposed with their actions (keyed as familiar): they bent their heads in pan-denominational American prayer poses (figure 4.4) or danced around an American-style Christmas tree. Such imagery was also made into participatory techniques. In 1953, for example, an author in *Child Evangelism Magazine* suggested a standard Sunday school activity to be performed for parents. Teachers were counseled to prepare a large cutout of the globe, which an older boy would hold in the center of the room while 15 smaller children in different national costumes joined hands around him to sing the familiar hymn, "Jesus Loves Little Children" (in the epigraph).[50] Whether children were of various origins or white Sunday schoolers mimicking "the nations," the replication of differently raced children doing the same thing at the same time—dancing in

FIG 4.3A AND 4.3B. Typical CCF Christmas cards for sponsors, c. 1956–1958. Courtesy of ChildFund International.

a circle, reading a declaration, seated together at a table—was a fundamental way that global consensus was reflected back to, and thus reproduced for, Americans at home. When the children's actions were legible to Americans as Christian, they seemed to demonstrate that there was indeed an emergent Christian "family" beyond the United States, through which mutual recognition and support were possible. And for this reason, incorporating a racially other sponsored child into one's family held value for U.S. Christians, regardless of their position on domestic racial politics. Americans incorporated "the world" into their families and churches in order to reaffirm their God's global reach.

Race was never invisible in these images, of course. Returning to Puar's "capacity for capacity," sponsorship organizations collapsed a triad of identity markers—white, Christian, American—into a generalized and privileged

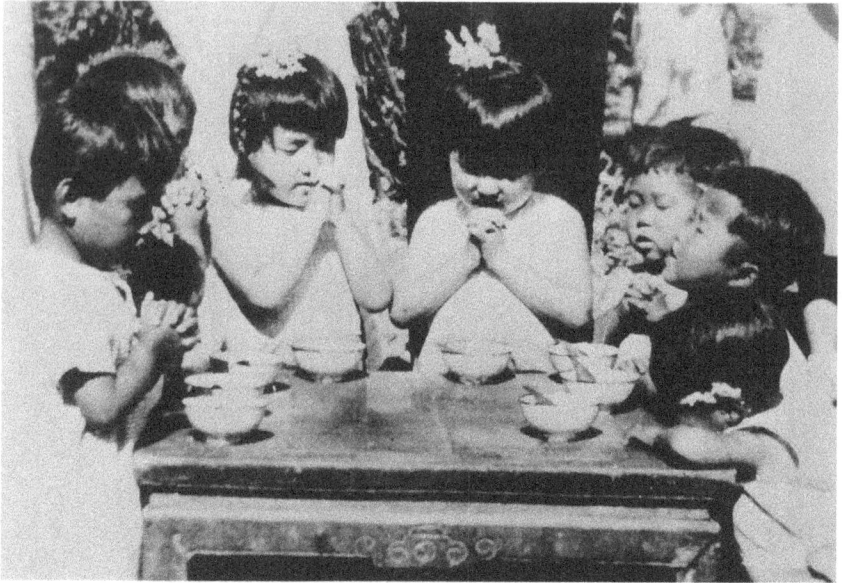

FIG 4.4. Snapshot of children in a prayer pose familiar to Americans, c. 1955. This photo reproduction was included in CCF publicity materials. Similar images remain popular today. Author's collection.

capacity for regenerative acts.[51] I am not suggesting that people who self-identified as white were the only sponsors at the time, although they were the vast majority. My point is that whiteness was an assumed characteristic of the prototypical mid-century sponsor in his or her role as charitable giver and substitute parent, and sponsors' unmarked personhood as white Americans accentuated the racialized difference of others by comparison. Put another way, any vision of post-racial unity that seems to transcend dichotomies between "us and them" still requires prior recognition of a polarity between things. This brings us back to the nineteenth-century legacy of colonialism and mission that laid the foundation for twentieth-century humanitarianism. Race was a central "sorting technique"[52] in these systems and racialized universalism rested on this inheritance, as much as any other. It made it seem like common sense that different races would "naturally" segregate. Yet, recall that most Christian sponsors believed that at some level God was implicated in their efforts. The children's difference therefore seemed a testimony to the miracle of God's globally circulating Love: despite what to many sponsors seemed like natural racial or cultural differences, God produced in them a kin-like longing for, and relatedness with, Asian or African children. This intimacy was one aspect of a god's eye view of creation.

Twentieth-century U.S. Christianity retained deep and unresolved tensions in this regard. Perhaps the most trenchant one concerned the impetus to pluralism (we are all different but equal) and universalism (we are all the same and thus equal). Many mid-century U.S. Christians paradoxically supported human rights and structures like the WCC or UN as measures to protect pluralism (the diversity of sociocultural formations) *because of* their assumptions about universalism (a core human sameness that overrode local particularities).[53] Sponsorship's genius as a fund-raising tool lay in its ability to cut across the tension, while also reinforcing it. Mirroring brought certain aspects of the child (such as skin color or clothing) keyed as "pluralist" together with others (such as the familiar prayer pose) keyed as "universalist." Americans could even performatively embody this duality when they engaged in pluralist activities like eating foreign foods or listening to "world" music as a mode of deepening their soul connection with God—the ultimate indication for them of a universal human essence.

LETTERS AS A TECHNOLOGY OF KIN-LIKE RELATIONS

Although nineteenth-century sponsors "hungered" for letters with "particulars" about their protégés abroad, the exchange of correspondence through missionaries was often unpredictable.[54] During World War I, the Fatherless Children of France created a better system, guaranteeing donors a set number of postcards per year (four, to be exact) by delegating the responsibility to French mothers and their children. The exchange was more direct, but it was plagued with translation problems. The Paris-based committee instructed children to write following a formula: "Thank [your sponsor], tell him what you do, what your father did, [and] where, when and how he was killed. . . . P.S. If your American benefactor writes in English you should not be surprised and if you can't have his letter translated, you should respond, to the address he indicates, in the manner we have told you above."[55] The result was an often-stultifying series of letters repeating the same thing in a language few U.S. sponsors could read. Finally, in the mid-twentieth century, organizations developed sufficiently robust systems to ensure translated correspondence and photos. Personal letters became sponsorship's most "thrilling" feature and the aspect that most distinguished it from its charitable competitors. These letters carried the weighty task of building a 1:1 relationship that would be familiar to Americans as kin-like and thus affirm the possibility of a unified Christian globalism. In other words, it was through letters that fantasies of kin-like intimacy and images of racialized universalism found a seemingly concrete expression.

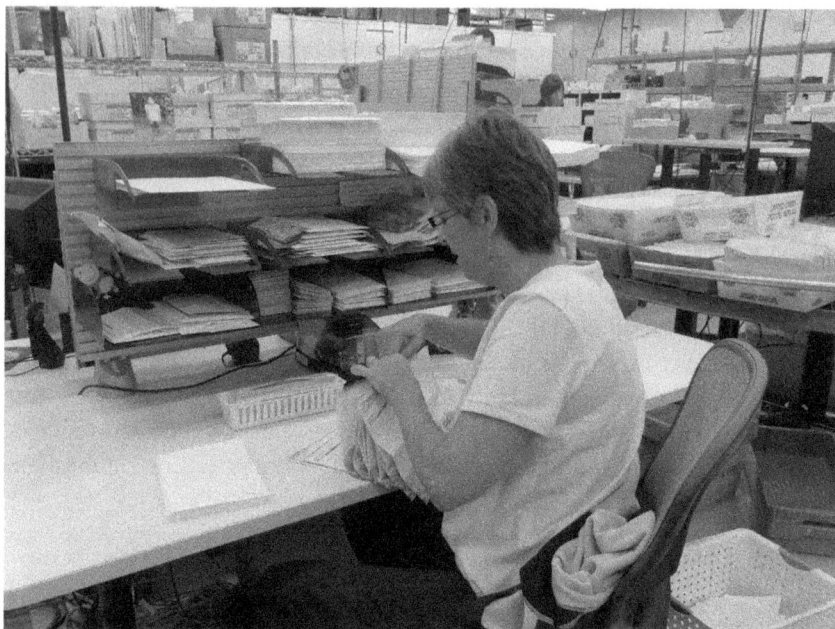

FIG 4.5. Systems developed in the 1950s endure today, as evident in the mailroom at Compassion's Colorado Springs headquarters. All U.S. letters transit through this central location, where employees check them to remove addresses, offensive comments, or bulky gifts. They are then sent overseas to be translated and delivered. The children's letters are processed through the same mailroom before they are sent on to sponsors. Photo by the author. Used by permission of Compassion International, Inc.

J. Calvitt and Helen Clarke at CCF were U.S. pioneers in this regard. They required that all children personally respond to their sponsors' letters and they developed a centralized system where correspondence and gifts were processed through their offices and in-house translators. Permutations of this system remain the standard today (figure 4.5). For the Clarkes, letter writing was political and religious work. It made sponsorship into a vital Cold War tactic that worked alongside other efforts to enlist citizens to construct an "ethical" side (or "friendly face") of U.S. statecraft and global power. The Eisenhower government called it "People to People" diplomacy, expecting that everyday Americans would win hearts and minds abroad through pen pal programs, tourism, and later, the Peace Corps.[56] Liberal church institutions embraced the concept too, for example in the 1948 collaboration between Church World Service, Lutheran World Relief, and the Catholic Rural Life Conference to run "friendship trains" across the country. When the train rolled into town, housewives and farmers would donate a portion of their foodstuff as a way to "convince the people of [starving] Europe that this food comes not from the United States Government but from every dinner table in America."[57] Whether or not people abroad were convinced, or even aware, of this method of gathering donations, the message resonated with Americans: it reiterated democratic, personalized giving—the basis of the systematic charity model developed in Europe three centuries before—as a seemingly natural attribute of the U.S. people.

Because Clarke viewed sponsorship in light of such efforts, he had little patience for those (including sponsors) who questioned whether the funds devoted to letters should be used for necessities overseas. "No money could be more blessed than this expenditure," Clarke fired back one time, "these letters of friendship, of kindness and brotherhood often contain more Christianity in them than in many a sermon . . . [It] is a far better investment for our country and our God than impersonal handouts."[58] While Clarke was thinking of the impact on foreign children, sponsorship letters, like the friendship trains, spoke most eloquently to U.S. people themselves about the type of kin-like Christianity they hoped to find and build in the world.

In this regard, the system faced two major challenges. The first concerned time. As anthropologists have pointed out, socially accepted intervals of time always elapse between a gift and its reciprocal return.[59] Whether a few months or a few seconds go by, those time intervals transform giving into an act of exchange that constitutes social relations. Sponsorship promoters also knew the value of time in the global kin-like relations they tried to foster. In the 1960s, letters took anywhere from 45 days to six months to be translated and shipped to their destinations. Surveys showed high levels of sponsor dissatisfaction in this regard. Time lags made Americans lose interest, question if the child was real, and sometimes withdraw their support.[60] One way that organizations dealt with the issue was to train foreign staff and children to collapse time by omitting dates, using indeterminate tenses, and making allusions to things not yet come.[61]

At CCF in the 1950s, thank you letters offer a good example. Sponsors were encouraged to send gifts at any time, though CCF held all items in Richmond until they could ship them in one batch, usually in army ships. Even gifts of money were only processed once a month. Yet the Clarkes wanted to mirror American kinship rituals in which adults often surprised children with spontaneous gifts and were gratified with an immediate response. Thus, the Richmond office would send a note overseas as soon as it received a gift. The child then wrote a thank you letter for a gift she had never seen in which she was told to "infer" in vague terms that it had already arrived and tell sponsors how happy it had made her.[62] In short, to create the thrill of kin-like intimacy, organizations tried to obscure their mediation—opening, checking, holding, translating, resealing—that caused delays, which ultimately required more intensive mediation than before. The indefatigable Helen Clarke and her team daily intercepted children's letters to erase dates, reject time-specific details, and catch violators of "every tabu" she instituted. "This means that we have to rewrite translations and make all sorts of devious, and I fear sometimes unconvincing, explanations," she remarked.[63]

The second major challenge to letter writing cut even deeper: Asian children and orphanage superintendents had to become at least minimally conversant with American expectations about the *tone* of kin-like intimacy. The difficulties involved are evident from the regularity with which Helen Clarke issued instructions to the superintendents. At a basic level, she required that children write "a courteous expression of appreciation for the sponsor's friendship." Yet a polite note—"I am obliged to you for your kindness"—that to superintendents seemed to fulfill the requirement, still failed from an American point of view. Americans, explained Clarke, expected children's letters to exude "spontaneity," a combination of chattiness and warmth, rather than formal deference. American intimacy had a particular cadence; it sounded as though one just happened to think of someone and dashed off a heartfelt word.[64] Other organizations faced the same problems, which World Vision later tried to address through a manual of 56 sample answers to the questions most commonly asked by sponsors, grouped into categories such as "Answering questions about what I will be when I grow up" or "Answering questions about animals." WV employees who understood little to no English could identify key words in sponsors' letters, copy the answers, and fill in the blanks.

C-4
My teacher's name is ____. I like her very much. There are ____ students in my class. During recess we have lots of fun.

F-1
I have a ____ (dog, cat, etc.). Its name is ____. I like to play with it very much.

K-2
We go to a ____ church. I like to go to church. I have many friends there and we play after the service. I am very happy that Jesus loves me.[65]

Despite such aids, or perhaps because of them, sponsors still repeatedly questioned if the children's letters followed a template (as they continue to do today).

In a 1969 report, Jae Kwon Ha, a former Compassion superintendent in Korea, noted the significant cross-cultural disconnect. He explained that Confucianism taught individuals to hide emotions and refrain from lengthy personal letters. Further, he clarified that sponsored children in war-torn Korea, especially orphans, had developed survival strategies based on their ability to please the adults around them. Trauma had taught them that "talking frankly and honestly about what they think and believe" could be detrimental.[66] Compounding the problem, most superintendents found it strange, and even ridiculous, that each child—especially a fatherless one—was uniquely important and of serious interest to a foreign adult. "You may think it too individualistic to write about one boy but you must," Helen Clarke urged them.[67] The issue crystallized around personal birthdays, a mark of individuation not generally celebrated in Asia. Besides, war and poverty had erased all traces of the year when most sponsored children were born, let alone the day. But no matter: superintendents were told to assign a birthday to each one. "Americans like to celebrate birthdays," Clarke explained, "and we receive many requests for birth dates from sponsors who wish to send their children birthday gifts."[68] Cecelia Costello was typical in that respect when she sent a card on the day marked in Jun Ya's file. The girl wanted to reciprocate: "I had an intention of sending [you] a birthday card, I can not find such a kind of card in our country. I think our custom doesn't have such one," she concluded astutely.[69]

One of the Clarkes' great insights was that individuality could be transmitted in multiple attributes of a letter, rather than content alone. Owing to the "tremendous appeal of something from the child's own hands," they required that letters be handwritten and Christmas cards hand drawn or colored. A childish hand, with its wobbly letters and ink splotches, produced a feeling of intimacy and allowed sponsors to better imagine a particular child, or as Clarke put it: "his quaint ways of speaking, his funny little thoughts."[70] Organizations made children's thoughts seem more childlike and amusing by translating their phraseology literally in English; it had the benefit of adding a touch of the exotic—"quaintly worded letters . . . bring a touch of the Orient into your home," promised WV. It followed with a typical example: "Dear My Sponsor, I hope you are well and happy in God's good caring. Tears of thankfulness poured from my eyes when I could have a precious mother who will pray for me . . . Your dearing little boy, Lee Chon Sik."[71] When they were successful, these (mis)translations combined professions of kin-like intimacy with racialized exoticism to forge the kind of relations upon which American sponsors could pin their hopes for a diverse and growing global church.

These translations became problematic in the late 1970s as sponsorship organizations shifted toward development models that discouraged overt paternalism. And they began to worry about sponsor letters too. At WV, sponsors were now counseled to write no more than four times a year since "too-frequent letters can cause a child to become too emotionally involved with you, instead of with the people in his own country." Sponsors were also told to minimize professions of love and kinship: "We should be careful of using too many overtly affectionate terms in our letters. As sponsors we are not meant to meet all of the child's needs, but rather to be a mirror reflecting the love of the One who can meet all their needs."[72] Too much human intimacy threatened to distort the mirroring effect, which could obscure the real relationship at stake—between the child and God.

FOREIGN LETTERS AT HOME

While the archives are filled with documents attesting to how sponsorship organizations managed letter writing, it is less easy to reconstruct the intimate conditions within mid-century homes as Americans received and composed their letters. And yet the home is in some ways the epicenter of our story. It was more than just a model upon which Christians based their hopes of kin-like globalism; it was the actual site in which they made and remade these aspirations. I turn for a moment, then, to Winola Wirt, her husband Sherwood, and their son Alexander. The Wirts were Presbyterians of a neo-evangelical bent, and it was during Sherwood's pastoral training in Scotland that the couple adopted Alex.[73] They brought the four-year-old back with them to the United States in 1950. Shortly after, Winola began sponsoring children through CCF, which had Presbyterian roots, and WV, which spoke to the non-denominational evangelical circles in which her husband worked.

Like many sponsors, Winola involved her son in the process. She linked intimate and global scales by weaving sponsored children's presence throughout their lives. She regularly reminded Alex not to tear his clothes so that she could send them to his "siblings" abroad. "I remember specific clothes I loved," laughed Alex when we spoke in 2015. "This hooded sweatshirt with an emblem on it, like a Mercedes logo. I wanted to keep it forever. But nope . . . it disappeared." Sometimes this system worked in his favor; to his great joy, a hated pair of shorts from his Scottish orphanage was finally packed up and sent abroad. Winola also asked Alex to add a line to her monthly letters and he recalls printing, "'I hope you're well and doing well in school.' Or if there was a disaster, like a typhoon, 'I hope you weren't near that.'" Most important, they prayed for the children by name every night at dinner, incorporating foreign names alongside familiar ones, binding faraway people to proximate ones in the same breath.[74] Because of these prayers, Alex told me, he never doubted that his mother's help was vital to the children—just as it had been for him.

Based on extant letters from the period, it is almost certain that Winola mentioned these prayers in her letters and that the sponsored children responded with assurances of their prayers for her family, including specific prayers for needs or events. As I discuss in chapter 5, most contemporary sponsors—especially evangelicals—unconsciously narrate global prayerways as a lopsided exchange, in which their prayers are an effective means of getting results whereas children's prayers are an expression of their gratitude and spiritual growth. This lopsidedness—or soft power—has a counterpart in how sponsorship unfolds within U.S. households too. Many sponsors told me about their children's reticence or eagerness to contribute to letter writing, which as parents they attributed to the child's sense of empathy for others abroad (or lack thereof). But looking back on his experience, Alex Wirt offers a sense of how a child's reaction might actually stem from the integration of these kin-like relations into domestic dynamics. When Alex was angry with his mother, he refused to add his note to her letters because he knew it would pain her. He would soon feel guilty for hurting his mother and neglecting the faraway children for whom they prayed by name. He always agreed to contribute the following month. Alex's ambivalence about sponsorship went deeper than that: occasionally he got the impression that his mother was looking to replace him. He was lucky to have been plucked from his orphanage by the Wirts, but could another child still take his place? Decades later, I laughed when Alex told me this, thinking he was joking. But he remained serious even after so many years: he *did* have that sense, he repeated.

In 1968, Alex was stationed in the Mediterranean with the marines. His mother's health was failing and she asked Alex to use his next leave to visit a girl she sponsored in Athens. The child and her chaperone joined Alex for a short meal. She spoke no English, but communicated that she knew exactly who he was and who his mother was: her American sponsor. Winola died shortly after and Alex returned to the United States. Statistically speaking, a single man in his early twenties was hardly the typical sponsor, but he felt that it was his inheritance. He called CCF to take over his mother's last remaining sponsorship—a girl in the Philippines. As we spoke, he kept returning to the idea of inheritance. "Maybe that's not the right word," he mused. "It was more like my parents demonstrated how this was part of a good character. I was helped [as an orphan] so there's a link . . . [But] inheritance means something you get whether or not you want it. This was purely voluntary. I *chose* to continue what she was doing." After he married, his wife set up direct deposit. As their two daughters were growing up, Alex never really mentioned sponsorship. "It's just something I do. It's not something I feel I have to do to be in good standing with God or with the Presbyterian Church or anything like that. I don't bring anyone else in on it." A generation after Winola's death her inheritance lives on. Currently, Alex and his wife support Nanoy, a boy in the Philippines.

Alex and Winola's story reminds us of the conditions of intimacy that bring foreign children into U.S. households and render them kin-like—the fissures where family dynamics blend into global commitments. A child's inchoate worry about being replaced. His stubborn refusal to sign a letter to Korea. His mother pronouncing foreign names and familiar ones together in prayer. The inheritance of a relationship sustained after death.

POSTSCRIPT: NOTES ON KIN-LIKE RELATIONS TODAY

The sponsorship model that Alex knew as a child was on the verge of collapse when his mother died in 1968. A seismic shift had been building in many corners of U.S. Christianity in response to the end of formal colonialism and the growth of churches in the "global south." Scholars have tracked how some liberal Christians responded by adopting foreign rituals and concepts to try to redress the Western impositions of a colonial past. Other globally minded Christians altered their language by incorporating words like equality and partnership; one study quotes the director of a Christian NGO describing his role as "just asking questions," rather than dictating to people abroad.[75] Responding to the same trends, in the 1970s the leadership of CCF and WV (and, later, Compassion) began to listen more closely to their local partners in the field. A number of these "Christian nationals," as they were called at the time, viewed sponsorship as paternalistic and even advocated ending it altogether.[76] At the same time, child psychologists now condemned wide-scale institutionalization.[77] All of the sponsorship organizations profiled in this chapter were receptive to the message, not least because they had recently dealt with major scandals in missionary orphanages (Compassion) or struggled through ill-fated attempts to build orphanages (WV and CCF). Each one was also transitioning away from the legacy of a pastor-founder to a more professionalized development model. These factors combined to convince them to abandon the missionary orphanage system and support children living at home instead.[78]

These changes had organizational and legal implications, but from sponsors' perspective what mattered most was that the children they supported were no longer portrayed as orphans in need of substitute parents.[79] In collaboration with their field partners, WV and CCF began to dismantle the 1:1 system even further. They started assigning sponsors a "sample" child—a kind of holograph 1:1 relationship where one child wrote heartfelt, personal letters that would be mailed out to a block of a few thousand U.S. donors. In 1982, WV staff confidently predicted that within a decade the "backlog of cultural assumptions around the concept of sponsorship" would fundamentally change.[80] Then famine hit. In the media frenzy surrounding the Ethiopian famine of 1984–1985, both organizations fell back on 1:1 sponsorship. The windfall of donations was too good to pass up. But something *had* changed. Although ironically the advertising campaigns to draw in new sponsors ratcheted up the shock images of abandoned children, organizations had largely succeeded in communicating to active sponsors that those they supported had biological kin.

This change intrigued me when I began my work with contemporary sponsors at Unbound and Compassion. What had it done to the promise of global kin-like relations that sponsorship had promoted so insistently in the 1950s and 1960s? In our conversations, I always asked sponsors whether they thought of sponsorship as a relationship and, if so, what sort. Very few compared it to their own child, as their mid-century predecessors might have done. Nurses and teachers likened it to their former patients and students, while other people mentioned godchildren, cousins, nephews, or nieces who lived far away.[81] Their responses evoked an absent/present quality; these were all children in whom they felt invested, but who were not (or were no longer) present with them. Most sponsors also said that, to use my terminology, a kin-*like* relation does important work—accent on the "like," rather than the "kin." Danielle, a 42-year-old Catholic in Kansas City, expressed it in a way that resonated across my conversations (with sponsorship organizational staff too).[82] She said, "I think the fact that they think that somebody in another country cares, will help them through, that would be sort of another gift from God. Like gee, somebody I don't even know is going to help me!" The kin-like position is crucial; if they were actual kin it would be clear why remittance payments or gifts came from abroad. For Danielle, this otherwise inexplicable generosity manifests the reality of a God with the power to move even strangers to reach out across the world.

As we got to know each other, sponsors and I talked about their children, we went to church or volunteered together, and we shared family meals. Like most U.S. Christians, they feel what could be called a kinship obligation—they might say, "a sense of responsibility"—to provide spiritual guidance and care for their children, grandchildren, and other young people in their lives. While hardly a novel discovery, it does lead to a key question for sponsorship's kin-like relations: do sponsors hope that the child they support will become a Christian? If so, what is their role in the process? At first I broached this question directly and got rather confused replies. Then I began to reword it: Did they think the child they supported *was already* Christian or from a Christian family? Few questions I asked elicited such a consistent response; nearly every sponsor said yes. This assumption is rather remarkable—and unprecedented historically. Nineteenth-century sponsorship was built on supporting a "heathen" child to encourage conversion. In the mid-twentieth century, WV and Compassion still explicitly promoted sponsorship as a way for homebound Americans to evangelize abroad. Even the liberal Clarke sometimes promoted this idea and it remained part of CCF's mission statement into the 1970s. Today, it is a non-issue for sponsors. What accounts for the change?

To one degree, sponsors' assumption that the child's family is Christian makes sense because they are usually right, at least at Unbound and Compassion. Unbound has always focused on Catholic majority places, and Compassion's program works through local evangelical and Pentecostal churches and schools. Neither organization restricts its aid, but Christian parents are most likely to take part and, at a more basic level, be aware such programs exist due to their social networks and proximity (indeed, it is a Compassion requirement that children live within walking distance of its Christian service providers).[83] Yet sponsors still assumed a child was Christian even when they knew little about the child's circumstances. They often told me it was based on their impression that churches are scattered everywhere in the global south. This idea, which would never have occurred to mid-century sponsors, is one result of the post-colonial ethos discussed above; as U.S. Christians grappled with provocations from their co-religionists elsewhere, they began to think of themselves as part of an expansive global network. Since the 1990s, popular media, Christian and secular, has devoted significant coverage to Christianity's much-vaunted demographic rise in the global south. In sponsorship more specifically, the assumption of a Christian milieu is also likely strengthened through silence: organizational materials have eliminated mid-century rhetoric about heathens (WV and Compassion) or communists (CCF) and left a gaping hole in its place. Current materials rarely discuss other religions or beliefs, leaving sponsors to assume Christianity is the norm.[84]

Sponsors' responses also indicate a profound shift on the issue of conversion. With only a couple of exceptions, no sponsor I met believed that non-Christians were consigned to Hell. Most denied any fundamental differences between religions at all. "No matter what, if you're honoring God in some way or another, this is what we're supposed to do," said Rose, a retired secretary in upstate New York. "If I wasn't raised in the Catholic faith, I probably wouldn't be Catholic." She meant that she may well have had another religion had she been born abroad—and from God's enlarged perspective it would not make a difference. Carrie, an evangelical homeschooler in Massachusetts, said something similar: "We are interconnected in that we were all created by the same God. No matter what religion [you are] . . . everybody believes that you were put here by one God." When I asked them to elaborate, Rose and Carrie included (even) religious rituals in a broad category called culture—alongside clothing, language, manners, and such—as varied and legitimate ways to acknowledge humankind's Creator. Such responses emphasize the necessity of God for all people *and* the necessity of protecting other cultures (including "religious" aspects), without viewing these goals as antithetical. It is one of the strange aftereffects of mid-century U.S. Christianity and the world it forged.

CHAPTER 5

Materialism and Consumption

Circulating Christian Love with American Things

> Sponsors don't adopt a child in the sense that they pull up their roots and make imitation Americans of them.
>
> —Shirley Boone, Compassion TV special, 1974

A BOX WITH MYSTERIOUS CONTENTS

> Outside it showed bright red and green / With a tag for a little boy
> He didn't know what to do, you see / He had never known the joy
> Of opening presents just for him / He'd never had a gift . . .
> He opened up and found a car / Some crayons and a ball
> But, best of all, because of that box / He met Jesus, Lord of all.
>
> —Poem by J.P. (Operation Christmas Child volunteer), Samaritan's
> Purse Processing Center Guestbook, December 3, 2014

Unitarian pastor Charles Rhind Joy was executive director of Save the Children Federation when he wrote "The Little Girl Who Had Never Smiled" in 1947.[1] The story was a simple but effective vehicle to create engaged empathy. It told of five-year-old Francine, a Jewish orphan in a refugee camp, who was so traumatized that she "didn't have the strength to smile, or the wish to smile." She remained impassive, even when an American woman from the Unitarian Service Committee promised to one day take her to an orphanage "where love is." The story reaches its climax as the woman hands the child an American chocolate bar upon departing: "It is something good to eat. Taste it." Francine hesitated over the unfamiliar food, then put it in her mouth: "She had never tasted anything quite so good before. Her warm hand melted the chocolate. . . . [and] something was happening to her as she ate it." The warmth spread through her, writes Rhind Joy, and standing there, covered in chocolate, watching the woman leave, Francine *smiled for the first time.* The piece ends by addressing "the good people of America" directly: children like Francine desperately craved the love that U.S. sponsors could provide.

Stories like this one impressed upon U.S. Christians that they could become a visceral part of other people's experience through their gifts. American-made chocolate was a rich example. Unavailable to poverty-stricken Europeans like Francine, the sugary, caffeinated treat seeped into her body, producing the endorphins that became happiness, perhaps even euphoria, leading to that elusive smile. Rhind Joy overlaid the physical reaction with spiritual significance, using the word "love" as a signpost: the Protestant orphanage is where love is found. The story championed the kind of humanitarian global politics that we have traced over the last two chapters, in which diplomacy's monumental mid-century failures seemed to prove that the way to secure a better future was to foster individual "heart-conversions" to a universal Love, which was implicitly or explicitly modeled on iterations of Anglo-Protestantism. When the chocolate seeped into Francine, according to Rhind Joy, it produced the first heart stirrings of that foundation for lasting peace. Many U.S. Christians believed that sponsorship could produce the same result.

While the story could certainly be analyzed for its troubling approach to refugee aid, I raise it here for a different reason: it foregrounds the bitter (sweet?) irony about luxuries like chocolate. Since at least the early nineteenth century, U.S. Christians taught their children to view candy as a morally ambivalent substance associated with privilege, pushing them to donate the pennies they saved for its purchase to support "needy" foreign children instead. Rhind Joy's story turns this very substance—a potent symbol of expendable luxury—into an embodied experience of U.S. love and generosity for a child abroad. This sleight of hand introduces the chapter's primary theme, which asks how the circulation of gifts and money raises fraught questions about U.S. "materialism" and the unjust global distribution of "abundance." These issues resonate with any Christian who cherishes an idealized communion of equally valued "brothers and sisters" in Christ within a system of stark and growing worldwide inequity. Does Love favor certain geographic regions and people over others? What does this say about Divine justice? The resulting moral challenges are not incidental to Christian globalism; they are fundamental aspects of its universalism.

There was also something historically specific about the way mid-century U.S. sponsors fused and confused God's Love with American gifts. The postwar economic boom made the United States the strongest economy in the world. A Cold War ideology of "citizen-consumer" positioned individuals as political agents by virtue of their consumption. In this view, exchanging money for goods carved out a sphere of personal autonomy and, moreover, was a morally benign and even positive aspect of sociality: spending money fueled the economy, which helped the nation as a whole. It is not hard to hear the echo of an earlier generation of Christian capitalists who sometimes defined the root of heathen "savagery" as the failure to want the consumer niceties of a civilized, Christian life.[2] In this view, Protestant Christianity and U.S.-style consumption were the twin pillars of any modern society. Thus, despite certain prominent Cold War cultural critics who lambasted middle-class suburbanites for their inward-looking consumerism, the prevailing logic posited a harmony between democratic egalitarianism, family love, and capitalist consumption.[3] Studies of transnational adoption and international humanitarianism argue that a similar mix of values encouraged U.S. citizen-consumers to objectify "Third World orphans" in "social relationships of exchange, meaning, and value that are both caring and consumptive."[4] Americans "purchased" Asia in miniature when they sponsored a child.[5]

U.S. sponsors have rarely (if ever) seen themselves as consumers of foreign children, but they have often considered the commodity logic of sponsorship. Their major focus has been assessing the impact of U.S. gifts abroad: do they risk remaking foreign children into U.S.-style consumers in the most negative sense? "Little Americans," as Shirley Boone says in the epigraph. To some degree, such concerns overlap with studies of globalization, which since the 1980s have bemoaned how U.S. cultural products swamp markets and lead to homogenization.[6] Few sponsors are bothered if a foreign child plays with a Barbie or listens to pop music per se. Their concern lies with the moral implications of *wanting*. Sponsors largely agree that some of what they define as "American values" related to individualism (Christian free will, democratic choice, capitalist aspirations) are morally good and should be applied universally, while other forms of individualism to which Americans seem susceptible (overconsumption, materialism) should be suppressed. The problem lies in the dense interweaving of these forms.

This chapter explores how U.S. sponsors responded to this challenge through "anti-materialist tactics." I adapt this term from literary scholar Mary Louise Pratt's "anti-Conquest narratives," which refers to nineteenth-century narratives that rejected colonial superiority, often by elevating colonized Others, while also conveying the speaker's power in relation to them.[7] The Noble Savage is a classic example. This rhetoric shares the flavor of how sponsorship has elevated foreign others as innocent non-consumers, while also reasserting U.S. Christians' economic and moral dominance as those who choose to give and, most important, co-labor with God to redistribute his resources around the world. This chapter thus approaches the dialogue between immensity and particularity somewhat differently than previous ones, which argue that the immensity of statistics or emergency needs is counterbalanced with the particularity of human-scale relations. Here it is the particular—the comparison of a U.S. donor's wealth with the poverty of a foreign child—that destabilizes and may overwhelm. It is tranquilized by enfolding the 1:1 comparison within a God-scale plan for circulating Love and resources globally—in which Americans are the central axis.

In what follows, I incorporate synchronic and diachronic modes of analysis in order to emphasize historical particularities as well as continuities over time. The chapter starts in the 1960s to 1980s, beginning with what I argue is a shift in how U.S. Christians conceived of materialism. I then explore three popular anti-materialist tactics related to choosing a child to sponsor, small and homespun gifts, and the rhetorical transfiguration of consumer objects into emotions like joy and love. I end by drawing on my contemporary fieldwork at Operation Christmas Child to explore the continued role of objects as points of contact in Christian globalism. Throughout is the bittersweet irony we tasted in Francine's story: U.S. Christians seek to overcome their anxieties about materialism by embracing materiality—the gifts, donations, and other objects of love that seem to provide the surest way to manifest and circulate Love across the world.

A NEW MATERIALISM

In their publicity materials from the 1950s and 1960s, Protestant sponsorship organizations regularly conflated terms like freedom, Christian, and democracy; these were juxtaposed with bondage, fear, paganism, communism, and materialism. Although the term "capitalism" was rarely invoked, it was implied on the side of good. The logic ran thus: God wants people to flourish, which undemocratic socialist-communist systems impede by destroying humankind's resources through war or (less straightforwardly) through nationalization programs that seize individual property, including U.S. foreign capital and investments. Or, God wants people to flourish, which undemocratic pagan systems impede by hindering free will as they bind individuals within rigid social structures, such as caste or ancestor cults, and teach them to fear the afterlife. By these lights, such systems were "materialistic" because they hindered individual advancement and more directly because they denied God's role in human affairs. In communism, this second failing was indexed by the seeming absence of religious material objects, whereas in paganism it was indexed by their fetishistic overabundance. U.S. Christians viewed their own country as potentially vulnerable to similar sins—one needed to guard against them—but not as materialistic per se, at least comparatively speaking. The newly declared People's Republic of China was perhaps the ultimate example, since it actually targeted U.S. investment and evangelism. And the issue was personal: Christian missions, including nascent sponsorship organizations, were pushed out en masse in 1951.[8]

Materialism held other meanings as well, which eclipsed earlier ones by the 1980s. At this point, sponsorship organizations rarely mentioned paganism or even communism. Materialism still referred to being estranged from God, but it became an internal state associated with personal and national overindulgence. Thus in 1989, for example, WV President Robert Seiple told his evangelical constituents that they were wrong to assume that materialism emerged from elsewhere to infect the church. U.S. Christians also had "an undue preoccupation with extravagance. It is an insidious form of idolatry that takes God's gifts and makes them more important than God himself."[9] For sponsors, the battle against materialism played out in their own lives, and among their families and friends. In this context, sponsors and the organizations they supported began to discuss materialism in three primary registers: egoism that wallows in an abundance of choices, including consumer products and life trajectories (e.g., the "spoiled" hippie or yuppie); the inability to distinguish consumer needs from desires, and consequent inability to "simplify" one's lifestyle; the focus on sensual pleasure through consumption and leisure (material "enjoyment") instead of Christian "joy."

Materialism was a corruption of the proper relationship to capitalism and consumerism, both of which were otherwise seen as necessary and morally benign engines of U.S. and global progress. In this view, sponsoring a child was a catalyst that could rupture and unsettle a "materialistic" life. It could bring one's actions back into right relation with capitalism and consumerism by redefining necessity and desire in order to curtail overindulgence. Writing of English families in the same period, anthropologist Daniel Miller notes that most consumption "comes from the gradual expansion of a sense of what ordinary people may ordinarily expect as their standard of living combined with the growth in their incomes." In other words, the capacity to need is a moving target in material terms, even if the moral implications of "over" consuming remain the same. He makes the point by comparing English consumers within a temporal framework: in the 1980s, an indoor toilet was considered as a need, whereas a short century earlier it was considered a luxury. Sponsorship made the same point within a spatial framework by offering a real-time comparison between Americans and people abroad. The goal was for sponsors to readjust their understanding of "need" in global terms such that they would come to realize that most of what they thought they needed was merely a consumer desire. In fact, other people in this period also struggled with anxieties about growing consumerism—anthropologist Webb Keane has discussed Indonesians under Suharto, for example[10]—but, from an American perspective, it seemed that people in the "West," and more specifically in the United States, were especially susceptible.

Evangelicals in particular embraced the word "lifestyle" in the mid-1970s as shorthand for this problem. In 1974, the landmark Lausanne Congress on World Evangelization included a paragraph in its *Covenant* that read, "All of us are shocked by the poverty of millions and disturbed by the injustices which cause it. Those of us who live in affluent circumstances accept our duty to develop a simple life-style in order to contribute more generously to both relief and evangelism." It led to the 1980 International Consultation on Simple Lifestyle in England.[11] Combining this new impetus with the older aesthetic of starving millions, World Vision told its supporters, "The fact that 800 million people are destitute and that about 10,000 die of starvation every day make any other lifestyle indefensible." Sponsors weighed in both for and against statements like these.[12] In general, however, globally minded U.S. evangelicals cultivated what is a now deeply embedded link between global engagements and self-castigation about "materialism, consumerism, narcissism, entitlement, meaningless distractions, and so much more."[13]

Sponsors rarely indicted themselves as materialistic before the 1970s, but they did worry about their children. A full-fledged "consumer culture" first developed in the late nineteenth and early twentieth-century United States, just as anti–child labor laws enforced new norms that naturalized a white middle-class ideal for children as a whole; that is, childhood innocence became equated with economic consumption, rather than production (as wage-earning workers).[14] Mid-century sponsors upheld this view of childhood, even as they balked at how their children (now targeted by marketers directly) clamored for more and more store-bought toys and clothes. To put it in the terms I used above, sponsors feared that their affluent offspring were unable to distinguish necessity from desire; all consumables seemed equally urgent.[15]

By comparison, foreign children seemed to embody the elusive ideal of economic innocence. They seemed "so pleased by simple things."[16] Contemporary sponsors echo this idea often. Mary, a working-class Catholic woman who raised eight children near Kansas City, recently started donating to Heifer International in lieu of buying Christmas gifts. She also reads her grandchildren the letters she receives from the child she sponsors and his family. "They are interested in such simple things. I mean, life is simple. That worries me that [my granddaughter] is like I want, I see, I want. That toy magazine comes at

Christmas, I want, I want." Abby, an evangelical mother of two teen boys in New Hampshire, feels the same way and used Marlin, the Guatemalan child they sponsor, as a heuristic tool to aid her boys' development. She imitates their whining:

> A: And when the kids were little and they'd be like, *Nyah, nyah, nyah*. I'm like, "Well, do you think Marlin would have . . . ? They were complaining and [I'd say] "Marlin doesn't even have a *fork*." (Ha)
>
> H: When they were asking for things like another ice cream cone or—?
>
> A: Right. Or "So and so has three-car garage." "Oh, really? How many garages do you think *Marlin* has?" (Ha)
>
> H: And did they—did they learn to hate Marlin or did they understand?
>
> A: No, they learned to be grateful for what they have. Right.

Abby might be optimistic. Neither of her boys ever agreed to write to Marlin, though she encouraged it, and recently they have refused to attend church as well. Nevertheless, the point is that sponsors like Mary and Abby mobilize global contrasts in order to short-circuit a vicious current whereby U.S. children lust after—and usually acquire—a multitude of consumer objects. This view is represented in the Lausanne document from 2010, in a passage that was significantly shaped by the advocacy of Compassion, WV, and other U.S.-based organizations. "*All* children are at risk," it reads, "Half of them are at risk from poverty. Millions are at risk from prosperity. Children of the wealthy and secure have everything to live with, but nothing to live for."[17]

Sponsorship has long perpetuated the view of foreign children as economic innocents, not least because field workers were instructed to omit any mention in the children's letters of "luxuries" or consumer desires related to objects such as brand-name clothing, televisions, and cars. Nor were photographs supposed to show "children in extravagant dress or environment or wearing excessive ornamentation."[18] The message was further reiterated because sponsored children were required to write letters of gratitude each time even the smallest gift was received. The seeming contrast between these children and their U.S. sponsors prompted two major questions or difficulties: the first was how to save Americans from the materialism to which they now viewed themselves as prone; the second was how to protect foreign children from the possibility that their sponsors, however unwittingly, would sway them from virtuous non-consumption into sinful overconsumption. The first of the tactics by which sponsors addressed these issues pertains to choosing a child to support—the very thing that sponsorship's critics point to as evidence of U.S. materialism run amok.

Tactic I: Choosing Children (or God's Plan in Action)

Choosing a child has been integral to sponsorship since the early 1950s. Some organizations printed children's photos in their advertisements and told sponsors to circle and mail back the one they liked best. Others sent sheets of stamps with children's faces for sponsors to glue onto a returnable form or mailed out envelopes of photos and asked sponsors to pick one and return the rest. Thus, a prospective sponsor in 1970 might have opened her mailbox to find an envelope filled with 3 × 5-inch cardboard cards from Compassion (figure 5.1a). Each one had a headshot and name on the front and a short story on the back.

No. 601- Fransisco–Venezuela.

Fransisco is 3 ½ years old and lives in Compassion's home for abandoned and orphaned boys in Venezuela, South America. He has good health, and so far he has a cheerful personality. Nothing is known of his parents' whereabouts.

No. 605- Suwarti—Indonesian.

This sweet little girl was born on March 23, 1959 in Salatiga, Java. Her father, a soldier, died in Salatiga in 1960, Her mother, though alive, is very poor and cannot care for the needs of her family since her husband died, as there is no source of income. The child lives with the mother. She is in 2nd grade, and is average in her studies. Her favorite subjects are math and reading and she enjoys sports and singing. Her duty at home is sweeping.[19]

By the 1980s, more informative "child packets" were sent to sponsors upon request or spread out on tables at recruiting events. They are still used today. Contemporary sponsors can also click through hundreds of photos online and search by sex, nationality, birthday, or special needs (figure 5.1b).

As images, these rows of faces evoke the statistics and landscape photos discussed in previous chapters, which order global immensity into a digestible form. They are a form of collection—the cultural equivalent of a taxonomic table, according to Jean Baudrillard—where the "aesthetic of seriality" strips each object of its own history and rearranges it according to the collector's whim. Adding to this insight, theorist Susan Stewart explicitly views collections as arising out of a "mercantilism" defined by extraction. Emblematic is the

FIG 5.1A AND 5.1B. Instructional card and photographs from a packet sent to Compassion sponsors, c. 1965. Used by permission of Compassion International, Inc. Copyright © 2014 by Compassion International, Inc. All rights reserved.

merchant of yore in whose cabinet exotic curios were completely decontextualized to become signifiers of the exchange economy itself.[20] It is this niggling idea (swap "curios" for "children") that so bothers sponsorship's critics. And to one degree the link with capitalist consumption is undeniable: sponsorship organizations developed technologies of choice precisely because it was a natural extension of how systematic/designated giving promised donors more accountability and control—a model that, as I have noted, arose from shareholding in joint-stock companies.

https://www.compassion.com/sponsor_a_child/

🏠 › Sponsor a Child Today

Sponsor a Child Today

✓ Trusted Charity Since 1952 | Over 1.9 Million Children Sponsored | BBB Accredited Charity

Questions?
Please call us at **(800) 336-7676**, Monday through Friday, 7 a.m. to 5:30 p.m. MT to speak with a Compassion Representative.

As you exchange letters, send photos and offer encouragement in Jesus' name, your love will bring hope to a child that will last a lifetime. Sponsor a child today for only $38 per month!

🕐 Urgent: Waiting Over 6 Months   🧍 AIDS-Affected Area   🛡 Highly Vulnerable to Exploitation

Sort All Children By: Age (Youngest) Age (Oldest) Longest Waiting Birthday Today

WAITING 303 DAYS — **Arnob** — Bangladesh — 6/15/2016 — CHOOSE ME
Marjorie — Philippines — 9/7/2002 — CHOOSE ME
Michele — Ghana — 11/27/2016 — CHOOSE ME

WAITING 306 DAYS — **Christina** — Tanzania — 3/12/2013
WAITING 305 DAYS — **Carlos Fernando** — Bolivia — 2/13/2010
Maria — Colombia — 1/2/2004

SEARCH FOR A CHILD
Where in The World — No Preference
Gender — No Preference
Age Range: 1-22 years old
Birthday — Select Today — Month — Day
Year
Show more search options (child name, special needs and more)
Search Now

Start Sponsoring a Child Today!
Your tax-deductible contribution of **just $38 a month** connects a child living in poverty with a loving, church-based Child Sponsorship Program.

Your support provides:
- **Medical checkups**, which often save lives
- **Nutritious food**
- **Health and hygiene training**
- **Educational assistance**
- Access to special **services** like

FIG 5.1A AND 5.1B. *(continued).* A screen shot of Compassion's website in 2019.

For many Christians, however, personal consumer choices ideally reinforce God's ultimate authority. In this respect, choosing a child is actually a tactic by which sponsors detach their actions from the morally ambivalent consumptive sphere and fix them within the sphere of prayerfully guided decisions instead. It echoes what scholars have found more broadly in U.S. evangelical consumerism, which at least in theory is guided by affective clues that reveal God's will—would Jesus want you to buy those jeans?—and in secular or liberal Christian modes of "ethical consumption," especially of organic and fair trade products. Liberal Christians, like the Mennonites at Ten Thousand Villages, first championed this form of anti-materialist consumption as an explicitly global project in mid-century North America, and since the 1990s it has become popular among more conservative U.S. Christians as well. By making certain purchasing choices, Westerners try to bridge the fissures that consumer capitalism creates between local private spending and global economic structures. (Gift giving is another way to moralize consumerism; not surprisingly, sponsors view choosing a child and giving a gift as interrelated tactics, as I show below.)[21]

Christian decision-making practices are everywhere in the sponsorship archive but are most pronounced among evangelicals. For example, a woman came across a WV advertisement in a 1966 edition of *Reader's Digest*. She prayed to God, opened her Bible, and put her finger on II Corinthians 9, where Paul urges God's people to give generously to the Macedonians. "I believe this has already been in His plan," she concluded. In another case, a 66-year-old widow flipped past an article about Compassion in a 1978 edition of *Eternity* magazine, but felt called back to it. "Christ Jesus spoke to me. 'Feed my lambs.' I read the Compassion plea again. And again Christ Jesus said to me, still in his soft voice, 'Feed my lambs.'" She responded to the call.[22] Organizations encouraged people to view their decisions in such terms. Compassion's advertising instructed in bolded font, **"If God has spoken to you simply fill in the coupon on the enclosed envelope."** In its publicity for mainline Protestants, it urged Christians to "obey your heart when it says 'yes.'"[23]

Evangelical organizations also maintained that God actually made the choice when they assigned a child, assuring sponsors that they, too, acted "prayerfully (see instructional card in figure 5.1a)." They further assured U.S. donors that if after gazing at the assigned child's face in prayer they failed to hear God's affirmation, the child would be exchanged for another.[24] This system could cause logistical headaches, which is perhaps why the same organizations emphasized flexibility. Stated one anonymous letter to WV magazine, "I do not want my dreams to interfere with whatever choice God has for me. And so I ask you to allow me the joy of helping to care for some child, boy or girl, of any age any place in the world as the Lord directs you. For I know it will be His choice for me."[25] Whether or not a real sponsor penned this letter, printing it was certainly to WV's advantage. Organizations counted on sponsors generally accepting the child that they (and God) assigned.

This rhetoric was never merely a clever way to do business. The men and women who work (and worked) for evangelical organizations abide by the same principles. When I volunteered at Compassion church events, we began by praying over the packets and asking God to bring a sponsor for each one. Reflecting on hundreds of hours staffing tables for World Vision, Bob Pierce's daughter Marilee Pierce Dunker told me she often witnessed what she called an "act of divine matchmaking"—a moment of synthesis between Spirit, organization, and sponsor. "People come up and say, 'I'm looking for a child that is *this* age or born on *this* day,'" she said. "And we have a limited number of packets but there it is—the *exact* child."[26]

Many evangelical sponsors had similar stories. Carrie, a real estate agent and homeschooler in her early fifties, told me about choosing Zara, a girl from Uganda. She felt drawn to the sponsorship table in her church lobby, but she knew she wanted to support a baby and none seemed to be available. "They said they only have one baby left and I said that's 'cause it's *my* baby. So she was chosen for me." I asked her to elaborate. "They had her, she wasn't even on the table like they have [packets] where you can look and that kind of creeped me out anyways that you, like, *shopped* for a baby. It kind of creeped me out and they said, well we only have one left [in a box under the table] and I said that's cause she's mine. So I didn't pick her. God did." For Carrie, choosing a child was no longer consumptive (shopping for a baby) or materialistic (making things more important than God). Instead, the experience became part of her ongoing efforts to actualize God's plan in her life.

Catholics and most mainline Protestants do not share the evangelical emphasis on trying to discern God in quotidian details, and (Catholic) Unbound never made choosing a child central to their program.[27] Nevertheless, when mainline Protestants and Catholics did tell me about choosing a child, many of them also highlighted coincidences and the inexplicable pull toward a certain packet.[28] I was present at sponsorship tables when prospective sponsors remarked in wonder about feeling drawn to the very child who shared their birthday or had the same initials as their grandchild. Whether they called it a "God moment," fate, or a funny occurrence, they meant that something other than randomness brought together two people from across the world.

Though sponsors may view themselves as (temporarily) devoid of agency, critics would argue that children are still objectified as passive vessels and are thus "purchased" by Americans. As Carrie implies, many sponsors are also "creeped out" by the similarities, even while they deny them. Literary theorist Lori Merish's work on emotion and nineteenth-century U.S. consumerism offers a helpful framework for thinking about the issue. Specifically, I am interested in her analysis of objects of love that eluded actual purchase, such as the country of the United States. Merish argues that in this case Americans developed "aestheticized possession" by engaging in acts that produced emotion (for example, walking through or gazing at the land) without possessing it per se (having a titled deed). Merish assumes that such objects are local: someone who did not possess land, a fancy dress, or a beautiful woman consumed them vicariously by coming into contact with them.[29] Yet aestheticized possession is useful for understanding Christian globalism too. It is echoed when sponsors talk about "their" child. More broadly, it connects to how they view God as governing his creation—a possession in which U.S. Christians share to some degree as God's co-laborers.

In the 1970s and 1980s, the sponsorship organizations under study became more committed to portraying the sponsored child and her family members as decision makers, and to communicate this fact to sponsors—even while their advertising to attract new sponsors communicated a very different message (which stoked much of the outside criticism). To my mind, however, what is at stake is not so much the question of a single child's agency, but the more general aestheticized possession in which sponsors participate by virtue of their presumed role as co-laborers with God. This "co-labor" is linked to the concept of stewardship, a theo-ideology that is less celebrated in the history of U.S. religion than the English Puritan "city upon a hill," perhaps, but is no less important in the making of American exceptionalism. It posits, or certainly implies, that God chose Americans as the axis through which (many) earthly resources are produced, consumed, and circulated globally. This idea has counterparts elsewhere, for example among Ghanaian Pentecostals who view globalization as a divine gift that enables them to spread spiritual and economic resources. Yet Ghanaians also struggle to block what they view as the corrupt influences that globalization brings from outside, including via the United States.[30] By contrast, U.S. Christians have generally approached global stewardship with an unalloyed sense of power: we spread and others receive.

The focus on stewardship emphasizes a contrast with other anthropological studies of Christians and globalization that highlight the charismatic promise that those who "give by faith" to God will reap abundant returns on "seed" money. As Simon Coleman emphasizes about Word of Life, a globalizing charismatic church in Sweden, the end result—who gets the money and how it is spent—matters less, if at all, compared to the *fact of circulation* as believers send resources into the world. The expected benefits to givers are seen as "almost automatic consequences of correct faith."[31] By contrast, sponsorship relies on a biblical principle derived from I Corinthians 4:2 that views the Creator as entrusting resources to human beings who must return a portion of it to further God's Kingdom (chapter 1), and do their best to ensure it is put to good use. In the United States, stewardship became a watchword in the nineteenth century with the growth of denominations. In U.S. churches, calls for "good stewardship" are still associated today with the diligent management of "time, talent, and treasure," as the expression goes. Sponsors give up treasure through regular tithing and proportionate giving. The organizations they support are "good stewards" when they streamline and lessen the costs of administration. Although stewardship has the ring of middle management and certainly does not produce the highs and lows of giving by faith, it too is expected to foster dependence on God. Sponsors often recognize that they sponsor "with God's help" and they manage resources carefully for His sake. "You do not want to waste since God gives you the money. Everything is His," Carrie told me, reflecting on her support for Zara.

Though stewardship has usually referred to personal finances or local church institutions—and has been studied as such by scholars of U.S. Christianity[32]—sponsors have no trouble upscaling the concept. If one thinks from a god's eye view, good stewardship dictates that one helps where the need is greatest—which is always abroad. Greg, a Catholic and a social worker in upstate New York, has spent his life working with and for people in need in the United States. He gave a response I heard many times: "Need is need. But I guess, probably, when you—in terms of objective truth, poverty in Africa is different than poverty in this country. It's not good in either place. It brings a lot of tension in either place but clearly it's more intense and pervasive in Africa and people are missing even more the basics than here." Sponsors are also aware that the global circulation of currency means that each U.S. dollar has higher impacts abroad. Richard, a civil engineer who attends a Lutheran church, exchanged curt words with his sister-in-law when she criticized his choice to help foreigners. He gave her what he calls "an engineer's response." The math just made sense: "Your money goes a lot further. Good grief, really? I can get somebody education, medical care and food for 40 bucks a month? . . . It's, these are the resources I have, I'd like to do as much as I can with it. And it's, you know, can I help one person versus ten? I'd go for ten."

Tactic II: The Anti-Materialism of Small Gifts and Homespun Objects

Until the 1970s, sponsors often wrote to organizations self-identifying as people of little means. Today this genre of letter has largely disappeared. "Although my financial resources are meagre," ran a typical letter from 1960, "I feel it is God's will that I help one of your orphans who has much less than I."[33] Older, single women were the primary authors and they followed a remarkably set format.

They often named their fixed monthly income ($101, $75, $130), specified what items they had sacrificed to sponsor—a new winter coat, cigarettes, the money for an AM/FM radio—and ended by self-deprecatingly noting the smallness of their donation and saying they wished they could do more. These letters circulated at a time when sponsorship and other humanitarian organizations continually juxtaposed post-war American prosperity with foreign poverty. The contrast, which was aimed at middle-class donors, almost certainly created ambivalence for lower-income Americans.[34] They were expected to recognize that they were financially elite in global terms, though in their daily lives they were poor (sometimes extremely so). Self-identifying as people of little means was an anti-materialist tactic that to some degree recognized their relative wealth in global terms, while reiterating their experience as marginal to the centers of U.S. wealth.

Mid-century sponsorship organizations commended and encouraged these letters. "We know that many, many of the gifts sent to World Vision this past year represented sacrifice as great as that of any valiant missionary across the seas," wrote WV to its supporters in 1959.[35] When it suited the occasion, organizations even transmitted this idea to their overseas partners. In 1966, Compassion's Korean staff demanded better pay and job security and Miriam Swanson, widow of the founder, chastised them in a moment of cringe-worthy disregard for what life was like following a harrowing war: "Many of our sponsors are so sacrificially giving to these children they are denying themselves many of the necessities of life . . . I only wish I could feel that you there in Korea are as concerned about your children as we are."[36]

The rhetoric of little means was linked to the production of homespun objects. U.S. women had been making clothing and other items for sponsored children since the 1820s.[37] As chapter 1 argued, for middle-class women the physicality of these tasks was seen as a sacrifice if one did not feel the pinch of penny donations. It was also an extension of women's domestic activities, and sewing parties remained popular into the mid-twentieth century. (For example, during Operation Winter in 1953, women's groups across the country knitted hundreds of Christmas gifts for Korean orphans in CCF's care.)[38] Yet by the 1960s, such labors became associated exclusively with elderly female sponsors of little financial means and great symbolic capital as "simple" Christians. Women wrote to organizations, describing the things they made, and organizations sometimes profiled the most industrious. Gladys Downing, for example, had hand-stitched more than two thousand quilts by 1976. "It is sometimes tiring," stated the WV newsletter, "but as she prays for strength, God enables her to keep working." Gladys described being in such intense arthritic pain one time that she had "to work with God in prayer" for two or three days before she could pick up her needle again.[39] These stories recall what anthropologist Liisa Malkki has recently found in Finnish Red Cross campaigns, where elderly women knit for humanitarian relief to relieve their own "claustrophobic solitude" and connect to a "lively world."[40] For Christians like Gladys Downing, homespun work was a literal way to co-labor with God. It joined them to that lively world, in which God was the center.

My sense is that when sponsorship publications featured these anti-materialist tactics, it allowed readers to share in the idea that Americans—themselves included—did sacrifice for others. However, the middle-class version of the same set of tactics was somewhat different: it focused on the heartfelt small gift. Hundreds of notes sent to organizational headquarters attested to the care with which a sponsor picked out a particular toy or inscribed a Bible. Even when they not ship objects abroad, sponsors often viewed small gifts as fundamental to kin-like relations. The same year that Gladys was featured for stitching her quilts, for example, Hope Friedmann, a middle-class retiree with adult children, wrote to *WV* at length about Sandor, whom she professed to love like her own and to whom she had recently sent money to buy a birthday gift and candy. She was especially happy he got some candy, which she associated with love and childhood. "I was filled with a mother's longing to send him treats," she wrote.[41] Like homespun things, small gifts evoked nostalgia for caregiving sacrifice in a world where consumer objects seemed overburdened with the signification of U.S. materialism.

Anthropologists note how handcrafts (and, I would add, small gifts) are often out of sync with professional NGO work.[42] In 1976, unbeknownst to Hope Friedmann with her birthday treats or Gladys Downing with her quilts, WV was repositioning itself within the NGO world, which meant revising its gift policy. Since the early 1950s, sponsorship field staff had complained about packages sent by well-meaning sponsors. No matter how lovingly chosen or stitched, such items could be gotten locally at a fraction of the cost. Now local staff also began to question the cultural appropriateness of American-style individualized gifts in the first place.[43] The fact that World Vision's global south partners were making such statements, and moreover were listened to at WV's head office, was testament to the sea change discussed at the end of chapter 4. This change signaled a shift away from an older, paternalistic sponsorship model to one that seemed to better express new ideas about mission following the end of formal colonialism, the growing recognition that Christianity's center was shifting southward, and the solidification of a professionalized "third world" development industry.

In June 1979, World Vision unveiled its new program: sponsors could donate to a common fund from which local WV staff would buy each child two gifts a year, one at Christmas and one on a special day in that child's country. Sponsors could no longer choose the gifts. They were asked to stop sending hand-crocheted items.[44] Within two years the field offices pushed back again; they disliked purchasing the frivolous toys and candy that Americans defined as Christmas gifts. In 1983, the gift policy was amended again: now Christmas would be celebrated with games and "a strong witness for Jesus Christ," rather than gifts. "You may send something small tucked inside a card for your child," WV staff acquiesced, albeit reluctantly, and they reminded sponsors, "You are already providing the gifts of life and hope, which mean the world to your child."[45]

Tactic III: Objects Transfigured (Or Love, Joy, and Christmas)

Christmas became fashionable in the United States in the 1850s, and two decades later female missionaries exported it to their orphanages and schools. They encouraged women's sponsorship circles to send boxes of Christmas gifts, which were highly anticipated by their recipients. Knowing that a box was on its way from Boston in 1873, Mrs. Parker, the missionary at Moradabad, India, even delayed Christmas altogether until it arrived.[46] After World War II, sponsorship organizations elevated Christmas to *the* annual fund-raising season. Children's letters and cards were timed to arrive in the United States at Christmas; sponsors were encouraged to send parcels of gifts. The holiday allowed mid-century sponsorship organizations to partly compensate for how good stewardship and regularized systematic giving left little room for the periodic and often lavish gift giving through which so many U.S. adults created intimate ties with children. But as Christmas soared in popularity, it also came under attack. As early as the 1920s, sponsorship-related publications condemned how it encouraged U.S. consumption. This criticism was so common by 1950 that President Truman's Christmas Message urged Americans to dedicate themselves to God rather than "turkey dinners and stacks of gifts."[47]

Christmas thus emerged as an especially good time to mobilize another anti-materialist tactic: a display of semiotic virtuosity that linked two forms of gift—U.S. Christians sent material gifts around the world because God sent the gift of his Son for all the world. This rhetoric shifted the focus from consumer objects or impersonal transfers of money and allowed U.S. sponsors to view themselves as *really* circulating love, joy, and hope. Banking metaphors further muddied the distinctions between actual money and affective gifts. "Dividends of gratitude and love will come back to you a hundred-fold," Save the Children told readers in a typical *Christian Century* advertisement in the early 1950s.

Sponsorship materials, then and now, rarely use "love" as a direct statement about one's feelings for a child ("I love John"). Instead, it is a euphemism for money ("your love makes a difference") or a reference to God's presence; a sponsor provides her "meager gifts and talents" so God can "pour out His miracles and love" on a foreign child.[48] Love also sacralizes U.S. money and gifts, which are "packed with love" or "sent with love."[49]

The ultimate purpose of these rhetorical transfigurations is to completely envelop sponsors' actions within positive affective registers, rather than negative ones like guilt, which is viewed as lacking the generative quality necessary for sustained giving and engaged empathy. For a similar reason, sponsors have been leery of the suggestion that they profit from giving, other than in a very general spiritual sense (being "blessed" by the experience). This concern speaks to how materialism is defined, in part, as seeking personal pleasure or social status; charitable giving is supposed to break this vicious cycle of materialism, not feed it.[50] At its most pronounced, I found that a persistent minority of contemporary Catholic sponsors did not mention their sponsorship, even to close relatives and grown-up children. "It would be a self-promotion. It wouldn't be right," one woman explained to me.

Sponsored children's letters occasionally cut through such anti-materialist rhetoric to show how, from their perspective, gifts were never fully transfigured into God's love: the actual consumer objects were precious and important. Consider the letters Kim Jun Ya sent from an orphanage in Seoul to her sponsor Cecelia Costello in California in the early 1960s (figure 5.2). When Cecelia sent her a doll, Jun Ya happily reported how much jealousy it provoked. She only allowed other children to play with it under her supervision. The following year, when Cecelia sent a record player to her three sponsored children, it was the two older girls who exercised their power by forbidding Jun Ya to touch it unless they were present. As she accumulated more American gifts, Jun Ya's schoolmates nicknamed her Ye Boon Ee. "It means pretty little girl," she wrote in March 1965, "They call me like this because I have all the thing that the girls of my age can have. Those thing are all from you. My friend envy me so much to see the pretty things you sent me." These consumer objects could make and break social ties. They conferred status and could even turn an orphan into a beautiful, envied person—though such good fortune could be ephemeral, as Jun Ya soon found out. Shortly after her letter in March, Compassion uncovered major corruption in the orphanage administration and cut ties, bringing the story of Jun Ya's pretty American things to an abrupt end.[51]

Although all the sponsorship organizations I studied employed similar terminology in their feats of rhetorical transfiguration, theological differences do create somewhat varied outcomes. In the contemporary context, blog writers

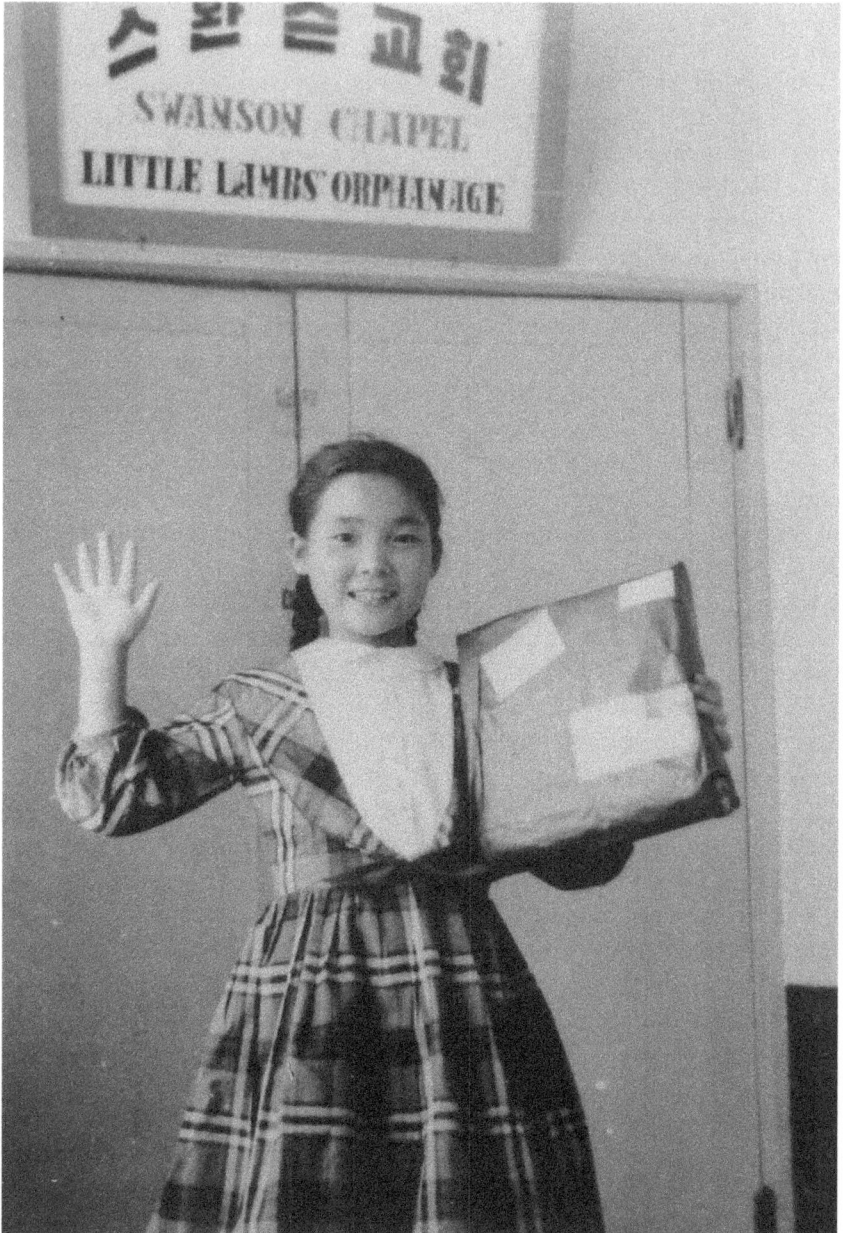

FIG 5.2. Kim Jun Ya with a gift from her sponsor, Cecelia Costello, c. 1964. Children sent a photo each time a gift was received. Used by permission of Compassion International, Inc. Copyright © 2014 by Compassion International, Inc. All rights reserved.

at the Catholic organization Unbound sometimes use the concept of "self-emptying," or *kenosis*, to talk about love. It refers to the intense humbling—even debasement—that God chose to undergo through the Son's incarnation and crucifixion. By filling oneself with the Eucharist, a believer "self-empties" in imitation of Christ to give in love for others. In Unbound's theology, giving up material attachments is also a form of self-emptying that creates room to be filled up with God. Their materials thus use "love" to refer to God's indwelling within people (instead of greed, materialism, etc.), which then allows Americans to send their "love" (money) through Unbound, which provides the hope and security necessary for Catholic people elsewhere to also empty themselves to God's "love."[52] Their Christmas gift policy fits this ethos of shared, almost Eucharistic, links across Catholic communities meant to encourage solidarity and dignity: sponsors can donate to a communal fund, but have no control over it. Parents abroad can choose to use the money to buy gifts for their own children (in their own names), pay for a community celebration, or purchase basic necessities. Everything must be bought locally and "contributions cannot be designated for specific individuals or families."[53]

In comparison, Compassion's gift policy reflects its evangelical ethos, which focuses on building up individuals. In its theology of gifting, God's love germinates when an individual donor feels prompted to give. She then sends her "love" (money) by way of Compassion's local staff members who act as the "hands and feet of Christ" on her behalf. At Christmas, they choose the perfect gift for each individual child in the program.[54] Of the organizations under study, Compassion limns closest to the individualism that lurks in materialism so it must work hardest to transfigure consumer gifts into "tangible expressions of God's love." It does so most often by equating gifts with childhood joy, as a staff member demonstrates on Compassion's blog: "There's no place better to see childhood than a Christmas party. The courtyard where the children gathered was full of shredded paper and shouts of excitement. Little boys played in the dirt with new cars and the girls gathered in clusters to exclaim over their dolls. Teenagers admired their new clothes. All was as it should be. It's about children feeling known, loved and protected."[55] The excitement generated by trucks, dolls, and fashionable clothes is transfigured into feelings of individual recognition, love, and security. In my conversations with Compassion sponsors, they acknowledged that such tokens were frivolous in material terms but nearly always emphasized that they showed how U.S. Christians (and thus God) genuinely cared, which gave poor people *hope*. As Compassion's website puts it, Christmas gifts provide "(1) Love in the name of Jesus! (2) Joy and lots of laughter. (3) A reminder that they aren't alone. (4) Hope that tomorrow can be better."[56]

The second result—joy and lots of laughter—is notable. In missionary liter-ature, Christians have long used "joy" to distinguish their religion from others. In the mid-twentieth century, mission-minded magazines regularly asserted that Christian joy made a deep impression on potential converts; literally, when Christians laughed and smiled, others began to wonder if they had found the secret to human flourishing.[57] Likewise, since the 1960s, sponsors have been told that exuding joy in their letters would give the words "a good spiritual tone."[58] Joy was echoed back in children's responses. (Wrote Helen Clarke in her instructions to orphanage superintendents: "Correct: I am sure that Santa Claus will bring me happiness. Incorrect: I am sure Santa Claus will bring me lots of presents.")[59] This impression was cemented through photography, which freeze-framed the moment of delight when a child received a spon-sor's gift (figure 5.2). These mid-century images date from a time when white Americans still routinely viewed racial others as emotionally defective, either because they displayed too much emotion or too little. Photos of joyful Asian children directly countered long-standing stereotypes of impassive "Orientals" and may therefore have seemed to testify all the more to an incipient Christian-ity. While today this stereotype has largely disappeared (or is no longer overt), the genre has a new life online. On WV's blog, for example, readers can scroll through a series of play-by-play images documenting young recipients' delight upon receiving a gift "packed with love" in the United States.[60]

OBJECTS AS POINTS OF CONTACT

Today, sponsorship organizations try to strike a balance between providing community development and gratifying donors' desire to give tangible things. At the time of writing, all the organizations under study had similar strategies. They allowed sponsors to send money with which in-country staff (or the children's parents) could buy gifts for that child's particular needs or wants. They also encouraged sponsors to send flat paper objects in their letters, such as stickers, hair ribbons, and craft projects. Recently, Compassion, ChildFund, and World Vision have also developed Christmas gift catalogues of practical items, such as goats or chickens. This fund-raising model, which not surpris-ingly also has Christian roots, has proven highly successful in a number of major charities, including Oxfam, Christian Aid, and Heifer International.[61] Sponsorship organizations view such gifts as part of a sustainable develop-ment model, and as good stewardship, since one animal breeds more. Given the restrictions on what they can send, many sponsors with whom I spoke also found livestock an attractive option since it materializes what is nonphysical in America—emotions like love or guilt, as well as the "intangible" money deducted electronically from their accounts each month. Yet, though giving a goat fosters a certain tie between here and there, sponsors still do not get to choose, touch, and wrap a gift that the foreign child later unwraps, touches, and uses.

The manipulation of objects is one of the most powerful ways to blur absence and presence. Making handcrafts as one pictures their global trajectory, as in the previously mentioned Red Cross knitting campaigns, is a particularly "evocative form of making virtual and enchanted connectivities."[62] The now ubiquitous campaigns to buy fair-trade handcrafts promote the same thing in reverse: consumers are encouraged to imaginatively trace an object's provenance to an individual maker, which creates an enchanted form of connection (hence the use of words like "unique" and "relationship" in their marketing). Although the context differs, Anderson Blanton's study of Appalachian Pentecostals sharpens this idea of long-distance virtual/enchanted connectivities in more explicitly Christian terms. The faith healers with whom he works use objects, such as scraps of cloth, as a "point of contact" with the holy. A preacher in one location prays over it, infuses it with Spirit, and then mails it to believers, for whom it retains efficacious power.[63]

Sponsorship objects are also "points of contact" in how human bodies collaborate with material things to produce more expansive forms of intimate globalism. Photography is a major part of this process, since it allows things that are touched and prayed over here to appear over there. Until the late 1970s, sponsors regularly received photos of the child holding or wearing the things they had bought or made. Sponsors also innovated methods to materialize intimacy. In 1964, for example, Priscilla Larson in Massachusetts asked a friend in the U.S. Army to visit Kwang, the Korean girl she sponsored. Before he left the United States, Priscilla gave him one-half of a paper heart she made. She mailed the other half to Kwang, telling her that "she would know when she put it together that it represented my heart of love for her." The soldier and the girl kept their half-hearts for nearly a year until they were finally in the same place. Her friend documented the heart in photos, which Priscilla enthused was "the next best thing to seeing our little girl in person."[64] Over the years, and still today, the most ubiquitous object along these lines are photos of the child holding a photo of the sponsor. Sponsors send a snapshot of themselves or their families with express instructions for the child to be photographed holding it in hand. Thus, American presence is materialized in the child's environment and reflected back to the sponsor, who can then incorporate the photo of the photo into her own environment, pinned to a bulletin board or pasted into a scrapbook (figure 5.3).

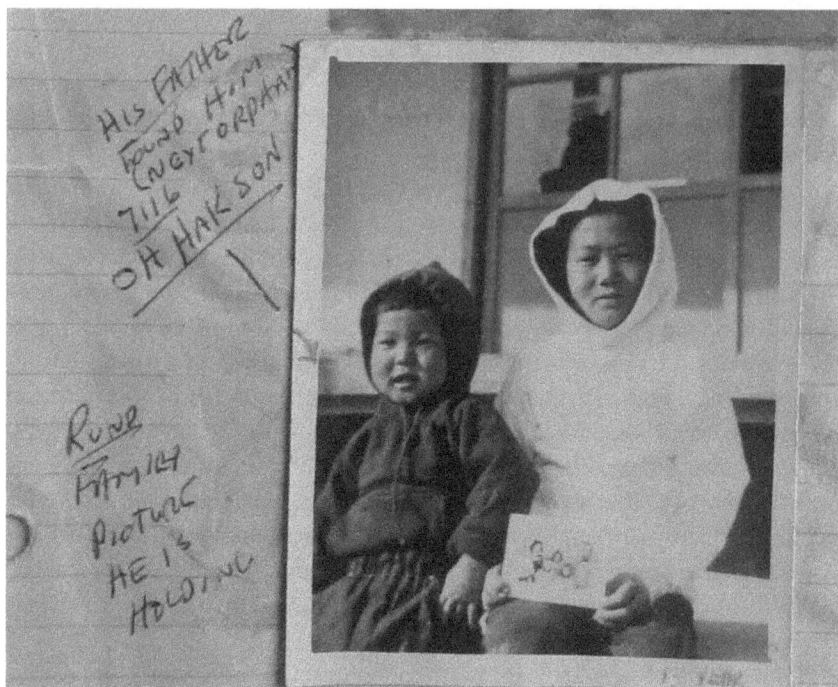

As Blanton intimates, touch can infuse traveling objects with presence. This process is especially interesting to observe at Operation Christmas Child (OCC), through which one can send a shoebox of gifts to a foreign child and even track its trajectory online. OCC is the flagship program of Samaritan's Purse, which was founded by Bob Pierce in 1970 after he left World Vision. Many of the evangelical families I worked with also assembled these boxes at Christmas and viewed it as an extension of the work they do through sponsorship. Samaritan's Purse sends the boxes to evangelical churches overseas, which are then supposed to invite recipients to follow a Bible study course. "We are continuing what Jesus started," says OCC's website, "Every shoebox . . . is a tangible expression of God's amazing love." During my research, I helped sponsors shop for their gifts and gather up boxes at church. I also volunteered at the main OCC processing center in North Carolina, where volunteers open each box to remove items that could break in transit or are deemed inappropriate, which at the time included those associated with Harry Potter (witchcraft) or Hannah Montana (actress/singer Miley Cyrus having embraced a different sort of darkness). Going through the boxes, one sees how Christian donors innovate points of contact. One included pretzels and equated their shape with arms folded in prayer. The note told the child to feel the donor's arms hugging her as she ate them. (Also included were Hershey's kisses for "the love that sweetens our lives," which I had to remove since chocolate melts, but not without recalling Rhind Joy's story about Francine.) Other donors traced their hands on the underside of the box tops and printed the words, "Put your hand on mine and we can pray together."[65]

The power of touch is linked to prayer. All Christians set certain objects apart and sacralize them through touch, prayers, and blessings—even those Protestants who may view prayer as unmediated and free from material conduits. At its most basic, this practice is a biblical one. Ancient Jews brought first fruits to the Temple as a sacrifice. Jesus took bread, blessed it, and passed it to his followers. Evangelicals and Pentecostals "wrap" or "cover" things with prayer to sanctify and implicate them in God's work. The link between money-things (coins) and prayer was so strong that in the 1950s, World Vision founder Bob Pierce viewed it as a major benefit of subscription charity: it was far preferable to have 80,000 people give one dollar and accumulate a prayer from each, he said, than to have someone give $80,000 with just one prayer.[66]

OCC honors covering prayers by instructing its volunteers to avoid changing the placement of items in each box. For example, if one removes a bottle of shampoo one should do so carefully and try to replace it with an object of a similar size in the same location; if one takes everything out of the box, one should repack it in the same configuration. The implication is that a covering prayer makes each consumer object in the box into something new, fusing them together into a whole that is united in the service of God. To make sure that each box is blessed, volunteers also pause during their day to pray over them collectively as they are loaded onto trucks. They talk about the object-in-motion as connecting people along its route. As one volunteer printed in the processing center guestbook after her shift, "What I tried to do today was feel the spirit of the person who packed the box initially; then thought of the child who would receive this gift box and know that we would all be somehow connected."[67]

In the Pentecostal/charismatic circles that Blanton studies, the Holy Spirit is the linking factor. It infuses word-objects or prayer cloths such that they produce blessings or healing for the person who receives them. In sponsorship and OCC gift giving, there is clearly a relationship between humans, objects, prayers, love/Love, and the divine figures in the Trinity, but these interrelations remain underdetermined so that each sponsor may interpret them as she wishes. Based on the OCC processing center guestbook from 2013–2014, however, evangelicals view God as the key figure in this immense project: in the comments they left behind, volunteers mentioned God 68 times (the Lord another 14 times) and Jesus only ten times and the Holy Spirit once. It is God's "awesome love" and "great work" that drive global connections through the distribution of American-bought gifts.

THE ROMANCE OF GLOBAL POVERTY

In the 1970s, many globally minded U.S. Christians were stumbling toward a reconceptualization of north-south relations as mutual partnerships within one Christian body. The move was not unprecedented, especially among liberal Protestants as previous chapters have shown, but it was articulated with new force at the time. Sponsorship programs adopted and promoted this idea, alongside emerging movements such as sister churches and short-term missions. Post-1960s Catholics began to celebrate all "national" manifestations of the Church as integral to a worldwide Body of Christ. By the late 1980s and 1990s, even conservative evangelicals began to talk about "the global church" in the singular.[68] In fact, the rhetoric sounded at times remarkably Roman Catholic. "We are one body," a Compassion Bible study lesson reminded readers in the early 1980s. The accompanying image showed the outline of a man on bended knee, his body filled with a collage of children's faces. "When a thorn is fixed in your heel, the whole body feels it and cares for it . . . *So the whole church works together*" (italics in original).[69]

Today's Unbound and Compassion sponsors are the heirs of this shift. Those with whom I worked often viewed sponsorship as a mutual partnership between far-flung Christians, which means they insisted that it was a global *exchange* of resources where both parties were givers and recipients: Christians with money circulate this form of abundance, while Christians without circulate their form of abundance—that is, their prayers and a model of faith to emulate. The goal of this kind of Christian globalism is to destabilize assumptions about U.S. power and privilege, but the end result is often the romanticization of poverty as an enviable state of material simplicity and spiritual riches.

The idea that those without earthly attachments are able to draw closer to God has been present within Christianity from its origins, reinforced through stories of early saints and hermits. It recurred strongly in mid-twentieth-century Catholic social teaching, which inspired Unbound's founders Jerry Tolle and Bob Hentzen. It provided a subtext for one of the organization's major inspirations today: Hentzen's epic 4,000-mile overland pilgrimage from Kansas to Guatemala, which he undertook in 1996 as "a tribute to the courage and prayerful simplicity of the poor."[70] Unbound portrays the poor in ways that cohere with iconic imagery of Hentzen walking with single-minded devotion and perseverance, his shoes in tatters (the image was sent to sponsors at the time and is still displayed at Unbound's headquarters). In its media for sponsors, poor children and their families are prayerful, sacrificial, and hardworking.

Unbound sponsors often described the spiritual qualities of the poor and did so more frequently than their evangelical counterparts. As I read through the letters they received, I realized how much the children and their families contributed to coproducing this framework. For example, Danielle, a 42-year-old Catholic mother of two and part-time nurse, sponsors Allan in Guatemala. "I think the family, their monthly income was $15 and then here's $30," she told me. "All I'm doing is giving this other Christian, this other soul, what they need to get by and what it happens to be is money." Then she turned to her pile of letters and randomly read one out loud: "I thank you for your help you give me every month and I'm happy and my mother feels blessed." Danielle looked up. "The relief that they must feel!" she said to me, and turned back to Allan's words: "I give you a thousand things, sponsor, for your help. We pray for you sponsor and for your family. We ask God to protect you and illuminate you and give you blessings." Danielle blesses Allan's mother with an extra $30 a month and they call on God to bring her blessings too, offering many "things" (prayers)—a thousand, in fact—in exchange for what Danielle gives them. Later, Danielle emphasized to me how this was an exchange between Christians, and Allan and his mother would almost certainly say the same. They share and reinforce for each other a framework for conceiving of mutuality within the rubric of Catholic social teaching.

As Allan's letter indicates, prayerscapes are fundamental in the romance of poverty, which is an entry point for some evangelicals too. Earlier scholarship generally assumed that Reformed Protestantism constructed "self-determined, impartible individuals," which meant that evangelicals prayed to create relations with God, rather than with other human beings. More recent work redresses that assumption by showing that evangelicals also "cultivate intersubjectivity, a form of communion among co-existing selves, an alternative reality that nearly approximates the divine . . . [through] prescribed forms of immersive sociality."[71] In this respect, even evangelical prayers have a "social life."[72] Chapter 4 noted as much, showing how many sponsors create intersubjective prayerscapes with foreign people they assume to be Christians. And for a subset of my evangelical interlocutors, this notion was amplified in the romantic register. For example, Christine, a 52-year-old mother of four, was raised a Baptist in South Carolina and now calls herself "just Christian" (nondenominational evangelical). She lives in a comfortable ranch-style suburban house in New Hampshire, where she homeschools the youngest of her teenage children. "I think about those prayers [by sponsored children] and I *know* God is listening to them and focused on their needs," she told me.

> And it's very humbling, you know, to know that these guys are praying for me, too. And I want us to have that, you know, this quality of knowing that they *need* God and knowing where our humble place is in this world and—because these guys *know*. It's knowing where you—your place is in the universe, because we're really all in the same place in the universe, you just don't know [as a wealthy American] . . . yeah, we think we're very safe and satisfied with our things [material possessions]. But we're all vulnerable!

Like all sponsors, Christine takes the children's prayers seriously in the sense that she views them as weighty in God's eyes. Like other sponsors with a romantic view of poverty, she views their prayers as *especially* weighty because they arise out of what she construes as true humility, where the materially poor better understand God as the only true source of stability and power. This characterization positions poor people's prayers as having a direct impact on U.S. lives insofar as they can be studied and emulated. American Studies scholar Melani McAlister has observed a parallel trend among contemporary U.S. evangelicals who hold up global south Christians as closer to a "longed-for numinous faith." In fact, the idea that the faraway poor are a spiritual example is so prevalent that U.S. Christians themselves sometimes lampoon it.[73]

It leads to a strange imbalance in the global prayerscape. While the global "poor" offer a vaunted ideal, U.S. Christians described a lopsided exchange in reference to actual relations with sponsored children and their families. What I mean is that all sponsors, but especially evangelicals, narrated their own prayers as an effective means of getting results for the child and his family, ranging from eliciting God's intervention for a concrete need (such as passing a school exam) to providing spiritual encouragement. By contrast, they narrated the child's prayers as an expression of his appreciation and part of his own personal spiritual growth. Not a single sponsor told me that a child's prayer for them had a specific and efficacious impact in their lives—although all considered it a "nice" and even moving gesture. While this pattern certainly reflects how adults view children's prayers in general, it did not change significantly when U.S. sponsors talked about the young adults they supported or a child's adult family members.

The materials I surveyed at organizational headquarters reiterated this message. In a set of 20 random sponsor letters that I catalogued during my visit to Compassion's mailroom, every one mentioned the sponsors' prayers for the child and 19 discussed aspects of the sponsor's personal life. But only one, penned by a woman in her twenties, connected both to indicate that the child's prayers could impact her life: "You also asked if I have any admirers. Well, currently I do and it could possibly lead to marriage! That is something you can pray for me for!" Catholics were somewhat more likely to view prayers as mutually efficacious, based on my survey of a set of 93 sponsor stories sent to Unbound after it solicited them in its *Impact* magazine in 2014. In this sample, 15% (n=14) did so. The following note, from an elderly woman, was typical: "She has offered prayers for my needs and that of my family in difficult times. I offer them for her and her family as well and so appreciate this caring support we have for each other." A few letters were specific in nature, among them an exchange between Morris and Maricela. In 2013, Maricela, a teenager in Guatemala, sent rosary beads to her sponsors, Morris and Judith, retirees in the Midwest. "For me it was so nice to give [the rosary] to you because in that way I will always know that God takes care of you every day," she wrote. Five months later, Morris wrote back to say he had recently developed a tumor. "I prayed using the rosary you gave me, and last week the doctor called and said it was NOT a cancer. The people in the doctor's office said it was a miracle." Maricela responded with satisfaction that the beads were efficacious, as she knew they would be, and promised to say more prayers on his behalf.[74]

While these stories are notable, they are by no means common. Few, if any, of my interlocutors seemed aware that they narrated a lopsided prayerscape—and they did not have the benefit of hearing the pattern echo across many conversations, as I did. This view is reinforced structurally by how organizations—especially evangelical ones that prize "intelligent" prayers—strongly encourage children to include specific prayer requests in their letters to cultivate engaged empathy. Sponsors are rarely encouraged to list prayer needs, and I found most were reticent to do so. Partly, it speaks to how they frame themselves as "givers" generally in the context of global relations, but at a more conscious level they refrain because they do not want to burden foreign people with what they view as their own comparatively inconsequential problems. They are also understandably chary of how much to reveal to a child.[75] The result is that sponsors and children "exchange" prayers, but the sponsor can pray specifically, based on the child's requests and needs, whereas the child's prayers remain general ("We ask God to protect you and illuminate you and give you blessings," Allan wrote to Danielle). Such prayers may be touching (or suspect, if sponsors think the children are being "coached"), but they are rarely seen as effective in the sense of moving God to intervene in American lives. Thus, sponsors implicitly reserve for themselves the role of co-laborers with God, which makes them into agents of change on a global scale. Prayers, like money, may circulate—but never evenly.

Despite the romantic way that the recipients of charity are often construed as closer to God or exemplars of humility, I do not want to paint all U.S. sponsors as completely out of touch with the nasty business of being poor. In response to the 2014 request from Unbound to send in their stories, one sponsor of three boys in India wrote, "I am so grateful to their parents for allowing them this opportunity [to go to school]. It was not an easy decision. They were needed at home [to work]." Many sponsors I got to know also volunteered with people in need in the United States. A fair minority were themselves poor or lower middle-class in American terms. A few had grown up in difficult, and even dire, situations. "I'm not saying that—that having material things is what makes happiness, but *not* being in poverty can *definitely* make life easier," one woman in her forties told me after narrating the harrowing details of a childhood filled with neglect, intermittent homelessness, and sexual assault. She laughed a little self-consciously, but she was right. Being poor is hard. Time and time again, sponsors acknowledged this fact and at those moments they emphasized the common human need for certain material things—bare necessities, of course, but also the small gifts and luxuries that make life a bit more pleasurable and humane. In a sense, this, too, is an anti-materialist tactic. And it is never a permanent fix. Sponsors continue to wrestle with the implications of their own abundance and power within a framework of idealized Christian equality, while finding ways to live within the status quo. It is a recursive tension built upon the hard facts of global inequity.

CHAPTER 6

Trust and Aspiration

Tracking the Results of Global Projects

God's got His fingerprints all over this. Sponsors wouldn't do it if that wasn't the driver.

—Paul Moede, Director of Global Communications, *Compassion*, Personal Interview, June 10, 2014

March 2017. I was in Ecatepec, a sprawling section of Mexico City where Compassion works with Cristiano Emanuel, an independent charismatic church. Its well-established project enrolls about 125 children from the surrounding neighborhood and is staffed by women from the church, about a dozen of whom were showing me around their orderly facilities. As we made our way through the church and its new childcare center, they told me a bit about the people they serve. Half the families attended Emanuel and most of the others were typical residents of the area: poor people who had left their natal villages to find work, which meant they were without the extended relations who would normally mind the children. Working mothers trusted Emanuel, its staff members told me, as the only dependable resource for free meals and childcare in the area. Yet one aspect of the program did sometimes pose a problem: despite the contract they signed, mothers could still be confused, and occasionally upset, when they realized their children's photos were being taken at the church and sent abroad. Sometimes they confronted the volunteers directly, worried that foreigners might take their children. What do you say to such fears? I asked. The most articulate of my hosts replied without skipping a beat, "We say, the sponsors are the people who give money to make the project run. That's it."

This chapter explores what anthropologist Anna Tsing argues is fundamental to any critical analysis of global connections, namely, "the friction between two subjectively experienced bridges, the friction between aspiration and practical achievement."[1] In sponsorship, these frictions are constantly in

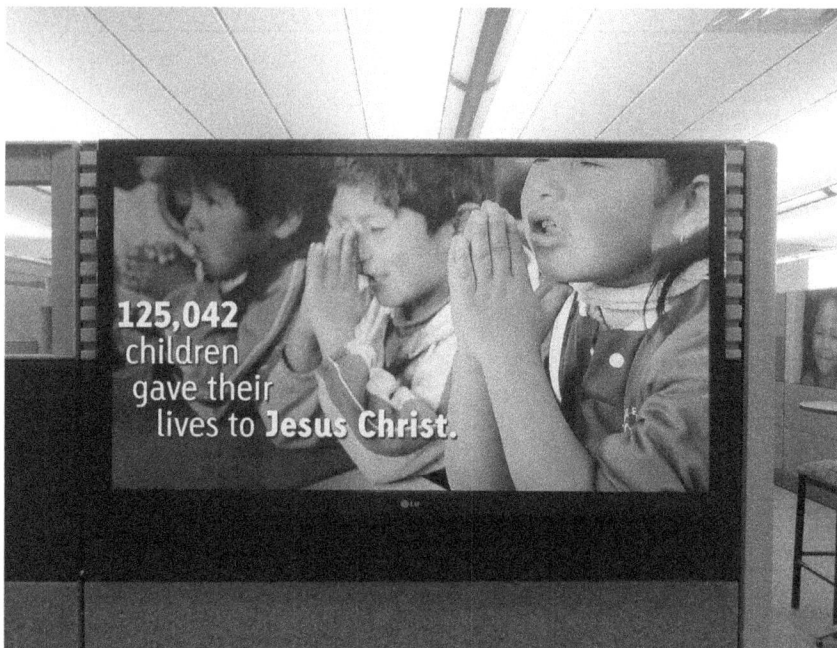

FIG 6.1. Screens tracking evangelical aspirations on cubicle walls in Compassion's headquarters, Colorado Springs, Colorado. June 2014. Since the time of my fieldwork, Compassion no longer reports on conversions. Photo by the author. Used by permission of Compassion International, Inc.

flux as stakeholders in different corners of the world negotiate varying expectations. At Compassion's headquarters in Colorado Springs, success means professional standards of child development, satisfied donors, and evangelical aspirations for born-again conversions (figure 6.1). Emanuel's project staff members undoubtedly agree, but in practical terms their baseline goal is simply keeping children enrolled. Given the focus of this book, my main interest lies how such factors pertain to sponsors and their role.

Compassion's materials assure sponsors that they are paramount: their good judgment ensures the high standards of a Christian organization; their love is the precious encouragement that ignites change in a child's life. As it has for two centuries, sponsorship subtly echoes an idealized Pauline model of faith transmission where a "mature" Christian mentors budding believers through letters. At Emanuel's project in Ecatepec, however, keeping children enrolled means assuaging parents' concerns, and the response above—"sponsors give money to make the project run"—accomplishes this end by displacing Americans from the center of things. They are the economic lifeblood, but that is all. For me, this moment of dissonance sparked the questions that led to this chapter. How do sponsors define and track aspirational models of success, and how do their rubrics correspond to those at organizational headquarters? How do sponsors and the organizations they support try to position U.S. Christian presence as central to what occurs in field sites and corporate offices where sponsors are, in fact, absent?

For child sponsorship organizations, and humanitarian organizations generally, successful outcomes refer to corporate responsibility and child development. They track efficiency in their budgets, for example, and gather data about whether sponsored children surpass their peers according to development indicators. All of the organizations I studied had sophisticated empirical methods for assessing these outcomes; in fact, although I was not aware of it at the time, Compassion staffers granted me access to their offices in Colorado Springs as a direct result of a recent, and unprecedented, decision to widen this empirical approach. Compassion allowed economist Bruce Wydick to conduct an extensive survey of its field sites to assess its program's long-term outcomes. His positive conclusions were a major publicity coup. As I write this chapter, their website footer reads, "Compassion International . . . is the only child sponsorship program to be validated through independent, empirical research."

This focus on tracking and evaluating success may seem natural and obvious, but it is actually a result of the long modern era. Christians historically understood poverty as a permanent feature of God's design; although charity was viewed as a moral obligation, there was little emphasis on measurable results.[2] As a product of the nineteenth century, sponsorship has always tracked outcomes to some degree. But it was in the 1960s and 1970s, in the transition away from supporting missionaries, that sponsorship organizations wholly adopted the "rituals of verification" that constitute today's "audit culture."[3] For my purposes, this system is notable, first, because of what it leaves out: sponsorship organizations have rarely, if ever, defined successful outcomes related to *sponsors*. Thus, while they collect piles of data on the children they serve and their own corporation, there is little or no information about how sponsors might be affected by their experience or how they define success. This leads me to a second point: in sponsors' lives, success and verification rely on a number of connections between hope and futurity that exceed the strictly "empirical." In this respect, I am inspired by studies that show how, from its earliest eighteenth-century forms, modern charitable fund-raising has depended on being able to produce rich imagined forms; potential donors invested if they could visualize, think, and feel their way into believing in desired outcomes. This point addresses an issue that studies of globalization have long recognized. Because global projects are characterized by temporal and spatial distance, they require that individuals extend trust to unknown persons and to forces beyond their immediate control. Investors in such projects must develop the ability to imagine trustworthy connections with people they have never met and feel excited about payoffs yet to come.[4] These imagined forms operate within the same cultural milieu that also enshrines empiricism.

This chapter begins by exploring how sponsors frame aspirations for foreign children's futures. It then turns to how sponsors cope when future plans are cut short because a child leaves the program—and then sometimes gets back in touch online. A subtheme in the chapter, reiterated in the interlude that follows, concerns the role of narrative gaps and silence. Sponsors imagine success within the confines of a system that ultimately severs their contact with sponsored children, sometimes abruptly. Sponsors never get to know the adult the child becomes. Ultimately, absence always haunts the imaginative forms they work into being.

The second half of the chapter turns to modes of verification. Since sponsors cannot personally verify the results of their giving, they expect detailed facsimiles in the form of audits, graphs, and Better Business Bureau or Charity Navigator reports. Yet in my experience, very few sponsors actually consult these documents. Instead, they and the organizations they support cultivate multifaceted modes of trust-creation using measures of success that might at first seem divergent, such as financial audits, answered prayers, and children's smiles. Sponsors also rely on aspirational talk (often in letters to and from the children) and on affective participatory techniques (for example, "experiencing" the triumph over poverty at Compassion's mobile exhibits, which I examine toward the end of the chapter). In short, then, verification and markers of success matter to sponsors, but not precisely in the way that assessment bodies or economists like Wydick might expect.

As Christians, sponsors' commitment to these efforts is driven by "a sense that the world we inhabit is not the world as it should or could be."[5] On that note, the chapter concludes with a short section about sponsors' hopes and fears for the world as a whole. It is the long view—or "immensity," to return to the book's central paradigm—that colors the experience of sponsorship and its shorter-term goals for the life of a single child. Throughout I underline God's bridging power: U.S. Christians view the (Holy) Spirit and (divine) Love as the forces that keep Christian organizations honest, animate sponsor-child relationships, and move human beings toward successful outcomes.

MAKING DREAMS AND PLANS

In recent decades, development professionals and the scholars who study them have coalesced around the idea that assistance must do more than save biological lives. It should also nurture "a concept of a future."[6] This view corresponds with what Appadurai calls "the capacity to aspire," meaning a culturally constructed ability to imagine a certain future and to hope, which then pushes one to act. The implication is that focusing on the past or present may problematically stifle economic and psychological growth.[7] Although the terms differ (swap "psychological" for "spiritual"), the sponsorship organizations and sponsors with whom I worked shared this basic view. Compassion describes its "holistic" model as aiming to create a "permanent, genuine, and significant change" in "character and lifestyle" of each child it supports.[8] In this view, economic development is inextricable from the internal transformations that evangelicals associate with psychological wellness and born again conversion. Paul Moede, Compassion's Director of Global Communications, sketched it out for me when we met in his office. "Poverty isn't a lack of things," he said, "Something else happens. Kids in poverty make conclusions about themselves, that they are worthless. Their psyche and self-esteem are damaged." Then he wrote on a piece of paper: *sponsorship builds esteem.* "I'm a great person, I have a purpose," he clarified, "which leads the child to realize . . ." He turned back to the paper and scribbled a makeshift flowchart: → 2. *I'm created by a Creator* → 3. *Jesus is the way of the Creator* → 4. *Salvation.* At Compassion, economic and psychological security culminates in being born again.

Unbound's social justice–oriented Catholicism provides a nice comparison point. Its team promotes what I came to think of as the "dignity" model, since that is one of the organization's preferred words. This model backgrounds the issue of salvation by positioning the child and his or her community as already deeply moral and unflaggingly hardworking (chapter 5). Paul Pearce, Unbound's Director of Global Strategy, explained to me that the people they support are *humble* rather than *poor.* "Poverty is defined as someone who has no hope," he clarified, "Being humble is a lack of material things you need at that moment, yet still with the dreams, the hope, and the resources to move forward." The statement echoes Pope Francis's call for a more equitable global system that allows "all peoples to become the artisans of their destiny."[9] Unbound's humble poor are stable workers full of economic aspiration—the "$2 a day manual laborer [or the] laundry women who have been living in a squatters' area for 15 years," says Pearce. Although there are significant ideological differences between this approach and the one at Compassion, ultimately both associate human sin and poverty with chaos and unpredictability. They envision sponsorship's role as providing the moral and economic stability that leads to progressive growth.

When I sat with sponsors and read through the children's letters with them, they emphasized much the same thing. And nearly all of them tracked progressive growth through two main indicators: the child's performance in school and the child's aspirations for adult employment. Both represent middle-class norms for defining and assessing universal standards for childhood, which are today enshrined in global organizations such as the United Nations and NGOs. These kinds of aspirations are also characteristic of a neoliberal form of capitalism that has propelled globalization since the 1970s. Neoliberalism refers to the advent of a system that views human well-being as best "advanced by liberating individual entrepreneurial freedoms and skills within an institutional framework characterized by . . . free markets and free trade."[10] It is often framed as the opposite of a moral order, but scholars of religion have traced a more complicated picture, in which it can "exhibit an extraordinarily ethical . . . face."[11] Anthropologists have employed neoliberalism to explain Pentecostalism's global growth since the 1980s.[12] Others discuss how it eased the way for religious broadcasting and other products that greatly increased U.S. Christian "outflows."[13] In this case, it helps us see how, in the 1970s, Protestant sponsorship organizations almost completely transmuted tropes about heathens trapped "in bondage to sin" into a neoliberal vision in which bondage referred to how other religions and cultures stifled the impulse to self-improvement. Only Christianity released individuals from fear such that they could choose to reach their "God-given potential" in spiritual and economic terms. Compassion's messaging most obviously reflects this transition.

Today, most U.S. sponsors view formal schooling as the single most important factor in cementing future success for the children they support. The emphasis on schooling fits with what they know from humanitarian fund-raising campaigns and often reflects their personal or family histories where education was the stepping-stone into the American middle class. School report cards translate foreign lives into familiar terms by quantifying children's progress. Sponsors also pay close attention to statements where children express what they want to do when they grow up. Such statements imply both the expectation that sponsored children will one day become economically self-sufficient and, more subtly perhaps, that they do not actually work *as children*. Organizations reinforce this idea since school attendance is a prerequisite for participation in most programs and, based on the sponsor letters I have read, paid work is coded as "chores."[14]

Regardless of their personal circumstances, most sponsored children and their parents are likely familiar with appropriate aspirational models from the middle classes in their own countries, and these models may in fact constitute a key theme if they attend an evangelical or Pentecostal church.[15] Local sponsorship fieldworkers also encourage this kind of thinking. For example, when Compassion's Indonesian staff traveled the country to interview children for the "It Works" publicity campaign in the early 2000s, they made sure to ask each child what he or she wanted to be. The children were recorded as dutifully naming jobs that far surpassed their parents' subsistence labor—a pilot, a police officer, or a teacher.[16] In my conversations with sponsors, they nearly always remembered and discussed what the children aspired to professionally: familiar middle-class careers such as engineering or nursing. Not one of them recalled a child describing a future of contingent and flexible labor—in other words, a future that almost certainly reflected the adult lives around them.

In Ecatepec, I heard something similar. I set up the visit as any sponsor would by going through Compassion's U.S. office, which assigned me a guide named Sarai from their Mexico office. A middle-class evangelical woman about my age, Sarai had never been to the project, but she was affable and quickly seemed at ease. Our afternoon was spent with Reina and Edgar, a couple with four children under age ten, who lived in a three-room cement house. Reina worked part-time in a market stall and Edgar did odd jobs, such as selling street tacos on Sundays. When we arrived, Edgar passed out orangeade in plastic cups, and to my surprise 11 church volunteers crowded with us into the small space. Sarai was in her element. Her job is to leverage sponsor visits to frame Compassion's approach for the local volunteers and families. "You are good, brave, and hardworking so God is blessing you through Compassion," she told Reina, and then turned to everyone and said ebulliently: "Compassion is releasing children from poverty in *Jesus'* name!"

Knowing a bit about my research, Sarai asked whether the boys had sponsors. Reina and the children were not sure. A volunteer interjected to explain that only one of the sponsors actually writes. Sarai pressed the point: Did you keep the letters? No. Do you remember the sponsor's name? No. The country? No. Reina seemed pained and Sarai deftly changed her line of questioning. "Tell us what the boys want to be when they grow up." Reina looked relieved and answered promptly, knowing what was expected. The oldest wants to be a truck driver, the other two want to be doctors. The baby girl might be a teacher, she added. Earlier I had asked the young project director, who also grew up in the neighborhood, whether it causes tension with parents when Compassion encourages children to imagine going to university and securing middle-class jobs that would almost certainly mean leaving Ecatepec behind. At first she answered firmly, *of course* parents want that future for their children. Then she paused and said: "Look, in reality it doesn't matter. So few go to university. Basically none, I'll be honest." The significant gap between local realities and the imagined futures sponsorship promotes makes Reina's facility with the expected answers all the more remarkable.

Sponsorship's aspirational models can pose problems, which was likely in my mind when I spoke with the project director. In the late 1950s, when Church World Service surveyed Christian work in Korea (including CCF, WV, and Compassion), it commended their vocational training in theory but noted that in practice there were simply no jobs in post-war Korea for program "graduates." Forty years later, anthropologist Erica Bornstein showed how at WV Zimbabwe former sponsored children were set adrift with education and expectations within a society where middle-class dreams do not make middle-class realities.[17] U.S. sponsors are not entirely ignorant of these facts. Yet when they think in terms of Christian globalism, they are also imagining big-picture aspirations for universal justice, prosperity, and peace. It leads them to operate in multiple temporal modes during sponsorship, where they may acknowledge present-day realities even as they persist in heightened expectations for future success.

DROPPING OUT AND GETTING IN TOUCH

For years, organizational surveys have shown that "the termination aspect" is "the most disturbing thing that happens in the sponsorship adventure."[18] Children are meant to age out (or "graduate") at age 18 or 21, but in fact sponsorship often ends abruptly, usually when a child quits school or moves away. In earlier generations, especially when sponsorship funded emergency relief in orphanages, the children not infrequently died. Other times, parents located their children and took them home when they could. Mid-century organizations began to cushion the blow to sponsors by providing a "substitute" shortly (or immediately) after a termination. They created updated lists of available children so they could propose a new child's name, often in the same letter that bore bad news. Whenever possible, U.S. office staff called sponsors directly to tell them of the loss and name a substitute.

The sponsors I got to know had a range of complicated feelings about such transitions, especially when a "child" quit the program as a teenager or young adult. Here, there was a gap between American endorsements of individual agency and sponsorship's aspirations. Sponsors acknowledged the now-grown child's ability to choose her future—a microcosm of a respectful north-south partnership, rather than Western paternalism. But they also yearned for her to fulfill what from earlier letters they understood to be shared goals for schooling and professional success. The most perplexing situation concerned teens who became pregnant and (often) got married. Nearly every sponsor who told me this kind of story recalled feeling saddened, even betrayed, that the young woman had not lived up to her "potential" (she was *so smart*, they always said), while also acknowledging that they had no right to feel that way. And yet, generally speaking, sponsors were less bothered by "termination" than I had expected. They tended to see it as a natural progression. Very few said they kept praying for a child after he or she left the program, even among those Christians who prayed daily for absent others. Most concurred with organizational justifications for ending ongoing contact: to protect children from predatory foreign adults and to guard sponsors from further demands for money. A fair number also told me that the substitutions made intuitive sense, since they viewed their contributions as part of a broad system that circulates Christian love, which by definition exceeds the discrete individuals that comprise it.

Genevieve, a Catholic statistician in her mid-forties, discussed how she came to understand sponsorship in this light. Ten years ago, her children came home from school to find her crying over a letter. The girl they had sponsored for five years had suddenly left the program with no reported explanation. "It was really sad," she says, "I don't know why, but I just felt like we failed. Because you were trying to save the world and she didn't [get saved]." When a letter proposing a replacement arrived shortly after, to her own surprise she felt better. "I kind of reconciled that that doesn't mean it failed . . . Having another one right away makes you feel [you're] not giving up." Since then, Genevieve has sponsored three more children and has come to view this practice as part of a much larger global project. "My work is in population analysis. I don't think individual, I think population wise. That's why—here's the whole world, here's the neediest." Her hands outlined the circle of a globe in the air and she thrust her index finger toward a single point. "I know the money is going straight there so I know it's not being wasted." Yet the initial loss bruised her and she no longer writes letters as a result. "When I wrote letters at the beginning and I would explain who my family was and say [the girl was] part of the family and . . . maybe it was after she left and it was so hard. So what happens after that? You're no longer part of our family because you're no longer even in contact?" Genevieve paused, "It's like I don't know about creating that type of relationship when I don't think I can keep it up either on my part or because they won't be eligible for the program, dadada and that's it." The many possibilities that Genevieve leaves hanging in the air remind us how, although Tsing's friction between aspiration and achievement is normally taken to refer to the expectations of various stakeholders, a similar dynamic may color individual experience. In this case the seeming impossibility of reconciling aspiration and achievement has stopped Genevieve from writing, although she is not exactly sure why.

Genevieve's shock at the impossibility of sustainable intimacy arose largely from the fact that she was not initially aware that she would cease communicating with the child once the sponsorship ended. Many first-time sponsors assume the financial responsibility ends but the kin-like relation continues. Thus, termination "disturbs" for two reasons. First, it is often the clearest moment when an organization's controlling mediation is made evident to sponsors, which directly undermines the fiction of intimacy. Second, it disrupts the telos of aspiration and progress where small failures can be understood as temporary vicissitudes on the way to a child becoming economically stable and spiritually secure. Indeed, sponsors who emphasize intelligent prayer find small failures intensely productive, since they are something definite for which to petition God. However, when sponsorship ends, they are left with complete absence: they no longer know what to pray for and they can no longer track its results.

Rapid shifts may be on the horizon as social media creates openings for continued contact. The sponsors with whom I spoke were generally intrigued by the possibilities. Quoting one woman, "I used to fantasize that, you know, as an adult he'd find me, with the state of computers now." In my 91 interviews, seven people told me that a former sponsored child had contacted them through Facebook or by finding their details online. In nearly every case, this contact was a prelude to requests for more money, which most Americans willingly gave at first. Each former sponsored child asked for a specific amount to accomplish a precise end, such as paying for a semester of tuition or buying a piece of land. Perhaps they cannily understood from their own experience as sponsorees how these goal-oriented projects fit within the aspirational teleology of sponsorship. Half of the relationships deteriorated after requests continued. (Although not all of them did, as I show in the interlude that follows.)

Eleanor, a 62-year-old grandmother in rural New Hampshire, sponsored a Ugandan girl named Angelus for many years. She and her husband even accompanied their evangelical church's short-term mission to Rwanda in 2011 and added a visit to Angelus's village. "She was always like another daughter to me," Eleanor told me, using kinship language that few other sponsors did. A year after the visit, Angelus went to Kigali to live with her mother and Compassion offered Eleanor a substitute. She contacted the organization, distraught. When Compassion's staff could not tell her Angelus's whereabouts, Eleanor got in touch with a Ugandan woman with ties to her church. The woman actually managed to find the girl, whose drug-addicted mother had since left town. Angelus was in her mid-teens, living on and off the streets with a cousin.

Years before, Angelus had written that she aspired to be a nurse, just like Eleanor. Whether she ever seriously imagined such a future is an open question; as noted, nursing is the kind of middle-class profession that sponsorship staff and sponsors applaud and that children often include in their letters. Nevertheless, like most sponsors, Eleanor took it at face value and was now determined to help her achieve this goal. She wired money to the Ugandan woman, who enrolled Angelus in a private evangelical boarding school with a nursing program. Then things went downhill quickly. Angelus repeatedly broke the school's strict rules. She was rowdy. She had boys in her room. The other students' sheltered lives differed markedly from her own. After consulting with Eleanor, the headmaster finally expelled her. Eleanor recalled that the headmaster said, "She had this attitude that because she had these people here [in the U.S.] she thought she was better than all the other kids." Angelus was back on her own, but she emailed constantly, begging for more money and to be given another chance. Eleanor described it:

> I just said, you know, at this point we can't—we can't send you any more money and, you know, we still love you, we'll always care about you but you don't get your trust back by just saying you're sorry. It takes time to earn trust back again and—it was very hard to let her go . . . and I said to [my husband] we have no idea what God is doing with her and what seeds were planted and how our sponsorship all those years, you know, what the final outcome's going to be.

Angelus's emails finally stopped. When I met Eleanor, it had been two years since they were in touch. I asked if Angelus would ever be able to earn back her trust, given the distance that separates them. She responded after a long pause:

> Yeah, I don't know. I just [pause] I don't know . . . Because I mean I would never give up on my own child. You know, she was sort of like another daughter to me but it's like we just felt like, well, we have to give her—put her into God's hands because we can't—it's just too far away . . . If she was closer to, you know, if there wasn't this big (distance) gap I probably would have worked harder.

We can only speculate about Angelus's interpretation of events; she may have seen the relationship as one of patronage where rich kin funnel money to their poorer relatives, which gave her status at the boarding school as she bragged to her peers. For Eleanor, this kin-like relationship entailed certain aspirations for a future like her own (as a nurse) and then a "tough love" approach where a wayward child must "earn trust back." Global distance necessarily causes breaks in trust and makes it nearly impossible for Angelus to earn it back—both because the concept is likely foreign to her (based on her baldly honest begging emails) and because she is not in New Hampshire to engage in the everyday behavior that for Eleanor is proof of real change.[19]

As I have noted elsewhere about trips to the Holy Land, most U.S. Christians view time as "meaningfully-forward moving" as Christian souls move toward heaven and history moves toward its ultimate end.[20] In Christian sponsorship, this modality is oriented toward "near future" results, rather than the immediate present of emergency relief work (although organizations that use sponsorship may engage it too) and the more distant future of prophecy (which even Compassion assiduously avoids).[21] When sponsors defer their hopes, they, too, picture a near future when a young life is turned around. Evangelicals, like Eleanor, often signal this idea with aphorisms about planting seeds. While the vocabulary is different, I found similar patterns among Catholics and mainline Protestants. In each case, it is after contact is severed that sponsorship is most clearly defined as a space of emergent possibilities that exceed human knowing. Sponsors entrust the near future to God's hands, rather than their own.[22] In Eleanor's case, reiterating her constant trust in the absent/present Deity occurs just as she loses trust in Angelus, the all too fallible absent/present human being. Extrapolating a bit further, anthropomorphizing God in kin-like terms—loving father or close friend—may assuage her regret or guilt as she extricates herself from bonds she once imagined as kin-like. Now shorn of material aid, the kin-like relation becomes purely metaphysical: sponsor and child are linked in God's global "family."

In other cases, ongoing contact was very positive, albeit bittersweet. John, who lives in a village outside of Hyderabad, India, found his former sponsor Nancy, who lives in Kansas City, on Facebook a couple years after he completed Unbound's program. For Nancy, this communication was a welcome surprise, although now she knows "it's not exactly a happy ending and he's struggling still. He has a lot of plans in his mind that he wants to do . . . He said that even with education, people cannot get jobs." John had excelled in school and he had eventually earned an MBA. But without connections, he wrote to Nancy, he could not secure a government post. Then the older brother who headed his mother's household fell sick and John returned to his natal village, where he remains without steady employment or the means to marry. A college education is no match for systemic corruption, chronic underemployment, and cultural expectations of family care. Nevertheless, Nancy says that both she and John retain hope as Christians, which they discuss in their correspondence: "He does have faith in God. I remind him of that. God is taking care of you. God will not leave you. Even in his last letter he spoke of that [and] I think that he'll be hopefully fine in the long run but right now it's a time [of] hardship."

CALCULATING SUCCESS: THE INTIMACY OF AUDITS

"Have you ever tried to chart the course of a single prayer?" asked Armin Gesswein, one of Billy Graham's associate evangelists, in a 1964 issue of *World Vision Magazine*. "Its range? Its reach? Its journey? . . . Its answer? . . . Thrilling thought—every true prayer is alive . . . If our eyes could be opened to see behind the veil of sense and space and sight, I believe we would see the whole universe shot through and through with prayer action."[23] Gesswein was right: it is a thrilling thought. But in practical terms, how does one follow a prayer overseas? How does one track the money that accompanies it? In global projects, the gap between here and there, between the immediate and the projected, always—necessarily—remains.

Pioneering sociologist Georg Simmel's work on capitalism did not explicitly engage globalism, but it did address the issue of verification and trust. His interest lay in how trust changed when capitalism created a credit-based system among attenuated networks of (often global) investors. Whereas "weak inductive reasoning" could account for more local forms of expectation (for example, in a barter system), Simmel viewed the trust required to convince someone to invest money as a quasi-religious type of faith. According to Simmel, "No matter how exactly and intellectually grounded [social forms of confidence] may appear to be, there may yet be some additional affective, even mystical, 'faith' of man in man . . . which [perhaps] goes back to the metaphysical sense of our relationships." Simmel never elaborated on this sense, and later scholars largely ignored this aspect of his work.[24] For our purposes, however, it raises the possibility that trust creation may include empirical and metaphysical factors at once. Along these lines, sponsorship tacks back and forth between two seemingly mutually exclusive modes of "audit"—the positivist/capitalist and the metaphysical/Christian.

Sponsorship grew into a permanent form of fund-raising after the Second World War, during the rise of "audit culture." The term refers to how modern capitalism compensates for the loss of direct relationships in small-scale economies by creating an ideal of absolute trust through transparency and immediacy of information.[25] Audit culture operates on an immense scale—and is thus crucial in global corporations—by investing the power of oversight in outside bodies and standardized financial reports. Clarke, Pierce, and Swanson initially had difficult relationships with audit culture. Part of the issue lay in how they viewed religious credentials as moral currency. For example, the National Information Bureau (NIB) repeatedly asked CCF to provide an operating budget in the 1940s. In fact, there were *no* reports about domestic or foreign spending. "A budget would be, more or less, an artificial thing,"

Clarke wrote back rather blithely in 1947. Anyway, he was a certified pastor, he repeated, and his partners in Asia were Christian missionaries.[26] As evangelical crusade preachers, Pierce and Swanson even more clearly saw themselves as divinely inspired apostles of God's projects on earth.

God's guidance and protection were not sufficient for the NIB and other bodies tasked with policing this new culture of corporate ethics. Audit culture expressly eliminates the relationship between humans and God as a sufficient guarantor of trustworthiness. (As a result, some Christian humanitarians still refuse to submit audits as an act of religious formation.)[27] Whatever sponsorship organizations initially felt about audits, they recognized that outside verification usefully compensated for the fact that they lacked the traditional backing of denominational mission boards. They began to prepare more significant audits in the 1950s, before fully adopting secular modes of financial accountability in the late 1960s—a negotiated process of professionalization that sociologists have tracked in many post-war Christian organizations.[28] In part, the push came from within as they grew beyond their often overbearing and idiosyncratic pastor-founders. Clarke and Pierce were forcibly retired in 1964 and 1967, respectively. Swanson died in 1965.[29] In the same period, they opted to receive varying amounts of government support (especially WV), which required new forms of governance.[30] Outside pressure also continued to build. In 1973, the Government Accounting Office undertook a series of audits of U.S. child-related charities in Asia and Africa, which led to "painful and most embarrassing" Senate hearings. Congressional bills demanded financial transparency of charities that solicited by mail and annual IRS-approved disclosure statements from public charities.[31] A 1977 media campaign pressured charities to make their accounts public. World Vision called it an oppressive "climate of suspicion and appearance of mismanagement."[32]

CCF embraced secular audit culture, while WV tried to deflect criticism without completely capitulating by co-founding the Evangelical Council for Financial Accountability in 1979, which collaborated with the NIB and Council of Better Business Bureaus.[33] By the early 1980s, all the sponsorship organizations I studied emphasized financial audits (Compassion laid it on thick, suddenly including in their publicity materials sponsors' statements such as, "I am very impressed by your financial statements!").[34] Today, it is nearly impossible to imagine Clarke's initial refusal to set a budget. Each organization features an "accountability" section prominently on its website homepage and displays credentials from a spate of institutions such as Charity Navigator and the Charities Review Council. Since the late 1980s, they have also publicized sponsor trips to their overseas projects as proof of their credibility, since they imply the possibility of personally evaluating the work.[35] That is why these trips so often feature in sponsorship media, although, according to staff estimates, fewer than 1% of sponsors actually participate.

Yet time and again, scholarship shows that economic trust is not based on informational flows alone—whether audit reports or detailed descriptions of trips to the field. Trust may be spirit-filled and contingent, rather than absolute. As WV president Robert Seiple put it in an address to sponsors in 1989, "When we have airtight budgets and perfect management strategies we are sanctimonious and safe . . . We suppress legitimate individual fears and doubts."[36] Of course, WV relied heavily on budgets in 1989—and sponsors demanded it. But his caution reflects the idea that a Christian should always doubt any promise of "airtight" or "perfect" accounting because these are always *human* forms of transparency. Retaining a certain distrust of purely human actions allows Christians to nurture a sense of deeper trust in God as ultimate overseer.

One way that sponsors and the organizations they support collaborate on spiritual modes of trust is through a dense network of mutual prayers. Since the 1950s, evangelical organizations have revealed (certain) administrative difficulties or challenges to their sponsors in order to ask for intercessory prayers. World Vision asked sponsors to pray for its office staff when they were overworked; for a new administrative department as it expanded; for a field office that was trying to discern who to hire. "We believe that our own staff [has] had the Lord working in their hearts, thanks to your prayers," it told its sponsors.[37] Profiles printed in *WV* magazine highlighted staff members who were everyday Americans trying to follow God—in short, people like sponsors themselves. In these profiles, female office employees were especially likely to describe their jobs as a vocation and their efforts as a small part of God's monumental work.[38] Prayer and vocation also formed an integrated part of corporate culture in overseas field offices, which sponsors knew were staffed by Christian "nationals" in each country.[39] This point is important because historical studies often focus on larger-than-life founders, like Bob Pierce. In fact, Christian credibility in these organizations was built by moving beyond one individual alone. It was the combined efforts of Christians at every level of the bureaucratic machine—from the founder down to the secretaries—that made it seem a trustworthy system. Everyone checked in with God and checked up on each other.

These portrayals of a U.S. staff that mirrored its Christian clientele were largely accurate. Statistically speaking, most sponsors have been middle-class white women who are active Christians. So were the secretarial staff who, according to CCF estimates in the late 1960s, comprised fully 90% of their office employees.[40] Thus, the mechanisms for creating intimacy in sponsorship—the personal "access points" in the global system[41]—brought together (mainly female) sponsors with (mainly female) employees who communicated and prayed with them. Today, the sponsorship organizations I profiled still keep open telephone lines for donor calls. I spent a couple of days listening to the calls and speaking with the (mainly female) telephone attendants at Compassion and ChildFund. Most sponsors called about basic administrative issues, but some did ask to pray over the phone. It occurred more often at Compassion than at ChildFund, though it was notable that such requests continued at the latter at all, since it had dropped the word "Christian" from its name in 2009. According to ChildFund call center operators, enough of their team was Christian that they could deal with prayer requests informally; those attendants who did not feel comfortable praying would signal their Christian colleagues in adjoining cubicles and pass the call through.

At Compassion, World Vision, and Unbound, staff members also circulate sponsors' prayer requests in weekly or daily memos—along with their own— and address them collectively in chapel services and small groups. At World Vision, a day is set aside each year during which its staff members across the world devote themselves to prayer; in the preceding weeks, sponsors are encouraged to submit their prayer requests for inclusion.[42] Unbound's Prayer Partners' emails, which go out weekly to nearly 7,500 sponsors, always end with a link to submit a prayer request. Dora Tiznado, in Sponsor Services, fields the 40 or so daily requests (or intentions, in Catholic terminology) from emails and the call center log sheets (figure 6.2). Nearly all of them come from women, and she estimates that 90% concern personal issues. She separates the prayers into three groups: those on a one-time basis, those marked "daily" that stay on the rolls for many weeks, and those on behalf of sponsors who have recently died (a typically Catholic concern that is not reflected at Compassion or WV). Dora and her team circulate the lists—which often run about six pages—over email and they pray every morning and noon in the chapel, calling other staff members to join them by ringing a small bell as they walk through the office. Sponsors tell Dora that the prayers are integral to their ability to continue giving. She told me, "Pretty typically they say because you are praying for our family it means we're able to support our sponsored child. Because you're helping us resolve our financial or health issue." Compassion's staff let me look through the emails that sponsors sometimes send after praying with their call center attendants. These messages also credit the prayers with improving a variety of difficult circumstances—surviving cancer, seeking full-time employment, or grieving a death.[43]

Staff members also pray for the needs of the corporation. While I was at Compassion, my main host—an administrative assistant—was part of a prayer team of female employees who gathered at lunch to pray for the successful

FIG 6.2. Dora Tiznado sorting through prayers in her cubicle at Unbound's headquarters, Kansas City, Missouri, August 2015. Photo by the author. Used by permission of Dora Tiznado.

completion of TCPT (Transforming Core Processes with Technology), which was an effort to streamline and improve Compassion's computer system. None of the women was directly involved with the technical or managerial aspects of this change. Instead, like sponsors themselves, the (mainly female, mainly low-level) employees are understood to play a vital role in the corporation by contributing unpaid prayer work to the paid work of (mainly male) employees. Over a number of decades, then, the Christian organizations I studied have nurtured the view that organizations benefit from prayers within and without the corporate structure—a point that is not lost on sponsors.

As a result of these interlocking strategies of faithful and financial accounting, nearly every sponsor I interviewed told me that Christian organizations are the most trustworthy. Even liberal Christians who refused the implication that they did sponsorship for any religious or spiritual reason said the same thing, although they were usually hard-pressed to express exactly why ("I just know the money will go where they say it will go!" one woman finally told me with some exasperation). The genius of Christian forms of trust making is that they subtly exceed the usual consumer-producer relationship. This idea became clearest to me when I transferred through the Houston airport not long ago and noticed World Vision prayer cards wedged into the plastic frames around wall advertisements in the terminal. Sponsorship itself was only mentioned in the fine print; the purpose of the cards was to recruit people to pray for the needs of a foreign child by name. Each one featured a child's name, photo, and a list of basic needs. Prayers offered up by sponsors or even non-sponsors (hence the cards in the airport) contribute to a dense "universe shot through and through with prayer action," to quote Armin Gesswein at the start of this section. This prayer structure admits the fallibility of an organization's human managers and therefore implies its reliance on a higher power. [44] In this sense, power relations are seemingly reversed: men at the top of the corporate structure are dependent on the people "below" who keep a line open to God.

AESTHETICS OF AUDIT: SHOWING GIFTS AND SMILES

A Christian organization inculcates trust at a general level, but sponsors may still harbor doubts about the particular benefits to the child they support. In this respect, photographs constitute a key aesthetic form of audit. In the 1950s, sponsorship organizations began to require their overseas affiliates to supply a yearly portrait of each child for sponsors. From the mid-1950s, they also began to require photographic verification each time the sponsor sent a gift or extra money overseas. "A picture is to be taken of the child showing him with the article purchased," instructed WV's Orphanage Manual in 1960. "The amount of the gift should be indicated at the upper right-hand corner . . . Items which were received should be mentioned in the letter."[45] The resulting letters had all the charm of a shopping list. "I am very much thankful to you," wrote Kim Jung Hi to her sponsor in 1959. "The package contained shoes, cookies, one-piece-dress, skirt, doll, hairpins, hand-bag, socks, necklace, picture-book, toys, shirt, pants and crayon. I am sending you a picture of me which was taken with the gifts from you and putting on the clothes." Writing to Cecelia Costello in 1963, Jun Ya even amended a previous letter: "I am very sorry that I missed to tell you that I have received one box of Kleenex. Please don't worry about it."[46]

Initially, I thought the posed photos and item lists would grate on sponsors since they disrupted the feel of kin-like relations. But sponsors repeatedly told me the opposite was true: they wanted verification of what was received. Their responses helped clarify for me a paradox of sponsorship letters: though sponsors invariably state that the purpose of exchanging letters is to benefit the child, they insist on receiving letters whether or not they write. Even among evangelicals—who put the most emphasis on writing as a form of Christian encouragement—sponsors have only ever sent one letter for every three they have received. Today, 40% of sponsors, or more, never write at all. In Compassion's surveys, 61–64% of sponsors reported writing letters. At Unbound, it was 50–70% (which their partners in the field thought was significantly too high).[47] In short, although sponsors say, and undoubtedly believe, that the purpose of letters and photos is to create kin-like relations and "encouragement" for the child, in reality they prize them as, or more, highly as a mechanism for tracking outcomes—in essence, as a form of "audit."

At some point during our conversations, nearly every sponsor spread out years' worth of photos in front of us. Most keep the older ones filed away and the newest ones posted as "power objects for warding off thoughtlessness."[48] Sponsored children, like all distant global objects, can too easily be forgotten. "The photo keeps that connection," a Catholic sponsor named Rose told me as she showed me the child she sponsors in Uganda, named Kalecki. "I see it and I think oh wow, how much you've grown! What a beautiful young lady." She told me something else I heard often: when she receives a photo in the mail, her eyes go to a *punctum*—the girl's face—which seems to reveal "a kind of subtle *beyond*" that stokes affective desire.[49] Many U.S. sponsors still expect that there is some correspondence between exterior and interior states, as discussed in chapter 3. They look at children's faces to discern imagined futures and feel more assured of desired outcomes. Rose pulls out a photo where Kalecki, perhaps ten years old, is smiling broadly. "Sometimes I'll say, oh she looks so sad! And at other times she looks very happy. I like certain pictures," she says. Rose has at times written expressly to encourage Kalecki to smile for photos. "Yes, I look for the smile very much . . . Boy, that makes you feel good that she's really going to go somewhere."

Looking for smiles has a history. By the late nineteenth century, it had become axiomatic for Americans that poor foreign children were joyless.[50] World War I relief work added the scientific heft of emerging child psychology, which argued that healthy children required happy, American-style play.[51] In the 1950s, the foreign child "who could not smile" became an iconic genre of fund-raising photography. *Life* magazine popularized the most famous story of this type in a 1951 piece titled "The Little Boy Who Wouldn't Smile" about Kang Koo Ri who lived at a CCF orphanage in Korea. Koo Ri became famous when Church World Service, the charitable arm of the National Council of Churches, featured his story in fund-raising slideshows throughout the United States.[52] Across the different Christian markets to which sponsorship appealed, unsmiling children were doubly meaningful since they seemed to indicate material want and spiritual brokenness. After seeing Koo Ri's unsmiling photo in *Life*, an elderly Christian widow in Los Angeles named Mrs. Cordelle Lefer was so "haunted" that, as she later told the magazine's reporter, "I got down on my knees and prayed and was told to adopt him." *Life* printed a follow-up that showed Lefer with her new son who was now grinning at an amusement park.[53]

The presumed relation between exterior and interior states (or, physiognomy and soul) required narrative and imaginative work. Mid-century sponsorship organizations coached their Asian orphanage directors to make sure that they described each child's personality for sponsors such that it matched the random snapshot they supplied. "Look at the photo of the child," CCF headquarters wrote in 1954, "and be sure your description is not made ludicrous by the look or expression on the child's face. Example: Do not say 'happy, good-natured child' when the look is a bitter, scowling one."[54] In other words, orphanage directors were told to study the photo—*not the child himself*—to discern personal characteristics. "The face of the child will tell a great deal if it is observed even briefly," wrote Clarke, "Shy with strangers," "a bit bashful," "somewhat nervous as yet" might be some adjectives that apply [to an unsmiling photo] . . . You will think of others as the face is studied."[55]

On the receiving end, sponsors studied the children's faces too. A serious photo could be a call to action, assuming it was one of the first received, and subsequent photos could seem to prove the effectiveness of the work. According to a couple sponsoring with Compassion in 1966, "there are no words that can adequately describe the overflowing joy and blessing of our hearts as we have seen him grow from the sad, disillusioned, suffering little face of his first snapshot . . . into a happy face radiant with smile and accompanied by a letter of testimony of his salvation—full of love for his Lord and his sponsors."[56] Children's smiles may seem to reveal a changed present but, moreover, as Rose intimated above, they speak volumes about the possible futures sponsors shepherd into being. Smiles seem to foreshadow the happy, productive, Christian adult the child will become, long after sponsors can no longer follow his trajectory through letters and reports. Because organizations understand the value of smiles, they have tried repeatedly (though often unsuccessfully) to impress upon their fieldworkers that children should smile broadly in the snapshots they were required to send overseas. Jun Ya's photo in the previous chapter (figure 5.2) was the ideal; a happy smile and jaunty wave as she clutched her sponsor's gift.[57]

Today, organizations are more apt to clarify why children do not smile— taking the snapshots is hectic, it is culturally foreign, it is their first portrait photo—but many of the old assumptions remain. Although Compassion's call center does not receive many calls about photos, when it does it almost invariably concerns a frowning face.[58] Such concerns echo in the comments that follow articles on Compassion's website, such as one that employee Becky Giovagnoni posted in 2008. Titled "Proof," it shows a series of yearly photos of Youvens, the boy she sponsors in Haiti. His face is serious each time, until the last one where he smiles broadly next to a birthday gift from Becky. The short text begins by suggesting that initially he did not smile because of his extreme poverty and ends with "That smile is all the proof I need that my sponsorship makes a difference." The context could imply the difference is solely material. But the comments generated over nine years show that sponsors immediately understood smiling as a sign of Christian love, change, and recognition. A small sample includes:

Debbie, April 2, 2008
Thanks for sharing Becky! I have had the exact same experience with my Selamawit from Ethiopia. When a picture comes that finally shows a beautiful smile on your sponsored child's face you know it is the illumination of love!

Vicki Small, April 2, 2008
The first two pictures that I got of my first girl in DR also were very serious . . . Now, I'm praying that God will protect her AND grab her heart, which I'm not at all sure He's done, yet. And I'm really happy for you, that you get to see that change in Youven!

Kelly @ Love Well, April 2, 2008
Wow. Now *that's* a testimony of God's grace and love.

Kathy, December 30, 2011
I so wondered why there were no smiles and it gives me extra hope that my sponsored child will be helped on the inside as well as the outside!!

Mike, January 8, 2017
I too am concerned about my child from Brazil. Her picture was not a happy time for her . . . [I saw] that [she] was not smiling. It's like Jesus spoke to me and said, "Mike she is your child to love and care for, she is the one I chose before the foundation of the world for you and your family." I know someday she will be smiling when she can understand what Jesus did for her.[59]

Over the years, I have collected many hours of tape recording the moment when sponsors spread out their photos before me. A quarter of the Catholics and mainline Protestants with whom I spoke pointed out smiles as proof of happiness and progress. Fully half of the evangelical sponsors did so too, and they framed it in more clearly spiritual terms, like the comments on Compassion's blog. In about a third of my interviews, sponsors also pointed

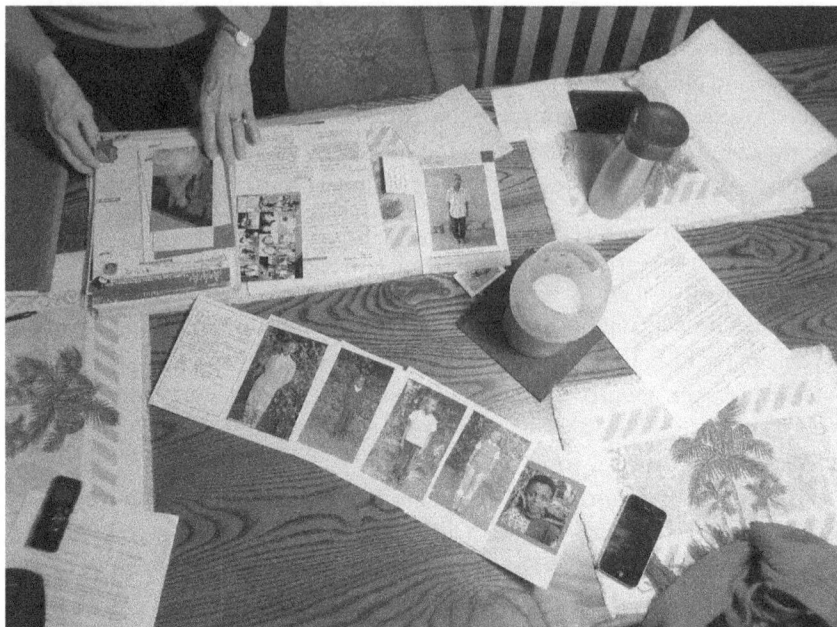

FIG 6.3. June in Westfield, Massachusetts, with photos of Firomsa in Ethiopia, spread out on her table to show his progress. Firomsa had recently and abruptly left Compassion's program. As we looked at the photos, June said, "His smile gave me the feeling that he was progressing quite well, although his academics were not. But I have to think that maybe he learned something in his [Compassion] schooling that . . . he had been exposed to the [Christian] Truth."

out physical growth. Putting photos next to each other, they created a time-lapse effect that enabled them to verify how a child gained weight, got taller and leaner (figure 6.3). Indeed, the physiological fact that children exhibit change much more rapidly than adults casts them as "paradigmatic embodi-ers of change" who are "in a constant and heightened state of becoming" that requires the moral attention of caring adults.[60] Although sponsors prefer photos in this regard, letters can serve the same purpose. Organizations attach the original letter to the translation as a form of audit—the child really wrote this—but sponsors also value the Amharic, Hindi, or Spanish script itself because they treat even what they cannot read as signs of a child's growing maturity. The printing becomes smaller and less wobbly. The child masters cursive. The exercise of placing photos and letters next to each other is often enormously satisfying for sponsors; it concretizes aspirations and seems to catalogue progress. As Rose said with the photos of Kalecki spread before us on the kitchen table, "Boy, that makes you feel good that she's really going to go somewhere."

COMPASSION EXPERIENCE: PERFORMATIVE TECHNIQUES
IN AN ASPIRATIONAL MODE

It was grey and cold—not how I pictured San Jose, California, in mid-May—when I arrived for my 9 am shift. In front of me was a massive 18-wheel truck parked in Westgate church's suburban parking lot. That weekend, five thousand people were expected to come and "experience" poverty through Compassion's multisensory stories of two children—Kiwi in the Philippines and Jey in Kenya. It is just the kind of participatory technique that lends itself so well to Christian globalism; popular metaphors of "accompanying" or "walking with" the poor become a felt experience within U.S. bodies as visitors literally walk through the site.[61]

Chelsea immediately came over and shook my hand warmly. As manager, she traveled with the truck and organized each new group of church volunteers into an efficient team for the weekend. She was in her late twenties, short like me, wearing the Compassion Experience t-shirt and yoga pants. We watched as the truck's sides were folded down. It was now three times wider than a regular 18-wheeler, and wooden walls were clicked into place to create rooms. Chelsea handed me a stack of photos and props. My job was to use the photos to recreate the scene in each room. A broken rattan chair placed just so. A woven rice bag slung over it just like that. Kiwi is a real person and she donated some of these objects. The beer bottles I artfully arranged in a corner to mimic their having been left by a drunk were, in fact, from Kiwi's father, who got sober when he found Jesus. Chelsea pointed to the garbage I was strewing about. "That's authentic. The team actually brought it back," she said, and I could see she was right; I recognized the brands from traveling in the Philippines a few years before.

Other humanitarian organizations have also utilized immersion experiences, ranging from a U.S. prison cell to a refugee camp. Antecedents lie more than a century earlier, for example in the recreations associated with "Oriental teas" (chapter 3). At the turn of the twentieth century, Anglo-Protestant mission societies took their immersive exhibits on the road. The World in Boston—where one could walk through elaborate recreations of mission stations staffed by costumed volunteers—filled eight freight cars in what may have been the largest mobile missionary collection in U.S. history.[62] Compassion's current endeavor is a partnership with Brewco Marketing Group, a Kentucky-based specialist in immersive events that cut its teeth working for NASCAR. In 2015, the Compassion truck at Westgate was one of four touring the United States, with two more in the works. Each one told the story of a child from a different location where Compassion works. The campaign was proving a major success: 50,000 Americans visited the trucks that year, netting about 7,500 sponsorships on site.[63]

The next day started early. I was in charge of conducting Compassion's entrance survey and cueing up the audio headsets that people wear as they walk through. Over the next months, having volunteered in four sites, I found that most people told me they had learned of the event on Facebook. Families made up the bulk of visitors, along with homeschooling groups. Most people self-defined broadly as evangelical Christians, but I also met hundreds of Catholics, including Catholic school groups. When I asked them about Compassion's evangelicalism, they were unperturbed or had mistakenly believed that when it said "Christian" it meant Roman Catholic. In another context, at Unbound's offices, I encountered the same fluidity: a confirmation class in Pennsylvania that raised money through a WV Planned Famine and then sent the funds to Unbound; a longtime Unbound sponsor who ran a Compassion Sunday in his parish after reading its publicity materials and concluding it was definitely a Catholic organization.[64] At the Experience, the youthful Brewco staff members also brushed aside differences. If families already sponsored through Unbound, for example, they brightly declared that it was all the same, as long as people in need were helped. In this case at least, theological fissures only seemed intractable to an academic.

During my breaks, I walked through with the visitors. The rooms I had set up felt transformed. They were dark, closed, and stuffy. The headphones blocked out everything except the track that played background noises of the villages or slums in which we were supposed to stand, with a child's voice narrating events. In Kiwi's story, we stood in her nipa hut in Bocol and then in the Manila slum housing where her family relocated. In Jey's story, we began in Nairobi's slums and then moved to a dank jail cell. Discussing an analogous "refugee camp" run by Médecins Sans Frontières (MSF) in New York City, anthropologist Peter Redfield identifies a tension between *zoë* (a state of being common to all animals) and *bios* (elaborated human experience). He argues that although MSF would like to privilege the human dignity that comes with *bios*, the camp was impactful precisely because it strips existence to *zoë*: here is a hole where people defecate; here is a tent that shelters them.[65] By contrast, the Compassion Experience elaborately reconstructed *bios* through personal narrative. If anything, it shared the ethos of an Oprah Winfrey makeover, with its cathartic tales of personal triumph in which the dispersal of material goods (a new car! a complete wardrobe! a home renovation!) galvanizes better lives. If those stories can be said to echo evangelical conversion narratives by dint of their disclosing testimonies and dramatic renewals,[66] then the reverse is true as well: Compassion's evangelical stories echo an American makeover where coming to God brings financial stability and family happiness. In fact, the culmination of both Kiwi's and Jey's stories was that they immigrate to the United States as adults, which securely binds Americanness to evangelicalness in the triumph over poverty and despair. These endings belied Compassion's usual message, which strongly discourages sponsors from expecting that the child might one day immigrate.

At a basic level, the Experience stories narrated a material and spiritual transformation from dark to light, which took on literal sensory dimensions. The story physically looped round, bringing visitors back to the same sites, now transformed. In the first room, Kiwi's nipa hut was miserable and dark; in the last room, the same hut was clean and brightly lit with family photos on the walls. Visitors ended by walking through a final curtain into a light-filled tent with smiling volunteers and Compassion packets lining the walls. Each one showed the face of a child who needed a sponsor. It felt reminiscent of a decision tent at an evangelical crusade. Walking through the Experience clarified God's actions by condensing a whole life into a series of moral events through which one could track progress over time; it was a multisensory equivalent of what sponsors evoked when they lined up a child's photos chronologically on the kitchen table.

The groups I accompanied often commented on how small and close the first rooms felt; one feels suffocated and trapped, a man told me. The atmosphere was deeply affecting. In one story, the Ugandan protagonist contracted malaria as a child, which caused her to go deaf. Suddenly the audio went silent ("deafening silence" in the true sense). It took my breath away and I choked back tears. Another time, a middle-aged woman and I sat down in the middle of the Experience and turned off our headsets because she was sobbing, recalling how the child she had sponsored years ago suddenly left the program. Could the girl's abusive father have *killed* her? she asked. I could only murmur something sad and indefinite. The Experience was remarkably effective at producing a visceral sense of the hopelessness that Compassion portrays as the main by-product of poverty. Visitors were often visibly relieved when we stepped into the brightly lit space of the reproduction Compassion center where the child first encountered sponsorship; it was double the size of the first rooms and the first optimistic turning point in each story. I began to turn off my headset as we entered: people sometimes breathed audible sighs of relief.

The Experience links the visual images of racialized unity-in-diversity discussed in chapter 4 with the immersive impersonations of "heathens" in chapter 2 and "famine orphans" in chapter 3. As anthropologist Laurie Denyer Willis has recently noted in her work on social discrimination in Rio de Janeiro, "race, constructed and experienced in infinite ways, is at least partly linked to the sensorial constructions of people and places . . . This becomes obvious when we consider that whiteness in Rio is almost always rendered as sensorially neutral or blank."[67] Likewise, foreign poverty (often, though not always, racialized as brown or black) has a particular feel, taste, smell, and sound for Americans. These sensory assumptions may shift over time; the feel of a loose silk sari against one's skin evoked spiritual poverty for nineteenth-century women putting on Oriental teas, and it has lost its ability to do so today. On the other hand, cacophonies of human-made noise (chapter 7) and the sight or smell of garbage produce abiding sensations of racialized poverty. Importantly, as Willis notes, prosperity (often, though not always, racialized as white) is "neutral or blank." Thus, it makes sense to middle-class U.S. sponsors, including non-white ones, that they might be able to *feel* what they imagine to be foreign poverty at the Compassion Experience. At no time do they walk through recreations or abstractions of their own lives, which therefore remain the "blank" sensory norm.

The Experience is also a microcosm of the relationship between immensity and particularity that undergirds Christian globalism. Visitors encountered the particular story of a child, but were then thrust into the tent filled with photo packets and a video on loop that talked about Bruce Wydick's study—"There is statistical evidence that Compassion *works*." It showed happy kindergarteners as the narrator promised that in Compassion projects "one child accepts Christ every four minutes." Many visitors seemed to feel a twinge of the overload that accompanies big numbers (chapter 2). I watched their faces as they emerged from the truck and hovered on the steps leading down into the tent (eyebrows raised, mouth forming a small "ohhh" as they saw the rows of packets). Some were motivated by the scene. Others were concerned. "It's so hard—there are so *many* of them," they often said. It evoked something fundamental about the place in which we found ourselves: how does one make sense of so many poor children staring down from around the room? When a child was chosen, my job was to replace the packet with another from the boxes stored out of sight under a table. "There are *more*?" one woman asked as she clutched the packet she had chosen and I restocked another. "I was so happy to see that hole," she said, "It was like, yeah, we're doing it! We're going to finish." She smiled ruefully.

ACCOUNTING FOR GLOBAL INJUSTICE

When sponsors pick up a child packet and imagine trajectories of individual success, they do so within a context in which humanitarian organizations and media outlets often pitch global connections in the superlative of emergency relief and disaster news. As a result, when sponsors picture the world from a god's eye view, they are often struck by its problems. Why do millions suffer? Christian globalism amplifies the problems of theodicy: sponsors credit a unitary God as the only certain power in the world, yet they refuse the idea that their God is capable of allowing such massive injustice. This type of thinking scales up the gaps and irresolution that mark sponsorship's 1:1 relations, as when Eleanor put Angelus "in God's hands" or when the Compassion Experience visitor broke down in tears recalling a child who abruptly left the program. To some degree, this unknowingness—both about the long-term trajectory of a child's life and the reasons for poverty—drives a desire for audits that track incremental outcomes. Yet, it also requires other ways of accounting for the state of the world.

When I spoke with sponsors, I always worded my questions about global injustice in personal terms: Why is [name of sponsored child] poor? Why aren't you? Does God have anything to do with it? I wanted to move theoria into the intersubjective realm. Like the Compassion Experience tent with its hundreds of photos on the walls, these questions were weighty because sponsors understood the metonymic quality of the comparison between themselves and the child: it was a small slice of a global problem multiplied countless times. Sometimes they joked, "Whoa, you're mean! How can I answer *that*?" Or, "So now you hit me with the million-dollar question!" But then they knuckled down and thought it through with me. Jesus said the poor would always be among us, they acknowledged. The question was, *why*?

Their responses were highly varied and often knowledgeable: some talked about how poverty was caused by the lack of arable land or a stable middle class, others mentioned the need for adequate education and medical care. But at some point, nearly all of them also offered a well-established Christian response: human beings make choices, are greedy, and do bad things as a result. Catholics called this free will, mainline Protestants often referred to human tendencies, and evangelicals were most likely to discuss inherent sinfulness. By a wide margin, the majority of sponsors blamed corrupt elites or government officials in the child's country for diverting aid money and resources for personal gain; this characterization persisted regardless of any given country's stability or social policies.[68] The view is attractive, first, because it associates foreign "elites" with political corruption, rather than the Christian NGOs that Americans support. No sponsor with whom I spoke noted that sponsorship organizations actually work closely with foreign governments; at different times, sponsorship has therefore effectively propped up failing states and dictatorial regimes by privatizing social services, while massive military spending continued unabated.[69] Blaming corrupt foreign elites also allows Americans to transfer culpability for poverty away from the child and his family, who are always cast as deserving and hardworking—a view that sponsorship organizations promote. By contrast, sponsors on the conservative side of the spectrum often told me that U.S. poverty had a different quality: it existed because individuals chose to engage in self-destructive behavior and then expected or cheated government "entitlement" programs. The places and people they talked about in this respect were almost always majority African American, although they rarely said so explicitly.[70] Thus the poorest Americans were seen to share immoral qualities with the wealthiest classes abroad—greed, laziness, corruption.

Liberal Protestants, Catholics, and evangelical women offered the widest range of responses about the causes of U.S. poverty, related to contingencies like illness or abuse, cycles of poverty and oppression, and the lack of legal protections. Yet even they drew few structural links between wealth in the United States and poverty elsewhere; to paraphrase Susan Sontag, they stopped short of locating their own privilege on the same map as other people's suffering.[71] Only a handful of sponsors addressed the issue directly. Barbara, an accountant in her late fifties who self-identifies as a social justice Catholic, was an example. She told me: "Pretty much the U.S. is in a state of permanent warfare. So what's the countervailing force? I can do nothing about the [foreign] politics of my country . . . [so] for me [sponsorship] is a political action, my social justice political act. Just trying to nurture one little being." Barbara sees herself as enmeshed in threats to world prosperity because she must pay taxes to a government that engages in war abroad. The "countervailing force" is a form of equilibrium in which she can also commit her money to global projects that privilege a specific life over generalized warfare. Barbara was unique in highlighting U.S. militarism as a cause of global poverty, but many sponsors did talk about economic factors, especially how Americans consumed inexpensive things without considering the negative impact on laborers abroad. At a larger level, however, few sponsors viewed U.S. people like themselves as culpable for the unethical practices of market capitalism; rather, *some* corporations benefited *certain* greedy American CEOs.

Blaming human behavior plays what is perhaps an even more important role: it buffers God from blame. Here we return to the key existential problem related to God's justice. A hundred years ago, sponsors commonly viewed natural disasters and massive poverty as God's method of supplying missions with orphaned and destitute children, making "this condition of things an open door for the entrance of missionary effort and the knowledge of a crucified savior."[72] Others suggested that God created disasters in response to pagan passivity: only a society-wide trauma could sufficiently rupture bonds of kin, religion, and law to create an opening for Christian truth. Such events, they believed, could move even notoriously stubborn Muslims to convert.[73] No contemporary sponsor viewed disasters and poverty in this light and every one emphasized that God abhorred when anyone suffered.

Catholics offered the most varied set of responses when I asked if God has anything to do with grinding poverty in the world. A large number argued that poverty could result in admirable qualities such as humility and dependence on the Creator (and many Protestants concurred). Others rephrased the problem around what they viewed as the central issue, namely how every human is impoverished in some respect because we all bear physical suffering and struggle with the same spiritual failings. Few spoke in explicitly theological terms, but the tenor of such responses bears the trace of Catholic social teachings that emphasize human alikeness as interdependent organs within one Body. A substantial minority (14%) of the Catholics I interviewed also suggested that God allowed poverty so that comparatively wealthy people like themselves could renew their faith by giving. About the same number raised this idea specifically to reject it as an outmoded form of paternalistic charity; they left the reason for suffering a mystery and focused on the call to action instead. Another 20% or so of Catholic sponsors (and not a single Protestant) noted that the afterlife should radically alter perspectives on material poverty. John, a 65-year-old Medicaid claim examiner from Utica, New York, put it well:

> God allows poverty to happen and I think that He sees the bigger picture, one that we don't see and that being, if heaven is eternal then our lives are very short. Just a tiny grain of sand . . . We see somebody that lives maybe 70 years in poverty and it's so horrible but I think that if we really could stand back and see the large, the big picture, maybe those of us that think we're living in non-poverty would see it differently.

Suffering disturbs on the intimate scale (why is *that* child poor?) so sponsors like John mobilize a classic form of Christian theodicy, reminiscent of Leibniz's famous response to the problem of evil: what appear to us as evils may in fact be doing good from God's enlarged perspective.[74] This logic is not limited to sponsors who project into the hereafter. Carl F. H. Henry, a key leader in mid-century U.S. evangelicalism, captured another aspect of this widespread sentiment in a letter to World Vision sponsors in 1976. "When I hear that . . . almost 650 million [people] subsist on an annual income of $50 or less, I am emotionally staggered," he wrote. And yet, he maintained, "superscribing and overarching all this human grief is an incomparable ***world vision of divine grace***."[75] Henry put the words in bolded italics so there was no mistaking where the emphasis should lie; awareness of large-scale evil could do existential work if Americans made it the basis for superseding the merely human scale.

This form of pulling back to a god's eye view is a kind of "phasing," to use Timothy Morton's term, referring to how humans glimpse only brief flashes of hyperobjects as they intersect with us. To explain this idea, Morton writes that global warming emits a "ghost" of itself when it heats up a thermometer, which is what humans can then observe.[76] Along the same lines, Christians try to interpret poverty and disasters as ghosts or glimpses of God's global project. For most sponsors, this thinking reinforces a vision of a "divinely invisible hand . . . as an optimistic generative force,"[77] despite the destruction and pain evident on the nightly news. It is this "incomparable world vision of divine grace," to quote Henry, that sponsors work into being when they contrast what we can see here with the next life or when they view poverty as having results beyond what we can track with audits and data—or even fully comprehend. Such answers are neither doe-eyed optimism nor apocalyptic pessimism. Engaged empathy is a more tense and hybrid thing.

Rizal Cruz (Baroy, Mindanao) and Carol Millhouse (Springfield, Massachusetts)

Following two sides of a sponsorship story, this interlude experiments with a narrative approach to further highlight the irresolution and silences that constitute global relations. It should be read alongside chapters 6 and 7, both of which raise questions about what it's like to keep in touch and lose touch during sponsorship. The interlude is based on interviews with individuals I have called Carol and Rizal in 2017 and 2018, respectively. My conversation with Carol lasted nearly three hours and was supplemented by her written recollections and follow-up emails. I contacted Rizal on Facebook and we were in touch for a few months before conducting a phone interview with the help of Kristel Kabigting, a colleague at my university who graciously offered to translate. Carmen Tomas, a Manila-based contractor with whom I have worked many times, transcribed and translated Rizal's responses into English. I underline phrases that are directly from the transcripts for both interviews (changing first person to third). The rest is paraphrased, with small details added for narrative flow. The final product is thus a result of its creation as I stitched together a patchwork of overlapping voices. Rizal's story is undoubtedly colored by mistranslations and emotions ("I was nervous," he said at the end, "This is the longest I ever spoke to someone from another country"). Carol's bore traces of her own multiple retellings, including a version she wrote in 2015 that I mention in the timeline below.

SPRINGFIELD, MASSACHUSETTS, AUGUST 1987

The TV screen flickered in the darkness. Tired though she was, the World Vision infomercial held her attention. There was something about the whole spiel, when they listed all the things they did. They didn't just feed and clothe kids, they taught them about Christ. "That's something I could get on board with," she thought. And she was finally making a reasonable amount of money, enough that she could put food on her table and have a bit left over.

At 35 years old, she knew not to take that stability for granted. She had survived an early marriage and five pregnancies. The first two occurred when she was still in her late teens—one was stillborn and the other a miscarriage. A couple of years later, her first baby was born, followed by another two years later, and then a third pregnancy four months after that. She remembered wanting to put a gun to her head. They didn't have a big enough apartment. The rural hospital close to her place had just shut its maternity ward. They didn't even have a car to get to an emergency room. "How are we going to do this?" she kept asking, "This isn't even possible. God, why did you allow this to happen?" But then she just kept praying and waiting and it really did work out. She was elated when the baby was born, though her marriage didn't fare so well. Money had been tight and he could be violent. She'd been in and out of abused women's shelters. They finally divorced and her kids, teens now, lived with him. Weird dynamics, she thought. She still had spells of loneliness.

Throughout it all, she'd kept her faith. She'd always attended church. The Bible was a beam down the middle of her core that steered her actions. Someone once compared it to a dog on a leash. When you get to a certain point you kind of feel that pull and you can't get too far from it because God doesn't let you get out of bounds. She smiled; she liked that image. She liked that World Vision gave poor kids the Bible. It would steer them as it steered her. The World Vision commercial made her think of other things too: she loved God's rainbow of people, and when she saw people of another race it was like a little party inside of her. She always thought, "God, it's just amazing that we have these different cultures, these different races. We're all one but we're different." She loved the reel-to-reel films her father used to show them as kids about life in Africa—the jungle, women dancing with bare breasts. During cowboy movies she always rooted for the Indians. "We're going to send you back to the Indians," her parents would say, and she'd reply, "Point the way, I'll take myself there!" She didn't know where it came from. Her father never told her why he had those films. They lived in a white suburb of Albany and her parents never talked about racism or went into black parts of the city. Still, her love of different nationalities persisted, even though she'd never traveled beyond New York State and New England.

There was one more thing that struck her about the World Vision commercial. She'd been getting really bothered by the lottery pool in her office. Everyone would talk about how they were going to win this big pot someday, and the plans they had for how they'd spend it. She hated gambling. Americans were always looking to enrich themselves. "What if we help these other people a lot less fortunate than us? What kind of country would America be then? The other thing that really bugged her was that concert with the Hollywood types, and they collected a lot of money for Africa during the Ethiopian famine. Then all of a sudden the focus was taken off that, as though a year later no one was starving. Sponsorship kept helping no matter what was on the news.

So she took a chance and dialed the number on her screen. "Do you want to designate a country or a boy or a girl?" asked the phone attendant. "You know, I'm just going to take whoever God gives me and let it go at that," she said. It would be easier to see the miracles God was going to work in her life if she let Him make the choice.

SPRINGFIELD, MASSACHUSETTS, SEPTEMBER 1987

A month later and Carol opened the brochure excitedly. The photo showed two dark eyes and a scowl. She began to read the details. Rizal lived with his parents, two sisters, and younger brother in the Philippines. He would turn nine years old on December 7. His father farmed and raised chickens. Then Carol paused and contemplated what she'd signed up for. It's really hard to write to somebody in another country, she thought, let alone a kid. What do you say? "Oh, I had a great time at the amusement park today." What do they care about all the wonderful things you get to do and they don't? And anyway, she reflected, I don't have an exciting life so I can't say, "Oh, I had just such a wonderful weekend. We went on a picnic and we went shopping at the mall," or something like that. I pretty much have a dull life. So what do I write? Should I say that one of the reasons I decided to sponsor is because I know what it's like to be rejected by people so I understand some of the things you're probably dealing with?[1] As she so often did, she turned her questions heavenward. "God," she asked, "*what do I do with this?*"

She took a breath and put pen to paper. "Dear Rizal . . ."

BAROY, LANAO DEL NORTE, MINDANAO, JANUARY 1989

Rizal held his brother's hand as they walked into Baroy with Pastor Abraham. He thought about how much had changed since Christmas Eve two years ago. December 24, 1987. The night his father was shot. Life had been difficult before, but never like this. His mother had found a new husband and stopped caring about what happened to them. She had another family now. She took his eldest sister and left. He and his younger sister and brother went to live with his Lola[2] in her house on the mountain. More than a year passed and then Pastor Abraham came to ask her to let him take the boys to an orphanage in town. He was 11 now and it was time he went back to school. Lola promised she would visit them often.

Rizal agreed because he trusted Pastor Abraham. He ran the born-again church where they went each Sunday, the church where his father had played guitar during worship. Pastor Abraham told them more about the orphanage as they walked. It belonged to Felise Lipsy, he said, a Christian lady from Texas who came every three years to visit.[3] Rizal knew the Pastor had many friends in America, and his wife, Evelyn, worked for World Vision. She first told them about World Vision more than two years ago: each child would have his own sponsor <u>who would pay for what was needed for school, notebooks, and an allowance</u>. Rizal <u>knew his family was very poor and he was very, very happy</u> to hear that. About 30 children at their church were sponsored, including him.

Ma'am Carol had been sending money since 1987 and now Pastor Abraham assured him that she would keep helping him while he was in the orphanage<u>. He felt better then. She had been so good to him, always shouldering his school expenses and never failing him</u>. She always <u>paid with regularity</u>. So few things had been predictable or regular in his life.

BAROY, MINDANAO, MARCH 1993

A few months ago, Ma'am Evelyn spoke to him at church, "<u>I don't know when World Vision will end. Just study hard and above all, have faith in God</u>." And now, suddenly, it was really over. She had just told them. World Vision was pulling out of the *barangay*. He was 15 years old and, after nearly six years in the program, he was left with no one to pay his high school fees. No more gifts of toys or *pasol*.[4] <u>So many small gifts, he could not count them</u>. He thought about Mommy Carol, as he liked to call her. <u>He thought of her as a good mother who was always there to help him.</u> He knew many things about her now, after six years of letters. She sent a photo one time, showing her children. He also knew she worked in an office, liked basketball, and was a born again like him. Now he was supposed to write to her one last time. "Please try to find me," he said in his letter. <u>It felt like the same thing as in the beginning before he was enrolled, when his father died. Life was really hard again.</u>

SPRINGFIELD, MASSACHUSETTS, DECEMBER 23, 2001

Carol looked up and blinked back tears as Olivia entered the church bathroom. She could feel God's hand at work. Why else would Olivia and her family have <u>literally dropped in her lap? What are the odds that a family from</u>

the same island in the Philippines, from Mindanao, would say, oh where do we go? To America, Massachusetts, Springfield, Springfield Evangelical Free Church, second service." *What are the odds*? A million to one. But here was Olivia, and she was asking why Carol was crying. "I finally have hope!" she replied, and the whole story poured out. She tried to condense more than a decade into a minute. A few months after she started sponsoring Rizal in 1987 his father was killed, she told Olivia. The boy had written, "It is hard to have no father." And that just really grabbed me," Carol said, "and then his mother left with another guy. I think it was mostly economics: a woman, in these countries, how are you going to support four kids on your own? But, you know, then she left town . . . So, when that happened it was one of those bonding moments, like, Okay, this is my kid. You touch my kid, I'm coming after you!" She paused and rephrased it for Olivia: "I just left it all up to God [to choose a child for me] and I get this kid, I'm like, "What do I do?" And a few months later he's got nobody, you know, and—and it's one of those things where you see God's hand afterwards."

She told Olivia how World Vision suddenly pulled out of his town when Rizal was 15. She didn't know it could do that. She spent six months calling until, to her surprise and relief, a World Vision operator gave her his address. She started sending him money and little gifts again, directly through the orphanage. Once she sent an inflatable globe so he could see where on the planet they both lived and the 12-hour time difference. She was never much good at prayer, but she used the time zones to help: she timed her prayers in the evenings so God would hear them right as Rizal started his day.[5] He sent her a photo in front of his high school with the clothes she had bought him. He looked so tall and grown up. She was filled with pride.

Then he dropped out. Math was hard and he wasn't doing well. His grandmother was sick and he went to help. Carol stopped getting any response to the letters she sent. "I knew Lanao del Norte was somewhere but I didn't know where," she told Olivia, "Trying to get information when you're a thousand miles away isn't easy." It was 1996 by that time and, shortly after, she first heard about the Internet. She tried to get help there too. A man [she met online] in Manila even put an APB on local TV. Finally, after four years, she gave up. She called World Vision on Rizal's birthday last year, the first year of the new century, to ask for another child in memory of the one she had lost. She still missed him a lot, especially on his birthday. She worried about him when typhoons hit his area. Was he alive? Married? Did he have any children? She wondered if he thought of her sometimes too.

Olivia didn't hesitate. They were going to visit family in Mindanao in April, she said to Carol. They would find a way to help her.

BAROY AND SPRINGFIELD, MAY 12, 2002

The line crackled and suddenly there were voices. Later, neither Rizal nor Carol remembered much of what they said during the short call. And in a way it didn't matter. Rizal stood with Evelyn at the orphanage, who translated. It was beyond explaining, he thought, the feeling that Mommy Carol had come back to him as a parent. She was the only parent who had ever come back to him. He knew it was special; the other kids at his church had all lost touch with their World Vision sponsors, but Mommy Carol had found him. For her part, Carol was deeply touched that it was Mother's Day in the United States. Olivia had been as good as her word: she managed to find him. She also passed along the notebook Carol made that contained all the emails she had sent to search for him since 1996. Over the phone, she tried to tell him that the notebook meant, "I've been looking for you. That's how precious you are to me that I have been looking for you all this time." She wanted him to know that he was her child in her heart, come hell or high water.

And it turned out her help was still needed. Rizal is starving, Evelyn told her, because he's no longer at the orphanage and has to make it on his own.[6] He'd gone back and finished high school, but there was no work in Baroy. Could she help him start a business, maybe send him to college? Carol was working two jobs and money was tight. "But I'm not starving," she thought, "and my kid is starving. I have to do something." She promised to send the money. The call was short, but they both felt God's presence.[7]

CANDIS, TUBOD, MINDANAO, SEPTEMBER 9, 2015

Rizal looked at his new cell phone. Internet access was still very bad in the mountains where he lived on his mother and stepfather's farm. Sometimes he had a signal, but often he did not. Still, this phone was much better than the one he had before. Really, it was the first time he had regular access to the Internet since he had left the computer college in Tubod in 2005. He glanced at the screen again, logged into his new Facebook account, and typed Mommy Carol's name into the finder. I'll just try it, he thought, I won't find her. But then there she was and she was actually active! Should he send a friend request? He considered it for a moment. They had fallen out of touch again, for nearly a decade this time. Since he had left the computer college, in fact. Maybe she's forgotten me, he thought, she almost certainly has. He decided to send the request anyway. He wondered what the response would be.

SPRINGFIELD, MASSACHUSETTS, SEPTEMBER 10, 2015

It was 9:58 pm. Carol's computer screen flickered to life. *A Friend Request from Rizal Cruz*. It had been ten years since they had been in touch, but it had been different than in the 1990s. She <u>hadn't been in a panic</u>. She felt she had <u>done everything she could for him. He was grown now, and the rest was up to him</u>. She thought about what had transpired after that phone call in 2002. She had sent money for Rizal to start a business raising chickens and then the tuition for computer college in Tubod. Pastor Abraham had kept her apprised. Rizal had been taking his chickens to cockfights and using the extra money he asked her for school projects to buy booze for his friends. Carol smiled wryly. <u>She hated gambling, but at least he was selling chickens!</u> And she understood what it was like to be <u>from the wrong side of the tracks</u> and <u>feel like you need to buy your friends</u>. <u>She'd been the outcast [growing up] so she understood how it could be when people didn't even get to know you before deciding whether they liked you or not.</u>

Looking at the screen, she felt elated and wary. Could someone be using his information? She sent him a tentative message, asking him about a few things only he would know. He told her Abraham was well, but Evelyn and his Lola had died.[8] He and his mother reconnected ten years ago, just after he finished college. Carol's <u>heart leapt for joy. It was definitely him!</u> *This time her child found her!* <u>She really had meant something to him.</u>

They kept trading messages and she had some moments of disappointment. He hadn't done anything with the college degree. <u>He seemed to be a houseboy or servant of some sort</u>. She could see on Facebook that Rizal's younger brother had a good job, a wife, and kids. <u>Why hadn't Rizal done more with his life? He'd always had low self-esteem, even as a child</u>. Maybe that was part of the problem.

SPRINGFIELD, MASSACHUSETTS, FEBRUARY 2016

<u>Carol loved writing, but she'd never sat down to actually write something out</u>. Rizal's Facebook request six months ago finally got her to start.[9] She decided to write their story.

<u>She'd learned a lot with Rizal, but she'd always been very reality-centered. No matter how much she sometimes fantasized that he'd come and live with her, she always knew he wasn't her kid.</u> There's no way she'd have put up with a decade-long absence from her own kids. <u>Her heart would be broken!</u> So there were differences, but there was also a bond. <u>When he screwed up,</u> she'd

think, "Well, my kids aren't perfect either. My kids do stupid things, too." You don't drop your kid because they buy booze for their buddies or gamble. After he contacted her on Facebook, Rizal asked her for money again. He was playing a borrowed guitar at church, could she buy him a new one? "Sure," she had written, "I owe you ten years of presents. Let's do a guitar." She got it for his birthday in December and she was happy to do it. She cherished a vision from a long time ago: Rizal with his sister and brother as little kids playing the guitar in church and singing, with God looking down going, "I love this little trio. I love the music they're making." Over the last few months, she and Rizal had settled into a pattern of sorts. He'd ask her for $50 here or $100 there. She didn't mind if she could afford it that month. I mean, who else was he going to ask? she reflected. A lot is that I'm the American. I have it and I've given it to him before. She remembered the thing with the booze so she sometimes double-checked with Abraham's son-in-law, who was Rizal's pastor and now her Facebook friend too. Was the money really needed? How was it used? Occasionally Rizal told her what he bought, but often he did not. At those times, she felt like he was using her in a way but she was aware of it so she wasn't mad. Again, she thought, who else is he going to ask when everybody there is in the same boat as him?

But none of that was going in the story she was writing. None of that was the point of her story with Rizal. The point was for it to be touching and spiritually moving. She wanted readers to become sponsors. She ended it with a plea that sounded a lot like the World Vision infomercial she saw 28 years ago as she lay on her couch, exhausted after work. "Millions of children around the world live each day hopelessly trapped in extreme poverty," she wrote, "The God Who Hears—hears the cries of children . . . It breaks His heart but He needs you to partner with Him to help make a difference . . . I am amazed at what God has done." As a child, Rizal had always scowled in his World Vision photos, so she added an uplifting postscript: "I've seen new pictures of Rizal and he looks happy and is no longer scowling!"[10]

When it was done, she sent the story to all her friends and a local paper. She sent it to Rizal with a note, "I wanted to put this story together and share it with you and then share it with the world." She also sent it to the 12-year-old girl she was sponsoring in Uganda because it was about sponsorship and about the difference you can make in a person's life. She didn't know if people would be inspired or ignore it. Whatever the reaction, it was still something Carol could share and say, "*This is something I've done.*"

* * *

At the time of writing, Rizal was in his early forties, living with his mother and older sister on a farm in the mountains. He went into town every weekend to play guitar at the born-again church his family attends, now pastored by Abraham's son-in-law. His Internet connection was still spotty, but he maintained contact with Carol over Facebook. Looking back on sponsorship, he said it had a "very big effect because [it made me feel] like I'm not nothing. It changed how I felt. Before, my life was very hard but . . . something positive came into my life." He hopes that Carol will come to visit. "By faith [I believe] that we will meet in person," Rizal told me, "I've been waiting a long time for that . . . That's what I am wishing for, to see Mommy."

At the time of writing, Carol was in her mid-sixties and working as an administrative assistant earning about $30,000 a year. She lived alone in a small apartment, with two of her adult children a short drive away and a third in Phoenix. She was very proud of her grandson who was serving in the navy. She sponsored two children and chatted daily with a boy from the Gambia who she met on Instant Messenger. She knows Rizal would like her to visit, but there are a lot reasons she doesn't think it will happen (she knows nothing about airports; she wouldn't know how to recognize dangers, ask for help, or use her cell phone abroad; she doesn't like heights or the idea of flying over water; adjusting to the time difference would be hard; she can't afford it; she'd have to get vaccinations; she worries about bird flu). Not wanting to disappoint Rizal, she has said to him, you never know what God will do. And who knows, she told me, perhaps someone will be so moved after reading their story that they will offer to pay for her trip.

CHAPTER 7

Synchrony and Territory

Spatiotemporal Elements of Global Unity

Joy to the world! The Saviour reigns
Let men their songs employ

Isaac Watts, "Joy to the World," 1719

We do not wear the face of any one nationality but rather reflect the beautiful diversity of God's Kingdom. We join our voices in a global chorus advocating for children in poverty. **We are citizens of God's Kingdom first, citizens of the world second, and citizens of our own nations third.** (bold in original)

—*A Good Name Is Compassion*, coffee table book for Compassion employees, 2009

Christian blogger Rosina Schmucker woke at 2 am in her Medicine Lodge, Kansas, home with Ralph S. Cushman's "Meditation at Midnight" running through her head: "Dear God, I cannot sleep!/ . . . Because so many hands keep/Beckoning me. And faces stare/And voices, piteous voices call/Upon the midnight air/ . . . many hands/Outstretched from all the lands." First published in 1945, the poem's familiar pan-denominational imagery eased its circulation through U.S. Protestantism: Cushman was a bishop in the Methodist Episcopal Church, Schmucker is a Mennonite, World Vision has used it for its evangelical audience. The visions it conjures play weird tricks with space and time. Faraway people become strangely close through their beckoning hands and voices. The wee hours, as the clock strikes 12, feel out-of-time, "for God and for eternity."[1] That night in Medicine Lodge, Rosina sat down at her computer and typed, "I thought of this poem at 2 am on Monday morning when I could not sleep. . . . Have you felt the pangs of that call?" Shortly after, an anonymous response was posted: "I have. And I long to feel it more."[2] The hands and voices that wake one up at night can be a welcome kind of haunting.

This final chapter secures Christian globalism more firmly within the discussions of space-time configurations that are central to globalization theory. In the early 1990s, two influential sociological studies set the tone in this regard. David Harvey famously defined postmodernity as "time-space compression," referring to how new technologies move capital around the globe, while also transforming one's sense of being in the world. Shortly after, Anthony Giddens used time-space "distanciation" to explore the difference between face-to-face encounters and the remote forms of sociality constitutive of globalization. He also underlined how time-space configurations fed universalism: the mapping of the globe and the concomitant construction of a single "human history" produced a "genuinely world-historical framework of action and experience," at least for Europeans.[3] At a basic level, this work rests on the foundation built by Durkheim, which moved the study of time-space beyond metaphysics by insisting that it was socially constructed. Durkheim argued that human beings became aware of the extension of space and the duration of time by encountering the boundaries and intervals that arise in social life. "We cannot conceive of time, except on condition of distinguishing its different moments," he wrote, "It is the same thing with space."[4]

Anthropological studies of Christianity have taken up spatiotemporal compression by examining the relation between global imperatives and local capacities, and between tangible infrastructure and conceptual maps. For instance, Simon Coleman's comparisons of Swedish and Nigerian Pentecostals show how they valorize what is distant to index spiritual power. Thus, to evoke "Africa" if one is in Sweden, or "Europe" if one is in Nigeria, recalls the diversity of Christians within a global "family" (chapter 4) as well as one's power to transcend the space between them (although Europeans are much more likely to have the passports and capital to actually do so compared with their Nigerian counterparts). To Coleman's studies of spatial compression, Joel Robbins's work on charismatic Christians in Papua New Guinea adds a sense of the temporal rhythm of globalism as it punctuates the week. Most of the time, Robbins notes, Papuan people are aware of the separation between Christians across the world, especially the inequality between whites and blacks. But during Sunday services "the lines of connection that bind community are drawn taut" as they imagine themselves in a worldwide communion of (largely white) people saying the same prayers for the same millennial hopes.[5] Robbins's point bears emphasizing because the tendency of anthropologists, and other scholars of global Christianity, to focus on self-consciously globalizing Pentecostal-charismatic churches (and, more particularly, their pastors) may create the impression of people permanently oriented toward the global.[6] To reiterate one of this book's central claims: a global subjectivity is better understood as wavering in intensity and requiring regular renewal.

Building on the work above, this chapter examines some of the boundaries and intervals (to paraphrase Durkheim) that shape Christian globalism. While there are many potential entry points into this topic, I focus on three key technologies and techniques that span the two centuries in which sponsorship has flourished: those associated with vocality (mainly songs and prayers), mapping (cartographic and conceptual), and long-distance communication (particularly social media). Loosely speaking, the first and last segments highlight temporal frameworks and the middle one explores the spatial. But as the quote in the epigraph from Compassion's self-published coffee table book indicates, Christians often interweave metaphors of voice ("a global chorus") and spatiality (citizens of God's Kingdom, the world, the nation). Indeed, it was as I was absent-mindedly flipping through this glossy book at Compassion's headquarters that the framework for this chapter began to emerge in my mind.

The chapter's first sections focus on the Anglo-Protestant use of choral singing and "concerts of prayer." As the last section about online technologies shows, U.S. Protestants continue to hone such techniques today. Harmonized hymnody and unified prayer are powerful tools because they extend space by constraining time when they bring far-flung Christians into imagined synchrony. Mapping also extends space by celebrating distant networks of influence, but it does so by constraining places and people through discrete categories ("nations") and subsuming individuals into larger groupings to produce global sites of familiarity—be they allies or enemies. Often, though, it is the gaps in these maps that attest most eloquently to how U.S. Christians live in the world; most places and people are neither "with us" nor "against us." These blank spaces shape the contours of Christian globalism.

At a basic level, these themes return to the dialogical relationship between particularity and immensity. In simulations of vocal simultaneity, a particular, individual voice—one's own, that of a single child—is harmonized in a chorus to create the affective power of immensity. In mapping techniques, the nation-state offers a discrete nodal point in relation to the world maps and imaginative exercises that approximate a god's eye view. It is helpful to think of globalism in this regard as scalar or fractal, a mode in which objects can be scaled up or down. This concept, in vogue among scholars of globalization, usefully highlights how constructions of space/time are relative and therefore relational. They can be proposed or evaded. They have the potential to shift in response to culturally embedded ideas about "normalcy, standardization, hierarchy, variation, and conflict."[7] The relationship between particularity and immensity is also always relative to the objects at play: a person is "particular" compared to a nation, while the nation is so compared to the globe, and the globe is so compared to God's universe. It is to this contingent and shape-shifting set of relations that we now turn.

SILENT GODS AND A HARMONY OF VOICES

Christians have found human utterances intensely interesting. Voice seems to reveal something essential about the self, akin to how sponsors scan foreign children's portraits for some clue about the soul (chapters 3 and 6). Unlike physical appearance, however, voice is an instrument that lends itself to spatiotemporal compression as it harmonizes with others. In Western Christianity, there is a biblical basis for connecting vocal forms with aspirations for global unity. Interpretations going back at least to Augustine suggested that the Deity and His creatures shared a single language in Eden; along with the physical expulsion from Paradise, humanity's punishment for sin was the rupture of pure linguistic harmony. Medieval theologians read Eden alongside Babel. Both events began in a state of primal perfection expressed through a single language and social order, which was fractured through sin. At Babel, God punished humankind by scattering them throughout the earth and introducing a cacophony of languages.[8]

Reformist-era Protestants tried to recover this lost harmony with God by constraining and unifying their prayers in contrast to what Luther called the "babbling and bellowing" of Roman Catholics. In the same period, Catholic clerics at the Council of Trent emphasized that prayers and songs praising God must be intelligible speech to best approximate the ordered expression of divine will. As Europeans encountered people hitherto unknown to them, there were even attempts to recover what Babel had destroyed. Early Pietist settlers in North America compared their own language and indigenous ones to discern any overlaps, which they believed to be vestiges of the tongue humankind once shared.[9] There are deep-rooted links between dreams of linguistic harmony and Christian globalism in Europe and its colonies.

Concerts of prayer became a key participatory technique in this respect. The initial impetus was the increased settlement of Scots in the North American colonies. For this now transatlantic community, the world's conversion seemed exhilaratingly possible, but also daunting. Christendom seemed far more extensible, but more fragile too. In 1744, a group of Scottish ministers developed a method to bind their far-flung churches to each other. They sent round a tract urging congregations to pray the same words each first Tuesday of the quarter. They hoped this clear expression of unity would hasten "an abundant affusion of [the] Holy Spirit on all the churches and the whole habitable earth, to revive true religion in all parts of Christendom . . . [and to] fill the whole earth with His glory."[10] The scheme was so popular that it was followed by another tract, "A Concert For Prayer, To Be Continued For Seven Years," that made its way through England and its colonies, where it captured the imagination of famed Congregational minister Jonathan Edwards, who penned a book on the topic in 1747.[11]

Over the next generation, concerts of prayer became a regular feature of Anglo-Protestant global engagements.[12] At a basic level, they suggested only that a group of Christians come together in "Congregations, Families, and other praying Societies" to pray agreed upon words at an appointed time, with the assumption that like-minded congregations elsewhere were doing the same.[13] There was a millennial cast to these exertions. Jonathan Edwards, like most early promoters, viewed them as the first step in fulfilling prophecies in the Hebrew Bible that foretold of a time when the nations would pray together in Jerusalem.[14] Instead of the nations physically displacing to Jerusalem, it was Anglo-Protestants who displaced as they settled across the world: through carefully timed prayer, they believed they could turn their isolated towns and, later, mission stations into a united front strong enough to move the world toward its appointed end.

Early child sponsors undoubtedly knew about, and likely participated in, such concerts. The year before the ABCFM missionaries at Bombay announced the first adoption scheme in an 1816 issue of the *Panoplist*, the same magazine called for a concert of prayer on their behalf. Later, the women's societies that supported sponsorship also set times to "belt the world in prayer."[15] Although the initial impetus had been to unite Europeans with each other, by the late nineteenth century the number of converts had risen and U.S. women viewed such concerts as uniting "European, American, and native missionaries of all Protestant churches . . . in all parts of the habitable world."[16] These techniques later became ecumenical World Days of Prayer, promoted by Anglo-Protestants on either side of the Atlantic.[17]

Harmonized vocality took another form in the construction of Christian globalism at the time. Foreign children in missionary schools were taught to sing hymns and chorus bible verses, prayers, and catechisms, which were performed for European and North American visitors on a regular basis and much remarked in their communications back home. The importance of these exercises rested on the Christian understanding of vocal unity as indexing religious truth, while its presumed opposite betokened sin, chaos, and brokenness. To this idea, missionaries added scriptural characterizations of other people's gods as without senses, based on Psalm 115: "Their idols . . . have mouths, but they speak not: eyes have they, but they see not . . . neither speak they through their throat." It was a tricky kind of falsity, according to biblical exegesis, because these gods' tangibility as statues at first implied their capacity to be present with human beings—when in fact the disembodied Christian deity, available *only* through his voice, was uniquely present on earth. Anglo-Protestants extrapolated by linking two meanings of "sense": when the gods were silent (without senses), human words ceased to have coherence or meaning (without sense). Heathens were thus "tortured by senseless incantations to senseless gods."[18]

Asian soundscapes seemed to fully manifest this principle. Late nineteenth-century U.S. visitors portrayed the streets as sites of "unintelligible jargon and filth." Public celebrations were full of "horrible . . . discordant sounds . . . a succession of sounds hard to describe and hard to endure." When translated into music, these tones seemed to indicate the bewilderment of a seeking soul. "[It is] the minor strain, the ending on an interval full of questioning," wrote a missionary from Japan in *HWF* in 1895. "We take to these seeking people [Christian] hymns . . . and teach them the noble harmonies, with major keys and full cadences, that express the glad certainty of our faith."[19] The vocal performances of heathen children in missionary care seemed a stark contrast. "Order and cleanly habits prevail, and we know that the knowledge of God and salvation is being taught and acquired," confirmed a U.S. laywoman to *HWF* readers after being treated to one such chorus in Peking in 1894.[20]

Although there may have seemed a particular urgency to regulating children's voices within missionary settings, these performances did not in fact originate in a Christian aversion to heathen sounds. They began in European charity schools that provided a template for missionary ones. The SPCK's yearly performance in St. Paul's Cathedral, London, was by far the most famous example. In the course of the eighteenth century, it grew into a spectacle that encompassed nearly seven thousand charity school children. Fixed on the symbolically resonant Ascension Day, commemorating Jesus's ascent to heaven, the children marched in orderly rows through the streets to St. Paul's, where they were seated on scaffolds high in its dome to sing hymns in unison—a not subtle rendering of London's poor as angelic hosts.

While scholars have focused on how such displays disciplined children into moral political subjects, I am just as interested in the participatory effect for audiences. William Vincent, a spectator in 1787, described his emotional response: "The union of five thousand trebles raises admiration and astonishment. . . . Compassion, benevolence, and Christian charity dilate the heart . . . and the aggregate of these several feelings contribute to render it one of the most heart-moving spectacles exhibited in this or any other country."[21] A better known recollection is William Blake's poem *Holy Thursday*: "Thousands of little boys and girls raising their innocent hands / Now like a mighty wind they raise to heaven the voice of song." It was a visceral experience of God's perfect order and unity through a vocal "performance of the mega," a phrase cultural theorist Robbie Goh uses for hymn singing in contemporary mega-churches with large crowds, massive sanctuaries, high amplification, and outsized video screens. This "mega," Goh writes, is a type of religious work: "The church body is . . . offered as an icon of God's body, reflecting in its own semiotic properties (enormity, dynamism, expansiveness) some of the qualities of an expansive and transcendent God."[22]

When similar performances were exported through missionary work—whether they included hundreds of children or a handful—many nineteenth-century Christians experienced a foretaste of the "mega" of a heavenly realm where "a great multitude, which no man could number, of all nations, and kindreds, and people, and tongues" would stand before God's throne and sing together, according to Revelation 7:9. Sometimes Americans saw themselves as choirmasters in God's service, as in this note by a Methodist woman, inspired by the revivals at a New Hampshire camp meeting in 1887: "And all at once it burst upon me like a vision—that the Church is working up the programme of the millennium! Just see how it opens: [With a song] by the 'World Chorus.' Now you see the exercises cannot begin until India's, China's, Japan's, Africa's, S. America's women shall have had terms of vocal lessons—*from us*."[23] Such visions were linked to participatory techniques. For example, U.S. missionaries on furlough from different stations sometimes performed Protestant hymns together "in the varied dialects to which they had been accustomed." Mrs. Hubbard of Clifton Springs, New York, was present for one such performance in 1884, where six missionaries from different fields sat at one tea table. Her husband proposed singing "Rock of Ages" and each one sang translations of the hymn: "Seven different tongues united, and yet not a discordant note, but one harmonious song," Mrs. Hubbard reported. She had often wondered what the songs in Heaven would sound like. "The mystery was solved! Every kindred, every tribe before the throne will unite in praise of Him," she wrote.[24]

THE PERFORMED SIMULTANEITY OF CHOIRS AND CONCERTS

These antecedents paved the way for popular innovations in the mid-twentieth century: calendars of prayer and Korean children's choirs. To varying degrees, all the mid-century organizations I studied circulated prayer bulletins and calendars to their sponsors to manage concerted prayer. In previous centuries, the concerts used formalized prayers framed in general eschatological terms and early promoters also suggested that, because prophecy said the nations would physically unite in Jerusalem, their vocal union must also be "visible" and "explicit"; in other words, congregational groups should ideally assemble to pray together.[25] The prayer calculus was different for non-denominational sponsorship organizations. Their mid-century donors were busy housewives and professionals who wanted to pray in concert with others, but from their home or workplace and on their own schedule, rather than at an appointed hour. Formalized prayers had also given way to informal ones in many U.S. Protestant churches, and evangelicals in particular wanted specific prayer targets that could nevertheless be spoken extempore. The resulting "chorus" needed a structuring mechanism that was also flexible and easily distributable. Calendars proved ideal.

Although the system was very popular, its individualism could also make it difficult for each person to experience the "somatic modes"[26] related to united prayer—that mystical amplification of human voices and visceral connection to globalism. Armin Gesswein, an associate evangelist with Billy Graham, was aware of this issue when he wrote a series of texts to accompany WV's prayer calendars in 1980. "There is *might in mass prayer*," Gesswein began, suggesting that readers let their bodies sense this immensity by focusing on something familiar: the affective charge when their local congregation prayed together— that "strange, strong, delightful response from all parts of the room. We feel lifted, almost as though an invisible arm held us up; our hearts burn, tears lie close." It approximated the feeling of heightened connection at Pentecost, wrote Gesswein, as he quoted from Acts 1:14: "*These all continued with one accord (unanimously) in prayer and supplication.*"[27] Ironically, then, sponsorship organizations' calendars decoupled concerts of prayer from congregational settings, yet the experience of congregational worship still provided its somatic framework.

The organizations I studied still circulate prayer calendars. At Unbound, nearly 7,500 sponsors receive its weekly Prayer Partners emails. At Compassion, 20,000 receive its downloadable monthly calendar. At WV, the 6,000 sponsors in the Hope Prayer Team have a mobile app and a monthly calendar. Other ministries use social media to sustain global concerts of prayer—the 24/7 Prayer, for example, coordinates people from around the world in a "nonstop" prayer chain[28]—and there is a resurgence of congregational concerts too. Many such events follow a loose format that uses human bodies as a proxy for "the world," effectively putting into practice what Gesswein suggested as an imaginative exercise. Participants begin the meeting by praying in partners for immediate acquaintances, then in small groups for their churches, and last as a whole group for the world's needs.[29] Tuning their voices and positioning their bodies, participants in such concerts of prayer embody the relational scale between particularity and immensity.

Sponsorship prayer calendars largely imply white, Western Christian sponsors praying with each other, in the mid-twentieth century and today. Another form of vocal simultaneity—the Korean children's choir—gave mid-twentieth-century U.S. Christians the chance to engage in the mirroring that, as chapter 4 describes, sought to produce experiences of unity-in-diversity. For more than a century, U.S. Christians had created "mediated spaces of live encounter" in which foreign Christians were toured through the country to edify church audiences. The Korean choirs built on this tradition.[30] Korean Christians affiliated with the YMCA likely started the first version in 1945, which toured the United States in the mid-1950s. World Vision created its own in 1958, followed by Compassion. In ordered, well-dressed rows, these groups of Korean children traveled across North America singing hymns, reciting scripture, and proclaiming their gratitude and Christian joy. The idea was so popular that even sponsorship organizations without a choir capitalized on it; in the late 1960s, for example, CCF recorded children in their orphanages singing a Christmas album.[31]

The evangelicals at WV and Compassion couched the choirs within publicity materials that implied defective soundscapes. Into the 1960s, they still associated Asia with "dumb idols."[32] More commonly, it was Asian children themselves who were portrayed as living in unnatural silence. This trope did not originate in the 1950s, but it was boosted by the affordances of technology. World Vision, in particular, produced a stream of disturbing photographs and film stills of a child in mid-cry, her mouth open wide but stripped of sound—an unsubtle sign of how nearby adults (and perhaps gods) failed to hear her pain. Silent shrieks had spiritual associations; the child had yet to hear (and therefore speak) the gospel. Sponsorship materials made this link explicit by drawing parallels to the Macedonian cry—Paul's vision in Acts 16:9 in which a man appears to him pleading for evangelization, "Come over into Macedonia and help us." For World Vision, U.S. Christians were especially attuned to the "wordless cry of baby voices that can mean only 'Come over and help us.'"[33] Like the landscape group photos described in chapter 3 where rescued children spelled out their thanks by arranging their bodies in orderly formations, the Korean choirs provided a compelling "after" in contrast to those silent screams (figures 7.1a and 7.1b).

The choirs produced Christian globalism in ways that correspond with the example above where missionaries performed immensity and unity by

FIG 7.1A AND 7.1B. Silent screams and a chorus of harmonized voices. A WV advertising campaign in *Christianity Today*, March 1957, compared to the Korean Orphan Choir in one of WV's "pictorial" pamphlets for sponsors, c. 1966–67. Courtesy of World Vision International.

singing the same hymn in many languages (without a single discordant note, as Mrs. Hubbard put it). Korean choirs sang "old familiar hymns," according to the brochures—that is, familiar to Americans, not to the children who learned them by rote—to produce experiences of linguistic unity. The choir programs emphasized interdenominational hymns and Christmas carols, including *The Old Rugged Cross, Amazing Grace,* and *Away in A Manger*; African American spirituals, such as *Old Black Joe* and *Swing Low Sweet Chariot*; and U.S. folk songs.[34] Familiar repertoires meant that U.S. audiences could sing "with" the children, whether out loud or in their heads. As a participatory technique, it brought East (the children) and West (the audience) into synchrony. Other times, the children became the bridge between these camps when they sang the same song in Korean and then in English or Anglo-Christian hymns translated into Korean and set to Asian-inspired music. "From over the seas [these hymns] come back to us," wrote Jeannette L. Hauser, a Methodist missionary in India, "echoes of our own songs of devotion, but mingled with strange, sweet notes, all telling of a Redeemer's love."[35] Americans heard their sacred music rendered global through the superimposition of musical forms, which seemed emblematic of the immensity of God and their central place in His creation. The same techniques buoy the Christian "world music" genre today.[36]

It seems that the Korean choirs did produce notable embodied experiences for mid-century listeners. Edith Wiebe of Dominion City, Manitoba, left a concert in 1962 and stepped into the cold winter air but "felt strangely warm all over" because of the blessings she received. She vowed she would never forget that night. Two years later, Janet R. Buchanan from Freedom, Pennsylvania, purchased the concert record and had a similar experience. "There hasn't been a time the record has been played that the eyes of my family have remained dry. The harmony is tremendous. I never knew that music so beautiful could come from earth."[37] Sunday school teachers used these recordings as pedagogical tools to inculcate globalism. They were counseled to pick from the album one of "our wonderful old traditional Christian children's chorus numbers . . . songs American kids cherish," and instruct their pupils to sing it. Then immediately cue up the Korean voices: "Play the record after your class has sung the same song. It's most effective!"[38]

WV and Compassion toured their choirs less often in the 1970s, and then ended them altogether.[39] However, the model persists. World Help, a large evangelical sponsorship organization, runs a "Children of the World" choir in which children from its field sites tour the United States in "native" dress. Echoing the silent sufferer of the 1950s, they are billed as representing "the desperate reality of millions of children who cannot speak for themselves." Another evangelical ministry, His Little Feet International Children's Choir, tours foreign children sometimes in partnership with Compassion and WV.[40] Americans also form their own "international" choirs, a model that has become more popular since the multicultural turn in the 1990s. In such choirs, U.S. children perform as the "great chorus of the world," often dressed to signal a "nation" to which they have a tenuous racialized link; for example, a Filipino American child wears a traditional Filipino outfit or a Jewish child wears an Israeli one. The symbolism is so widespread and plastic that it appeals to very liberal Christians and non-Christians too, for whom the young singers in their "colorful authentic native costumes . . . symboliz[e] diversity, peace and unification."[41] For conservative evangelicals, the choirs "invite audiences to expect an encounter with God . . . [As] the children will share stories of how their lives have been changed . . . from darkness to light; from despair to hope."[42]

Contemporary sponsors are familiar with such imagery and sometimes showed me relevant online tools. Eleanor, the 62-year-old evangelical woman who had sponsored Angelus (chapter 6), introduced me to a video she had recently seen on Facebook and forwarded to friends. "You kind of well up [when] you see these beautiful people from all over singing together," Eleanor told me as I opened my laptop and we clicked through to the website of OMF International (formerly Hudson Taylor's China Inland Mission). On February 21, 2016, the site informed us, OMF teamed up with U.S. evangelical hymn-writers Keith and Kristyn Getty to lead "an estimated 1.1 million believers together across 100 countries" in a "Global Hymn Sing" featuring the hymn *Facing a Task Unfinished*. The four-minute video opens with Kristyn Getty singing the first lines in Grace Community Church in California. It then turns to a montage of congregations around the world singing the same lyrics with Getty on the appointed day (figure 7.2). Simultaneity is heightened as each image fades into the next one, leaving a precious moment when the faces are blended. This type of video was familiar to me since sponsorship websites also use it. For example, Compassion's website features short videos showing rapid shots of children around the world praying the same words in English: "Heavenly Father, thank you for giving us this day. Amen." A chorus builds as children in separate locations seem to finish each other's sentences. "Prayer unites us as a family of believers," intones an American woman's voice. The last frame cuts to a girl in El Salvador who stares directly into the camera with tears in her eyes: "Every day I pray for you."[43]

As Eleanor and I watched the OMF video, a few things came to my mind. The first was a comparison with the televisual media that anthropologists often study in the context of globalizing charismatic Christianity. Such videos usually feature a pastor in one location who prompts listeners elsewhere to pray aloud with him; by contrast, the OMF video seemed designed to evoke an affective

FIG 7.2A-F. Screenshots from OMF's video of a global hymn. It begins with U.S. evangelical singer Kristyn Getty and it ends with a children's choir in New Zealand. Top right: between each shot, the images blend together to heighten a sense of simultaneity.

SAITAMA INTERNATIONAL CHURCH
SAITAMA, JAPAN

REFORMED CHURCH OF AVONDALE
AUCKLAND, NEW ZEALAND

FIG 7.2A–F. *(continued)*

mood rather than elicit a verbal response.[44] The second thing I noticed concerned the hyperbole in Christian claims to globalism; in this case, despite the
touted 100 countries, nearly all the churches in the video were majority white
and located in the United Kingdom, United States, Canada, New Zealand, or
Australia. Kristyn Getty's professionally trained and American-accented voice
sang over the others—"We go to all the world, His Kingdom, Hope Unfurled!"—
and thus Americans seemed to lead the charge. Her voice faded only at the end
as a ragtag group of children sang the last lines in wavering tones—the embodiment of human intimacy after the rapid shots of congregations and swelling
hymnody lifted one up to a god's eye view.

Eleanor and I discussed my observations, but she did not find the video
less compelling. Instead, she noted what theorist Lauren Berlant would call an
"intimate public" that shares "a worldview and emotional knowledge" through
the circulation of common texts, like the OMF video. Berlant writes that such
publics offer members "recognition and reflection."[45] Eleanor made this point
as she validated her interpretation (over mine) by turning my attention to the
broad online audience that concurred with her assessment. We scrolled through
the positive comments posted under the video and she pointed to a few that
she correctly identified as germane to my study:

> LuAnn Graber
> I just want to hop on a plane and visit every one of these beautiful brothers
> and sisters. What a wonderful family I have!

> Bev Grove
> It's lovely to see all the nations worshipping God together in their own
> language.

> Ruth Christner
> We are a very small church in Wisconsin, USA. Often we feel so alone. How
> encouraging to see believers all over the world!

Eleanor lingered on Ruth Christner's comment. "I get that. We're like that too,
out here in the woods [in New Hampshire]! There's this world and you want
to know it better and be more . . . something . . ." She trailed off: "Connected.
I'm not sure that's the word exactly, but I think you see." For sponsors who
used social media, including sponsorship organizational blogs, the comments
section, where users contribute and usually include their physical locations,
operates as both "icon and interface" of globalism: it symbolizes a broad Christian network and also creates it.[46]

Eleanor was sufficiently moved by the combination of these comments and the synchronized voices that she forwarded the OMF video to her friends, brought it up with me, and wanted to watch it multiple times. It is emblematic of technologies and techniques that bridge two complementary forms in this book. The viewer is attuned through the tuning of multiple voices to the immensity of global Christendom—or at least, to its potential—and, in this sense, it operates like the statistical exercises in chapter 2, which were expected to create an affective charge to lift one up to a god's eye view. At the same time, the comments section reinforces the assumption that Christian viewer-participants around the world feel the same emotions as those in the United States. In that sense, it evokes the universalism of, say, the NER's Golden Rule dinners in chapter 3, which rested on the assumption that all human bodies share certain basic sensations and emotions in common. The combination of these facets led Eleanor to feel that longed-for *something*—a collective effervescence, an expansive empathy that strengthens each individual voice while clarifying the immensity of a God that encompasses so many believers at once.

MAPPING NATIONS

In the late 1950s, World Vision described an affecting scene for its sponsors. A. B. Simpson, founder of the Christian and Missionary Alliance, began every day by slowly revolving the globe on his desk while praying aloud "for all the lost multitudes of earth as the various countries of the world passed before him." Then (according to an eyewitness), he would suddenly fling his arms around the globe, hugging it to him and bending over it to weep. "The tears that now ran freely down Dr. Simpson's cheeks struck the top of the globe and there divided so that it seemed that one went down one side and another down another until the whole earth was wet with the tears of compassion."[47] The story may well have been apocryphal, but what mattered to WV was the example it provided. Simpson's prayers were as emotionally and physically affecting as the harmonized prayers above, but instead of temporal compression, the emphasis was spatial: by spinning the globe and hovering over it, Simpson experienced a god's eye view that made the world's places and people into a coherent whole.

U.S. Christians have long made use of maps and globes. Nineteenth-century missionary promoters printed striking wall-sized maps on cloth, which they used in fund-raising tours, fairs, and expositions. The aesthetics of this mapping reflected various theologies. In the 1920s, Near East Relief maps were covered with arrows arcing out from their U.S. headquarters to illustrate the

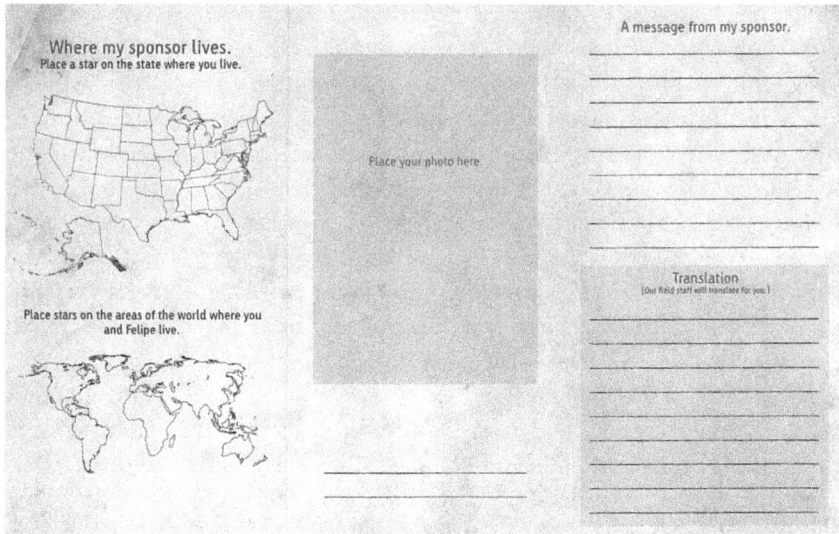

FIG 7.3. Map in an insert within a Compassion child packet from 2014. Sponsors are encouraged to use the insert to craft their first letter, including the maps, a personal photo, and a short message that is later translated by Compassion's field staff for the child. Used by permission of Compassion International, Inc. Copyright © 2014 by Compassion International, Inc. All rights reserved.

worldwide spread of liberal Protestantism's Golden Rule (see figure 3.6).[48] At the same time, Catholic sponsors were instructed to draw a world map, mark it with 288 crosses for each place the missionaries supported children, and then drip the ink from a red pen onto each one: "To your surprise you will find that your alms and prayers have helped to spread the merits of the Precious Blood over practically the whole pagan world."[49] Mapping exercises are still common today, especially among evangelicals.[50] During my time at its headquarters, Compassion had just rolled out a new template for sponsors' first letter that featured a blank world map so that Americans could mark where they lived in relation to the child they supported (figure 7.3).

Maps have fascinated scholars too, as they began to deconstruct the relation between signs and their objects. Map is not territory, Jonathan Z. Smith reminded religionists, while post-colonial historians emphasized that modern maps were never merely informational; like the statistics in chapter 2, they were tools of world making and instruments of power. At the same time, early studies of globalization celebrated what seemed like the accelerated demise of the borders shaped by those maps: the future would be transnational, extranational, or postnational.[51] While much of this work has focused on technology (the Internet) and economy (global corporations or finance), cultural critics have weighed in too. Politically left historians mobilize the term "transnationalism" to "provide the conceptual acid that denaturalizes" the nation.[52] Ecotheorists argue that the hyperscale of ecological change makes nation-states into "an illusion or a small colored patch on a large dark surface."[53]

The problem with these deconstructions is that for many people maps still matter. Moreover, maps of nation-states still matter. This is perhaps unsurprising since the nation as an imagined community, to paraphrase Benedict Anderson, arose coterminously with recent globalization; nation was not pitted *against* globalization, but was a fundamental aspect *of* it. Many scholars recognize this fact, of course. Tsing remarks that nationalism frames contemporary activists' dreams of social change. Historians say the same of "religious internationals," Christian progressives in the mid-twentieth century who "transcended the borders of the nation state, but also presupposed it as the indispensable springboard for a supra-national identity and as the key module for concrete actions."[54] These so-called internationals were part of the zeitgeist surrounding the rapid proliferation of post-colonial states and the expansion of UN-affiliated networks and NGOs. There was an uptick in cultural representations of multinational cooperation in this period too: the Miss Universe pageant (founded in 1952), the Olympics (founded in 1896 and first broadcast on television in 1956), and Disneyland's "It's A Small World" ride (a salute to UNICEF in 1964) are just three examples.[55] Each one used a human body—the woman, the athlete, or the child—as icon of the nation.

In sponsorship, this mid-century moment marked an organizational change along the same lines. Whereas an earlier generation supported a child at Oodooville or Rosario mission station, mid-twentieth-century Americans sponsored a child in Korea or Indonesia.[56] Today, organizations still sort children's profiles according to country and encourage sponsors to choose on that basis. Events like the Compassion Experience (chapter 6) map the world into countries and continents; visitors walk through the story of a child from the Philippines or Uganda and at the end they face shelves divided into Asia, Africa, or South America with child packets labeled according to nation-state. The buildings in which sponsorship professionals work are often mapped along these lines, with floors or conference rooms named after countries ("Let's meet in Kenya." "Is there a screen in Bolivia?"). The churches that sponsors attend may also feature maps (figure 7.4), especially in Sunday school classrooms. Occasionally, sponsors have even refused alternate organizational models of the world. In the 1970s, for example, WV redefined its prayer targets according to "unreached people groups," rather than nation-states. In December 1974, it unveiled a lengthy alphabetized list to encourage sponsors' prayers for the Afar, Bororo, Kurds, Ligbi, and such. Feedback poured in, which led to the

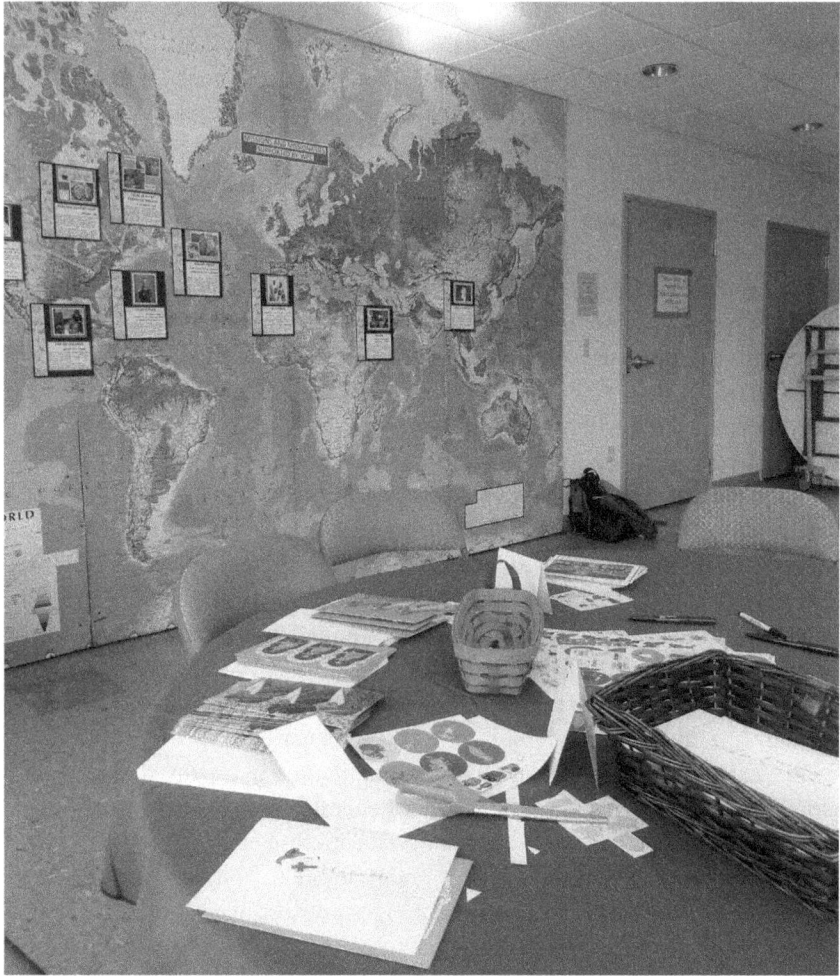

FIG 7.4. Church meeting room in New Hampshire with wall-sized map showing the locations of the missionaries the congregation supports. Another wall (not pictured) displays sponsored children's photos. The table in the foreground is set up for the annual gathering when each sponsor writes a Christmas card to the child he or she supports.

list being reissued two months later with the same groups, now alphabetized according to country—Brazil (Bororo), Ethiopia (Afar), Ivory Coast (Ligbi), Turkey (Kurds).[57] U.S. Christians conceived of the world as divided by nation-state and they wanted their prayer aids to reflect it.

The nation means something particular from the vantage point of Christian globalism because it superimposes secular and sacred terminology: when sponsors discuss "nations," they do mean sovereign states in the contemporary sense, but they are also aware of the Bible's repeated use of "nations" in English translations of the Hebrew *goyyim* and Greek *ethnesin*. Thus, for example, when WV's director of International Intercessors issued its 1983 prayer list organized according to nation-state, he averred that it was God's preferred system. Why else would Jesus have said, "My house shall be called a house of prayer for all the nations (*ethnesin*)"?[58] The word "nation" also appears in the prophetic passages of Revelation where it describes the multitudes around the Heavenly Throne, giving eternal weight to a modern political construction.

For contemporary sponsors, nation-states are one part of how they make global space legible as nodal points. In this respect, I am thinking of what scholars of globalization have called a certain "patchiness to the global map," referring both to imagined connections and to the uneven spread of resources.[59] Scholars of Christianity have contributed significantly to fleshing out what this means in cosmological terms. Writing of the same missionary contexts in which sponsorship first emerged, historian Frank Hatje argues that, because Protestants defined the Kingdom of God as the incarnation of Christian piety in societal forms, one could travel *in* the Kingdom by making a beeline between "bright spots of Protestant fellowship." That was how most Christian travelers—itinerant preachers, missionaries, or tourists—moved about and, consequently, mapped the world for their co-religionists at home.[60] Anthropologist Thomas Csordas has made a similar observation about church websites that map out their global affiliates by pinpointing "hot spots, safe zones, or high points" to make the Kingdom of God "traceable in a preliminary sense."[61] Many other studies track how globetrotting Protestant pastors still hop between churches and conferences and beam this vision of "the world" back to their congregations.[62] The same is true of prominent Catholic leaders; the Pope's national tours map out a Catholic world for his audience. It is by joining these points on the globe that Christians can trace the tendrils of divine authority and the institutional linkages (including those fostered by sponsorship money) that make up "the global church." Though most of the time Christians harness the structuring logic of the modern nation-state to create this map, God's Kingdom also keeps a tension in play: it maps *divinely inspired* human networks, which always take precedence over the merely human-made.

To better understand how this "bright spot" approach works, we can add anthropologist Kevin Lewis O'Neill's analogy of a patchwork quilt. The Guatemalan Pentecostals with whom he works discursively and literally mapped their connections to particular countries with growing churches like their own; Guatemala was envisioned as "stitched" to South Korea or Zimbabwe, rather than to Iran or Iceland.[63] Sponsors also view certain patches on the quilt as

textured or "bright." The others lack distinguishing features but are often integrated into larger agglomerations. Thus, a sponsor may know nothing about
Indonesia, the country where the sponsored child resides, but she will view
it as constitutive of a larger "patch" colored by impressions of Asia. In my
conversations with U.S. sponsors, they most often organized the global map
into four of these agglomerations: patches of cultural affinity (e.g., Asia or "the
West"); patches linked by economic investments and trade; a bipartite division
into "have" and "have not" countries; and patches linked through common
environmental problems, such as tornados or overfishing.[64] Although some
of these patches stitched together geographically contiguous places, many did
not. It is an important point, since scholars of the U.S. often focus on areas
such as the hemispheric Americas, the Atlantic World, or the Pacific Rim that
reinforce a vision of transnational spatiality as linked by land or sea.[65] There are
good reasons to do so if one is tracking politics and trade. But for U.S. people
and groups such as churches, a bright spot approach more closely resembles
their experience of a globe that flexibly "expands or contracts, reveals certain
vistas and conceals others."[66]

This approach also foregrounds the ad hoc legibility of certain places over
others. Places become bright because of political or technological exigencies (if
the United States is waging war or encouraging trade; if ships or airplanes travel
there) and because of humanitarian disasters in the news. There are Christian
linkages as well. For example, U.S. Catholics have strong ties to Latin America through institutional missionary work, humanitarian partnerships, and
immigration, which make their approach to the "global" largely hemispheric.
More than 80% of U.S. Catholic sister church partnerships are situated in this
region. In my interviews, so were 46% Unbound sponsorships (with another
17% in the Philippines).[67]

While such links are important, the focus in studies of global commitments
on congregations or denominations (or, in this case, humanitarian organizations) can result in an overly institutionalized picture that obscures how
individuals use "situated particularity as their point of entry to the universal."[68]
Jenna, a 43-year-old mainline Baptist in Kansas City, is one example. Over the
course of our conversations, she discursively mapped the following places: the
United States (where she was born and lives), England and Germany (where
she visited and has ancestors), Jamaica (where her family vacationed twice),
Spain (where her daughter went on a school exchange), Kenya (home to a
family of recent immigrants at her church), Tanzania (where World Vision
assigned her a child to sponsor), Haiti and Palestine (where her church supports projects). These locations are not uniformly bright. For example, Jenna
felt very connected to the Haitian church partnership, whereas the Palestinian

one remained dim; she did not even know its precise location. Bright spots also fade. Twenty years later, she could not remember where the first WV child lived, although she wrote to him regularly at the time (after some searching in her file folders, we found it: Uganda). Jenna's narrative approach contrasts with the mapped coherence of, say, the "domestic" and "foreign" spheres of U.S. law and statecraft or the much-studied "10/40 window," a contiguous global swath that certain evangelicals target for proselytization.[69] Bright spot mapping is less immediately arresting, perhaps, but it helpfully jumbles up those connections roughly classed as political, personal, religious, and touristic. Such are the varied, experiential ways that most people map the world.

This brings us back to the dialogical relation between particularity and immensity. Mapping creates particular bright spots, but it also promotes an aesthetic of immensity. Certain maps background the nations altogether to approximate a god's eye view. The most ubiquitous map of this type is the blue-green orb suspended in space. Others are highly personal, even dreamlike cartographic deconstructions; Coleman records how the head pastor at Word of Life beheld a vision in which the map of Sweden exploded into a firework spreading in all directions.[70] Some of the most successful participatory techniques tack back and forth between immensity and particularity by utilizing spinning globes.[71] A. B. Simpson's daily routine is a good example. Because globes spin, geographic points whirl and blend into immensity. Arresting its movement to direct a prayer on a single point is an exercise in particularity. In my fieldwork, I encountered similar practices. A women's prayer group at a Baptist church in North Carolina experimented with circling around a globe and placing their hands upon it as they prayed. In upstate New York, Stephanie, a busy mother of three who supported Unbound, kept a small globe hanging from her rearview mirror to prompt her to pray for big "things that plague the world." As we were chauffeuring her sons around one afternoon, she showed me what she meant. Glancing over at the globe, she caught sight of the Middle East and, eyes still on the road, murmured a quick prayer for those caught in the violence in Syria. At another prayer group, this time at the San Jose evangelical church where I was a Compassion Experience volunteer, one member spun a globe and then stopped its trajectory by bringing her finger down onto a point. Any other member could then call out a relevant prayer. When her finger landed on East Africa, we prayed for AIDS victims. On Russia, for broken families. When it landed on the ocean, I suggested a prayer for clean water. (The group liked the idea so much they told me they might work it into their regular rotation.)

In his famous essay on the Eiffel Tower, Roland Barthes expresses the kernel of what I am suggesting here. Walking the streets of Paris, he writes, is being "thrust into the midst of sensation . . . [to] perceive only a kind of tidal wave of things." By contrast, climbing the tower and looking out from on high is a way "to transcend sensation and to see things *in their structure*," which, according to Barthes, makes the warren of city streets intelligible and thereby asserts a certain mastery over it.[72] In her study of Wall Street, Karen Ho identifies something similar about the discursive mapping of place names. When bankers talk about being "global," they list the places where their banks are established, along with a litany of "faraway and unlikely places." Protestant pastors may likewise incorporate multiple place names into their sermons to map Christian expansion, or at least its potential for infinite deterritorialization.[73] Sponsorship organizations employ the same kind of linguistic and cartographic gigantism, though even the most widespread only cover a comparatively limited number of actual points on the globe. (As of 2019, the largest is World Vision, which provided services in about 65 out of 195 countries.) Mapping immensity in these ways invokes the "tidal wave" of places and then makes it intelligible. It is the imaginative glue that allows sponsors to think of themselves as "masters of a world," as Barthes puts it, even while they take a bright spot approach.

Ho and Barthes remind us that a god's eye view is power. Coleman's work on Sweden's Word of Life church also reminds us of the stakes for Christians: when church leaders map the rapid expansion of Christianity, he writes, their congregants "marvel."[74] In Christian globalism, immensity is meant to provoke marvel and awe as affective responses that recognize the miracle of God's work. In this regard, there is some irony in sponsorship's use of mapped immensities to produce a god's eye view. After all, maps erase people. Sometimes this serves an explicit ideological purpose (for example, early maps of the United States progressively erased imagery related to Native inhabitants to create the semblance of "open" space),[75] but mostly it is a symptom of how maps make lived places into graphic spaces. The irony lies in the way sponsorship is built on Christian sentimentalism's conception of human relations as the mechanism by which God's Love travels. Thus, maps erase people to create a god's eye view, which necessarily falls short of sponsorship's Christian ideal in which a living God is understood to be closely involved with his creatures. As a result, maps have value in sponsorship insofar as they are framed within a larger set of techniques that bring the particular back into play. Prayer is one of the most important.

Building on Mauss's insight that prayer is a social process, anthropologists of Christianity have recently called attention to its function as "a way of mapping affect." One contribution to the discussion tracks how fundamentalist Protestants in Scotland pray for intercession along a widening trajectory that begins with family, moves on to community, and from there to the nation. Each level varies in its affective register from anguish to resentment to resignation.[76] While sponsor prayers differ, the larger point is that affective "prayer mapping" should be considered alongside other conceptual and cartographic maps since it clarifies the multiple registers through which Christian globalism is reinforced. Throughout my fieldwork, I jotted down the beings to whom sponsors prayed, usually when I was with them for grace before meals. I also asked if they directed their personal prayers differently when they prayed about local needs and global ones. Sponsors gamely tried to identify patterns, although it was not a familiar exercise for them. (Unlike, for example, asking a born-again Christian to narrate the story of her conversion.)

The Compassion sponsors with whom I worked most closely attended an Evangelical Free Church of America and a Presbyterian (PCUSA) church that was effectively non-denominational evangelical. The Unbound sponsors came from a variety of parishes and were nearly all cradle Catholics. They have more potential options for intercessors than their Protestant counterparts, yet when it came to global concerns, they used fewer variations than I expected. They reserved saintly intercession for day-to-day and personal needs, often related to a specific family member. (In just two cases, sponsors addressed St. Jude, patron of "hopeless causes," about an especially desperate disaster in the world.) They, and their evangelical counterparts, also rarely mapped the Holy Spirit onto a global prayerscape. My evangelical interlocutors called on the Spirit to sort out confusion in their own hearts or in group settings, for example during a tense church administration meeting or (in a more positive sense) to animate group prayer. For Catholic sponsors, the Spirit was a mood of serenity and a driving impulse internal to the self. The relative absence of the Holy Spirit offers a notable contrast to the better-known examples of globalizing Pentecostal and charismatic churches.

Among the sponsors I got to know, then, Father and Son were by far the most active agents in the global prayerscape. Evangelicals were split evenly about whether they prayed to God or Jesus on a regular basis. Catholics were more likely to address God (58% said they did so, compared to 21% who prayed to Jesus or Mary, respectively). This difference largely disappeared, however, when it came to global needs. In that case, 58% of evangelicals told me they addressed the Father, as did 60% of Catholics. Abby, a 44-year-old evangelical in New Hampshire, was typical in emphasizing Jesus's earthly ministry and thus his "heart" for personal, human-level well-being. When expressing the role of the Father, she laughed, "He is just like the one who can take care of things and fix them. I don't know, like the big daddy!" Danielle, a 42-year-old Unbound sponsor in Kansas City, employed similar imagery: "I think of God as the watcher over the whole world and then I think of Jesus as being like our brother and—He's walked our lives. Jesus [is] how I connect to *my* Christian faith." Repeatedly, sponsors mapped Jesus's presence onto the intimate places of heart, home, and hospital. When they called on Jesus in prayer for global targets—including for the child and his family—it was most often for needs in similarly intimate spaces far away. The Father, on the other hand, was mapped onto less precise needs requiring general "fixing" or "watching," to paraphrase Abby and Danielle.

These prayer patterns diverged most significantly when it came to Mary, the mother of Jesus. The 42% of evangelicals who told me they did not address God for global needs all directed their prayers to Jesus; instead, of the 40% of Catholics in the same position, nearly 30% addressed Mary. In part, as a number of Catholic sponsors told me, they mapped Mary globally because she already affiliated herself with nations. She was the protector of particular countries and each of her apparitions or manifestations had "designated areas of responsibility" in the world, to quote one sponsor. For example, some U.S. Catholics called on Our Lady of Guadalupe when they prayed for the children they sponsored in Mexico or Central America since they viewed her as implicated in and protector of that region. As the recipient of global prayers, Mary most clearly reinforced a view of the world as segmented into nation-states.

VIRTUAL PRESENCE

The Internet combines the most resonant elements of Christian globalism's spatiotemporal compressions. Like synchronic prayers and choruses, it projects seemingly limitless, instant global communication. Like map exercises, it is a graphic medium with a capacity for intertextuality through the incorporation of videos and other media. Contemporary sponsors recognize the impact of the Internet and other communications technologies in cementing global ties: in our discussions, 40% brought up its role in this respect. It was rivaled only by the frequency with which they talked about ties we might think of as cosmic through the "body of Christ," the "global church," or the Creator. Flying in the face of globalization theory, but in keeping with their own experience, only 7% brought up ease or rapidity of travel as a factor in creating global connections.[77] In other words, it is the virtual and cosmic spheres that offer the primary "tools with which ordinary individuals create global culture in a local context."[78] Sponsorship organizations know this and since about 2010 they have rapidly augmented their online applications. Compassion runs especially sophisticated campaigns across multiple platforms, including its blog, a Pinterest board, coordinated hashtags on Twitter and Instagram, mobile phone apps, and a Vimeo channel with nearly 900 videos at the time of writing. Across these platforms, women are the most engaged users.

One might expect online technologies to significantly impact sponsorship's infrastructure and sponsors' outlook. However, I found something more akin to the recent, and rather sober, assessments by media scholars whose work suggests there is strong affinity between offline and online behaviors as users reinforce a holistic identity in multiple modes simultaneously.[79] We can return, for example, to Coleman's work on Swedish charismatics. He tracks how they hone an "expansive" self that projects things (words, prayers, money) outward in order to receive a return from God. They put this self into practice as they say prayers for others, give away money, and such. They also use new media as "a symbolically rich" space in which to project the same unconfined self.[80] Sponsorship organizations differ from globalizing charismatic churches, but they too share an "elective affinity" with the Internet as an expansive space that suits what they already cultivate offline. In fact, the promoters of non-denominational Christian sponsorship and many promoters of new media platforms share overlapping visions of a worldwide network that circumvents old institutions to unite humankind (one thinks of Marshall McLuhan's "global village" or Mark Zuckerberg's rhetoric about Facebook).[81]

At a more practical level, too, the Internet has not altered sponsorship's basic model. At the time of writing, all the organizations under study had developed methods for sponsors to pay online and email letters and photos through an intranet system. Sponsor letters were then printed out and translated for the children, who responded with a physical letter as before. For organizations, the system saved on postage, potentially improved sponsor experience, and ideally retained their control by circumventing other forms of social media. However, as many sponsors told me, from their perspective the difference was minimal. At Compassion, emailed letters were printed at its Colorado Springs headquarters and then sent on as before; the process took two to three months, clocking in at just one week faster than sending it by post. At Unbound, e-letters shaved off a bit more time since they were transferred directly to the field, but then they were also printed and mailed in the child's country.

The other major online tools for sponsors—organizational websites and associated social media—reiterate participatory techniques that have defined Christian globalism for generations. For example, mid-century sponsors received photos of foreign children in familiar prayer poses with captions that said they pronounced their U.S. sponsor's name "in quaint accents." Now Compassion's website embeds footage of it. A two-minute video titled "Does My Sponsored Child Know My Name?" features a series of back and forth cuts in which the viewer watches as a U.S. sponsor reacts emotionally to a video of a foreign child pronouncing his or her name. Big numbers are also rebooted on Compassion's Sponsorship Board, which was launched in July 2014. "Each day, at exactly 12:00 am MST, our story starts with a blank page," it states, "As new children are sponsored, this page will populate with their smiling faces, serving as an ever-building visual story of the hope and possibility that sponsorship creates." A ticker is updated in real-time and users can scroll through the rows of photos (about 100 per day when I monitored it in July 2018). Other online features enhance the vocal simultaneity discussed above. Compassion's "Joyful Songs" page features images of children in Burkina Faso in mid-song—mouths open, blurred hands in motion—with embedded sound clips. "Hear sponsored children sing it in their country's official language, French!" reads the caption. Click and one hears a worship song with lyrics that are familiar to U.S. evangelicals, sung in French with an African beat. Scroll down and Bolivian children offer the same experience in Spanish. The lyrics to each song are printed in English so users can "sing along" (figure 7.5).[82]

Although I did not find that the Internet reshaped existing cultural frameworks, it certainly mediates Christian globalism in especially convincing ways. One reason is its capacity for "transmedia storytelling."[83] The term refers to the ability to substantiate a meta-narrative—that is, a narrative already familiar to users—by reinforcing it through multiple forms of media at once. Sponsorship websites do this by combining video, audio, and print, as evident on the "Joyful Songs" page. They also create multiple online access points for the same messages through their blogs, emails, and alerts. I signed up for each organization's emails from October 2013 to July 2017, during which time I received approximately 11 individual emails from Compassion per month, 10 from ChildFund, 5 from World Vision, and 2 from Unbound. The last two organizations also have prayer ministries that send emails from separate accounts, which added another email per month from the WV Hope Prayer Team and three more from Unbound's Prayer Partners. Even at the low end, the number of communications far outstrips the pre-Internet era during which a sponsor would have received a quarterly magazine and perhaps one monthly mailing. Organizations expect that the stream of semi-tailored emails, along with the proliferation of blog content, will hold sponsors' attention and generate greater investments.

Every study is a product of its time, and this was especially evident to me as I spoke with sponsors about virtual presence. When I was conducting research from 2014 to 2016, Compassion, Unbound, and World Vision had only really rolled out their internal email systems in the last two years and started to build integrated social media platforms within the last five. Further, many of the sponsors I got to know were older—the average age of an Unbound sponsor was 55—and varied markedly in their level of online activity. Yet regardless

FIG 7.5. A detail from the "Joyful Songs" section of Compassion's website. Participatory techniques are now integrated online, combining visual images, embedded video, and sound files. On the left are links to recipes so parents and their children can taste foods similar to those the sponsored child eats (compare to chapter 3).

of age or actual usage, nearly every sponsor told me that they would welcome online tools *if* these could deliver on sponsorship's promise to compress spatiotemporal distance and create more robust 1:1 relationships. (Sponsors have viewed new media in this light for 150 years, ever since they began to request photographic portraits.) Sponsors' responses, and frustrations, largely reflected the halfway email system then in place. Because it did not radically disrupt the letter writing process (recall that children and sponsors still received paper letters), it is hard to know how online tools might impact sponsorship moving forward.

Nancy, a 68-year-old Unbound sponsor, was one of the few people I met who could compare paper letters to a completely online form of communication: she had been in contact with John in Hyderabad, India, since her sponsorship of him ended (chapter 6), and she received regular Facebook updates from Carlos, the father of the girl she now sponsors in Honduras. "The Facebook thing was a blessing and a downside," she reflected. Although she was no longer sending money to John, she felt that their ongoing communications were a "very practical way of helping in a spiritual way . . . [I can] still say, God is always with you and I'm praying for you too." At the same time, she felt her own insignificance: the obstacles John faced were so massive that she often did not know what to say. Once, when John was at a low point, he asked if he could come to the United States to be her servant. Nancy, who worked as a computer analyst for the Kansas school system, never had nannies or cleaners while she raised her two kids. She rolled her eyes self-deprecatingly as she told the story, sitting with me in her modest home in suburban Kansas City. An Indian servant was clearly a ludicrous idea. But she understood the depth of John's desperation at that moment and, in this case, the rapidity of online interactions felt like a detriment to thoughtful spiritual encouragement. "With a letter you have time to prepare an answer, to think what's the best thing to say to help him. Normally if I get a message [on Facebook] I'll answer right away but in that case I thought whoa, I have to wait . . . I [have to] just let this sit and I'll answer this tomorrow."

With Carlos, Nancy appreciates that she is no longer beholden to Unbound's lengthy mail system. Now she can send an e-birthday card for each member of his family, not just the sponsored child. She has been able to learn much more about them too, and vice versa. She and Carlos message each other in (almost) real time to request prayers or tell each other if they have prayed for one another. Nancy and I scrolled through her Facebook feed and, sure enough, Carlos and his family had just posted to tell her they were praying for her daughter, who was about a week away from giving birth. The volume of messages also meant more information, which in one instance allowed Nancy to surmise that the sponsored child needed glasses; she intuited it from how Carlos wrote that his daughter had trouble with certain tasks. She contacted Unbound to send extra money to get the girl's eyes checked and Carlos sent pictures of her sporting new glasses a few weeks later. Nancy's main complaint about Facebook is the language barrier. She puts the messages through an Internet translator, but Unbound's translations are much better. Recently, she and Carlos have begun to address the issue by sending more photos and fewer messages.

Only about 10% of the sponsors I met had been contacted by the children they supported, but this balance will likely change as sponsored children and their families have greater access to the Internet and as sponsors become more active on social media. For sponsorship organizations, the challenges will be enormous, especially if scholars are correct in arguing that social media is making users more intolerant of obvious mediation in an age of "immediate" connection (though emails are in fact mediated through complex technical apparatuses).[84] One way to stem the tide will be to convince sponsors that it is in their best interests to rebuff any attempts at contact outside of organizational systems. Currently, organizations do so by warning sponsors that it is "surprisingly common" for an adult—someone who knows the child vaguely or an uncle or cousin—to pretend to be the child on social media to elicit money. They add that refusing contact outside of their systems also protects children from potentially predatory sponsors and, more commonly, helps sponsors "navigate the ocean of cross-cultural sensitivities [to] avoid inadvertently writing something inappropriate."[85]

These challenges strike directly at the promise of a globalism mapped onto those "bright spots" of Christian fellowship. As sponsorship organizations have less ability to mediate and monitor access points, it will be increasingly difficult for them to explain to Americans at home why the foreign people that are portrayed as mirroring their fundamental ideas, prayers, and aspirations may not always act in ways that are legible to them. And yet individuals like Nancy are a good reminder that U.S. people can be flexible and sophisticated in their understanding of these exchanges too. They take them day-by-day and, implicitly perhaps, recognize them as one aspect of the emerging and shifting relations that comprise Christian globalism.

Globalism, Made and Remade

You are sitting at the bank, or the bus station, or the post office. The chair is hard plastic, sculpted to fit someone else's frame. You shift a bit, cross and uncross your legs. As you wait, your eyes wander to the wall. A row of clocks. Each one with a nondescript face, neatly ordered and identical—except for the hands, which are conspicuous in their different orientations. One in the afternoon. Eight in the evening. Four in the morning. Below each one block letters indicate a place. New York, Tokyo, Oslo. Then your town or city, with the local time. You feel a surge of intimacy. You are here, others are there. Collaborators in this global thing, this standardized time. Somehow knowable to each other. You could transfer money, or travel, or mail a letter to those people far away. You probably won't, but you could. A fleeting sensation of globalism embedded in an everyday space. There it is, there on the wall.

*　　*　　*

As I was working on this project, I began to notice rows of clocks (figure 8.1). Then I began to notice other ways that globalism's forms impinged on me. Down the street, there is a mural where children of many colors, wearing t-shirts and beatific grins, hold hands as they circle the globe. On my bike ride to work, hotel lobbies hang dozens of national flags together over grand entries. At an art show just after Leonard Cohen's death, I stood in an installation where participants hummed his song, "Hallelujah," while numbers flashed on a screen showing how many hundreds of others around the world hummed along at the same time. On Twitter, evangelical crossover company TOMS shoes alerted me to its annual One Day Without Shoes campaign where one goes barefoot for a day to "experience a bit of what is a daily challenge for millions around the world." The aesthetics of big numbers saturate my newsfeed, announcing the growth of Christian populations, worldwide inequity, or environmental decay.

The forms and techniques I associate with Christian globalism are by no means confined by some bright line to a sphere called "U.S. religion." They have developed through transoceanic encounters, and in contexts where Christianity and culture are entangled and mutually reinforcing. They complement

FIG 8.1. Clocks in the Montreal bus station. June 2018. Photo by the author.

and contribute to other attempts to reify global community; the United Nations, the Olympics, rhetoric about social media, ecological activism, and humanitarian campaigns are a few examples mentioned in this book. In U.S. politics, there is still a belief in "people-to-people diplomacy," to use the mid-century term; the Peace Corps program remains strong; U.S. celebrities are photographed as UN goodwill ambassadors. These forms are interwoven with sweeping assessments about global "allies" or "enemies." None of us who live within these forms should take them for granted. They come from somewhere specific and they have significant impacts in the world. With child sponsorship plans as its starting point, *Christian Globalism at Home* alerts readers to their presence.

At a basic level, my goal is denaturalization. Revealing the labor that goes into global projects redresses the persistent assumption that "global Christianity" is somehow organic and even inevitable, leaving scholars to catalogue it and marvel at its spread. Partly, I am thinking of those Christian scholars and commentators whose subtle Providentialism has helped shape the study of (especially Pentecostal and charismatic) Christian growth.[1] However, anthropologist Anna Tsing makes a similar point more broadly; many social scientists, she argues, have been seduced by their own vision of globalization as a progressive and seemingly unstoppable force that "flows" unhindered across the world. They have written about globalization the way they want it to be.[2] Another, not unrelated, issue that needs "denaturing" is the tired assumption that globalization originates in the (Christian) West and cascades out to engulf other people who then grapple with its results.[3] In this view, U.S. Christians may at first seem to be natural global subjects.

Since I started this project in 2012, more scholars of U.S. Christianity have begun to deconstruct this idea by evaluating the impact of globalization on U.S. Americans, as I do here. *Christian Globalism at Home* builds on and reframes this work. It does so by moving away from the overarching emphasis on written media such as sermons, news headlines, or speeches at international conferences. It attempts to look beyond the notable, but still small, number of U.S. Christians who travel abroad as pastors, statesmen, missionaries, humanitarians, and tourists. It asks, what about everyone else? What is the texture of global commitments in the time between Sunday sermons and newspaper headlines? Globalism is fleeting. Intensity wavers. Techniques must be repeated.

In tracking one type of fund-raising, I link organizations and people across a number of Christian affiliations. Initially, this approach may seem surprising since it traverses boundaries that scholars often use to clarify and narrow their work. It also covers a comparatively long time frame, which leapfrogs the fissures that separate liberal and neoliberal or modern and postmodern. By contrast, previous studies of child sponsorship have tied it closely to particular periods, viewing it as indicative of a paternalistic post-war moment in U.S. foreign relations, for example, or an individualist neoliberal one since the 1980s.[4] While I do not disagree with these assessments, ultimately I found a long-term, comparative approach was more revealing of sponsorship's substructure: it provides an archive of the development of a particular form of universalism, shaped by modern orientations and aspirations, and expressed through U.S. Christian conceptions of body, self, and soul.

As with any situated case study, my findings will not be equally relevant for all Americans or for every Christian. I want to be very clear about this point: we need more comparative work on varieties of globalism. For example, the kind I have examined does not track neatly onto African Americans' aspirations for Christian racial solidarity or onto the experiences of global south Christians who insist that universalism also encompasses the specificity of national struggles.[5] Sponsorship itself also continues to appeal to new (usually middle-class) publics; the contemporary organizations I profiled here have growing numbers of U.S. sponsors who are Hispanic and Korean American. There are more sponsors in select countries outside of the west, such as Korea and Singapore. Besides non-religious sponsorship organizations, there are a growing number of Muslim-run ones. Subsequent studies will undoubtedly uncover new aspects about this fund-raising model and its participatory techniques.

Yet my contention is that we can still pinpoint a broad pattern in U.S. Christianity (and likely other places where the subject is viewed as an agentive "I" in the world): globalism operates in the unstable space between God-scale immensity and human-scale particularity. Global commitments are therefore fragile things—balanced between "the precariousness of being" and "the possibility of hope."[6] It is the dialogical relation between immensity and particularity that gives globalism its tensile strength and creates highly effective tools for engaged empathy, as attested by the billions of dollars that American individuals give to overseas projects each year.[7] This relation also affirms what for U.S. Christians is the connection between God and his creation. It is the feeling of awe in God's presence, the fleeting awareness of the world and its fate as a whole, and how it relates to human efforts to cultivate intimacy (or "sentiment"). In other words, sentimental Christianity did not displace Divine majesty in U.S. Christianity, as earlier work suggested. Instead, it produced a dynamic and culturally contingent Christian universal, which this book breaks down into four core aspects.

Circulating Love/Love

Love is a foundational concept in U.S. Christian globalism. Building on studies that demonstrate the links between affect, sentiment, and foreign and domestic politics, my argument is that the intimacy of sponsorship's promised

1:1 relation is a counterpart to immensity—or more precisely, a facet of it—because it refuses to disentangle God from his human creation. Put differently, sponsorship insists on an organic link between what I shorthand as (human) "love" and (Divine) "Love." Chapter 1 traced this loose theology of love to white, middle-class Protestants living within the radical economic and political changes of the nineteenth century. Sponsorship developed to encourage women, children, and others with new access to small amounts of cash to view themselves as personally responsible for global projects of moral uplift. These givers came to understand their impact on faraway places through the new logic of "sentimentalism," as scholars now call it, which celebrated the intuitive felt-life of love and emotion. Moreover, it argued that parental (and especially maternal) love was deeply consequential in how it opened a channel for God's grace to penetrate a child's passive soul. Once this idea was scaled up, it began to seem self-evident that the actions and emotions associated with a Christian's love opened a channel for God's Love to penetrate heathens' souls as well.

U.S. Christians made this globally circulating, pre-cultural love the bulwark of their globalism. Though the metaphors differed—some nineteenth-century Christians talked about sensations traveling through a body's nervous system, others referred to sowing seeds in a field or infusing light into darkness—they all implied something natural about the spread of Christianity and its relation to divine Providence. These were the precursors to metaphors of "flow" in later theories of globalization. They bequeathed a moral framework to twentieth-century humanitarianism too. In the nineteenth century, when heathendom still "darkened" the world, Christians found a necessary relation between disgust and love. As heathendom lost its cultural traction in the mid-twentieth century, love was left to buoy aspirations for transglobal intimacy (chapters 4 and 6) and rhetorically transfigure money into Christian joy (chapter 5).

Today U.S. sponsorship is inexplicable without the idea that a Christian person's loving actions provide an entry point through which God's Love travels. Sponsorship's enormous growth in the last half of the twentieth century, despite widening splits between liberal and conservative U.S. Christians on many international issues, testifies to the plasticity and ubiquity of this theology of love: for liberals, it seems to sidestep the problem of U.S. crypto-imperialism by going back to the individual—affirming that good U.S. individuals *can* make a difference; for conservatives, it seems to sidestep the problem of waning direct, one-to-one evangelism by going back to the individual—affirming that good U.S. individuals *can* make a difference.

Being a Global Body

Scholars know that many Americans at home find global projects compelling, but the day-to-day mechanics of these commitments are poorly understood. This brings me to the connection between love, discussed above, and the body. The body is a well-known metaphor for a global church of believers, and U.S. Christians have circulated photographs of victimized or joyful foreign bodies since the late nineteenth century (chapter 3). However, I also emphasize the body itself as a key site for the physical manifestation of globalism. The premise has two components. On the one hand, it refers to the affective charge that Christians view as human beings' (limited and fleeting) connection to a god's eye view. This is the sense of vertigo and wonder as one is confronted by big numbers, a massive chorus, or a spinning globe. On the other hand, bodies also manifest globalism through their assumed connection to each other: U.S. Christians have come to trust the body as a site of deep knowledge about others based on the idea that all humans share certain basic sensations and emotions by virtue of their single origin point in the (Christian) Creator.

In the sponsorship literature, this idea goes back to the late nineteenth century, but it first appears prominently among liberals in the 1920s. It seems to run parallel to the growing acceptance of cultural relativism. What I mean is that nineteenth-century U.S. Christian aspirations for transglobal intimacy focused largely on their own missionaries or on "native protégées" (to use sponsorship language) who adopted familiar names, clothes, and customs. This changed as early twentieth-century liberals began to view culture as a positive aspect of human diversity; since the 1980s and 1990s, U.S. Christians have (often emphatically) celebrated marked cultural differences between Christians across the world. Most of the sponsors with whom I worked found this idea highly invigorating, but it also planted seeds of doubt about the possibility of really knowing faraway others. The body universal provides a solution: one's body can feel what seem to be visceral reactions shared by all bodies—sadness, joy, fear, or hunger. To that end, as this book shows, U.S. Christians have developed myriad bodily techniques using food, dress, prayer, or song. A variant extends the body through points of contact, which are understood to transfer spirits/spirited objects across vast distances (chapter 5).

For U.S. Christians, God is never an interloper, although most sponsorship staff and many sponsors acknowledge that the U.S. government, military, and even missionaries may very well be. This basic premise about God meant that, while I often heard sponsors and staff members question the role of U.S. people and culture abroad, I never heard them dissect the underlying universalism that associates a common Creator with a shared set of human feelings and sensations. Persistent issues relative to race also shape these acts of imagined unification. Ultimately, foreign poverty (often racialized as brown or black) has a particular look, smell, and sound for U.S. people, whereas American prosperity and capacity (often racialized as white) is sensorially blank.[8] This unspoken norm welds together a set of techniques, including immersive impersonations of "heathens" (chapter 2) and orphans (chapter 3), and the multisensory displays of poverty at today's Compassion Experience (chapter 6). Sponsors often recognize this ambivalence, albeit obliquely, which leads to another set of techniques that I call mirroring to tranquilize the problems posed by racialized inequality.

Mirroring Universalism

Christian globalism declares that there are likeminded believers far away. Philip Jenkins, among other heralds of a "global Christianity," has argued that contemporary U.S. Christians are now significantly more likely to view foreign Christians as "just like the person in an adjacent pew at one's own church."[9] Like all aspects of globalism, unity-in-diversity is actually the product of sustained labor as Christians rhetorically and visually invoke their presumed "ideological and ritual soulmates."[10] As I have shown through sponsorship, unity relies upon the regular invocation of racialized difference. I broach this idea most clearly in chapter 4, which examines sponsorship's mid-century overlap with transnational adoption, so-called GI babies, and rising tensions related to systemic segregation in the United States. In this atmosphere, organizations like CCF increased the use of imagery depicting children as the nations, which circulated alongside similar imagery in nascent NGOs and the UN. Depictions of unity-in-diversity are thus by no means limited to Americans, although they certainly appeal to them strongly.

These images invoke racialized difference without foregrounding race itself. The usual assumption—pace Jenkins—is that they do so because unity-in-diversity *overcomes* racial difference and prejudice. More helpful is Ann Stoler's description of race as a "sorting category" in colonial systems, and of course in the United States. Sponsorship media has created, or certainly reinforced, the premise that "races" (or "nations") are internally coherent and naturally separate. Thus, unity-in-diversity provokes joy and wonder precisely because it seems to make visible how God's system—Christianity—overcomes humankind's natural state. It is the tenacious assumption of difference that creates the miracle of sameness. Today, U.S. sponsors often conceptually map the globe into "West and the rest" or "have and have not countries" (chapter 7) and many find the implicit racial implications deeply unsettling. It is not hard to understand the continuing appeal of unity-in-diversity imagery and the hope it suggests.

These images, and related participatory techniques, do more than merely depict people getting along: they mirror back to Americans the culturally diverse but ultimately familiar moral forms that make others knowable as fellow believers. Otherwise, diversity could seem to augur chaos and threat. Mirroring appeals to U.S. Christians across the spectrum (and thus to sponsorship organizations) because it keeps its Christianity vague. Sometimes it includes what is explicitly Christian but nonsectarian, such as prayers or hymnody. Other times it invokes unmarked moral categories, such as aspirations for future employment or "meaningful" lives (chapter 6). Its globalism is just as vague, and generally hyperbolic, claiming that people "of every tribe and nation" collaborate with U.S. Christians—reading the same publications, supporting the same causes, praying for the same things—even though sponsorship supporters have, historically speaking at least, often been U.S. and European ex-patriots stationed abroad.[11] These claims are notable not because they (necessarily) reveal Christian expansion, but because they reveal the construction of its global forms.

The Immensity of Injustice

Immensity is the god's eye view, the cascade of statistics, the swelling chorus of voices, the faces crowding into a frame. It is a feeling of awe and infinitude, a sensation of vertigo, a "quake in being."[12] It, too, evokes the deepest kind of knowing. Besides delight and wonder, however, immensity risks provoking despair about the enormity of the world's problems. Studies have tracked increased American pessimism about the state of the world, but my work with sponsors shows a neutral and often optimistic view, especially once we look beyond white, conservative evangelicals. Through sponsorship, Christians work to turn potentially negative emotions into engaged empathy, and they usually succeed. And yet immensity does provoke a lingering question: Why do war and poverty occur and why do these burdens fall most heavily on some of the world's people and not others?

Sponsors grapple with this question from their vantage point as citizens of a global powerhouse. Even in the nineteenth century, U.S. Christians understood themselves as significantly more blessed than the people to whom their missionaries traveled. As might be expected from a study that takes a fund-raising method as its basis, the uneven distribution of material resources is often foremost in sponsors' minds. In the nineteenth century, they viewed their pennies as (more) moral through systematic means of collection (chapter 2). In the mid-twentieth century, a different issue arose: large segments of sponsorship's audience—especially working-class people and elderly pensioners—had to reorient their sense of self as wealthy within a global context. This challenge remains even among upper-middle-class sponsors who, like U.S. people in general, persist in seeing themselves as "comfortable," rather than rich. They find ways to make money moral by reiterating earlier claims about systematic giving and stewardship, making handcrafts (chapter 5), or mixing prayer with audits (chapter 6).

Sponsors raise questions about other inequalities too. While a nineteenth-century sponsor might have asked why God leaves some places mired in heathendom, her twenty-first-century counterpart is more likely to ask why poverty, war, or natural disasters decimate places that are already struggling. While such questions clearly differ from each other, at base they point to a major ontological conundrum: Why would an omnipotent and completely loving Deity allow injustice? What if God is less great than Christians believe? More worrisome perhaps, what if God is less good? There are many ways to finesse an answer, as chapter 6 shows. Most commonly, sponsors settle on a call for human action, and more specifically for action by those who have been "blessed" by resources—in essence, sponsors themselves. Therein lies a fundamental irony: Americans profess to extricate themselves from the center of things through a global outlook, yet the kind of globalism they cultivate re-centers them as the axis through which God's resources flow.

* * *

Christian globalism yearns for a certain kind of future. In its modern American form, these expectant hopes are inseparable from intimate human relations that are understood as an expression of, and channel for, the ultimate relation of human beings to their common Creator. This is what has driven U.S. people at home to support children abroad for more than 200 years. These are the aspirations, sometimes ineffable, often bodily and concrete, that make and remake global subjects.

ACKNOWLEDGMENTS

Many people spent countless hours telling and showing me what they do as sponsors. They generously welcomed me into their homes, churches, and volunteer sites. The first acknowledgment is to them, without whom there could not have been a book at all. A few individuals also went out of their way to help me organize trips to their hometowns: I am very grateful to Ted and Sue Filipiak, Susan Mitchell, Karen Aliphant, and Dan and Marianne Denson.

The historical portions of this text relied on a group of dedicated archivists and family history keepers. I am indebted especially to archivists Chris Anderson, Mark Shenise, and Dale Patterson (United Methodist Archives Center at Drew University), Karrie Dvorak (Nebraska United Methodist Historical Center and Archives), Steve Gray (World Vision), Joan Losen (ChildFund), Frances O'Donnell (Andover-Harvard Theological Library), and Shawn Weldon (Catholic Historical Research Center of the Archdiocese of Philadelphia). Other people enthusiastically helped me with unprocessed collections, including Lorie Lee (Compassion), Rev. Dan Lewis (FUMC in Los Angeles), and Paul Rosstead (Calvary Baptist in Washington, DC). And yet others shared their own documents and memories with me, including Bruce Berney, J. "Jay" Calvitt Clarke III, José Chipenda, the Dooley family in Kansas City, Marilee Pierce Dunker, Mariana Gomez-Simpson, Susan and Rob Johnson, Bill Kliewer, Lindy Lybarger, Mary and Kent Moran, JoAnn Stroud, Louis Weeks, and Alexander Wirt. Another big thank you to the volunteers and Brewco staff at the Compassion Experience trucks, Jesse Cernak and her team, Carmen Castro Tomas and Kristel Kabigting, Kate Marley, and to Heidi Baumgaertner at *The Christian Century* who generously waived the fee to post my request for sponsors.

It took a leap of faith for sponsorship organizations to let me mine their archives and spend time in their offices. It meant trusting me with their stories, both past and present. The past—especially at Compassion, World Vision, and ChildFund—does not always represent what these organizations strive for today. A contact of mine at WVI aptly described it in an email after she read a draft of the manuscript: "It does make for uncomfortable reading at times for those of us still battling to help shift people's understanding about our work and why and how we do it. To that end, is there any chance you could run an acknowledgment of our willingness to engage with this project as part of our commitment to accountability and transparency?" I want to make that acknowledgment here: The people who welcomed me at World Vision, Compassion, Unbound, and ChildFund did so because they believe deeply in their programs and in the possibility that academic research can contribute something to understanding them better. In response to concerns that some Compassion and WV staff raised, I also want to emphasize a couple points I make in the book. First, neither organization defines itself as actively evangelizing today. Second, they rarely feature images of screaming or starving children (e.g., figure 7.1). All the organizations under study strive to show children "with dignity," to use Christian inflected language. On that note, I am grateful especially to Suzy Gliebe, Paul Moede and Christy Janssen at Compassion, Tennille Bergin at WVI, and Scott Wasserman, Paco Wertin, Paul Pearce, and Loretta Kline at Unbound. Dozens of other employees took time out of their busy schedules to speak with me, show me around, help me fix the photocopier, and take me out on weekends. They contributed to this book in innumerable ways.

In crafting an interdisciplinary project, I depended on the input of an especially wide array of colleagues. I asked historians, sociologists, anthropologists, and U.S. cultural studies experts to comment on chapters or send me lists of sources. I am incredibly lucky to have such generous conversation partners—those I name below and those I may have inadvertently missed. A few people who shaped my thinking at key junctures include my wonderful peers and mentors in the Young Scholars in American Religion program who gave me valuable feedback on a very early project proposal. Although they almost certainly do not remember, Tom Tweed and Tisa Wenger also offered thoughtful comments on the first iteration of this work at the American Society of Church History meeting in 2014. More recently, the yearly meetings of Sally Promey and Sarah Rivett's Material Economies of Religion in the Americas project at MAVCOR have given me the chance to workshop ideas as I wrote (and rewrote). I have also presented aspects of the project at the University of Edinburgh, Princeton University, McGill University, Memorial University in Newfoundland, Columbia University, Queen's University, the Taking Exception conferences at Indiana University (Bloomington) and Universidad Nacional Autónoma de México, and the Biennial Conference on Religion and American Culture in Indianapolis. I am so grateful for those stimulating exchanges, especially with graduate students. Thanks to organizers including Sarah Imhoff, Cooper Harris, Judith Weisenfeld, Philip Goff, Courtney Bender, Gale Kenny, Naomi Haynes, Barry Stephenson, and Ian Cuthbertson. Courtney, Sarah, and Naomi in particular also offered helpful insights over meals and drinks. John Modern and Elijah Siegler organized High Theory at the American Academy of Religion meeting in 2018, which prompted revisions to chapter 2. James Bielo and Kristy Nabhan-Warren's edited SI in *Exchange* sharpened my thinking, as did expert editorial comments by Brooke Blower and Courtney Bender, who invited me to write pieces in, respectively, the *Journal of Modern American History* and *The Immanent Frame*. Other colleagues generously shared their ideas and even materials with me at early stages of the project, including Sara Fieldston, Emily Baughan, Heather Curtis, Kate Carté Engel, Julia Irwin, David King, Amanda Moniz, and Bertrand Taithe. Jess Farrell kindly cast her expert eye on my interlude about Liberia.

Many colleague/friends read parts of the manuscript or articles that arose out of this research, which helped me clarify what ended up in the book: James Bielo, Katharine Gerbner, Britt Halvorson, Courtney Handman, Jessica Hardin, Sonia Hazard, Lucia Hulsether, Fred Klaits, Dana Logan, Kelsey Moss, David Walker, and Tisa Wenger. The unparalleled Simon Coleman and my mother, Maureen, each read the whole draft. So did two insightful anonymous reviewers for Princeton University Press. Fred Appel and his team have been a pleasure to work with throughout. Fred is a sharp, funny, and dedicated editor, as well as a delightful lunch companion. One could not ask for more. At Concordia, I have had the good fortune to be in conversation with David Howes and especially Jeremy Stolow, my collaborator on the Material Religion Initiative. I am also lucky to have departmental colleagues who encouraged and congratulated me every step of the way. I am grateful especially to Carly Daniel-Hughes. A number of our excellent students worked with me as research assistants: my thanks to Cal Boog, Georgia Carter, Chloé Collier, Ashely Crouch, Lindsey Jackson, Seila Rizvic, Daniel Saenz, and Rhee-Soo Lee at Harvard. This project was made possible by generous grants from the Social Sciences and Humanities Research Council and the Fonds de recherche société et culture du Québec. I do not take for granted living in a place where the government supports academic research. It is a privilege that lets me do what I love doing.

As always, my heartfelt thanks to my family, which has grown bigger since I began this project. A warm welcome to my niece, Annie Goldie, and my daughter, Charna Evi. I finished fieldwork and started writing with Evi by my side. None of that would have been possible without Jesse. This book is for him.

APPENDIX A

Methodology

Since there are different disciplinary conventions regarding summaries of methodology, I have opted to include a substantial appendix on the topic. Research took place from 2012 to 2017, with the most concentrated period from January 2014 to May 2016. The historical portions of the book are based on university archives, mainly at Drew, Columbia, Harvard, Stanford, and Virginia. I consulted a half dozen smaller archives as well, which are listed in the notes if cited. This multi-sited approach helped round out a portrait of attenuated networks. For example, the nineteenth-century mission boards that I cover in chapters 1 and 2 operated through a centralized Women's Foreign Missionary Board. Each board was divided into regional branches, which were further subdivided into local auxiliaries and mission circles, generally of about 10–20 members. To study these circles, I began, with the help of diligent research assistants (see the acknowledgments), to survey monthly missionary periodicals *The Panoplist* (1805–1820), *The Missionary Herald* (every second year from 1821 to 1899 and every year from 1900 to 1951) and *Heathen Woman's Friend* (1869–1896). The first was one of the earliest such periodicals in the United States, published by Congregationalists in New England. It gave rise to the ABCFM's official organ, *The Missionary Herald*, which was read widely by Protestants in a number of denominations. *Heathen Woman's Friend* (HWF) was the periodical of the Methodist Women's Board for Foreign Missions and reached a circulation of more than 20,000 by the late nineteenth century. My RAs and I focused especially closely on the short notes at the end of each issue of *HWF* where local secretaries discussed each circle's activities.

Based on these sources, I contacted some still-extant churches to see if they had retained any unprocessed materials by women in the circles. I was able to visit seven of these churches in Los Angeles, Washington, DC, and Minneapolis. I sat in Edwardian church parlors and empty Sunday school classrooms; once I was driven to an offsite storage unit packed to the rafters. My most memorable experience was a two-day stay at the Fellowship Deaconry in Liberty Corner, New Jersey, where aging deaconesses from a German faith mission helped me comb through diary entries related to the sponsorships they ran for the China Inland Mission in 1936—two years before CCF, generally recognized as the first U.S.-based plan, was founded in Virginia. Today, they still run 17 sponsorships, which they track on hand-written cue cards. My other tactic, inspired by historian Judith Weisenfeld, was to compile lists of sponsors named in archival sources and mine Ancestry.com for evidence of the networks within which they worked and lived. I was able to find some living relatives, through which I obtained a few extant letters from World War I–era sponsorship. I repeated the process for the 1950s–1960s and was able to interview 16 people who had sponsored or (in two cases) been sponsored themselves. My research assistants also catalogued relevant articles and advertisements in the flagship neo-evangelical magazine, *Christianity Today* (1956–1998) and in the liberal Protestant *Christian Century* (1952–1980).

I base the rest of my discussion of the mid-twentieth century on extant archival materials at four organizational headquarters: ChildFund (Richmond, Virginia), World Vision (Monrovia, California), Compassion International (Colorado Springs, Colorado), and Unbound (Kansas City, Missouri). Each one had cabinets and closets filled with documents, only some of which was processed (mainly at WV and ChildFund). My stay at each site varied from two weeks to two months, during which time I also attended any meetings and prayer groups to which I was invited and spent time in a number of locations, such as mail-sorting rooms and call centers. Compassion and Unbound both kindly gave me a desk among their cubicles, so I spoke informally with employees over lunch, at breaks, and when I was invited out on weekends. I also conducted taped interviews with staff members, focusing on those who were implicated in sponsor outreach and communications. I gathered nearly 70 hours of tape from 31 such interviews at ChildFund (7), Compassion (13), Unbound (8), and World Vision (3). I also surveyed these organizations' magazines and newsletters from the 1950s to the 1980s and their contemporary online materials. I signed up for sponsorship email lists from October 2013 to July 2017 and did an in-depth review of those materials during 24 months (January 2014 to December 2015). An RA coded posts on each organization's blog and Twitter feed according to themes I identified as most relevant (e.g., "Gifts" or "Conversion") and created a database of user comments.

The last type of research I conducted was ethnographic—of the roving variety. I opted to focus mainly on Compassion and Unbound, which represent diverse ends of the U.S. Christian spectrum and about which little scholarship has been written. I participated in any sponsorship-related events at the churches in which I conducted interviews, including going shopping for Operation Christmas Child gifts, letter writing events, and Compassion Sundays. I volunteered for Samaritan's Purse sorting through Operation Christmas Child boxes in Boone, North Carolina, for two Christmas seasons. I volunteered with the Compassion Experience mobile exhibit in four locations (Western Massachusetts, Denver, San Jose, and Atlanta). In each case, I stayed a week to attend church and Compassion Sunday events. I also visited a Compassion project in Mexico, which I mention in chapter 6. The bulk of the time I spent with sponsors was in their homes. As I have found with conversational interviews in the past, the structure (or unstructure) depends greatly on the person to whom I am speaking. In some cases, I spent a day with sponsors talking, making dinner, going to church or volunteer work. I saw some sponsors on return trips and we kept in touch over email. Others responded to the questions I had provided and we finished the interview in a bit under two hours.

Over the course of the project, I conducted 91 interviews with 118 people (accounting for spouses) and gathered 196 hours of tape. I identified sponsors in three main ways. Unbound generously mailed out hundreds of letters on my behalf in two key locations (Kansas City and Schenectady, New York). People then contacted me to set up a visit when I was in the area. I returned to the New York location three times and conducted the Kansas interviews in the evenings and weekends while I was at Unbound's offices. I conducted 20 interviews in upstate New York and 19 in Kansas, interviewing a total of 52 sponsors (including spouses). With Compassion, I met people when I volunteered at the Compassion Experience, who then invited me to their churches. I worked most with an Evangelical Free Church in Western Massachusetts and a Presbyterian Church in New Hampshire. Both congregations included people who had grown up in evangelical and fundamentalist households, alongside those from Catholic or mainline Protestant backgrounds. In Massachusetts, the pastor let me recruit sponsors by introducing myself on stage after his sermon. In New Hampshire, the Compassion Advocate (a volunteer at the church) sent me a list of sponsors and I emailed out my request. I recruited more individuals when I participated in their annual card-writing event a few months later. I conducted 12 interviews in Massachusetts, 13 in New Hampshire, and 8 in San Jose (where I also volunteered at the Compassion Experience), with a total of 43 Compassion sponsors.

Mainline Protestants were the hardest to find. CCF, now ChildFund, no longer views itself as a Christian organization and was not able to help me recruit on that basis. Many liberal Protestants also sponsor through non-religious organizations or through those I classify as evangelical (especially World Vision) and Catholic (Unbound has recently had some success drawing Episcopalians). None of these sponsors are identified in organizational records per se. In the end, I was able to identify some interviewees thanks to contacts at ChildFund headquarters. I found others through word of mouth, and a few more after I put an advertisement on the *Christian Century* website and magazine in 2015. I conducted 19 interviews (with 23 people), 8 of which were in person. Taken together, the sponsors I interviewed hailed from 22 states across the country. I note other basic demographic data in the introduction.

It is always useful to state one's positionality at the outset. As I have noted in my earlier work, I see myself as an outsider and insider to the communities within which I work. I am an insider in the sense that I am North American, Anglophone, middle-class, and white. Many sponsors self-identify in these ways too. I differed from them because I am Canadian (although I lived in the United States for six years and still cross the border regularly) and, most evidently, because I am Jewish. In the context of this project, my experience also differed from most sponsors because I have traveled widely, including in most of the countries highlighted in this book (with the exception of India). I mention this fact not to claim some kind of expert knowledge about those places—far from it—but to underline that I actually fit what some studies call "nomadic cosmopolitanism," which as I point out in this book is nonstandard in North America.

Methodologically speaking, the scope of this study poses a few explicit challenges, which I raise just briefly. First, since I focus on sponsors' perspectives, I try to limit my discussion of foreign political and social circumstances to what is evident to them. I also limit my discussion of the inner workings of organizations, including disputes between marketing and programming wings. Marketers need unified messages for public consumption, while their counterparts in the field may strive for a less coherent and generally more accurate portrayal of their projects. Recognizing such complexities within any given organization is important but less relevant for a book, like this one, that focuses on the message as it is ultimately transmitted to sponsors. A second challenge follows: it is hard to gauge sponsors' own experience, especially in the archives, when it is filtered through organizational materials. Where possible I use non-published sources; attentive readers should consult the notes for each chapter. Another major challenge concerns the children who are supported. In many ways, sponsors create a composite child through recursive means as letters, media, and objects circulate globally. Although I am sympathetic to arguments that children should be studied in their own right, I only rarely infer what children might make of the experience (I have read hundreds of children's letters, but these are shaped by program requirements). Yet even though this book is not about those children, the marks of their presence are everywhere. As I was writing, I sometimes paused to remind myself that they are never only names on a page or faces in a photo. One subtle but important rhetorical move is my refusal to use the possessive, although sponsors consistently follow organizations in referring to "their" child. Wherever possible I also use children's personal names. I hope these measures serve as reminders, however inadequate, for readers too.

A final challenge is the lot of historians and anthropologists more generally: I tend to focus on people for whom sponsorship matters because they either strongly support it or emphatically do not. (This is especially true of the historical sections of the book that depend on what was preserved in archives.) Yet as a fund-raising tool, sponsorship's genius lies in its capacity to draw thousands of Americans for whom it may be a largely unnoticed aspect of monthly or yearly giving, especially in an age of direct deposit. Although people in this category do not always appear in my content-driven chapters, it is helpful to signal their presence since sponsorship, like Christian globalism generally, is characterized by varying degrees of intensity. Even committed sponsors move through periods of more and less engagement.

APPENDIX B

Organizational Summaries

AMERICAN BOARD OF COMMISSIONERS FOR FOREIGN MISSIONS

The ABCFM was founded in 1810 as the first foreign missionary organization in the United States. From its headquarters in Boston and Salem, it published a periodical (*The Panoplist*) and settled missionaries in Bombay (India) in 1813 and Jaffna (Ceylon) in 1816. Missions to the Cherokee began shortly after. Its main supporters were Congregationalists, but the ABCFM comprised a variety of denominations. By 1850, it had sent 157 ordained male missionaries (usually with wives) to foreign posts. Most missionaries discussed in this book lived and worked in "stations" that contained their homes, schools, churches, and medical facilities. The ABCFM continued as its own entity until the 1950s; this book discusses its first 50 or so years.

WOMAN'S BOARD OF MISSIONS AND WOMAN'S FOREIGN MISSIONARY SOCIETY

After 1868, women in a number of denominations established foreign missionary boards, which maintained their own accounts and supported female missionaries. I focus on two such boards: the Congregationalist Woman's Board of Missions (WBM), which cooperated with the ABCFM, and the Woman's Foreign Missionary Society of the Methodist Episcopal Church (WFMS). They were founded in Boston in 1868 and 1869, respectively. Each national board oversaw regional branches, which oversaw local auxiliaries. The latter were generally groups of about 10–20 women or children that fund-raised through dues, donations, and events. This money was sent to the boards for redistribution across mission sites. Each organization also published millions of pages of missionary literature, including monthly periodicals initially called *The Heathen Woman's Friend* (WFMS) and *Life and Light for Heathen Women* (WBM). The WFMS was the largest organization of its type at the time. Both organizations continue in new permutations today, but this book focuses on their work in the nineteenth century.

NEAR EAST RELIEF

The American Committee for Armenian and Syrian Relief (ACASR) was founded in 1915 to provide emergency relief for Armenians in the Ottoman Empire. Championed mainly by former ABCFM missionaries and prominent Presbyterian laymen, in 1919 it became the second American humanitarian organization to be chartered by the U.S. Congress (after the Red Cross). At that point, it was renamed Near East Relief (NER). Its massively popular grassroots fund-raising campaigns raised more than $116 million during and just after World War I. It fielded its own overseas workers and disbursed funds through established Protestant missionaries who often ran orphanages. This book follows NER's trajectory into the late 1920s. It ended emergency aid operations in 1930 and became the Near East Foundation, which is the name it retains today.

FATHERLESS CHILDREN OF FRANCE

Émile Deutsch de la Meurthe, a wealthy Paris-based industrialist, established *La Fraternité franco-américaine* in 1915 to secure patrons in the United States for the children of war widows. Translated to the Fatherless Children of France (FCF), the fledgling organization sent two English women, Florence Scho-field and Elinor Fell, to travel the United States establishing voluntary committees, many of which were headed by wealthy socialites. By 1918, FCF had 180 committees across the country. Sponsors committed $36.50 a year, which doubled the French government's war widow pension. Money was remitted to Paris, via New York, and sent by money order to families in the program. Unlike most other sponsorship organizations in this period, FCF only supported children living at home. Its plan was the largest at the time, supporting more than 286,000 individual children by the war's end. FCF discontinued its appeals in 1920 and disbanded shortly after.

CHRISTIAN CHILDREN'S FUND

Presbyterian pastor J. Calvitt Clarke founded China's Children Fund (CCF) in Richmond, Virginia, in 1938. It began by supporting Pu Kong Orphanage, an institution run by a Southern Baptist missionary in Shiu Chow (Chaozhou). CCF expanded to other Chinese orphanages but was forced out of the country in 1951. It changed its name to Christian Children's Fund, set up a regional office in Hong Kong, expanded to South Korea and, shortly after, moved into Latin

America, Europe, and the Middle East. Appealing mainly to liberal, ecumenical Protestants, its budget ballooned to more than $2 million by 1955 and within five more years it had established regional offices in Canada, England, Korea, and Japan. It was the world's largest Protestant NGO of its type at the time. The Clarke family was forced out of leadership in 1964, at which point CCF began to professionalize and discard the orphanage model. In the 1990s, it transitioned away from its Christian affiliation, a process signaled by its becoming Child-Fund International in 2009. Still based in Richmond, it now operates as part of the ChildFund Alliance, a global network of child-centered development organizations in 58 countries. This book focuses on CCF before the 1980s.

WORLD VISION

Pastor Bob Pierce founded World Vision (WV) in 1950 after touring as a Youth for Christ evangelist in China and Korea. Based in Portland, Oregon, and then Monrovia, California, WV was a major part of an emerging neo-evangelical network. Its relief program began in South Korea, where it supported missionary orphanages and paid local evangelists' salaries. Within a decade, it had expanded its operations to more than 20 countries. Bob Pierce was forced out in 1967 and WV transitioned from the orphanage model to Christian-based humanitarian work. It also grew massively, thanks to television advertising; its sponsorship plan increased tenfold, to exceed 300,000 children by the early 1980s. After another major growth spurt in the 1990s, World Vision began to identify as the largest privately funded relief and development agency in the world.

Since the mid-2000s, about 30% of WV's funding comes from sponsorships and more than 60% from government grants and gifts-in-kind. (By contrast, Unbound and Compassion receive little or no such income.) From a governance perspective, World Vision International (WVI) was founded in 1977 with a separate board and president; in 1994, World Vision US moved to Washington State, while WVI remained in Monrovia. Today, WVI is the coordinating entity for global field operations and the World Vision Partnership, which is a network of interdependent national offices. World Vision US remains responsible for fund-raising in the United States and monitoring the field programs it supports. This book focuses on the period before WVI, and when I do refer to "WV" after 1977 it means World Vision US, unless I note otherwise. In 2018, World Vision US raised $1 billion and Americans sponsored more than one million children. In total, WVI had about 3.5 million sponsored children in its program that year.

COMPASSION

Baptist pastor Everett Swanson started the Everett Swanson Evangelistic Association in his Chicago home in 1952 after returning from a preaching tour with U.S. troops in South Korea. Before his death in 1965, Swanson renamed the organization Compassion. Until 1968, Compassion operated exclusively in South Korea, using the same orphanage model as CCF and WV. Corruption, strikes, and a major fraud investigation in its Korea headquarters led Compassion to begin transitioning out of the country and partnering with other missionaries, mainly in India, Thailand, and Indonesia. It grew significantly during the 1970s and expanded its donor base into the UK and Australia. In 1980, it adopted its current name—Compassion International Incorporated—and the following year moved from Chicago to Colorado Springs. Today, its U.S. employees and overseas partners are born-again Christians. In the field, local church partners implement its "holistic child development and discipleship model" through after-school and weekend programming. Compared to World Vision and Unbound, this program is less varied and more consistent across field sites, as well as more focused on direct aid to individual children. Its leadership is largely centered in Colorado Springs, although in 2008 it established a Global Partner Alliance with its own charter and board for donor countries in Europe, Canada, Australia, New Zealand, and South Korea, along with a new Global Ministry Center at its headquarters. Today, Compassion works with about 6,500 local partners and receives about 81% of its income from individual sponsorships. As of December 2018, it supported 2 million sponsored children.

UNBOUND

In 1981, Bob Hentzen and Jerry Tolle, former priests who had worked in Latin America, collaborated with other members of the Hentzen family to found the Christian Foundation for Children in Kansas City, Missouri. One of the first plans for the U.S. Catholic market, it initially supported Central and South American children who lived at home by sending payments through their parishes and Catholic schools. Growing slowly in its first decade, it expanded to a few sites in the Philippines and Andhra Pradesh, India. In 1994, it was renamed the Christian Foundation for Children and Aging (CFCA) after introducing sponsorships for elderly people. It also developed its main fund-raising tool: retired priests volunteer to travel around the country giving guest homilies and promoting the program. In the late 1990s, CFCA established its own legal entities to administer programs in the field, making it independent from other Catholic institutions. Today, its programs are often tailored in response to local needs and it considers itself the most "personalized" U.S. sponsorship program because 89% of its income is collected from individuals and it receives no government funding. It is also much less growth-oriented than its evangelical counterparts since it calibrates expansion based on its field sites' needs; indeed, its numbers have remained largely static since 2006. Bob Hentzen headed the organization until his death in 2013. The following year, it was renamed Unbound. In 2018, it sponsored about 300,000 individuals in 21 countries (9% of whom were elders). Its 270,000 sponsors are all based in the United States.

NOTES

INTRODUCTION

1. Barber, *Jihad vs. McWorld*. "Fundamentalist Americanism" in Brouwer, Gifford, and Rose, *Exporting the American Gospel*. Permutations of this question arise in missiology, in the subfield of World Christianity, which seeks to decouple the spread of Pentecostalism from assumed U.S. (or Western) influence. There is often a strong Christian inflection in this field, for example in Mark Noll, *The New Shape of World Christianity*.

2. New work is starting to address the issue in the interdisciplinary subfield devoted to U.S. religion. Notably, three books came out as I was finishing this manuscript in 2018, which are cited throughout: Halvorson, *Conversionary Sites*; McAlister, *The Kingdom of God*; and Curtis, *Holy Humanitarians*.

3. It is not clear how many U.S. people have been abroad during their lifetimes, especially since Mexico, Canada, and areas of the Caribbean did not require passports until 2007. At the time of writing, about 40% of U.S. people had a passport (whether or not these had been used). More accurate statistics show where U.S. travelers go. In 2018, of 54.5 million individual trips (including multiple trips made by one person), 83% were to Mexico (39.5%), Canada (14.8%), the Caribbean (10%), and (largely Western) Europe (19%). "Two-thirds" is based on a 2,000-person survey of churchgoers that showed 62% had lived or traveled outside the United States during their lifetimes, in Wuthnow, *Boundless Faith*, 3, 251–58. "U.S. Citizen Travel to International Regions, 2018," National Travel and Tourism Office, accessed October 27, 2018. https://travel.trade.gov/view/m-2018-O-001/index.html; "Valid Passports in Circulation," U.S. Department of State-Consular Affairs, accessed October 27, 2018. https://travel.state.gov/content/travel/en/passports/after/passport-statistics.html.

4. I draw inspiration from Tsing ("The Global Situation") and Meyer ("Aesthetics of Persuasion," 754–55) on structures of power.

5. Compassion's staff estimate 1%, Unbound's estimate 0.5%, and World Vision's reports "a small fraction of 1 percent." Based on my interviews with sponsors, their travel is statistically typical of U.S. Americans and therefore rarely to the places in which sponsored children live (apart from Mexico). In short, very few sponsors renew their commitment to global projects through face-to-face encounters. Cf. O'Neill, "Left Behind," 217.

6. Tsing, "The Global Situation," 347. On the Forbes 2015 list of the 15 largest charities in the United States, three use Christian sponsorship (Food for the Poor #8, World Vision #11, Compassion #14).

7. I do not use this term as some Christians might within their own theologies and, in fact, sponsors rarely employ it. Nevertheless, it is useful for me here to put this book into conversation with scholarship about the production of "human oneness," including Tsing, *Friction*; Ticktin, "Transnational Humanitarianism," 279; Malkki, *The Need to Help*, 79. Englund ("Universal Africa," 12) calls on scholars to "make explicit how universals are made." I had that line in mind when I wrote, above, that this book's goal is to show how Christian globalism is made.

8. Along with the sources cited just above, I am thinking of Fassin, *Humanitarian Reason*, xii; Hulsether, "Buying into the Dream"; Keane, *Ethical Life*, 215–16; Ilana Feldman and Miriam Ticktin, eds., *In the Name of Humanity: The Government of Threat and Care* (Durham, NC: Duke University Press, 2010), 5.

9. Michael Carrithers, "Seriousness, Irony, and the Mission of Hyperbole," *Religion and Society: Advances in Research* 3 (2012): 60.

10. Paul S. Rees, *Missions Today: Ten Urgent Needs*, 1967, pp. 17–20, Folder 7, Sunday School-Missions Literature, WVIA.

11. The study of globalization in this tradition grew out of "world systems" approaches in the 1970s that traced how a nation relates to international politics or a local producer becomes a multinational corporation; the next generation of scholars examined local rejections and appropriations of global cultural forms.

12. Appadurai, *The Future as Cultural Fact*, 299.

13. "Pleasurable swept-up-ness" in McAlister, "What Is Your Heart For?," 881. I use "awe" advisedly since it recalls Rudolph Otto's *The Idea of the Holy* and I do not mean to reproduce his ideas about a *sui generis* numinous or the distinction between sacred and profane. Yet in another respect, evoking Otto makes sense in empirical terms since such notions arose out of his Christian convictions. Likewise, U.S. Christians are familiar with the word awe based on its biblical usage.

14. (Western) scholars experiment with making the same claims, for example, George Lakoff and Mark Johnson, *Metaphors We Live By* (Chicago: University of Chicago Press, 1980), 3, 14; and Lefebvre, *The Production of Space*, 213–17. In Religious Studies, see Kim Knott's repurposing of Kant in *The Location of Religion: A Spatial Analysis* (London, Equinox: 2005), 17.

15. The most important are Save the Children (founded in 1919) and Foster Parents Plan (1937). There are innumerable smaller examples, such as the German deaconesses in Liberty, New Jersey, who brought sponsorship to the United States in 1936 to support the China Inland Mission.

16. On evangelicalism being "favorable," note that evangelicals also started Kindernothilfe (KNH) in Germany in 1959, which is today one of Europe's largest Christian organizations. The statistics about "substantial" organizations are from Wydick, Glewwe, and Rutledge, "Does International Child Sponsorship Work?" 401.

17. Tyrrell, *Reforming the World*, 15.

18. Roswel P. Barnes to J. Calvin Clarke (hereafter JCC), January 19, 1939; JCC to Barnes, February 1, 1939, folder 4, box IB22, CFA. On working for NER: Letter from JCC, February 1, 1926, folder 2, box 15, series II, NER.

19. Edmund W. Janss, *Yankee Si, the Story of Dr. J. Calvitt Clarke and His 36,000 Children* (New York: Morrow, 1961); "Light a Life for Christ, Bring a Sunbeam to Him" Poster-Pamphlet, c. 1960, folder 1, Marketing Korean Sponsor Promos, 1956–1965, WVIA; Swanson to "Dear Friend" c. 1964, Promotional letter, USA1960.09.06.01, folder "1960–1966 Form Letters," box USA, CIA.

20. Edmund Janss became a director at WV after 7 years at CCF. Ervin Raetz was also poached from CCF to help WV in Korea. On competing: Seiji Giga to V.J.R. Mills, June 29, 1964; Erwin Raetz to V.J.R. Mills, July 9, 1963, Seiji Giga to J. Calvin Clarke, April 5, 1961, misc. folder 1, CFA; V.J.R. Mills to Bob Pierce, December 22, 1961, folder 9, box IB24, CFA. On computers: Mills (CCF) to Ted Engstrom (WV), August 3, 1964, April 20, 1964, and June 15, 1966; Engstrom to Mills, June 10, 1966, folder 27, box IIB5, CFA. On meeting and training: Ted Engstrom to G. A. Hemwall, November 22, 1965, USA1962.02.01.0927, folder "Correspondence, 1962–1967," CIA; "Christian Child Care Training, 25–26 October 1962," folder 7, box IB22, CFA.

21. Mills to Engstrom, June 15, 1966, folder 2, box IIB5, CFA; V. E. Kemp to Harvey Henry, August 22, 1967; V. E. Kemp to Robert Sweeney, October 5, 1967, folder 10, box IIB5, CFA. On the code of ethics: "25 Years of Compassion," 1977, p. 26, folder 1977–1982, box USA, CIA.

22. In both cases, the primary donors were French. The Spiritans used sponsorship in the 1880s and 1890s too. Kollman, *The Evangelization of Slaves*, 53–54; Taithe, "Algerian Orphans," 240–59.

23. "The Friend Makes Friends," *Heathen Woman's Friend*, February 1874: 608; "Notes Toward a Christian Christmas," *The Living Church* 153, no. 26 (1966): 12; Florence Wedge, "Children of Compassion," *Franciscan Message*, 27, no. 7 (1974): 1–6, folder 1965–76, box USA, CIA; W. Herbert Scott, Letter to Dear Friend in the Family of Prayer, June 1977, folder Ministries "Int. Intercessors," January–December 77, WVIA; "A Mission Outreach for Vacation Bible School," *Heartline*, June 1971, back cover. On CCF, for example, "Keep the True Meaning of Thanksgiving Alive and Well," *Visitor* (November 15, 1981): 7; "It's Scary that Her Life Depends on This Ad," *St. Anthony Messenger* (1992): 53.

24. Ken Waters, "How World Vision Rose from Obscurity to Prominence: Television Fundraising, 1972–1982," *American Journalism* 15, no. 4 (1998): 79.

25. Bob Hentzen was a Christian Brother and Jerry Tolle was a Jesuit. "The Christian Foundation for Children and Aging," *Publicity Pamphlet*, n.d. (1980s), 2, folder 6/72, National Catholic Reporter Publishing Company Records CNCR #2000 148; "Spirit of CFCA," *Pamphlet*, 1994, folder 7/03, CNCR #2001 165; Jim Hentzen to Sister Anne McCarthy, Letter, March 8, 1993, folder "Christian Foundation for Children and Aging, 1992–1993," Pax Christi USA Records, CPAX 35/26, NDUA.

26. Laney Haake (Director of U.S. Marketing, Unbound), Personal Interview, July 24, 2015.

27. A Guatemalan woman named Cindy Sales-Ortiz started a small "Adopt a Granny" program in London, which, according to archival documents I found, inspired Unbound to offer sponsorships of elders in 1984. This program is a key example of its different ethos (what I call the "dignity" model in chapter 6) but, because it only accounts for 9% of Unbound sponsorships today, I do not focus on it in the coming chapters. On statistics for children: Christian Foundation for Children, Newsletter, Winter 1983: 5; CFCA, Annual Report, 1993; CFCA Annual Report 1994; CFCA Annual Report, January to December 1998, 4. On the elderly: "President's Note," CFC Newsletter, Summer 1984, 2; "Help the Aged: Adopt a Granny," attached to Fred McCaffrey, letter to Jerry Tolle, Personal note, n.d., Unprocessed archives, UA. Laney Haake, Personal Interview, July 24, 2015.

28. Wydick, Glewwe, and Rutledge, "Does International Child Sponsorship Work?," 394, 401.

29. Immanuel Wallerstein, *The Modern World-System* (New York: Academic, 1974). On religion, two notable exceptions (with remarkably similar titles) from 1991 are Robertson and Garrett, eds., *Religion and Global Order*, and Roof, ed., *World Order and Religion*. On the anthropological side see Thomas J. Csordas's introduction to *Transnational Transcendence*.

30. Hopkins et al., *Religions/Globalizations*, 2–3.

31. Appadurai, *Modernity at Large*. Sociologists such as Roland Robertson and José Casanova had made similar arguments about religious imaginaries a few years earlier, also influenced by Anderson.

32. Coleman, *The Globalisation of Charismatic Christianity*, 59; Tsing, "The Global Situation." Many others levied similar criticisms, including Clifford, *Routes*, 36; Vásquez, "Studying Religion in Motion," 151. Valentina Napolitano makes this point vis-à-vis Catholicism in *Migrant Hearts*, 13. Appadurai acknowledged the model's limitations (*Modernity at Large*, 52) and addressed them in *The Future as Cultural Fact* (198). On the term "sacroscape," see Tweed, *Crossing and Dwelling*, 61.

33. Rose, "Geometries of 'Global' Evangelicalism."

34. Quote above in Coleman, *The Globalisation of Charismatic Christianity*, 61; Also, Coleman, "Constructing the Globe," 189. Recent work offers some discussion along similar lines focused on U.S. Christians at home, notably Halvorson, *Conversionary Sites* and McAlister, *The Kingdom of God*.

35. Ho, "Situating Global Capitalisms."

36. Mahmood, *Politics of Piety*. This "turn" has proven so popular that there is some danger in seeing all aspects of Christianity, or even all religions, as operating this way. I am not making that argument here. Further, not all of Foucault's insights are equally relevant. For example, although sponsors are intentional about their actions, it would be too far to claim that their "innermost feelings become objects of scrutiny and then articulation" (Foucault, *Ethics*, 223). However, there is more awareness than Mauss ("Techniques of the Body") and Bourdieu (*The Logic of Practice*, 66–67) posited, both of whom viewed individuals as largely unconscious of socialization. In thinking about self-making in charity and voluntarism, I have found especially helpful Muehlebach, *The Moral Neoliberal*, 7–8; O'Neill, "Left Behind," 204–26. On a similar note, Beliso-de Jesus, "Religious Cosmopolitanisms," 705.

37. Morton sees Christianity as an obstacle to hyperobject thinking (*Hyperobjects*, 42, 168–69), although ironically there are significant overlaps between his ethical project to "upgrade" people to think as he does (19, 101) and the goals of Christian sponsorship promoters. Notably, my work and Morton's differ in how we situate human beings. Morton argues that we must cease to think in terms of human significance, whereas my work is human-focused and intersubjective.

38. Morton, *Hyperobjects*, 15. Section above based on ibid., 70, 74, 139, 152–53. I follow Morton in his use of "global warming," rather than climate change.

39. Lloyd, *Charity and Poverty*, 8, 10, 16–18.

40. Italics added. Tsing, "The Global Situation," 330.

41. Joseph Nye, "Globalism Versus Globalization," *The Globalist*, April 15, 2002. Accessed July 22, 2016. https://www.theglobalist.com/globalism-versus-globalization/.
42. Giddens, *The Consequences of Modernity*, 14–15; *Modernity and Self-Identity*, 21.
43. As always, I am inspired by Orsi, *History and Presence*, 198.
44. Stewart, "Still Life," 405.
45. Miller, *The Anatomy of Disgust*, 8. On studies of emotion/affect, I am thinking of Berlant and Stewart, noted above, as well as Morton.
46. Certeau, *The Practice of Everyday Life*, 130.
47. James Bielo ("Replication as Religious Practice," 142) notes something similar, as does Birgit Meyer about the charismatic Christian belief in the body's "truthfulness" ("Aesthetics of Persuasion," 756). On Christian origins of the humanitarian "body universal," also Zito, "Secularizing the Pain," 20.
48. Among others, Burman, "Innocents Abroad," 241; Cartwright, *Moral Spectatorship*, 34; Ticktin, "A World Without Innocence," 583.
49. I am indebted to foundational work by scholars such as Susan Sontag, Edward Said, and Johannes Fabian that clarified how the European or Western self is constructed in contradistinction to an Other. More specifically, the term "mirroring" is partly an homage to a classic essay by Joan Jacobs Brumberg, "The Ethnological Mirror." Yet I hesitated to use "mirror" since it brings to mind psychoanalytic theory and continental philosophy, especially Jacques Lacan and Paul Ricoeur. In different ways, each one discusses the necessity for self to distinguish its existence from other, which they (or their interpreters) have used to promote and critique humanitarian approaches. Perhaps what is most useful here is how both thinkers lead back to Freud and his notion of the uncanny—experiences of things that are strangely familiar and thus unsettling. Mirroring evokes this idea in reverse: seeing the familiar located in a new context reinforces it—rather than unsettles it—by emphasizing its global resonances. Mirroring also raises the Freudian idea of "projection," which some critics have employed to discuss how humanitarians project their expectations onto others. While sponsors also project certain aspirations (chapter 6), when I use "mirroring" I refer to how U.S. sponsors see what they believe *already exists* abroad. In emic terms, it means that mirroring can contribute to the idea that Christianity spread thanks to the Holy Spirit or spirit-filled missionaries (even the first apostles), which bolsters the Christian view of their religion as *already belonging* in other places, rather than imposed by the West. On that note, I should underline that, in the sponsorship I studied, many recipients were in fact Christian (chapter 4). Whether they contribute to the forms I call mirroring, these Christians may certainly be invested in producing the mutual recognition (to use Ricoeur's term) that fuels Christian globalism.
50. O'Neill, "Beyond Broken," 1104.
51. Bornstein, "Child Sponsorship," 600; O'Neill, "Left Behind," 217; Fieldston, *Raising the World*, 203.
52. For example, Melvin Van de Workeen in Emilie Tavel Livezey, "Child Sponsorship Dollars: How Much Goes to Him?" *Christian Science Monitor*, August 6, 1981.
53. Anthropologist Erica Bornstein and historian David King have both studied World Vision and their work is cited throughout. Other notable sources include Lori Henry Lee, "Now That You Have Seen": A Historical Look at Compassion International, 1952–2013" (Ed.D dissertation, Southeastern Baptist Theological Seminary, 2014); Susan Mary McDonic, "Witnessing, Work, and Worship: World Vision and the Negotiation of Faith, Development, and Culture" (PhD dissertation, Duke University, 2004); J. Calvitt Clarke III, *Fifty Years of Begging: Dr. J. Calvitt Clarke and Christian Children's Fund* (Bloomington, IN: Archway, 2018).
54. "Naming and Educating Heathen Children," *MH* 35, no. 2 (February 1839): 74.
55. Peter G. Schreck, "GN Study," submitted to Cliff Benzel, March 25, 1977, p. 5. MIN/WIV 1–GN Study–FY77, WVIA. My tallies of archival records bear out the importance of women's role too. For example, CCF's lists c. 1950 show sponsors (N=165) broken down by individual women (N=60), women on behalf of a group or Sunday school (N=80), co-signing couples (N=11), and individual men (N=14) (Boxes Misc, Unprocessed Documents, CFA). My research assistant also tallied 108 identified sponsors whose letters were published in World Vision's magazines (*Scope, Heartline, WVM*) from 1958 to 1980: 72% (N=78) were women and another 7.5% (N=8) were women signing on behalf of a couple. While women may be overrepresented if they responded more to surveys, it is safe to say that sponsorship has largely, although certainly not exclusively, been their responsibility.

56. Kemp to "Members of the Board of Directors of Christian Children's Fund," March 3, 1969, folder 2, box IIA3, CFA.

57. Notes in John Meredyth Lucas, "Compassion," *Television Script*, 1974, p. 13, folder "To Compassion—Specials for Compassion," box USA, CIA. This does not mean that African American Protestants ignore global problems; indeed, Wuthnow shows that they are somewhat more likely to respond favorably to surveys on this question than their white counterparts. Wuthnow, *Boundless Faith*, 151.

58. Evangelical organizations skew younger than in the 1970s because of ad campaigns with celebrities and their partnerships with music festivals. Unbound skews older because 70–80% of their sponsors are recruited through a pitch made during the homily, and older Catholics attend mass in the United States. Statistics from Raamses Rider (Market Research Manager, USA group, Compassion), Personal Interview, June 30, 2014, and Laney Haake (Director of U.S. Marketing, Unbound), Personal Interview, July 24, 2015.

59. "Homes Operated or Assisted by Christian Children's Fund, Inc.," May 30, 1958, folder 6, box 3, UVL; Joyce Morgan to Miriam and Everett Swanson, Robert Swaney, Dr. G. Hemwall, September 14, 1965, folder USA1962.02.01.0927 "Correspondence, 1962–1967," box USA, CIA.

60. Robert E. Swaney to Ann Landers, December 20, 1966, Landers to Swaney, March 7, 1967 and March 16, 1967; "Dear Friends—Ann Landers Said It!," Pamphlet, 1967; "God Bless the Teens," *Moody Monthly* clipping with Richard Borth to Swaney, April 10, 1967, USA1960.09.07.01, folder "Advertising Documents 1960s," box USA, CIA; On Dear Abby, see Charles Benbow, "Prime Time Unties US Purse Strings," *St. Petersburg Times*, January 7, 1976: D1.

61. This misconception is widespread, not least because organizations like CCF and Save the Children make this claim. For example, Fieldston, *Raising the World*, 42; Baughn, "Every Citizen of Empire," 131.

62. Bakker, *Sister Churches*, 27–29, 50–52, 135, 145; Mary M. McGlone, *Sharing Faith Across the Hemisphere* (United States Catholic Conference, 1997), 109, 111; Tara Linn Hefferan, "Deprofessionalizing Economic Development: Crafting Faith-Based Development Alternatives Through United States–Haiti Catholic Parish Twinning," (PhD dissertation, Michigan State University, 2006); Napolitano, *Migrant Hearts*, 8, 51–52, 61, 69. A good overview is Sarah Elizabeth Johnson, "Almost Certainly Called: Images of Protestant Missionaries in American Culture, 1945–2000" (PhD dissertation, Duke University, 2007). Antecedents go back to the 1920s: Robert, "The First Globalization," 52; Hollinger, *Protestants Abroad*, 61–66.

63. "Distant and Majestic" in Rabinowitz, *The Spiritual Self*, xxix. Also, R. Pierce Beaver, "Missionary Motivation Through Three Centuries," in *Reinterpretation in American Church History*, ed. Jerald Bauer (Chicago: University of Chicago Press, 1968), 139–47; Chaney, *The Birth of Missions*, 226; Hutchison, *Errand to the World*, 48.

64. Berlant, "Introduction: Compassion (and Withholding)," 6.

CHAPTER 1: LOVE AND SIN

1. "Report from 3 November 1910," *WFMS Secretary's Report March 1904–September 1912*, pp. 146–47. First United Methodist Church, Pasadena, California, unprocessed archives.

2. Dipesh Karmarkar, "Towards a Colonial Urban Space of Bombay: A Perspective in Historical Geography" (proceedings of the Indian History Congress, 67th Session, Calicut, India, March 2007): 7; "Table 4. Population of the 46 Urban Places: 1810," U.S. Bureau of the Census, accessed January 2, 2016. http://www.census.gov/population/www/documentation/twps0027/tab04.txt.

3. Worcester to Judson, Nott, Newell, Hall, Price, November 10, 1812, ABC 1.01, vol. 1, ABCFM.

4. Reprinted as "Thoughts on Various Methods of Advancing the Cause of Christ by Missionaries at Bombay," *Panoplist* 12, no. 1 (January 1816): 34–39.

5. Worcester to Hall and Newell (at Bombay), October 16, 1816, ABC 1.01, vol. 1; Worcester to My dear Brethren, December 18, 1816, ABC 1.01, vol. 2; Jeremiah Evarts (possibly Worcester) to Newell, and Hall, January 4, 1817, ABC 1.01, vol. 2; Worcester to Newell and Hall, December 10, 1816, ABC 8.1, vol. 4, ABCFM.

6. Phillips, *Protestant America*, 42.

7. For more on this custom in nineteenth-century sponsorship, see Kaell, "Renamed."

8. Worcester to Warren, Richards, Meigs and Poor, December 8, 1817, ABC 1.01, vol. 1, ABCFM.

9. Conroy-Krutz, *Christian Imperialism*,14. On a similar point regarding Enlightenment liberalism, see Mehta, "Liberal Strategies of Exclusion," 59–86; Stoler, *Carnal Knowledge*, 154.

10. Hutchison, *Errand to the World*, 47.

11. Berlant, *The Female Complaint*, 32. "All sentiments have a history" paraphrased from Foucault, "Nietzsche, Genealogy, History," 153. My thinking in this chapter has been shaped by a growing body of work on intimacy and emotion in Protestant colonialism. Along with formative studies by the Comaroffs, see Rai, *The Rule of Sympathy*; Stoler, *Carnal Knowledge*; McLisky, Midena, and Vallgarda, eds., *Emotions and Christian Missions*. On a different note but helpful is Ahmed, "Collective Feelings." On domestic missions in the United States, see Schuller, *The Biopolitics of Feeling*.

12. Campbell, *The Romantic Ethic*, 131, 218–19.

13. "Science of Subjectivity" in Poovey, *A History of Modern Fact*, xv, 148–49; Noll, *America's God*, 94. Scholars of humanitarianism often carve out a strangely secularized history of these sentiments (e.g., Ticktin, "A World Without Innocence"), but one should not overemphasize only its religious aspects either; as Laqueur ("Bodies, Details") has noted, inventions such as the novel and medical autopsy also contributed to new conceptions of body, sympathy, and suffering.

14. Morton, *Hyperobjects*, 28, 31–32, 103.

15. Barbara Pitkin, "The Heritage of the Lord: Children in the Theology of John Calvin," 167, and Catherine A. Brekus, "Children of Wrath Children of Grace Jonathan Edwards and the Puritan Culture of Child Rearing," 304. Both in Bunge, ed., *The Child in Christian Thought*.

16. *Eleventh Annual Report of the Topeka Branch of the WFMS of the Methodist Episcopal Church, 1894* (Fairmont: Nebraska Signal Printers, 1894), 17, WDG, GCAH; On the same pattern in U.S. schools: Anne M. Boylan, "Sunday Schools and Changing Evangelical Views of Children in the 1820s," *Church History* 48, no. 3 (1979): 320–33. Other details in this paragraph from: John Locke, *Some Thoughts Concerning Education and Of the Conduct of Understanding*, ed. Ruth Grant and Nathan Tarcov (Indianapolis: Hackett, 1996), 1, 139, 110; Jonathan Edwards, *Faithful Narrative of a Surprising Work of God* (1737), section III on Phebe Bartlett; Marcia J. Bunge, "Education and the Child in Eighteenth-Century German Pietism Perspectives from the Work of A. H. Francke," in Bunge, ed., *The Child in Christian Thought*, 247, 268–71, 275–76; Richard P. Heitzenrater, "John Wesley and Children," " in Bunge, ed., *The Child in Christian Thought*, 295. John MacKay Shaw, "Poetry for Children of Two Centuries," in *Research about Nineteenth-Century Children and Books*, ed. Selma K. Richardson (Urbana-Champaign: University of Illinois Press, 1980), 135.

17. Hutchison, *Errand to the World*, 39; Robert V. Williams, "George Whitefield's Bethesda: The Orphanage, the College, and the Library," *Library History Seminar Proceedings*, no. 3 (1968): 47–72; Eleazar Wheelock, "A Brief Narrative of the Indian Charity-School in Lebanon in Connecticut, New England," 2nd ed. (London: J and W Oliver, 1767), 5; Hatje, "Revivalists Abroad," 73.

18. In British India, missionaries also ran thousands of day schools, which were taught by locals and did not have adoption plans. "History of the Female Boarding School at Oodooville" and "Catalogue of Pupils," *MH* 37, no. 1 (January 1841): 39.

19. Johannes Ferdinand Fenger, *History of the Tranquebar Mission Worked Out from the Original Papers by J. Ferd. Fenger* [1842]," trans. Emil Francke (Tranquebar: Evangelical Lutheran Mission Press, 1863), 19–20, 36, 52, 78. The Danish/German Lutherans replicated this strategy in other colonies, such as Greenland in the 1720s. Claire McLisky, "Affective Circuits," in McLisky, Midena, and Vallgarda, eds., *Emotions and Christian Missions*, 153.

20. Carson, *The East India Company*, 8, 10–11, 194, 212. Rev. A. Westcott, *Our Oldest Indian Mission* (Madras: Diocesan Committee of the Society for Promoting Christian Knowledge, 1897), chap. 1. Background on Tranquebar in Katharine Gerbner, *Christian Slavery* (Philadelphia: University of Pennsylvania Press, 2018), 140–46.

21. An important reason was the passage of Resolution 13 (the "pious clause") in 1813, which specified that the Company had an obligation to support religious improvement in India and resulted in more licenses for non-SPCK missionaries.

22. In their *Panoplist* letter, the missionaries remarked on the Tranquebar and African missions. The latter reference is unclear, since they almost certainly did not mean missions in Africa. It likely refers to the mission in "Black town," the native part of Madras, also started by the Tranquebar Pietists. Worcester to Newell, Hall, and Nott, October 12, 1815, ABC 1.01, vol. 1, ABCFM. Another version in Worcester to Newell, Hall, and Nott, October 13, 1815, ABC 8.1, vol. 4, ABCFM.

23. "The Rev. Dr. John on Indian Civilization, being a report of a successful experiment, made during two years on that subject, in fifteen Tamul (*sic*) and five English native schools," *Missionary Register* 11, no. 1 (November 1813): 369–83.

24. See note 21. Despite the "Pious Clause" of 1813, different governors still encouraged or blocked access to missionaries. Governor of Ceylon Robert Brownrigg (1813–1819) encouraged the Americans when the governor of Bombay (briefly) expelled them. Brownrigg allowed them to settle stations around Jaffna—where child sponsorship would first prove so successful. Under his successors, however, the Americans remained confined to this outpost in part to keep them far from the capital, which was prime territory for English missionaries.

25. Reprinted as "Thoughts on Various Methods of Advancing the Cause of Christ by Missionaries at Bombay," *Panoplist* 12, no. 1 (January 1816): 34–39.

26. J. E. to Hall & Newell & Bardwell, December 9, 1817, ABC 1.01, vol. 2, ABCFM.

27. Harriet Lathrop Winslow (and Miron Winslow), *A Memoir of Mrs. Harriet Wadsworth Winslow, Combining a Sketch of the Ceylon Mission* (New York: Leavitt, Lord & Co., 1835), 148–49.

28. Missionaries usually had to choose whether to cater to elite or destitute children; parents of the former would not allow them to mix with the latter. Fannie Sparks, "In the Mountains," *HWF*, January 1875, 773.

29. "Fanny Garretson Hyde, "An Account Written by Herself." *HWF*, October 1871, 190–91.

30. William Butler to J. P. Durbin, July 16, 1858. 2540-3-4:03 Correspondence: Butler, William to Durbin, J. P. 1856–62, GCAH.

31. Bushnell, *Christian Nurture* (Cleveland: Pilgrim, 1861,1994), 9–10, 20, 40; "Unconscious Influence, A Sermon Preached by Rev. Horace Bushnell, DD, of the United States" (London: Partridge and Oakey, 1852), 11, 19, 23. Barbara Cross, *Horace Bushnell: Minister to a Changing America* (Chicago: University of Chicago Press, 1958), 52–72; Margaret Bendroth, "Horace Bushnell's Christian Nurture," in Bunge, ed., *The Child in Christian Thought*, 312, 353, 359; Edwards, "My God and My Good Mother," 117–18.

32. Stoler, *Carnal Knowledge*, 81. "Sensorial Discipline" in Schuller, *The Biopolitics of Feeling*, 18; Kaplan, *Anarchy of Empire*, 16, 19.

33. Cunningham, *Children of the Poor*, 48. The WFMS recognized this too, e.g., "Twig-bending," *HWF*, February 1892: 186–87. "Enlarged" in Corrigan, *Business of the Heart*, 174–75, 292.

34. Emily C. Pearson, "The Little Hindu," *HWF*, March 1870, 71.

35. Mrs. Baldwin, "The Habitations of Cruelty," *HWF*, September 1870, 28. Baldwin's feelings about the Chinese were complicated; she later vigorously campaigned against the Chinese Exclusion Act in the United States.

36. For example, in the work of Locke and Francke. Schuller, *The Biopolitics of Feeling*, 9.

37. "Unconscious Influence, A Sermon Preached by Rev. Horace Bushnell, DD, of the United States" (London: Partridge and Oakey, 1852), 17.

38. Mrs. G. E. Doughty, "Report" (Cincinnati Branch), *HWF*, July 1874, 681. Chaney, *The Birth of Missions*, 183, 232.

39. J. F. Willing, "Under Bonds to Help Heathen Women," *HWF*, August 1869, 22, and "Money Enough," *HWF*, September 1869, 29–31.

40. By contrast, earlier thinkers such as Edwards and Locke saw motives as *external* ideas that compelled obedience. See Corrigan, *Business of the Heart*, 83, 103, 294–95; Noll, *America's God*, 94; Rabinowitz, *The Spiritual Self*, 164, 169, 171–72.

41. "Sympathy" is the terminology of the time, rather than empathy. In this chapter and the next one, I therefore avoid the word "empathy" and use "sympathy" when my sources do.

42. Ngai, *Ugly Feelings*, 6–7, 11.

43. Miller, *The Anatomy of Disgust*, 10–12,184; Ngai, *Ugly Feelings*, 354. Hence the reason U.S. missionaries were so insulted when the upper classes in "cultured" places like China and India found that

Americans smelled disgustingly of milk (China) or defiled food with their touch (India). Competing notions of the noxious fueled missionaries' ambivalence about heathen adults and their rosy portrayal of the mission children who lacked such "prejudices."

44. Quotes in this section in order: M. Mc, "New England Branch" (on Mrs. Dr. William Butler's closing remarks), *HWF*, August 1881, 45; No Title, *HWF*, October 1871, 193; Mrs. E. E. Baldwin, "View of China and the Chinese Social Life," *HWF*, December 1874, 760.

45. Miller, *The Anatomy of Disgust*, 195; Modern, *Secularism in Antebellum America*, 80, n. 89. Below I depart from Miller in his contention that love is not readily communicable or vicarious. This is not the case from a Christian perspective, which envisions love as an extension of God's work made immanent in human beings.

46. "Reprint from China's Millions," *HWF*, November 1884, 107.

47. *WFMS Secretary's Report March 1904–Sept 1912*, 79, 136, 142. First United Methodist Church (Pasadena), unprocessed archives.

48. Italics added. "The Children's Offerings," *HWF*, March 1871, 107.

49. L.M.H., No Title, *HWF*, December 1894, 151.

50. For example, see Tanya Murray Li, *The Will to Improve: Governmentality, Development, and the Practice of Politics* (Durham, NC: Duke University Press, 2007); Muehlebach, *The Moral Neoliberal*.

51. Jane Schneider, "Spirits and Spirits of Capitalism," in *Religious Regimes and State Formation: Perspectives from European Ethnology*, ed. Eric R. Wolf (Albany: State University of New York Press), 194–95.

52. John A. Andrew, *Rebuilding the Christian Commonwealth: New England Congregationalists and Foreign Missions, 1800–1830* (Lexington: University Press of Kentucky, 1976), 72–73.

53. Mauss, *The Gift*, 65–78.

54. Cf. Michael J. D. Roberts, "Head versus Heart?" Voluntary Associations and Charity Organization in England, c. 1700–1850," in *Charity, Philanthropy and Reform: From 1690s to 1850*, ed. Hugh Cunningham and Joanna Innes (New York: St. Martin's, 1998), 70.

55. Sermon from c. 1810 in Andrew, *Rebuilding the Christian Commonwealth*, 78.

56. Italics added. Rufus Anderson, "Economy and Curtailments in Missions," *Report of the American Board of Commissioners for Foreign Missions* (Cleveland, Ohio), October 1–3, 1861 (Boston: Press of TR Marvin and Son, 1861), 10–13. Such ideas could be more eschatological, as detailed in Elsbree, *The Rise of the Missionary Spirit*, 125.

57. I. H., "Systematic Giving—Study for November," *HWF*, October 1888, 95.

58. Miller, *A Theory of Shopping*, 108–10.

59. Lyon in Robert, *American Women in Mission*, 100. Also, Mary Lyon's own *A Missionary Offering, or Christian Sympathy, Personal Responsibility, and the Present Crisis in Foreign Missions* (Boston: Crocker and Brewster, 1843). Work on this topic is voluminous and includes: Hill, *The World Their Household*, 65; Crowley, "The Sensibility of Comfort," 759–61, 771; Corrigan, *Business of the Heart*, 142–43.

60. Bushnell, *Unconscious Influence*, 17–18.

61. Mary Nind, "Annual Address," reprinted in *Fifth Annual Report of Work of the Western Branch of the Woman's Foreign Missionary Society, For the Year ending April 21, 1875* (Des Moines, Iowa: State Journal Book and Job Printing House), 13, 2599-2-4:12, WDG, GCAH. Also, Beaver, *American Protestant Women*, 13, 33–34; Hill, *The World Their Household*, 69.

62. Mrs. J. F. Keen, "Philadelphia Branch Annual Report," *HWF*, July 1875, 5.

63. J. F. Willing, No Title (Northwestern Branch Report), *HWF*, February 1882, 189.

64. D., "Philadelphia Branch," *HWF*, May 1878, 256; M.T.L., "Northwestern Branch," *HWF*, February 1881, 184–85.

65. J. F. Willing, No Title (Northwestern Branch Report), *HWF*, August 1881, 48.

66. Sarah Leonard, "What Maidie Did," *HWF*, November 1873, 576; E.J.K., "New York Branch," *HWF*, January 1877, 160; Branch reports (various), *HWF*, January 1876, 135–40. On similar trends, for example, Lum, *Damned Nation*, 96.

67. Italics in original. Mrs. U. B. Wilson, "State of Missouri," *Third Annual Report. Saint Louis Branch of the Woman's Foreign Missionary Society for the Year Ending April 3, 1873* (Barns and Beynon Printers), 18, 2599-2-4:12, WDG, GCAH.

68. Ernst Bloch, *The Principle of Hope* (vol. 1), trans. Neville Plaice, Stephen Plaice, and Paul Knight (Cambridge, MA: MIT Press, 1995), 74–75; Ngai, *Ugly Feelings*, 210.

69. No Title, *HWF*, January 1888, 178. For an example of an unpublished source on middle-class anxieties about the potential loss of wealth, see Hume to Miss Child, April 23, 1878, folder 3, Box 1, Series 1, WBMR.

70. No Title, *HWF*, January 1888, 178.

71. Italics added. Mrs. W. W. Fink, "Reply to the Address of Welcome," *Seventh Annual Report of the Western Branch of the Woman's Foreign Missionary Society of the Methodist Episcopal Church For the Year 1877–'77* (Minneapolis: Johnson, Smith, and Harrison Printers), 52. 2599-2-4:12, WDG, GCAH.

72. Manufacturing wages averaged $345 a year. Women made much less; a female educator in 1880 averaged just $54.50. Clarence D. Long, *Wages and Earnings in the United States, 1860–1890* (Princeton, NJ: Princeton University Press, 1960).

73. "Minutes," *HWF*, July 1881, 11 and 13; Mrs. Kennard Chandler, "The Appeal," *HWF*, September 1886, 72–74. On parallels in English missionary circles, see Rosemary Seton, *Western Daughters in Eastern Lands: British Missionary Women in Asia* (Denver, CO: Praeger, 2013), 91–92.

74. Mrs. John Talbot Gracey, *Eminent Missionary Women* (New York: Eaton and Mains, 1898); "Pioneer Story # 17," Pamphlet, c. 1913. 2599-4-3: 11 Ann Wilkins, Undated, WDG, GCAH.

75. Schuller, *The Biopolitics of Feeling*, 9.

INTERLUDE: BELINDA COLES

1. *Travel Sketches from Liberia: Johann Büttikofer's 19th Century Rainforest Exploration in West Africa*, ed. Henk Dop and Phillip Robinson (Leiden: Brill, 2013), 296.

2. On "Sunday suits" at Heddington: Park, *"White" Americans*, 97–98.

3. A chief's "stranger" was a guest under his protection. Wilkins did know King Zoda Quee. "Two hours' walk" from John Seys's diary entry (it was about 10 km). "Extracts from the Journal of the Rev. John Seys," *Missionary Register*, vol. 31 (January 1843): 22–23; Dop and Robinson, eds., *Travel Sketches from Liberia*, 659.

4. Literally: "negotiation" or "talk" with God. The Liberian term at the time for church services.

5. In 1839, the Queah under a newly converted King Zoda Quee formed Robertsville, likely when they converted en masse to Methodism. The girl Belinda was from the town and was about three years old when it was founded. "Journal of the Rev. John Seys," *Missionary Register*, vol. 31 (January 1843): 22–23; Park, *"White" Americans*, 101, 104; Carl Patrick Burrowes, *Power and Press Freedom in Liberia, 1830–1970* (Asmara: Africa World Press, 2004), 22, 34.

6. In 1839, there was a major revival at Heddington and in February 1840 at Robertsville, during which people were almost certainly encouraged to burn gris-gris—talismans to ward off evil spirits. In March 1840, there was a battle against the Boatswain people and half the town scattered. John Saillant, "Missions in Liberia and Race Relations in the United States, 1822–1860," in Bays and Wacker, eds., *The Foreign Missionary Enterprise*, 22. Also, Park, *"White" Americans*, 95–96.

7. Dash are presents. A suitor would supply them to his prospective bride's family until she came of age. Converts in this area were pushed to accept only the first wife and, according to Park (*"White" Americans*, 98, 106), local people viewed the schools as enhancing their daughter's marriageability and bride price. I have imagined this backstory for Belinda.

8. My version of Seys's speech paraphrases his colleague George Brown's speech at Heddington in 1839. Park, *"White" Americans*, 91, 105. On the king's palaver house for preaching, A. F. Russell, letter dated September 29, 1845, reprinted in *Africa's Luminary*, November 12, 1845, 74. Courtesy of Jess Farrell.

9. Robertsville was a Queah town and Heddington was Pessah, with Goulah and Vey. "Native" was the term for Africans and "colonist" for the approximately 2,500 African American settlers. The Methodist missionaries were mostly white, like Wilkins and Seys. Millsburgh, Heddington, and Robertsville were small but notable "native" Methodist towns.

10. Wording from quote and description of Belinda's hair in Ann Wilkins (hereafter AW) to Rev. George Coles (GC), November 14, 1845, 1646-6-2:54, Ann Wilkins Correspondence, GCAH.

11. Ibid. "Mantle of white . . ." from George Coles, *My First Seven Years in America* (New York: Carlton & Phillips, 1852), 97.

12. Wilkins was the first single white woman missionary to Africa. Her school opened in 1842 for about 45 students, including African American colonists. Belinda and five other girls who arrived in 1845 were identified as the first natives "out of the bush"—although they actually came from the converted Queah and Pessah. Edwin Williams, "Colony of Liberia," in *A Comprehensive System of Modern Geography and History* (New York: Bliss, Wadsworth and Co., 1835), 485; "Christian Missions in Liberia," *Maryland Colonization Journal* 1, no. 5 (October 15, 1841): 79; "Annual Report of the Liberia Mission," *The African Repository* 14, no. 3 (March 1838): 80–81.

13. "Camp meeting" refers to a usually annual revival in Methodist communities. Other details based on George's autobiography and the 1830 census, which places the Coles in Queens, New York, with two "Free colored persons" living with them as servants. Other details in Mrs. John Talbot Gracey, *Eminent Missionary Women* (New York: Eaton and Mains, 1898), 45–49; "Ann Wilkins (1806–1857)," in *Portraits of American Women in Religion*, ed. Connie King (The Library Company of Philadelphia, 2005), n.p. Available at http://www.librarycompany.org/women/portraits_religion/wilkins.htm.

14. In 1845, the Coles children were: Hester (age 15), Electa (age 20 or 10), Phebe (age 12 or 8), George (age 9), James (age 7). There is some discrepancy in the census reports regarding Electa and Phebe: *1850 US Federal Census, Records of the Bureau of the Census*, Roll M43_614, page 196B, image 319; *1860 US Federal Census, Records of the Bureau of the Census*, Roll M653_806, page 164, image 169, National Archives, Washington, DC.

15. These facts about Mary Mason are true, and Belinda almost certainly knew her from the Coles's time in New York. "Treasurer's Report," Methodist Episcopal Church Missionary Society, *Annual Report of the Missionary Society, vol. 18* (New York: J. Collard Printer, 1837), 36; Mary Mason to Mr. [John] Kahbeege, March 15, 1840, 1646-6-8:09, Mary W. Mason Correspondence, GCAH.

16. Coles, *My First Seven Years in America*, 126.

17. In his autobiography, Coles quotes from the diary entry in 1819. The rest of his speech is from his reflections on this entry in Coles, *My First Seven Years in America*, 86–88.

18. Electa became a music teacher. *1860 US Federal Census*, 164.

19. Paraphrased from AW to Miss Mary [Rutherford] Garrettson, June 22, 1846, 1646-6-2:54, GCAH.

20. A girl did come from Robertsville with Belinda and was renamed Suzy-Ann Pitman. AW to GC, November 14, 1845, 1646-6-2:54, GCAH.

21. Quote from Ibid.

22. Belinda Coles sent these things to her namesake, who did like to sing. However, the wording is from AW to Miss Mary [Rutherford] Garrettson, June 22, 1846, 1646-6-2:54, GCAH.

23. Park, *"White" Americans*, 93.

24. AW to GC, November 14, 1845, 1646-6-2:54, GCAH.

25. This story is about girls renamed Joanna and Caroline Curtis. AW to Garrettson, June 22, 1846, 1646-6-2:54, GCAH.

26. The passage upon which this paragraph is based reads, "Belinda and Suzy-Ann Pitman are children of pious mothers who are among the native converts at Robertsville; they were here to see their daughters the other day, and heard them read, and seemed quite pleased with their improvement in learning and appearance, and also with their fare. The children often say they do not want to leave me till they "get plenty of learning," and then "go teach their people." AW to GC, 14 November 1845, 1646-6-2:54, GCAH.

27. In 1850, the Coles family had a 14-year-old black servant named Caroline Spaulding. She may have been with them in 1846. *1850 US Federal Census, Records of the Bureau of the Census*, Roll M43_614, page 196B, image 319, National Archives, Washington, DC.

28. AW to George and Belinda Coles, June 25, 1846, 1646-6-2:54, GCAH.

29. It was actually knitted by Caroline Curtis and sent to her patron, Mary. AW to Garrettson, June 22, 1846.

30. AW to GC, November 14, 1845, 1646-6-2:54, GCAH.

31. Based on Wilkins's letter, which reads: "I think Bro. Coles [*sic*] reasons for wishing a little girl of Africa, named Belinda, are very good ones; I do not wonder that he and his family now feel a greater

interest in Africa, than they would without such attraction; and yet I am pleased to think that he felt an interest for Africa's children, as fellow beings possessing immortal souls bound to the same destinies as other human beings first, that caused him to wish so favorite a name to be perpetuated on a pupil here." AW to George and Belinda Coles, June 25, 1846, 1646-6-2:54, GCAH.

32. The revival was in 1847, but I do not know the precise date. Ann's words about the "Congoes" in Wilkins to Garrettson, June 22, 1846. The Pons was an American-built ship captured by the USS *Yorktown* on December 1, 1845 with about 900 slaves on board. "Congos" was the term for people rescued from slave ships after the transatlantic trade was banned and "repatriated" to Liberia (or Sierra Leone if rescued by the British). Wilkins was given 33 children from the Pons for her school. Louise M. North, "A Lovely Sisterhood of Missionary Spirits," *Woman's Missionary Friend*, vol. 41–42 (October 1909): 347; C. Herbert Gilliland, "Deliverance from This Floating Hell," *Naval History* 17, no. 6 (2003): 48–51; "Extracts from letters respecting the capture of the slave ship Pons . . . on the 16th of the twelfth month, 1845, from Capt. Bell to the Secretary of the Navy," *Quaker Broadsides*, HC10–12179_01, Haverford College Quaker and Special Collections & Friends Historical Library of Swarthmore College, http://triptych.brynmawr.edu/cdm/ref/collection/SC_Broad/id/2124.

33. North, "A Lovely Sisterhood," 347.

34. All details including the girl's pleased countenance and response from AW to George and Belinda Coles, June 25, 1846, 1646-6-2:54, GCAH. I have incorporated it here to fit my imagined timeline.

35. Ibid. This is a close paraphrase of the letter.

36. Charles Pitman was a Queah orphan raised at the girls' school. He became a major "success story" as the one native preacher the mission produced. There is no evidence that Belinda was asked to marry him, although missionaries strongly encouraged the children to marry each other. Park, *"White" Americans*, 106.

37. Dop and Robinson, eds., *Travel Sketches from Liberia*, 593.

38. In 1846, John Benham became superintendent of the mission and ended Seys's policy of giving the kings dash, which did cause a break with Zoda Quee. I do not know if his people left Christianity as a result, but missionaries reported that this did regularly occur. I also imagined a "Zoda town," but it was common for a tribe to desert an old settlement and name a new one after their king. It is also a fabrication that Belinda had a child (although she was about 15, so it would not be surprising). Anthony D. Williams, "Intelligence from Liberia," *African Repository* 14, no. 3 (March 1838): 65–66; Park, *"White" Americans*, 101, 105; Burrowes, *Power and Press Freedom in Liberia*, 35.

39. Belinda left the school in 1847 or 1848, and I have embellished a reason why. Of the six native girls Seys brought in 1845, four went back to their kin after two years. This may have been due to tensions with Zoda Quee or because the girls were of marriageable age or because their parents left Christianity. Parents regularly withdrew their children from missionary schools for all these reasons. Details from AW to Mary R. Garretson, October 26, 1849, 1646-6-2:54, GCAH. On the presents Americans liked: Park, *"White" Americans*, 105–6.

40. In the same letter, Wilkins notes that Belinda's people did not allow her to wear "civilized" dress upon her return but does not say why.

41. "Boundary of Liberia," *Thirty-Second Annual Report of the American Colonization Society*, vol. 28 (January 1849): 14; *Travel Sketches from Liberia*, 307; A. F. Russell, letter dated September 29, 1845, reprinted in *Africa's Luminary*, November 12, 1845, 74.

42. It was Mary Garretson who sent Belinda a Bible in 1849, and Wilkins did forward it to her after she had been back with her people for a year and a half. On plastering the walls with religious tracts, I draw inspiration from Dop and Robinson, eds., *Travel Sketches from Liberia*, 296.

CHAPTER 2: SYSTEMS AND STATISTICS

1. M.L.S., "The Story of a Beginning," *HWF*, January 1886, 161.

2. Porter, *Trust in Numbers*, 49. On governance and the colonies: Michel Foucault, *The History of Sexuality*, vol. 1 (New York: Random House, 1978), 138–46; Hacking, "Biopower"; Daston, *Classical Probability*, 15, 127, 9; Desrosières, *The Politics of Large Numbers*, 148.

3. Porter, *Trust in Numbers*, 78; cf. Hacking, "Biopower," 290.

4. My definition draws on A. T. Pierson in the *Homiletic Review*: "*The systematic way* [is] to lay aside as an offering to God a definite portion of our gains . . . This is adapted to all, whether poor or rich." Reprinted as "Seven Ways of Giving," *HWF*, September 1890, 63. It continued to circulate in sponsorship circles, e.g., A. T. Pierson, "7 Ways to Give," *WVM*, July 1960, 15.

5. "Report of the Prudential Committee," *MH* 17, no. 1 (January 1821): 2–12. Catharine Beecher argued the same regarding democracy in her chapter "On giving in Charity" in *A Treatise on Domestic Economy* (1841).

6. Lum, *Damned Nation*, 45.

7. The context is different but the idea is helpful: Ralph Cintron, "Rhetoric in the Moral Order: A Critique of Tropological Approaches to Culture," in *Culture, Rhetoric, and the Vicissitudes of Life*, ed. Michael Carrithers (New York: Berghahn Books, 2009), 140.

8. Morton, *Hyperobjects*, 136–37.

9. Taylor in Edwin L. Frizen, *75 Years of IFMA, 1917–1992: The Nondenominational Missions Movement* (South Pasadena, CA: William Carey Library, 1992), 149.

10. No Title, *HWF*, September 1879, 49. This concern continues today, according to the profiles in Wuthnow, *Boundless Faith*, 183–84.

11. J. F. Willing, "Money Enough," *HWF*, September 1869, 30.

12. Hill, *The World Their Household*, 5, 186–91. Cf. Robert, *American Women in Mission*, 302–15.

13. Morton, *Hyperobjects*, 47.

14. Brigitte Resl, "Bequests for the Poor," in *Medieval Christianity in Practice*, ed. Miri Rubin (Princeton, NJ: Princeton University Press, 2009), 209–13.

15. M. G. Jones, *Charity School Movement: A Study of Eighteenth Century Puritanism in Action* (Hamden: Archon Books, 1964), 12–13.

16. Andrew, *Philanthropy and Police*, 47–49, 198; Roberts, "Head versus Heart?", 66–86; Lloyd, *Charity and Poverty*, 27, 38.

17. William Webb Kemp, *The Support of Schools in Colonial New York by the Society for the Propagation of the Gospel in Foreign Parts* (New York: Columbia University Press, 1913) 30, 104 fn. 168. On the SPCK: Sarah Lloyd, "Pleasing Spectacles and Elegant Dinners: Conviviality, Benevolence, and Charity Anniversaries in Eighteenth Century London," *Journal of British Studies* 41, no. 1 (2002): 33; Thomas Bray's "General Plan" (1697) in Kemp, *The Support of Schools in Colonial New York*, 13. On antecedents: Resl, "Bequests for the Poor," 209–13.

18. It should be noted that although Anglo-Protestants often disparaged "stagnant" forms of European Catholic charity, Catholics instituted equivalent methods of systematic subscription in the Society for the Propagation of the Faith and Holy Childhood Association in the 1820s–1830s. The French Revolution also pushed them to recognize the need for non-state voluntary societies to support missions, even under republicanism.

19. Beaver, *American Protestant Women*, 25; Kaell, "Evangelist of Fragments."

20. Anderson to David Abeel, 1835, ABC 1.0, v.14, ABCFM. Cited in Pruitt, *A Looking-Glass for Ladies*, 215n.12.

21. Hannah Hume to Mrs. Leonard, May 10, 1871, folder 2, box 1, series 1, WBMR. All Hume citations in this chapter are in the same folder unless otherwise noted.

22. Hume to Mrs. Bartlett, May 10, 1871; Hume to Mrs. (Lemuel) Bissell, May 30, 1871; Hume to Mrs. Bartlett, June 13, 1871. On renaming see chapter 4.

23. Hume to Mr. Riggs, January 24, 1876; Hume to Miss Strang, April 25, 1876. By 1874, Branch affiliates supported: 13 girls in Marsovan (Armenian Mission, Turkey), 16 in Madura (South India/Tamil Nadu), 4 in Ceylon (Sri Lanka), 3 in Ahmeddgar (India), 6 in Foochow (China), 3 in Inanda (Zulu Mission, South Africa) and 1 in Harpoot (Armenian Mission, Turkey). The number of circles and adoptees is my estimate based on Hume's sources.

24. Hume to Miss Child, March 24, 1876.

25. Hume to Miss Child, September 28, 1874. Also, Hume to Miss Child, May 20, 1892, folder 4, box 1, series 1, WBMR.

26. Hume to Miss Child, May 15, 1876.

27. Hume to Mrs. Kimball, May 27, 1876; Hume to Mrs. Page, June 23, 1876.

28. Hume to Miss Leitch, November 5, 1884; Hume to Miss Child, December 24, 1884; Hume to Miss Child, March 14, 1885; Hume to Miss Child, December 26, 1885, folder 4, box 1, series 1, WBMR.

29. Hill, *The World Their Household*, 96, 99–100. By 1885, the Congregational Women's Board down-played adoptions, and a decade later the Presbyterians and Methodists did the same. This did not actually stop adoptions, but it undoubtedly slowed them down.

30. Mrs. J. T. Gracey, "An Orphan It Must Be," *HWF*, June 1884, 278.

31. Luthera Whitney, "Special Objects," *HWF*, September 1884, 57–58.

32. "New England Branch, Giving," *HWF*, May 1878, 254.

33. "A Word to Western Women," *HWF*, July 1869, 13; "Much from Little," *HWF*, January 1872, 227–28; Miss L. L. Coombs, "The Peking Hospital," *HWF*, June 1876, 271–73; Mrs. T. S. Johnson, "Then and Now," *HWF*, June 1877, 272.

34. Modern, *Secularism in Antebellum America*, 16, 67.

35. N.A. "A Dun," *HWF*, May 1878, 252–53; N.A. "Vow-paying," *HWF*, November 1883, 111.

36. Mrs. Esther Tuttle Pritchard, "Stewardship and Systematic Giving," *HWF*, October 1885, 81.

37. Excerpt printed in "Proportionate Giving—A Methodical Plan," *Life and Light for Woman*, May 1894, 226–27.

38. "Cincinnati Branch" (Trinity Auxiliary), *HWF*, January 1882, 164.

39. Slack, *From Reformation to Improvement*, 80.

40. Rudnyckyj and Osella, *Religion and the Morality*; Chu, *Cosmologies of Credit*.

41. "Extracts from Bishop Thoburn's Report," *HWF*, June 1892, 280–81; Mrs. Easter quoted in R.B.B., New York Branch, *HWF*, March 1880, 208.

42. "The Human Family," *HWF*, February 1895, 228.

43. Meyer and Verrips, "Aesthetics," 29. In the same key, Christopher Pinney uses the term "corpothet-ics" to refer to "sensory corporal aesthetics." Although I do not use his neologism here, it is certainly relevant.

44. Meyer, "How to Capture the 'Wow.'"

45. Pandey, "The Prose of Otherness," 205.

46. Desrosières, *The Politics of Large Numbers*, 22–25, 86–87.

47. Foucault, *The Order of Things*, 67–75.

48. In reference to population tabulations and statistics, James S. Dennis, *Foreign Missions After a Century* (New York: Revell, 1893), 13.

49. Desrosières, *The Politics of Large Numbers*, 9–10; Asad, "Ethnographic Representation"; Rowse and Shellam, "The Colonial Emergence of a Statistical Imaginary."

50. Morton, *Hyperobjects*, 73, 75.

51. John Cameron Lowrie's Presbyterian *A Manual of Missions* (1854). These maps were ubiquitous, for example, John Scudder's *Tales for Little Readers about the Heathen* (American Tract Society, 1849). In Lum, *Damned Nation*, 136–37, 64–65.

52. William Carey, *An Enquiry into the Obligations of Christians to Use Means for the Conversion of the Heathens* (Leicester, 1792); "Accurate computing" from Gordon Hall and Samuel Newell, "The Conversion of the World: or, The Claims of Six Hundred Millions and the Ability and Duty of the Churches Respecting Them," (Andover: Flagg and Staff, 1818), 10. On the tract's influence: Andrew, *Rebuilding the Christian Commonwealth*, 94, 114; Elsbree, *The Rise of the Missionary Spirit*, 180, 229.

53. Conroy-Krutz, *Christian Imperialism*, 29, 34.

54. I draw this point from historian Mary Poovey, who notes that early economists and statisticians like Adam Smith prized "precision" (meaning systematic coherence) over accuracy; his goal was to create in readers a *feeling of satisfaction* at seeing the potential of a perfectly moral system. Ac-cording to Poovey, this goal shifted in the 1830s when government statistics were emancipated from Christianity and philosophy. By contrast, in missionary texts it lingered throughout the nineteenth century. Poovey, *A History of the Modern Fact*, xxi, xxiv, 215–17, 265, 267, 273. On this note, Engelke, "Number and the Imagination," 819, 821.

55. Mrs. H. Benton, "Uniform Study for September," *HWF*, August 1886, 41–42.

56. Mrs. J. B. Johnson, "July Report [1904]," WFMS Secretary's Report March 1904–September 1912, pp. 8–9, in unprocessed archives, First United Methodist Church (Pasadena, California).

57. Mrs. I. M. Hartsough, "NW Iowa Conference," *Eighth Annual Report of the Western Branch of the Woman's Foreign Missionary Society of the Methodist Episcopal Church Held in Mount Pleasant Iowa, April 18–21 1878* (Illeg.), 39–40, 2599-2-4:12, WDG, GCAH.

58. "Uniform Readings for January, 1883," *HWF*, January 1883, 160–61.

59. Hume to Mrs. Leonard, November 19, 1875.

60. Samuel Worcester to Hall, Newell, Bardwell, June 11, 1818, ABC 1.01, vol. 3, ABCFM.

61. Worcester to Edward Payson, February 28, 1816, ABC 1.01, vol. 1, ABCFM.

62. He uses the term "devotionalist" but I use "sentimentalist" to keep the terminology consistent. Rabinowitz, *The Spiritual Self*, 159, 1601–62.

63. Luhrmann, *When God Talks Back*.

64. Hume to Miss Dodge, February 18, 1879, folder 3, box 1, series 1, WBMR.

65. Hume rarely disentangled missionaries from the foreign children sponsored; to be familiar with one was to be familiar with the other. Quote in Hume to Miss Parsons (Bardezag, Turkey), April 22, 1876.

66. Hume to Miss Payson, November 23, 1874.

67. Ibid. "Peculiar and tender," in Hume to Mrs. Chandler, February 5, 1874.

68. Ibid, and Hume to Mrs. Clarke, (December?) 11, 1873 (Manissa, Western Turkey).

69. In the order they appear in this paragraph, the performances are from: Secretary's Report, March 26, 1880, folder 1, box 4, series 2, WBMR; "Philadelphia Branch," *HWF*, March 1888, 252; "New England Branch," *HWF*, November 1882, 110; A. R. Thompson, "New York Branch," *HWF*, October 1882, 85.

70. Frank J. Wagner, "Minneapolis Branch," *HWF*, February 1884, 192.

71. Philip J. Deloria, *Playing Indian* (New Haven, CT: Yale University Press, 1998); Mark C. Carnes, *Secret Ritual and Manhood in Victorian America* (New Haven, CT: Yale University Press, 1989), 14, 95–97. On summer camps, I am thinking of children's camps, such as the Boy Scouts, and the performance of Israelite rituals at evangelical institutions like Chautauqua after the mid-1870s.

72. Lott, *Love & Theft*, 6.

73. Elise Boxer, "Review of Real Native Genius: How an Ex-Slave and a White Mormon Became Famous Indians by Angela Pulley Hudson," *Mormon Studies Review* 5 (2018): 110–14.

74. Kenny, "The World Day of Prayer," 134.

75. J.M.O., "Little Things" *HWF*, September 1872, 333–34; On pennies: "Supplement to Heathen Woman's Friend: Please Read This," *HWF*, June 1888, n.p.

76. I. H., "Systematic Giving—Study for November," *HWF*, October 1888, 95.

77. Italics added. "Compassion" script by John Meredyth Lucas, TV special Pat Boone and the Little Ones, 1974, pp. 11–12, folder "Specials for Compassion," box USA, CIA.

78. For CCF, the tipping point was the Central Political Administration Council's policy in December 1950, called "Rules Governing Registration of Cultural, Educational, Relief Organizations and Religious Bodies Accepting Foreign Subsidies or Being Operated by Foreign Funds." It required these bodies to submit to government surveillance and asset liquidation. CCF moved to Hong Kong in 1951. By 1953, the PRC was imprisoning the (mainly) Catholic missionaries who remained under charges of espionage. "Crown jewel" in Ruble, *The Gospel of Freedom*, 27.

79. This collage exemplifies what I call landscape portraits in chapter 3. "Pray for China," *Heartline*, July–August 1971,1; "Asia: Where 57 percent . . ." *Heartline*, September 1971, cover story.

80. Frank Farrell, "Two Prayer Requests," *WVM*, November 1971, 1, WVIA.

81. Paul S Rees, "The Chinese Quarter," *WVM*, November 1971, 31. Although evangelicals used this sort of language in the 1950s and 1960s, this wave of interest was sparked by the hope that "ping pong diplomacy" would pave the way for missionaries.

82. For example: "Larry Ward Founds Food for the Hungry: Statistics Have Names," *Heartline*, April 1971, 12–13; Donald E. Vasey, "Sponsorship: A ministry of Love," *WVM*, January 1973, 21; Carl F. H. Henry, "Grief, Grace, and Grist," *WVM*, April 1976, 16–17.

83. *A Call To Prayer* (Newsletter), February 12, 1960, Folder "Ministries Call To Prayer, Jan–Dec 1960"; W. Herbert Scott to "Dear Friends in Fellowship," c. November 1976 and "World's millions . . ." in Scott Letter to "Dear Fellow Intercessor," March 1976, Folder "Ministries Int. Intercessors Jan–Dec

76"; Scott, "Daily Prayer Reminders: Nov 5 China," Nov 1980: n.p., Folder "Ministries Int. Intercessors Jan–Dec 80," WVIA.

84. The database was created by the Missions Advanced Research and Communications Center (MARC). It is discussed elsewhere, including Hutchison, *Errand to the World*, 151; King, "Heartbroken for God's World," 80; McAlister, "The Global Conscience."

85. Ju Hui Judy Han, "Reaching the Unreached in the 10/40 Window: The Missionary Geoscience of Race, Difference and Distance," in *Mapping the End Times: American Evangelical Geopolitics and Apocalyptic Visions*, ed. T. Sturm (Burlington, VT: Ashgate, 2010), 188.

CHAPTER 3: FOOD AND FAMINE

1. Berlant, "Introduction: Compassion (and Withholding)," 5; Sontag, *Regarding the Pain of Others*, 18, 105; Niebuhr, *Experiential Religion* (Eugene, OR: Wipf and Stock, 1972), 3–4.

2. Hannah Arendt, *On Revolution* (New York: Viking Press, 1962), 85.

3. Hugh Dellios, "The Miracle Merchants: For Sponsors, Image and Reality Worlds Apart," *Chicago Tribune*, March 15, 1998: 8. Quoted in Moeller, *Compassion Fatigue*, 9. Similar criticisms in, for example, Burman, "Innocents Abroad," 247; Bornstein, "Child Sponsorship," 601–2, 606; Briggs, *Somebody's Children*, 158–59; Zarzycka, "Save the Child." Related work includes Berger, "Photographs of Agony"; Malkki, "Speechless Emissaries"; Boltanski, *Distant Suffering*.

4. Sontag, *Regarding the Pain of Others*, 51–52; Halttunen, "Humanitarianism," 303–8; Curtis, "Depicting Distant Suffering."

5. "From French 'Mascots' to Their American 'Godfathers," *Pamphlet* (Paris, France: American Red Cross, 1919), 5–6, PAM D639 C4, Hoover Library, Stanford University.

6. James Barton was its chairman and Cleveland Dodge its treasurer. Barton was a former missionary in Turkey and secretary of the ABCFM. Dodge was chairman of the board of the ABCFM college in Istanbul. The cost of sponsorship was later raised to $100 to cover financial losses in the early 1920s.

7. Luisita A. Leland, "Report" in Report of the Operations of the Fatherless Children of France, 1915–1916," 14–15; "Fatherless Children of France, Annual Report, 31 December 1918," 2; "Report of the Operations of the Fatherless Children of France, 1920–21," 6. All in folder 2, box 1, LEC.

8. Among others, Ussama Makdisi (*Artillery of Heaven*, 169–79) tracks how U.S. Protestant missionaries united U.S. exceptionalism, racism, and liberalism in the late nineteenth and early twentieth centuries (in his case, among the ABCFM workers who later collaborated to create the NER). The trends discussed in this chapter are one aspect of this key historical shift. On the "tight link" between Christianity and NER's humanitarianism, see Torchin, "Ravished Armenia," 214–20.

9. Christopher Tilley, *The Materiality of Stone: Explorations in Landscape Phenomenology* (London: Bloomsbury 2004), 16.

10. Bold in original. The missionaries at Kollegal Girls School and Faith Brethren sources date Bird's trip north to 1888, but it may have been the famine of 1896–98. Lilo and Ron Penny (Kollegal Girls School), Personal Correspondence, March 8, 2014; Helen S. Dyer, *Revival in India: "Years of the Right Hand of the Most High"* (London: Morgan and Scott, 1907), 112, 116–18.

11. Dr. Abbott of Bombay, "Famine Children in India," *MH* 10 (May 1901): 182. A series of major famines made headlines in U.S. Christian media, notably the Turkish famine in 1875, the Chinese famine in 1876–79, and the Indian famines of 1876–78 and 1896–98. These were the testing ground for famine-related fund-raising in child sponsorship programs (unlike Russia, where there was famine but no major missions).

12. James Smith, "Industrial Training in India," *MH* 4 (April 1900): 168–72. Other stories in R. S. Hoskins, "Famine in India," *HWF*, June 1869, 5; "Children's Corner," *HWF*, September 1869, 39.

13. "Madura Mission—Southern Hindustan, The Terrible Famine," *MH* 73 (December 1877): 401.

14. "Famine Rescue Work in India," *MH* 8 (August 1901): 316–18.

15. For example, "Orphans in Turkey," *MH* 4 (April 1900): 136–37.

16. Halttunen, "Humanitarianism," 306; Curtis, "Depicting Distant Suffering," 163; Sontag, *On Photography*, 26; Corrigan, *Business of the Heart*, 234; cf. Laqueur "Bodies, Details."

17. Lindsey, *A Communion of Shadows*, 23.

18. Mrs. Dr. Butler, "Buried Alive," *HWF*, November 1870, 59–60.

19. Hannah Hume to Mr. Riggs, November 20, 1876, folder 2, box 1, series 1, WBMR; "Our Post-Office Box," *HWF*, March 1894, 305.

20. Stewart, *On Longing*, 136–38.

21. Griffith, *Born Again Bodies*, 58–61; Lindsey, *A Communion of Shadows*, 41–45.

22. Mollie S. Pilcher, "Northwestern Branch: Helping Our Medical Education Fund by the Sale of Photographs," *HWF*, January 1880, 162–63.

23. FRJ (Pittsburgh, PA), "One of Our Orphans," *HWF*, October 1872, 350–55.

24. Schuller, *The Biopolitics of Feeling*, 19.

25. Lindsey, *A Communion of Shadows*, 28.

26. Pilcher, "Northwestern Branch."

27. Fanny Garretson Hyde, "Bible Reader in Moradabad, Account Written by Herself," *HWF*, October 1871, 190–91. Fanny's story appears in chapter 1. She did not mention the Sepoy rebellion (1857–1858), which resulted in massive violence in the region where she lived. However, her mother's death and her displacement likely occurred at that time when she was about six or seven years old.

28. Luisita A. Leland, "Report" in "Report of the Operations of the Fatherless Children of France, 1915–1916," 14, folder 1, box 1, LEC.

29. "Report April 1 1917–1918" in MSS S83 (vol.1)–1917–1922, Letters received and records of payments: regarding Marcel Huiban, the Athenaeum "godchild," 1917–1924, BAA.

30. "Famine Relief," *MH* 5 (May 1900): 179.

31. Castelli, "Praying for the Persecuted Church," 326.

32. "Sixteen Striking Scenes," 1917–18, folder 10, box 4, series 1, NER. History of the genre in June Rose, *For the Sake of the Children: Inside Dr. Barnardo's: 120 Years of Caring for Children* (London: Hodder and Stoughton, 1987), 38, 57–58.

33. N.A. "India Photographs," *HWF*, February 1883, 182.

34. Bernard Mandeville, *The Fable of the Bees: Or, Private Vices, Public Benefits. With an Essay on Charity and Charity Schools. And a Search into the Nature of Society* (London: J. Tonson, 1729).

35. "The Golden Rule" (pamphlet), 1925, p. 11, folder 2, box 18, series II, NER.

36. Anna Granniss, "America, Great Mother," Reprinted in *Preliminary Report: International Golden Rule Sunday Observance,* 1924, p. 17, folder 1, box 18, series II, NER.

37. Rev. James Smith, "Industrial Training in India," *MH* 4 (April 1900): 168–72.

38. Harold B. McAfee letter to Dr. O.S. Morgan, October 6, 1925, folder "Unnamed," Harold B. McAfee Papers, HIA. Also, "Making History," Pamphlet, folder 7, box 17, series II, NER. Background on the coalescing of these ideas in Makdisi, *Artillery of Heaven*, 169–79; Hollinger, *Protestants Abroad*, 94–116, 119.

39. "The Cry of a Million," American Committee for Armenian and Syrian Relief (later NER), June 1916, folder 1, box 2, series 1, NER; Malkki, "Speechless Emissaries," 377–404.

40. According to my survey, the Golden Rule first comes up regularly in the children's sections of HWF and MH in the mid-1880s. The man who wrote this story did not specify the church in which he was raised, but it was undoubtedly liberal (or "modernist," to use more historically specific terminology).

41. Golden Rule dinner manuals offered a choice of Protestant, Catholic, or Reform Jewish prayers. I invented two small details in the description: the age of the second child and the idea that war relief campaigns made the father recognize global needs (he says he became aware after *serving* in the war). Everything else from "Why and How I adopted an Orphan Child by a Would-be Christian," Docket of Executive Committee Meeting, May 28, 1925, pp. 83–85, folder 5, box 14, series II; "Suggestions and Meditations for Golden Rule Sunday," booklet, 1926, pp. 35–37, folder 2, box 18, series II, NER.

42. "Preliminary Report: International Golden Rule Sunday Observance 1924," p. 14, folder 1, box 18; Charles Vickrey (likely) to Executive Board, December 1923 or 1924, folder 6, box 7; Vickrey to Talcott Williams, November 25, 1924, folder 1, box 18; "Minutes 93rd Meeting of the Administrative Committee Near East Relief, Caucasus Branch 22 April 1925," p. 36, folder 6, box 14; "Finances Report," folder 2, box 14; Vickrey to Talcott Williams, April 16, 1925, folder 3, box 14, series II, NER.

43. "Suggestions and Meditations for Golden Rule Sunday," booklet, 1925, pp. 7, 44–45, folder 2, box 18, series II, NER.

44. Ole S. Quammen to NER, November 16, 1925, folder 8, box 14. Other events in "Christmas Appeal," December 3, 1923; John D. Rockefeller to Vickrey and Vickrey to Talcott Williams, December 13, 1923, folder 6, box 7, series II, NER.

45. "Significance of International Golden Rule Sunday," *Team Work*, vol. 3, no. 1, 3 January 1924, p. 8, folder 1, box 7, series II, NER. On similar trends two decades earlier, see Curtis, *Holy Humanitarians*, 83, 253.

46. Vickrey, "Sailing of Christmas Ship," December 12, 1916, folder 1, box 2; On Billy Sunday: Vickrey to Rockwell, May 26, 1917, folder 5, box 2, series I, NER.

47. "Notes on a conversation with Dr. Talcott Parsons, January 29, 1916, Concerning the Work of the Publicity Campaign," folder 1, box 1, series 1, NER.

48. On the YMCA, an important example is Joseph and Corinna Lindon Smith. On church groups: Caroline Hill to Constance Hall, May 3, 1916 and Caroline Hill to President of Shepard Memorial Church Relief Committee, Cambridge, MA, May 3, 1916, A/H174, folder 2, Constance H. Hall Papers, Schlesinger Library, HUA.

49. Elizabeth Wallace, "Introduction," in *Letters Written by the Fatherless Children of French to their American Godparents* (Chicago: Allied Bazaar Committee, 1917), 5.

50. Jimmerson to Luisita Leland, November 5, 1917, folder 1, box 1, LEC.

51. Campbell, *Romantic Ethic*, 118; "Unmarked Protestantism" in Tracy Fessenden, *Culture and Redemption: Religion, the Secular, and American Literature* (Princeton, NJ: Princeton University Press, 2007), 3, 6.

52. "International Golden Rule Observance," Cooperation of Organizations in Near East Relief, NER booklet, c. 1926–1927, p. 46, folder 14, box 7, series II, NER.

53. Inboden, *Religion and American Foreign Policy*, 10, 108.

54. Tyrrell, *Reforming the World*, 114. "Friendly neighbors" in S. Parkes Cadman (vice-chair of National Golden Rule committee), "Dear Brother," form letter, November 24, 1925, folder 8, box 14, series II, NER.

55. Translation mine. Le Comité, "Les Dons Américains aux Orphelins de la guerre," 1916, folder 9, box 1, LEC. On "friendship" in missions: Robert, *American Women in Mission*, 273, 279, 284; Klassen, *Spirits of Protestantism*, 18. On "friendship" as a broader trend: Irwin, "Teaching 'Americanism'" and *Making the World Safe*, 170, 174, 196 n. 37; Fieldston, *Raising the World*, 56–58.

56. "Special Golden Rule Docket," unpublished minutes, 1924, folder 2, box 18, series II, NER.

57. Sharon Stephens, "Introduction," in *Children and the Politics of Culture*, ed. Sharon Stephens (Princeton, NJ: Princeton University Press, 1995), 8. Liisa Malkki extends this argument in "Children, Humanity," 72.

58. *The Fellowship of the Golden Rule* (newsletter) 1, no. 1 (July 1, 1925) p. 2, folder 3, box 18, NER.

59. "International Golden Rule Observance," in Cooperation of Organizations in Near East Relief, NER booklet, c. 1926–1927, p. 46, folder 14, box 7, series II, NER.

60. First quote: Jonathan Davies (Governor) letter to "Dear Friend" October 11, 1924; Second quote: Arthur J Carruthers, *Golden Rule Day News Service*, October 10, 1924, folder 10, box 13, series II, NER.

61. H. B. Skidmore, "New York Branch," *HWF*, February 1883: 185.

62. Marlene D. LeFever, "Mission Saturation," *CEM*, February 1973, pp. 6–7, folder 23–24, box 31, collection 20 Papers of Herbert J. Taylor, 1916–1979, BGCA.

63. Aoki, "Singing Exoticism," 943–55. See Yuko Tanaka's work on page 945.

64. Bennett, *Vibrant Matter*, 39–40, 42–43, 50. Marcel Mauss intimated much the same thing in "Techniques of the Body," 83.

65. "Golden Rule Booklet, 1924," folder 1, box 18, series II, NER.

66. This is a rather literal and thus intriguing example of what David Morgan ("The Ecology of Images," 86) calls "material acts of seeing that enfold humans into large and extended networks."

67. "Suggestions and Meditations for Golden Rule Sunday," 1925, p. 32 and "Suggestions and Meditations for Golden Rule Sunday," 1926, p. 38, folder 2, box 18, series II, NER. Background in Paul Weindling,

"From Sentiment to Science: Children's Relief Organisations and the Problem of Malnutrition in Inter-War Europe," *Disasters* 18, no. 3 (1994): 204–12.

68. "Guiding Principles," *The Fellowship of the Golden Rule* 1, no. 1 (July 1, 1925): 3.

69. Mary Bowers MacKorrell, "The Boy Who Made Me Diet," *Scope*, June 1969, 12–13. Reprint from *Guideposts Magazine*.

70. *Childcare Notes*, November 1974: 2. COM/WVI 4–1 FY73–79, Childcare Notes Newsletter 1973–1979, WVIA. On Hatfield see D. G. Hart, *From Billy Graham to Sarah Palin: Evangelicals and the Betrayal of American Conservatism* (Grand Rapids, MI: William B. Eerdmans, 2011), 57–64. There is significant work on current child rescue, which remains a facet of evangelical aid campaigns. Sponsorship organizations have varying levels of involvement. See Rosenberg, "Rescuing Women and Children"; Briggs, *Somebody's Children*, 3–5; Marc Lacey, "Haiti Charges Americans with Child Abduction," *NYT*, February 4, 2010; Karen Swallow Prior, "The Great Tiny Baby Rescue," *CT*, January 25, 2013.

71. JCC to President Johnson, April 24, 1964, folder 8, misc. correspondence 1964, box IIB3, CFA; Mark O. Hatfield, "World Hunger Is a Spiritual Problem," *WVM*, March 1983, 7–8.

72. JCC to President Johnson, April 24, 1964; Peter Adamson, "By the Year 2000: Two Billion New Arrivals," *ChildWorld* (CCF), July–August 1980, 10, 16, misc. documents, CFA.

73. Hatfield, "World Hunger Is a Spiritual Problem"; King, "The New Internationalists," 935–36.

74. For example, in a 1989 survey of 20,772 CCF sponsors, the majority said that "famine" should be the organization's first priority. "Record Response to Child Survival Survey," *ChildWorld*, Spring/Summer 1990, p. 10, misc. box, CFA.

75. "Family Project for India," *Scope*, January 1967, 10. Such exercises persist: Valerie Hopkins, "Could You Eat Like Your Sponsored Child for a Week?" *Compassion Blog*, last modified March 5, 2012. https://blog.compassion.com/could-you-eat-like-your-sponsored-child-for-a-week/.

76. Hatfield in King, "The New Internationalists," 934.

77. "Sally Struthers to Help Impoverished Children Worldwide," CCF press release, August 27, 1976, and "This Meal Not for Eloise—Poorest Fare in Hotel History Underscores Starvation," CCF Press Release, December 31, 1975, misc. box, CFA; "25 Years of Compassion," booklet 1977, p. 15, folder 1977–1982, box USA, CIA.

78. "Planned Famine" (advertisement), *WVM*, February–March 1990, 17. On Catholics: "From Our Mail," *CFCA Newsletter*, July 1988, 3.

79. Les Wagner, "A Rumble with Hunger," *WVM*, December 1984–January 1985, 16–17. For more on Planned Famine in the contemporary context, see Kaell, "Immobile Global."

80. Kleinman and Kleinman, "The Appeal of Experience," 2.

81. Admittedly, I am playing a bit fast and loose with the phrase "Body of Christ" vis-à-vis an evangelical like Mary MacKorrell. Yet the language is not absent among evangelicals either, especially in popular discourse about globalism. For a good overview from a theological perspective, see F. LeRon Shults, "The 'Body of Christ' in Evangelical Theology," *Word & World* 22, no. 2 (2002): 178–85.

CHAPTER 4: FAMILY AND FRIENDSHIP

1. Clarence W. Cranford (pastor) to JCC, January 14, 1952, folder 2, box IB22, CFA. Other details from the *Calvary Caller*, Calvary Baptist Church, unprocessed archives, Washington, DC, especially the following articles: "Calvary in Korea," October 12, 1951, 3; "Christian Education Notes," October 26, 1951, 3; "Special Offering for Korean Relief," November 16, 1951, 1; Clothing for Relief," January 4, 1952, 3; "Calvary's Korean Relief Fund," February 8, 1952, 2; "Your Adopted Orphans," October 31, 1952, 2.

2. Fassett, "More than Forty Years of Life Sustained through Your Response to Calvary's Korean Offering," *Calvary Caller*, December 21, 1951, 1; Frances F. Nickels to JCC, March 17, 1952, folder 2, box IB22, CFA.

3. Clark H. Phillips, "How Methodists Give Relief," *Michigan Christian Advocate*, November 11, 1954, p. 9, folder 8, box IB22, CFA.

4. "Do Relief Work Through Your Church," *Yearbook and Annual Report 1958, Board of World Missions, Presbyterian Church in the U.S., 1959*, folder 10, box IB22, CFA.
5. Fieldston, *Raising the World*, 3.
6. There were crackdowns and even closures to prevent their foreign employees from unionizing or securing more control over operations, for example with CCF in India, WV in Laos, and Compassion in Korea. On WV, see folder "WVI/ORG 18 World Vision History WV Laos," WVIA; On CCF, see JCC to Mills, May 25, 1954 and JCC to Mills, June 1, 1954, folder 3, box IIB10, CFA. These issues nearly ended Compassion, since it operated solely in Korea at the time: Robert Morgan to Gustav Hemwall, January 12, 1966; Edward Kimball to Robert Swaney, October 13, 1966; Kimball to Hemwall, January 3, 1968, folder 1965–76, box USA, CIA. On anti-communism at CCF, WV, and Save the Children Fund: Fieldston, *Raising the World*, 80–87; Barnett, *Empire of Humanity*, 121–122.
7. Stoler, "Intimidations of Empire"; Klein, "Family Ties," 38. Also relevant are Howell, *The Kinning of Foreigners*; Briggs, *Somebody's Children*; Catherine Ceniza Choy, *Global Families: A History of Asian International Adoption in America* (New York: New York University Press, 2013).
8. Perry, *Growing God's Family*, 33, 100.
9. These racialized designations are messy, but I opted not to use quotation marks around the word "white" in order to underline how U.S. sponsors perceived and wrote about these categories. In the war and interwar periods, most sponsored children were continental Europeans or Armenians (who were viewed as "white" compared to Muslim Turks). In the 1930s, new opportunities emerged to sponsor Chinese children caught in the civil war—including through the nascent CCF.
10. I am referring to European culture more generally, in which the enlightenment ideal of the "universal man," and its relation to emerging national consciousness, assumed a priori a white subject constituted in relation to a racial other. For example, Da Silva, *Toward a Global Idea of Race*.
11. I follow Kwame Anthony Appiah (*My Father's House*, 13) in his use of "racialism." When I say "natural" I am referring to a biologized view of race. As many scholars have pointed out, race is a political category, so reproducing and reformulating it (more races, fewer, what counts as "race," etc.) has never been left to heredity alone. For much the same point about UNESCO's Statements on Race in 1952, see Jenny Reardon, *Race to the Finish: Identity and Governance in an Age of Genomics* (Princeton, NJ: Princeton University Press, 2005), 19–29.
12. Berlant, *Cruel Optimism*. On unity-in-diversity, anthropologist Mary Hancock ("Short-Term Youth Mission") makes a similar point, which she calls "identity-in-difference." I prefer "unity" to "identity" since it underlines the ultimate goal of Christian globalism.
13. Mrs. Samuel Etchings, "Letters from Our Readers," *WVM*, January 1961, 14; Anon (Larry Ward), "I Heard My Daughter Pray," *WVM*, October/November 1957, 12; Mrs. Dorothy Greiser in "Feeding Jesus' Little Lambs," *WVM*, February 1976, 14–15.
14. Mrs. Samuel Etchings, "Letters to 'Box O,'" *Scope*, October 1969, 12; Ward, "Open Letter to Two Little Girls," *WVM*, June 1960, 8–9.
15. Faubion, "Introduction," 12–13, 21. "Relatedness" is most associated with Carsten, *Cultures of Relatedness*.
16. I avoid "fictive kin" (cf. Bornstein, "Child Sponsorship," 616 n.15) because anthropologists use it most often in the context of literal adoption. "Kin-like" signals how sponsorship is far more removed. Faubion, "Introduction," 8; Robert Parkin, "Relatedness as Transcendence: The Renewed Debate over the Significance of Kinship," unpublished paper, 2013.
17. Kaell, "Renamed."
18. "Dear My Sponsor," pamphlet, c. 1955, Sponsor/Childcare Historical Promotions, 1950–1970, WVIA.
19. Rev. and Mrs. Orin Biley, "A Son Dies but Hope Comes to a Refugee Boy," *Scope*, September 1967, 6; "From Box O," *WVM* January/February 1958, 10; Mrs. L.C., "Letters to Box O," *Scope*, August 1968, 6; "Meet Mrs. Duffield," *Scope*, October 1968, 8.
20. These letters were sent to Unbound's office before my arrival and I was given permission to copy them. Of the organizations under study, World Vision is the most likely to include such stories in its publicity today, albeit less often than in the past. The man referred to above is Lindy Lybarger (North Manchester, Indiana), Personal Interview, May 2, 2015.
21. For example, Scherz, "Seeking the Wound."

22. "Impact of Sponsor Communications, Final Report Prepared by Dr. Alistair Sim," June 2011. Courtesy of Alistair Sim, Program Effectiveness Research Director, Compassion International.

23. "Roses: Letters compiled by Cecelia Costello (American Sponsor to Four Korean Orphans)," Scrapbook. See letters from March 4, 1961, November 23, 1962, May 29, 1964, KR1965.02.03.01, Box Korea, CIA.

24. On the first wave: "Many Seek to Adopt Children of France and Belgium," *The News Letter* (American Red Cross Atlantic Division), 39 no. 1 (September 30, 1918): 4, folder 8, box 1, LEC. On the second wave, see letters in IB26, also JCC to V.J.R. Mills, January 16, 1951 and Mills to JCC, January 29, 1951, folder 1, box IB1, CFA. Kim, *Adopted Territory*, 51, 53, 60; Nancy Ota, "Family Matters: Family and Race and the Post-World War II Translation of 'American,'" *International Review of Social History* 46 (2001): 229.

25. Mrs. Scotty Mitchell to Robert Swaney, January 2, 1966, USA1962.02.01.0927, folder "Correspondence, 1962–1967," box USA, CIA.

26. Kim, *Adopted Territory*, 47, 69, 71, 74; Oh, *To Save the Children*, 54.

27. It took three months to bring a child over using the proxy method and three years or more through regular channels. On the Holts: Briggs, *Somebody's Children*, 153; Kim, *Adopted Territory*, 35, 42–44. On proxy adoptions see Herman, *Kinship by Design*, 218. For a balanced view from the time, LeRoy Bowman, Benjamin A. Gjenvick and Eleanor T. M. Harvey, *Children of Tragedy: Church World Service Survey Team Report on Intercountry Orphan Adoption* (New York: National Council of Churches of Christ in the USA, 1961), 42, 49.

28. Carl G. Karsch to JCC, April 29, 1955 and Noel Braga (U.S. Embassy, Seoul) to JCC, April 7, 1955, folder 10, box IB22; Mills to JCC, September 26, 1952 and JCC to Mills, October 25, 1952, folder 2, box IB2, CFA; Swanson to "Dear Friend," USA1960.09.06.01, "1960–1966 Form Letters," box USA, CIA.

29. "What Is a Sponsor?" *Heartline*, March 1971, 4–5. Unbound and CCF focused on creating productive citizens, rather than missionaries.

30. "Ann Landers Said It!," Compassion pamphlet, 1966, p. 2, folder "1966 Publications," box USA, CIA.

31. Mrs. R. D. Mullins (Clifton, VA) to JCC, February 22, 1950 and April 14, 1950; JCC to Mullins, February 28, 1950 and April 20, 1950, folder 1, box IB26, CFA.

32. Okazawa-Rey, "Amerasian Children."

33. Mills to JCC, April 27, 1951, folder 4, box IB1, CFA; Larry Ward (anon.), "Open Letter to an Unknown G.I.," *WVM*, December 1958, 3.

34. Puar, *Terrorist Assemblages*, 34–35, 200. Klassen (*Spirits of Protestantism*, 209) says something similar about white middle classes in this period, whose social location gave them "the space in which to imagine and to work toward a cosmopolitan world that would be founded on peace with justice."

35. Klein, *Cold War Orientalism*, 152–59; Fieldston, *Raising the World*, 107.

36. Seiple, "Strangers in Their Fathers' Land," *WVM*, August–September 1990, 5–9. Seiple was not alone in romanticizing racial hybridity as a reaction to racial violence in this period. See for example Gary Nash's 1995 Organization of American Historians presidential address, "The Hidden History of Mestizo America."

37. Stoler, *Carnal Knowledge*, 13, 24.

38. Sara Ahmed, "Forward: Secrets and Silence in Feminist Research," in *Secrecy and Silence in the Research Process: Feminist Reflections*, ed. Rosin Ryan-Flood and Rosalind Gill (New York: Routledge, 2010): xvii. "Race blindness" in Fieldston, *Raising the World*, 105–6.

39. For example, Conroy-Krutz, *Christian Imperialism*, 16; Takaki, "The Tempest in the Wilderness," 906; Mary A. Renda, "Conclusion," in *Competing Kingdoms: Women, Mission, Nation and the American Protestant Empire, 1812–1960*, ed. Barbara Reeves-Ellington et al. (Durham, NC: Duke University Press, 2010), 367–77.

40. Chang, "Marked in Body," 138; Curtis, "Popular Media," 1054.

41. Thomas A. Askew, "The New York 1900 Ecumenical Missionary Conference: A Centennial Reflection," *International Bulletin of Missionary Research* (2000): 149; Bramen, *The Uses of Variety*; In U.S. Christianity specifically, Mislin, *Saving Faith*.

42. Sullivan quote in Kaplan, *Anarchy of Empire*, 30–31. I take inspiration from Napolitano, *Migrants Hearts*, 54–55.

43. Bramen, *The Uses of Variety*, 205.
44. Watershed moments include the World Missionary Conference in Edinburgh in 1910, which led to the World Council of Churches in 1948; the Second Vatican Council and the 1971 Catholic Synod of Bishops; the Lausanne Committee for World Evangelization in 1974 and subsequent Lausanne Movement (in which the leaders of WV and Compassion were involved). Mainline Protestants and Catholics were also actively involved in the formation of the UN and, although scholars may debate whether the UN is a form of cultural imperialism or a "global discursive flow" (Appadurai, *The Future as Cultural Fact*, 63), they largely concur that if one traces the lineage of documents like the Universal Declaration of Human Rights (1948), one finds its roots in Christianity. In the period under study, many conservative Christians rejected this language of rights, which they viewed as ignoring the human subjugation to God (in the 1940s, Everett Swanson, soon to found Compassion, even preached that the UN was Satan-inspired). The issue was not the human creation of global institutions per se, but which of these seemed to ignore God. By the 1970s, organizations like World Vision, and even Compassion, became more comfortable situating themselves at the center of power. More optimistic about their ability to impact the UN, they largely embraced it. For liberals, the ethos is so consistent with their own that, as Unbound's team told me, when the organization crafted appeals for mainline Protestants, it found it could just replace the words "Catholic social teaching" for "UN Millennium Goals" with no significant change to its core message. Among other studies, see Moyn, *Christian Human Rights*; Gene Zubovich, "Where Is America in Human Rights History?," last modified July 8, 2015. https://tif.ssrc.org/2015/07/08/where-is-america-in-human-rights-history/; Nurser, *For All Peoples and All Nations*.
45. Oliver et al., "Exploring the Global History," 1039; Miller-Davenport, "Their Blood Shall Not Be Shed," 1111; McAlister, *The Kingdom of God*.
46. Otávio Velho, "Missionization in the Postcolonial World: A View from Brazil and Elsewhere," in *Transnational Transcendence*, ed. Csordas, trans. David Rodgers, 36–37; Ruble, *The Gospel of Freedom*, 65–68; Hollinger, *Protestants Abroad*, 72–86, 323 n.75.
47. Barthes, "The Great Family of Man," in *Mythologies*, 196–99.
48. "Readers Right," *WVM*, October 1965, 26, WVIA; On CCF: Kemp to Miss Ruth E. Vaughn, June 10, 1964, folder 17, box IIB6, CFA.
49. Tsing, *Friction*, 78; Malkki, *The Need to Help*, 79, 89–94; Malkki, "Children, Humanity, and the Infantilization of Peace," 72–73; Englung, "Universal Africa," 2–15; Hulsether, "Buying into the Dream," 483–508. On the UN photo, see an example from 1950 on "History of the Document," United Nations website. Accessed June 28, 2017. http://www.un.org/en/sections/universal-declaration/history-document/index.html.
50. "Visualized Songs," *CEM* May 1953: 21.
51. By including race, I build on what other studies have noted: U.S. Christian global ambitions have often collapsed what is "American" and "Christian." Wuthnow, *Boundless Faith*, 94; Miller-Davenport, "Their Blood Shall Not Be Shed," 1109–32.
52. Stoler, *Haunted by Empire*, 2–3.
53. Zubovich, "Where Is America in Human Rights History?"; Robert, "The First Globalization," 52.
54. Missionaries wrote all these communications, to a greater or lesser degree depending on their workload and interest. Quotes in Hannah Hume to Miss Dodge, February 19, 1878, folder 4, box 1, series 1, WBMR.
55. Translation mine. Le Comité, "Les Dons Américains aux Orphelins de la guerre," 1916, folder 9, box 1; "Fatherless Children of France, Annual Report, 31 December 1918," p. 1, folder 2, box 1, LEC.
56. "Ethical" is inspired by Muehlebach, *The Moral Neoliberal*, 7. On people-to-people diplomacy: Klein, *Cold War Orientalism*, 49–56; Herzog, *The Spiritual-Industrial Complex,* 78. Cf. Inboden, *Religion and American Foreign Policy*, 6, 8–9, 15. Fieldston offers a more in-depth discussion of anti-communism and sponsorship in *Raising the World*.
57. Daniel Sack, *Whitebread Protestants: Food and Religion in American Culture* (New York: Palgrave Macmillan, 2000), 141.
58. JCC to Edward Postma (The Banner), February 25, 1963, folder 9, box 9, UVL.
59. Bourdieu, *The Logic of Practice*, 98–99.

60. All three archives feature regular pamphlets for sponsors addressing the reasons for time lags. Survey in Jae Kwon Ha, "A Study of the Ministry of Compassion of Child Care in Korea," MA paper, Mc-Cormick Theological Seminary, May 1969, pp. 39–40, 45, 59, folder 1965–76, box USA, CIA.

61. Anon (likely Helen Clarke), "Requirements from Superintendents of Orphanages Operating under Christian Children's Fund Inc., 1950s," p. 4, misc. box 3 of 4, CFA. On the same guidelines as WV: Edmund Janss, *Manual for World Vision Superintendents*, 1975, pp. 17–18, 20–21, folder 9, ORG/WVI 16 FY-74 Sponsorship Programs Manuals, WVIA.

62. Robert Arculli (PR secretary, CCF HK office) to "Dear Friend" (to all orphanage superintendents), October 1, 1956, folder 1, box IC1, CFA.

63. Helen Clarke to Mills, June 17, 1957, folder 2, box IC1, CFA.

64. Helen Clarke (probably) to superintendents—"Your Annual newsletter . . . ," c. 1956, misc. box 3 of 4, CFA.

65. Janss, "Instruction Manual for Children's Letters," in *Manual for World Vision Superintendents*, 45, 53.

66. Jae, "A Study of the Ministry," 64–65. By this time, sponsorship organizations were trying to express these ideas to sponsors directly, as was evident in the letters in "Folder: 1969 Publications," box USA, CIA.

67. "Your Annual Newsletter . . ." c. 1956, misc. box 3 of 4, CFA. Fieldston, *Raising the World*, 123–24, 219–21.

68. "Requirements from Superintendents of Orphanages Operating under Christian Children's Fund Inc., 1950s"; Noel Braga to JCC, November 3, 1952, folder 4, box IB2, CFA; Janss, *Manual for World Vision Superintendents*, 20–21.

69. Kim Jun Ya to Cecelia Costello, September 15, 1962, "Roses: Letters Compiled by Cecelia Costello (American Sponsor to Four Korean Orphans)," Scrapbook, KR1965.02.03.01, Korea Box: Photos and Photo Albums, CIA.

70. "Your Annual newsletter . . ." c. 1956. Quote above in Helen Clarke to Ernest T. Nash, August 10, 1956. Both in misc. box 3 of 4, CFA.

71. "I Want to Belong to You," pamphlet, c.1958, Sponsor/Childcare Historical Promotions, 1950–1970, WVIA. Contemporary sponsors still prize letters that reflect modulated idiosyncrasy and often suspect a too "neat, precise, evenly written note" (Cf. O'Neill, "Left Behind," 213–14) was merely copied from a template.

72. Patricia Hershey, "Tuck a Little Love in Your Letter," *WVM*, August 1977, 12–13; Janss, *Manual for World Vision Superintendents*, 20–21.

73. Alexander Wirt, *Personal Interview*, May 1, 2015. Sherwood Wirt was a well-known Presbyterian pastor, Billy Graham associate, and editor of *Decision Magazine*.

74. The intimacy of these prayers contrasts with current military idioms in Pentecostal and charismatic "spiritual warfare," which reminds us that Christian globalism engages multiple affective moods. On spiritual warfare, see note 49 in chapter 7.

75. Klassen, *Spirits of Protestantism*, 190; Halvorson, *Conversionary Sites*, 38–52, 215–17; Hollinger, *Protestants Abroad*, 82.

76. Dave Toycen, "Analysis of Sponsorship Communications Questionnaire," 1981, 2, 16, WV 6–3–Organizational Structure: Ques & Stud. Sponsorship Communications Analysis–FY81, WVIA. On this shift more broadly in institutions and leadership: McAlister, "The Global Conscience of American Evangelicalism," 922–49; Ruble, *The Gospel of Freedom*, 49–52, 82–85; Swartz, "Embodying the Global Soul," 887–901; David C. Kirkpatrick, *A Gospel for the Poor: Global Social Christianity and the Latin American Evangelical Left* (Philadelphia: University of Pennsylvania Press, 2019).

77. Lori Henry Lee, "Now That You Have Seen": A Historical Look at Compassion International, 1952–2013" (Ed.D dissertation, Southeastern Baptist Theological Seminary, 2014), 98–99; Fieldston, *Raising the World*, 206–223. The National Council of Churches actually raised this issue more than a decade before. "Notes on a NCC Consultation," December 23, 1959, folder 3, box IB22, CFA.

78. CCF tried "Family Helper Programs" in Korea as early as the mid-1950s because so many parents were enrolling their children as "orphans" to access the free education. This was the kind of system CCF and the others introduced on a wider scale in the 1970s; see J. Calvitt Clarke III, *Fifty Years of Begging: Dr. J. Calvitt Clarke and Christian Children's Fund* (Bloomington, IN: Archway, 2018), 245.

79. The approach was not always consistent, but the first WV media stories noting the children actually had parents date to the late 1960s. E.g., "Djar Decides on a Career," *WVM*, December 1967, 10; "What Is a Sponsor?" *Heartline*, March 1971, 4–5; "Some Orphans Have Parents," *WVM*, May 1972, 18–19. Some liberal Christians had earlier leveled criticisms along the same lines: "When 'Adoption' Is Not Adoption," *CC*, December 2, 1959, 1396. CCF advertisements also swapped the word "adopt" for "sponsor" in the mid- to late 1960s.

80. A Presentation on a New Childcare Offer," October 5, 1982, ORG/WVI 4 Child Sponsorship Task Force—FY 82, WVIA.

81. The main categories were the following. Pen pal, student, patient: Protestants (38% n=25), Catholics (27% n=14). Nephew, niece, cousin: Protestants (32% n=21), Catholics (27% n=14). Godchild: Protestants (0%), Catholics (31% n=16). Others had no answer, or their responses did not fall into a distinguishable category.

82. Bornstein, *The Spirit of Development*, 53.

83. I include Catholics as Christians, although Compassion does not (at least in terms of its service providers). The question about whether children are already Christian is most delicate at Compassion, with its evangelical base. It does not gather statistics in this respect, but a number of my interviewees did confirm a high probability of self-selection into the program by already Christian parents (e.g., Alistair Sim, Program Effectiveness Research Director, June 12, 2014; Mark Hanlon, Senior Vice President of Global Marketing and Engagement, June 12, 2014). On walking distance, Wydick, Glewwe, and Rutledge, "Does International Child Sponsorship Work?," 396. Bornstein (*Spirit of Development*, 52) notes that WV employees resolved the issue by saying that people may be Christian but they are not "real" or "deep" ones. This idea was common in historical sponsorship-related materials, but I did not hear it among contemporary sponsors.

84. When they do discuss other religions, there is a liberal/conservative split. Unbound told positive stories about Hindus and Muslims, for example in "Celebrating World Inter-faith Harmony Week," *Unbound Blog*, February 6, 2015. https://blog.unbound.org/2015/02/celebrating-world-interfaith-harmony-week/#more-20958. By contrast, Compassion's website continues to associate indigenous traditions, Vodou, and even Hinduism with fear and helplessness. The authors I found who write in this vein are fieldworkers (Christians from the country in question), not its U.S. staff. Examples include Vera Mensah-Bediako, "There's No More Idol Worship and the Difference Is Jesus," October 3, 2011. https://blog.compassion.com/theres-no-more-idol-worship-and-the-difference-is-jesus/; David Adhikary, "Serving the Santal Tribe of Bangladesh," March 12, 2010. http://blog.compassion.com/serving-the-santal-tribe-of-bangladesh/; Bernard A. Gbagba and Amber Van Schooneveld, "Trapped in a Voodoo Temple," February 16, 2017. https://www.compassion.ca/blog/trapped-in-a-voodoo-temple/; Willow Welter and Bernard Gbagba. "Delivered from Darkness," n.d. https://www.compassion.com/for-sponsors/stories/delivered-from-darkness.htm. All accessed December 3. 2018.

CHAPTER 5: MATERIALISM AND CONSUMPTION

1. Charles Rhind Joy, "The Little Girl Who Had Never Smiled," unpublished manuscript, 1947. Charles Rhind Joy papers, bMS 347, box 28, Andover-Harvard Theological Library, Harvard Divinity School.

2. Hulsether, "Buying into the Dream," 484.

3. One of the most trenchant was David Riesman, *The Lonely Crowd: A Study of the Changing American Character* (New Haven, CT: Yale University Press, 1950) and *Abundance for What?* (New York: Doubleday Day and Co., 1964). Many historians have discussed this period, including May, *Homeward Bound*, 13; Jason W. Stevens, *God-Fearing and Free: A Spiritual History of America's Cold War* (Cambridge: Harvard University Press, 2010), 169–70.

4. Sara Dorow quoted in in Kim, *Adopted Territory*, 12. Also Briggs, *Somebody's Children*, 160; Woo, "Imagining Kin," 39.

5. Klein, *Cold War Orientalism*, 158. On a similar note, O'Neill, "Left Behind," 208.

6. Hannerz, "Notes on the Global Ecumene," 70.

7. Pratt, *Imperial Eyes*. I am also loosely inspired by de Certeau's "tactics" in *The Practice of Everyday Life* to refer to how consumers disrupt the structural forces that seem to constrain them. The attitudes and practices I describe may or may not be consciously engaged.

8. CCF was concerned about communism as materialistic; WV and Compassion worried about paganism too. Regarding China, Bob Pierce got the idea for WV while there, but he could not gain a toehold since the PRC had just been declared. CCF was based solely in China and left with the last remaining U.S.-run organizations in 1951. Clarke was deeply bitter. On the wider context, see Ruble, *The Gospel of Freedom*, 27, 46–47.

9. Robert Seiple, "Seduced by the Numbers," *WVM*, February–March 1989, 3.

10. Keane, *Christian Moderns*, 272.

11. "International Consultation on Simple Lifestyle," *Lausanne Movement: Connecting Influencers and Ideas for Global Mission*, accessed December 2, 2016. https://www.lausanne.org/gatherings/issue -gathering/international-consultation-on-simple-lifestyle-2. Also, David R. Swartz, *Moral Minority: The Evangelical Left in an Age of Conservatism* (Philadelphia: University of Pennsylvania Press, 2012) 153–69; King, "The New Internationalists," 929, 934–35. This is part of a broader rhetoric with longer roots, e.g., David E. Shi, *The Simple Life: Plain Living and High Thinking in American Culture* (New York: Oxford University Press, 1985).

12. Quote in "Globe at a Glance," *WVM*, June 1980, 22. Sponsors debate, for example, in the *Readers Right* section of *WVM*: John H. Walton (Haddonfield, New Jersey), "Turn-off," August 1979, 18; James Greenelsh (Sierra Madre, California), "Response," September 1979, 16.

13. O'Neill, "Left Behind," 205; Elisha, "Saved by a Martyr," 1070; Wuthnow, Boundless Faith, 184, 245.

14. Lears, *No Place of Grace*; Richard Butsch, *For Fun and Profit: The Transformation of Leisure into Consumption* (Philadelphia: Temple University Press, 1990); Curtis, *A Consuming Faith*; Zelizer, *Pricing the Priceless Child*; Marjorie Elizabeth Wood, "Emancipating the Child Laborer: Children, Freedom, and the Moral Boundaries of the Market in the United States, 1853–1938" (PhD dissertation, University of Chicago, 2011), 198–266.

15. On urgency, I am thinking of Campbell's definition of consumerism as "a deferment of gratification punctuated with moments of indulgence when a longed-for object is possessed." He argues that fears about consumption arise in wealthy societies when the period of deferment is radically shortened. Campbell, *The Romantic Ethic*, 203, 215; Miller, *A Theory of Shopping*, 139.

16. Patty Duncan, "Rejoicing in Little Things," *WVM*, October 1980, 12–13.

17. According to Menchit Wong, Compassion's Director of Leadership Engagement for Global Advocacy, who was present at Lausanne in 2010. Wong, Personal Interview, June 3, 2014. Quote in "The Cape Town Commitment: A Confession of Faith and a Call to Action," *Lausanne Movement*, accessed December 2, 2016. https://www.lausanne.org/content/ctc/ctcommitment.

18. Janss, *Manual for World Vision Superintendents*, 17–18, 20–21.

19. Loose photos, USA1960.01.05.03, folder 1952–1964, box USA, CIA.

20. Jean Baudrillard refers to how seriality ("la satisfaction sérielle") has an aesthetic component in *Le système des objets* (London: Verso, 1996), 146–48; Stewart, *On Longing*, 153, 159.

21. Zaloom, "The Evangelical Financial Ethic," 334–35; Zwissler, "Markets of the Heart." On fair trade among conservatives, see for example the Southern Baptist missions-related organization, World Crafts. James Bielo (personal communication) notes that about a third of the items in the Ark Encounter gift shop are also fair trade. On ethical consumption more generally: Hann and Hart, *Economic Anthropology*, 171; Carrier, "Introduction," 18.

22. "Can Hardly Contain Myself," "Letters to 'Box O,'" January 1967, 10; "Letters from Sponsors," *Compassion Magazine*, March–April 1978, n.p.

23. "Choose Your Own Orphan," card set, c.1966, KR1954.03.03.01, box USA, CIA; Compassion (advertisement), "Your heart-concern can turn his grief into joy!" *CC* 7 (February 1968): 169.

24. "Choose Your Own Orphan," Card set, c.1966.

25. "Letters From Our Readers," *WVM*, November 1961, 14.

26. Marilee Pierce Dunker, Personal Interview, April 24, 2015.

27. Today, a prospective sponsor can choose a child on Unbound's website, but it only shows one portrait at any time with a paragraph of personal description. In other words, there are no rows of faces (compare this aesthetic to Compassion's site in figure 5.1b). However, Unbound does use child packets at tabling events in parish churches.

28. I should not overemphasize the point. Many sponsors could not recollect why they chose a particular child. Based on 30 volunteer hours at sponsorship tables, I tallied a rough list of the reasons sponsors gave me for choosing a particular child, from most to least common: (a) shared birthday; (b) facial expression; (c) country of origin; (d) sex; (e) highest need, as indicated on the child packet; (f) name. A substantial minority of evangelicals chose a child because he/she looked sad, which they viewed as a call to change those children's lives (chapter 6). I met only a few African American sponsors, but every one of them prioritized sponsoring a black child.

29. Merish, *Sentimental Materialism*, 2–4. Although Merish's analysis of U.S. Christianity is superficial, she helpfully argues (pp. 89–90) that pious consumption appealed to a wide variety of Christians from the 1820s onward—thus throughout the whole period covered by sponsorship. By contrast, following Lears's influential analysis, many earlier studies dated a shift from Protestant "asceticism" to consumption only to the 1880s. See note 14.

30. Daswani, "The Globalization of Pentecostalism."

31. Coleman, "Charismatic Christianity," 246. An associated concept encourages spending beyond one's means in order to depend on God's intercession. Some sponsors have given "on faith" (most famously, WV's founder Bob Pierce subscribed to a version of this theology in the 1950s), however, neither it, nor prosperity theology, has ever been the norm in sponsorship.

32. Bielo, "The Mind of Christ," 329–33; Bialecki, "Between Stewardship and Sacrifice," 378–85; Zaloom, "The Evangelical Financial Ethic," 325–38; Gary Scott Smith, "Evangelicals Confront Corporate Capitalism: Advertising, Consumerism, Stewardship, and Spirituality, 1880–1930," in *More Money, More Ministry: Money and Evangelicals in Recent North American History*, ed. Larry Eskridge and Mark A. Noll (Grand Rapids, MI: William B. Eerdmans, 2000), 39–80; James Hudnut-Beumler, *In Pursuit of the Almighty's Dollar: A History of Money and American Protestantism* (Chapel Hill: University of North Carolina Press, 2007), 65–72. Cf. Wuthnow, *Boundless Faith*, 184.

33. "Letters From Our Readers," *WVM*, June 1960, 14. Based on my surveys of online materials, WV is the only one that sometimes reiterates this message today. For example, Marilee Pierce Dunker, "World Vision Works" (initially in *WVM*), email newsletter, July 13, 2015.

34. Marla Frederick ("Neo-Pentecostalism," 388, 391) makes a similar observation about African Americans. Regardless of their social location in the United States, they are reframed as people of means in a comparative global light.

35. "World Vision's Stewardship," *WVM*, January 1959, 3.

36. Miriam Swanson, "Letter to Superintendents and Staff Members," December 2, 1966, USA1962.02.01.0927, folder "Correspondence, 1962–1967," box USA, CIA.

37. "Donations to the Board," *MH* 17, no. 1 (January 1821): 4–5.

38. "Warmth for the Orphans of Korea," *McCall's*, October 1953. In Kim, *Adopted Territory*, 63.

39. "Love Is a Warm Blanket," *Childcare Quarterly*, Spring 1976, n.p., folder Marketing: Childcare Quarterly, January 75–Fall 77, WVIA.

40. Malkki, *The Need to Help*, 137–39, 160.

41. Hope B. Friedmann, "Sandor's Second Mother," *WVM*, November 1976, 7–8. Cf. Jae, "A Study of the Ministry," 23.

42. Halvorson, "Woven Worlds"; Malkki, *The Need to Help*, 123–24.

43. Edwin Moll (Lutheran World Federation Near East Branch) Memorandum to V.J.R. Mills, 1952, folder 2, box IB2, CFA; Peter G. Schreck, "GN Study" submitted to Cliff Benzel, March 25, 1977, pp. 1, 3–4, 7–8, Appendix B. MIN/WIV 1—GN Study—FY77, WVIA.

44. Mary Erickson, "Sincerely Yours . . ." *Compassion* (newsletter), November–December 1980, 2–5, Folder: 1980: Publications Newsletter, box USA, CIA.

45. "Questions Sponsors Ask," *WVM*, October 1983, 6–7 and May 1984, 7.

46. *Third Annual Report. Saint Louis Branch of the Woman's Foreign Missionary Society for the Year Ending in April 3, 1873* (n.p.: Barnes & Bennon, Printers), 30. 2599-2-4:12 Annual Reports 1873–1882, WDG, GCAH.

47. Herzog, *The Spiritual-Industrial Complex*, 79.

48. Brandy Campbell, "Three Things I Learned at My First Compassion Christmas Party," Compassion website, October 23, 2015. Accessed March 10, 2019. https://blog.compassion.com/3-things-i-learned-at-my-first-compassion-christmas-party/.

49. Love is used differently in Christian globalism than in sentimental evangelicalism. Cf. Brenneman, *Homespun Gospel*, 6–7, 73.

50. Muehlebach, "The Catholicization," 517; Cf. Rudnyckyj and Osella, "Introduction," 18.

51. Jun Ya was at Little Lamb Orphanage in Seoul under Kwon Eng Pal, with which Compassion broke ties in 1965–66. The sentiment of "jealousy" or "envy" likely had less strong connotations than in English; other Compassion child letters in this period also used it. Kim Jun Ya letter to Cecelia Costello, November 5, 1961, November 23, 1962, March 24, 1965. "Roses: Letters Compiled by Cecelia Costello," KR1965.02.03.01, CIA.

52. Olivia Hoopes, "Emptying Yourself for Christ," Unbound e-newsletter, May 11, 2015; Tom Hornbeck, "Imitating the Self-Emptying Love of Christ," Unbound e-newsletter, March 23, 2015.

53. "Share the Joy of the Season," Unbound website, Accessed August 23, 2017. https://www.unbound.org/DonationFunds/Christmas. And yet Mary Geisz, Director of Sponsor Experience, told me that sponsors still ask to purchase large individualized gifts for the family (e.g., a washing machine or new roof) and Unbound does its best to facilitate these requests. Geisz, Personal Interview, July 28, 2015.

54. N.A. "See What Christmas Means to Children in Poverty!" Compassion website, December 18, 2017. Accessed March 10, 2019. https://www.compassion.com/christmas-gift-for-needy-children.htm?referer=165453.

55. Campbell, "Three Things I Learned." This idea has a long history related to the importance of play, as shown in Fieldston, *Raising the World*, 125–31, 217–18.

56. N.A. "See What Christmas Means!"

57. "Our God Is Different," *WVM*, June 1962, 9; "Letters From Our Readers," *WVM*, November 1961, 14.

58. Mrs. Cecille Miller, "The Woman's Page," *WVM*, July 1962, 13.

59. "CCF Christmas Material Procedure" booklet, c. 1953, misc. folder 21, CFA.

60. Eugene Lee, "Packed with Love: From thousands of miles away, a letter and a package means the world to a sponsored child," WV e-newsletter, October 12, 2015.

61. Rather than livestock catalogues, Unbound encourages microfunding campaigns on a case-by-case basis. The first livestock-sending program was likely Heifer International, the brainchild of a Church of the Brethren worker in the 1940s. The gift catalogues have soared in popularity since c. 2005. Kelley Holland, "Symbolic Charity: When Is a Goat Not a Goat?" CNBC online, December 6, 2013. Accessed October 15, 2018. http://www.cnbc.com/2013/12/05/oat-not-a-goat.html.

62. Malkki, *The Need to Help*, 124.

63. Blanton, *Hittin' the Prayer Bones*, 53–62. On a similar point: Coleman, *The Globalisation of Charismatic Christianity*, 170–71, 177.

64. Priscilla and Warren Larson, "Two Halves Make a Heart," Letters to Box O, *WVM*, September 1964, 20.

65. It was not unique. I saw two other such boxes during my week at OCC. In the volunteer guestbook (2013–2014), people noted having seen the same type of boxes on five separate occasions.

66. "Jet-Propelled Preacher," *WVM*, September 1960, 16, 18.

67. Catherine Cudra, Guestbook comment, Operation Christmas Child, October 3, 2013.

68. According to Menchit Wong (Director of Leadership Engagement for the Global Advocacy, Compassion International), Personal Interview, June 3, 2014. Bakker, *Sister Churches*, 27–29, 50–52, 135; Mary M. McGlone, *Sharing Faith Across the Hemisphere* (United States Catholic Conference, 1997), 109–11.

69. G. R. Balleine, "Faith of Our Fathers," reprinted in *Compassion International Bible Study Booklet: Lifelines of Love, 1982*, UA1982.03.00.01, box "Memorabilia and Awards," CIA.

70. "Walking 4,000 miles in their shoes," CFCA Annual Report 1994, back cover. A nice summary of Catholic social teaching is Manini Sheker, "What Good Is Religion?" *Aeon Magazine*, May 22. 2018. https://aeon.co/essays/is-there-a-role-for-religion-in-international-development.
71. This and quote above in Elisha, "Personhood," 43.
72. Bandak, "The Social Life of Prayers."
73. McAlister mainly refers to the idea that they face physical persecution, but poverty is also a factor. Quote in "What Is Your Heart For?" 883; Howell, *Short-Term Mission*, 200; Bornstein, "Child Sponsorship," 608–9.
74. Maricela to Morris, March 23, 2013, Morris to Maricela, August 25, 2013, Maricela to Morris, November 27, 2013. This set of letters was in Unbound's file of responses to their 2014 Sponsor Stories prompt.
75. At Unbound, sponsors can choose to support an "elder," who is usually close to their own age. In this case, sponsors were much more likely to communicate about death or illness and feel supported by the sponsoree's thoughts and prayers.

CHAPTER 6: TRUST AND ASPIRATION

1. Tsing, *Friction*, 8.
2. Andrew, *Philanthropy and Police*, 197–98.
3. Strathern, "Introduction," 3.
4. Malcolm Waters, *Globalization* (London: Routledge, 1995), 63–64; Eriksen, *Overheating*, 139. Above from Lloyd, *Charity and Poverty*, 2, 15, 18. See also Stevens, *The Poor Indians*,14–15, 198.
5. Naomi Haynes, "*The Future as Cultural Fact*: Book Review," *AnthroCyBib*, April 18, 2013. https://www.blogs.hss.ed.ac.uk/anthrocybib/2013/04/18/the-future-as-cultural-fact-book-review/.
6. Nauja Kleist and Stef Jansen, "Introduction: Hope Over Time—Crisis, Immobility and Future-Making," *History and Anthropology* 27, no. 4 (2016): 385. Amartya Sen's *Development As Freedom* (New York: Anchor Books, 1999) led the way for many of these approaches to human flourishing among development experts.
7. Appadurai, *The Future as Cultural Fact*, 179, 293.
8. Quotes from Menchit Wong (Director of Leadership Engagement for the Global Advocacy, Compassion), *Personal Interview*, June 3, 2014; Wydick, Glewwe, and Rutledge, "Does International Child Sponsorship Work?," 395. On this idea at WV: Bornstein, *The Spirit of Development*, 46. Antecedents in Klassen, *Spirits of Protestantism*, 100–107.
9. "Apostolic Exhortation *Evangelii Gaudium*," of the Holy Father Francis. The Holy See, November 24, 2013. Web, §190. The link is not random. Unbound's founders Bob Hentzen and Jerry Tolle (a Jesuit) served as priests in Latin America in the 1960s and embraced the idea of a "preferential option for the poor," a phrase first used in 1968 by the superior general of the Jesuits and then adopted by Liberation Theologians. Pope Francis, also a Jesuit, was interpreting the same principle in the quote above. Today, Unbound celebrates both Francis's papacy and the preferential option for the poor, although it views the phrase itself as too Catholic for its marketing materials aimed at a broad-based audience.
10. Harvey, *A Brief History of Neoliberalism*, 2; Tejaswini Ganti, "Neoliberalism," *Annual Review of Anthropology* 43 (2014): 89–104.
11. Muehlebach, *The Moral Neoliberal*, 19.
12. For example, John and Jean Comaroff's path-breaking *Millennial Capitalism and the Culture of Neoliberalism*. More recently, Marlene de Witte, "'Buy the Future': Charismatic Pentecostalism and African Liberation in a Neoliberal World," in *Pentecostalism and Politics in Africa*, ed. Adeshina Afolayan, Olajumoke Yacob-Haliso, and Toyin Falola (Cham, Switzerland: Palgrave MacMillan, 2018), 65–86; Stephan Lanz and Martijn Oosterbaan, "Entrepreneurial Religion in the Age of Neoliberal Urbanism," *International Journal of Urban and Regional Research* 40, no. 3 (2016): 487–506.
13. Frederick, *Colored Television*, 22–23. On child sponsorship itself, see O'Neill, "Left Behind," 204–26.
14. For example, a sponsor showed me the Unbound report from a project in Guatemala that recorded a nine-year-old child doing "chores" after school. In the notes section, the in-country staff described

it as, "Alivar brings vegetables and other stuffs [sic] to the market to sell for his mother." Clearly, the child is integral to his family's paid labor. Unlike Compassion, Unbound does not make school attendance compulsory, although cases where a child is not in school are very rare.

15. Howell, "Practical Belief," 241; Meyer, "Make a Complete Break," 320; O'Neill, *City of God*, 164.

16. "Indonesia Reports" (for "It Works" campaign), 2001, folder "2001 Internal Documents," box USA, CIA. Wydick's surveys of sponsored children in Bolivia, Kenya, and Indonesia showed they were 10–25% more likely than their peers to name a white-collar job as their goal; studies of former sponsorees showed a 5.1–6.7% increase in the likelihood of white-collar work as an adult, although Wydick notes that parents may also choose to enroll the child they think will most likely succeed in this respect. Wydick, Glewwe, and Rutledge, "Does International Child Sponsorship Work?," 397, 427.

17. LeRoy Bowman, Benjamin A. Gjenvick, and Eleanor T. M. Harvey, *Children of Tragedy: Church World Service Survey Team Report on Intercountry Orphan Adoption* (New York: National Council of Churches of Christ in the USA, 1961), 22–24; Bornstein, "Child Sponsorship."

18. Toycen, "Analysis of Sponsorship Communications Questionnaire," 11; *Childcare Notes*, February 1977 and May 1977, COM/WVI 4–1 FY73–79, Childcare Notes Newsletter 1973–1979, WVIA. Also, Bornstein, "Child Sponsorship, Evangelism, and Belonging," 602.

19. As Omri Elisha ("Moral Ambitions of Grace") has pointed out, these breaks also occur in local instances of 1:1 charity, which he views as an inevitable gap between evangelical (donor) compassion and (recipient) accountability. Eleanor echoes the Christians in Elisha's study, perhaps because of her close tie to Angelus, which was unusual in sponsorship since it circumvented the organizational apparatus.

20. Crapanzano, "Reflections on Hope"; Hillary Kaell, "Can Pilgrimage Fail? Intent, Efficacy, and Evangelical Trips to the Holy Land," *Journal of Contemporary Religion* 31, no. 3 (2016): 393–408.

21. Zaloom, "Future Knowledge," 444–46. Cf. Guyer, "Prophecy and the Near Future."

22. Luhrmann, *When God Talks Back*, 272. On the same ontology among World Vision staff, Bornstein, *The Spirit of Development*, 126.

23. Armin R. Gesswein, "The Biography of a Prayer," *WVM*, August 1964, 6–7.

24. Simmel, *The Philosophy of Money*, 179; Möllering, "The Nature of Trust," 406, 409.

25. Strathern, *Audit Cultures*; Giddens, *The Consequences of Modernity*, 26, 83–85; Corsín Jiménez, "Trust in Anthropology," 180.

26. Quote in JCC to Mrs. E. R. Goodwin (National Information Bureau), February 26, 1947, folder 9, box IB21. In the same folder, see also JCC to Sponsors, c. 1941. Also, Dr. Jay Clarke, Personal Interview, December 11, 2014; Janss, *Yankee Si*, 2, 30.

27. Scherz, "Let Us Make God Our Banker," 626–27.

28. Perry, *Growing God's Family*, 200.

29. Clarke and Pierce can both be described as overbearing and idiosyncratic; both were ousted unwillingly. As far as I am aware, Swanson did not share those traits. He also prepared the organization to continue after his death by removing his own name and renaming it Compassion.

30. Partnerships between NGOs and government (specifically related to agricultural and military surplus) arose through a series of legal shifts from 1954 to the late 1960s (see Wuthnow, *Boundless Faith*, 124–25). WV has utilized these funds since the early 1960s, more than the other organizations under study. Cf. Barnett, *Empire of Humanity*, 127.

31. Bruce R. Hopkins, *The Law of Fundraising*, 3rd ed. (New York: Wiley, 2002), 331–33. Emilie Tavel Livezey, "Child Sponsorship Dollars: How Much Goes to Him?" *Christian Science Monitor*, August 6, 1981.

32. Milton H. Kohut, "Dollars and Disclosure Sense," *WVM*, October 1980, 15–16. Background in William P. Marshall and Douglas C. Blomgren, "Regulating Religious Organizations Under the Establishment Clause," *Ohio State Law Journal* 47, no. 2 (1986): 293–331.

33. Ted Engstrom, "Monthly Memo," *WVM*, June 1979, n.p.; Ted Engstrom, "Charities Establish Financial Disclosure Standards," *WVM*, April 1969, 19.

34. "Letters from Sponsors," *Compassion Magazine*, September–October 1983, n.p.

35. Quote from Jo Ann Stroup (International Trip Specialist, Compassion International) recalling what President Wess Stafford said when he started such trips in the 1980s. From Stroup, Personal

Interview, August 7, 2014. Compassion ran a few tours in the 1960s, picked them up again in 1986, and institutionalized them in 1989. Unbound also ran its first trip in 1989. WV ran some trips in the 1960s–1970s, but since the 1980s has opted to coordinate visits for sponsors traveling independently. They estimate that "a small fraction of 1%" do so. Tennille Bergin (WVI Director of External Communications), Personal Communication, April 25, 2019.

36. Robert A. Seiple (President of WV), "Seduced by the Numbers," *WVM*, February–March 1989, 3.

37. A Call to Prayer (Newsletter), December 18, 1959: Ministries "Call to Prayer," January–December 1959, WVIA. Although CCF rarely asked for sponsors' prayers, the pattern is not limited to evangelicals. In its early years, Unbound asked sponsors for prayers, although in more general terms (cf. evangelical "intelligent prayers"). Bob Hentzen, Letter to Dear Friend, June 4, 1982; Bob Hentzen, Letter to Dear Friend, December 3, 1982, UA.

38. "Carrying on the Vision," *WVM*, March 1982, 8–11.

39. Bornstein (*The Spirit of Development*, 60, 62) notes that in Zimbabwe in the 1990s, there was even "a Christian Witness Coordinator" for local staff. Today, many of these field officers play a key role in this prayerful system through the posts they write on sponsorship blogs.

40. Kemp to Miss Nancy Partridge, February 14, 1968, folder 7, box IIB7, CFA.

41. Giddens, *The Consequences of Modernity*, 85–88.

42. "How can we pray for you?" WV E-newsletter, September 23, 2015.

43. From emails forwarded to me by Rich Van Eaton (Sponsor and Interrelations Director), on October 7, 2013, March 23, 2014, and May 13, 2014.

44. This argument draws on work by Susan Harding, Tanya Luhrmann, and others, as outlined in Kaell, "How Distrust Begets Asking and Giving."

45. "Orphanage Manual for Sponsorship Programs," August 1960, 15, Marketing Korean Sponsor Promos, 1956–1965, WVIA.

46. Kim Jung Hi quoted in "Letters From Our Readers," *WVM*, December 1959, 14; Kim Jun Ya to Cecelia Costello, letter May 22, 1963, "Roses: Letters compiled by Cecelia Costello," KR1965.02.03.01, box Korea, CIA.

47. "One for every three," in Jae, "A Study of the Ministry," 23. Present-day statistics are estimates because organizations do not have mechanisms to track sponsor letters (unlike the children's letters, which are highly regulated). On Unbound: Laney Haake (Director of U.S. Marketing), Personal Interview, July 24, 2015; Mary Geisz (Director of Sponsor Experience), Personal Interview, July 28, 2015. Compassion: Raamses Rider (Market Research Manager USA), Personal Interview, June 30, 2014. At the same time, a multi-country study of Compassion showed that 71.8% of children reported having received a letter at some point (Wydick, Glewwe, and Rutledge, "Does International Child Sponsorship Work?," 403). There is no clear reason for the 8-point difference between this finding and Compassion's sponsor surveys.

48. Malkki, *The Need to Help*, 130.

49. Italics in original. Barthes, *Camera Lucida*, 59.

50. Mrs. C.L.R. Hoskins noted that "people often say" so in "Something about the Little People of India," *HWF*, April 1886, 257.

51. In my surveys, the first mention I found of this idea concerned Armenian child survivors of famine. N.A. "Taught to Play," *MH* 4 (April 1903): 147. On a later period, Fieldston, *Raising the World*, 125–32.

52. Kang Koo Ri was at Taegu Bo Yook Won home. His name was actually Ri Kang Yong, according to CCF. Michael Rougier, "The Little Boy Who Wouldn't Smile," *Life*, July 23, 1951, 93; National Council of Churches, "Will You Help Keep Kang Koo Ri Smiling by Giving to the United Relief Appeal?" *CC* 12 (March 1952): 323; JCC to Editor, *New York World Telegram*, September 24, 1952, and JCC to Wynn C. Fairfield, March 19, 1952, folder 10, box IB22, CFA. Other relevant examples include Save the Children Fund, "The Boy Who Never Laughs," *CC* 19 (September 1956): 1085 and (October 17, 1956): 1908; CCF, "In Korea—The Boy Who Can't Stop Crying," *CC* 23 (April 1952): 509. "The Little Boy Who Never Smiled," *Bob Pierce Pictorial 1: Going With God*, c. 1953, folder "Unfiled Pictorials 1950s," WVIA.

53. "A Famous Orphan Finds a Happy Home," *Life*, May 14, 1956, 129–30.

54. Ruth Fisher letter to V.J.R. Mills (Hong Kong office), March 8, 1954, box 3: 5—letters—1954–62, UVL.

55. JCC, "Notes for Hong Kong Office," c. July 1952, folder 1, box IB2, CFA.

56. Mr. and Mrs. F.H.J., "No Words Can Describe Blessing," *Compassion Magazine*, November–December 1966, back cover.

57. Janss, "Rules for GNs," in *Manual for World Vision Superintendents*, 42.

58. Rich Van Eaton (Sponsor and Interrelations Director), Personal Interview, June 30, 2014.

59. Becky Giovagnoni, "Proof," *Compassion Blog*, last modified April 2, 2008. https://blog.compassion.com/proof/.

60. Mayblin, *Gender, Catholicism, and Morality*, 149.

61. On these metaphors, Caldwell, *Living Faithfully*, 74–77; Halvorson, *Conversionary Sites*, 48–50.

62. Hasinoff, *Faith in Objects*, 144; Eric Reinders, *Borrowed Gods and Foreign Bodies*, 6; Christopher Wingfield, "Reassembling the London Missionary Society Collection: Experiments with Symmetrical Anthropology and the Archaeological Sensibility," in *Reassembling the Collection: Ethnographic Museums and Indigenous Agency*, ed. Sarah Byrne, Anne Clarke, and Rodney Harrison (Sante Fe, NM: School for Advanced Research Press 2013), 61–87.

63. Compassion International, *The Compassion Experience Guide for Volunteers*, PDF document, c. 2015. World Vision also runs "experience" trucks, but theirs evoke an interactive museum exhibit about hot-button issues, such as sex trafficking or AIDS.

64. On the Planned Famine: "From Our Mail," *CFCA Newsletter*, July 1988, 3; On the Compassion Sunday: Laney Haake, Personal Interview, July 24, 2015.

65. He draws on Giorgio Agamben. Redfield, "Doctors, Borders, and Life."

66. Lofton, *Oprah*, 86–89.

67. Willis, "It Smells Like a Thousand Angels Marching," 327.

68. Brenneman, *Homespun Gospel*, 139.

69. For example, South Korea in the 1950s and Zimbabwe under Mugabe in the 1990s. See Kim, *Adopted Territory*, 47, 69, 71, 74; Oh, *To Save the Children of Korea*, 54; Bornstein, "Rituals Without Final Acts," 87; Wydick, Glewwe, and Rutledge, "Does International Child Sponsorship Work?," 402. The view that humanitarian work is apolitical is prominent in Christian NGOs, but it is also a basic assumption in the development sector, as James Ferguson underlined in his classic *The Anti-Politics Machine*.

70. Scholars of U.S. evangelicalism have explored these ideas in depth (Emerson and Smith, *Divided by Faith*; Perry, *Growing God's Family*, 215). I found this view characteristic of political/social conservatives, whether or not they were "evangelical" per se—but people who self-identified as born-again Christians did make up the majority in that camp.

71. Sontag, *Regarding the Pain of Others*, 102.

72. Address by Miss Classon in *Minutes of Public Meetings N.H. Br. Of W.B.M. Nov. 12 1872–Dec 11 1883*, entry on July 9, 1874, folder 1, box 4, series 2, WBMR. On similar ideas among U.S. Catholics: Fr. Paul de Fresonora, Letter extract in *Annals of the Holy Childhood* 111 (March 1873): 15–17. Special Collections, UNDA.

73. Cousin Alice, "The Story of Leila," *HWF*, February 1878, 188–89; Rev. James Smith, "Industrial Training in India," *MH* 4 (April 1900): 168–72.

74. Leibniz in Campbell, *Romantic Ethic*, 113–14.

75. Carl F. H. Henry, "Grief, Grace, and Grist," *WVM*, April 1976, 16–17.

76. Morton, *Hyperobjects*, 74, 152–53.

77. Caldwell, *Living Faithfully*, 19.

INTERLUDE: RIZAL CRUZ AND CAROL MILLHOUSE

1. I am taking some poetic license: It was Carol, not Rizal, who said these words when talking about her motivation to sponsor a subsequent child in Uganda.

2. Grandmother in Tagalog.

3. Carol thought that Pastor Abraham started the orphanage, however Rizal identified it as run by "Felice Lipsy" from Texas. A quick Google search confirmed that Phyllis Livesay, a graduate of

Oklahoma's Rhema Bible Training College (founded by Assemblies of God preacher Kenneth Hagin), started the orphanage in 1983. Today, she is the pastor emerita of Christian Faith Center, an independent Pentecostal church in Texas. "History," http://christianfaithcenter.church/our-history/.

4. *Barangay* is an administrative region (e.g., a district). *Pasol* is a fishing line.

5. Carol gave the globe to Rizal, but her time zone prayers were actually for the child she now sponsors in Uganda.

6. According to Carol, Evelyn and Abraham wrote this in a letter to her (rather than saying it over the phone). Though it is hard to imagine they said he was literally starving, since he was still living with his grandmother and attending Pastor Abraham's church.

7. Although neither one used this exact phrasing, both told me that they felt God during the call.

8. Evelyn had just died at this point, but his grandmother actually died in c. 2003 when he was still in touch with Carol.

9. She started writing in November 2015, two months after Rizal's Facebook message, but I have shifted the timeline a bit so I could talk more about their relationship at this stage.

10. "The God Who Hears," November 2015. Provided courtesy of Carol.

CHAPTER 7: SYNCHRONY AND TERRITORY

1. "Eyes to See," *WVM*, April 1960, back cover, BGEA.

2. Rosina Schmucker, "Meditation at Midnight," *Arabah Rejoice*, August 15, 2016. Accessed August 22, 2018. https://arabahrejoice.com/2016/08/15/meditation-at-midnight/.

3. Harvey, *The Condition of Postmodernity*; Giddens, *The Consequences of Modernity*, 14–15. Jonathan Xavier Inda and Renato Rosaldo, "Tracking Global Flows," in *The Anthropology of Globalization: A Reader* [2002], 2nd edition, ed. Jonathan Xavier Inda and Renato Rosaldo (Hoboken, NJ: Wiley-Blackwell, 2008), 30–35.

4. Durkheim, *The Elementary Forms*, 10–11.

5. Coleman, "Only (Dis-)Connect," 381, 385; Robbins, *Becoming Sinners*, 175.

6. An example of pastors' role is O'Neill, *City of God*, 181–82.

7. Jennifer L. Roberts, "Introduction: Seeing Scale," in *Scale*, ed. Roberts (Chicago: University of Chicago Press, 2016), 22. Eriksen, *Overheating*, 28–29, 132–33; Tsing, *Friction*, 58 and "The Global Situation," 327.

8. MacKendrick, *The Matter of Voice*, 71.

9. Luther quoted in Keane, *Christian Moderns*, 181, n.1; 190; Council of Trent in Mladen Dolar, *A Voice and Nothing More* (Cambridge, MA: MIT Press, 2006), 49; Erben, *A Harmony of the Spirits*, 10–11, 17–18, 103.

10. Beaver, "The Concert for Prayer," 425–26; Chaney, *The Birth of Missions*, 156–57.

11. Edwards, *An Humble Attempt To Promote Explicit Agreement And Visible Union Among God's People in Extraordinary Prayer, for the Revival of Religion and the Advancement of Christ's Kingdom on Earth* (Boston: D. Hinchman, 1747). Available at http://name.umdl.umich.edu/N04757.0001.001.

12. The initial concerts were aimed at those the Scottish ministers considered "brethren . . . within the British Dominions" (Edwards, *An Humble Attempt*, 24). Shortly after its founding in 1795, the London Missionary Society introduced the first large-scale concert, which reportedly included groups in "Holland, Switzerland, Germany, America, India, Africa, and wherever there are any missionaries from the Societies in England." Beaver, "The Concert for Prayer," 425–26; Chaney, *The Birth of Missions*, 156–57; Andrew, *Rebuilding the Christian Commonwealth*, 86. Although concerts of prayer are often related to Christian globalism, they can have local goals (e.g., Elisha, "The Time and Place for Prayer").

13. There was some question about whether participants could engage in "secret prayer" (at the same time, but alone). Early Scottish promoters concluded that it was possible, but visible union in "social prayer" was far preferable. Edwards, *An Humble Attempt*, 17–18.

14. Chaney, *The Birth of Missions*, 68.

15. Samuel Worcester to Nott, Hall, Newell, March 20, 1815; Jeremiah Evarts to Nott, Hall, Newell, April 17, 1815, ABC 8.1, vol. 4, ABCFM; Also, Worcester, "Report of the Prudential Committee,"

MH, vol. 17, no. 1 (January 1821): 8–9. "Belt the world" in Gertrude Howe, "Notes from Abroad," *HWF*, April 1876, 234. Hill, *The World Their Household*, 81–82; Beaver, "The Concert for Prayer," 427. I focus on Protestants, since this tradition is the source of sponsorship organizations' concerts of prayer. Catholics organized "unions of prayer" in this era to unite laypeople for causes, including the conversion of heathen, but such "unions" did not suggest a shared time or day upon which to pray, as far as I know. Hickey, "The Society for the Propagation of the Faith," 3 n.5, 13; Cf. Wemyss Brown, "Unions of Prayer," *The Catholic Encyclopedia*, vol. 15 (New York: Robert Appleton, 1912). Online, accessed December 30, 2014.

16. Mrs. J. T. Gracey, "A World Missionary Conference," *HWF*, April 1888, 269. Initially, the concerts' role in spreading God's Kingdom was not linked to converting non-Christians. Writing before the evangelical missionary push, Edwards (*An Humble Attempt*, 47) assumed that, as the number of "saints" (Puritans) increased in proportion with the general population, they would fan out to inhabit "every nation" and thus fulfill scriptural prophecy.

17. Beaver, *American Protestant Women*, 159–61; Kenny, "The World Day of Prayer."

18. Mollie S. Pilcher, "Northwestern Branch: Helping Our Medical Education Fund by the Sale of Photographs," *HWF*, January 1880, 162–63.

19. First quote: Mrs. S. L. Keen, "In Peking," *HWF*, March 1894, 273; Second Quote: Ella Johnson, "Heathen Wedding at Hok Chiang," *HWF*, February 1892, 192–93; Third quote: Anna Vanzandt Bing, "Music in Missions," *HWF*, June 1895, 343–44. I am inspired by work on soundscapes, especially by Brian Larson, Charles Hirshkind, and Isaac Weiner. Other work helpfully notes how in the nineteenth-century, U.S. voice training—including performing choral hymnody—was a method to aspire to full moral citizenship. Ashon T. Crawley, *Blackpentecostal Breath: The Aesthetics of Possibility* (New York: Fordham University Press, 2017), 140; Mark Smith, *Listening to Nineteenth Century America* (Chapel Hill: University of North Carolina Press, 2001), 10.

20. Mrs. S. L. Keen, "In Peking," *HWF*, March 1894, 273.

21. Cunningham, *Children of the Poor*, 41–42. Also, Lloyd, *Charity and Power*, 40.

22. Parenthesis in original. Goh, "Hillsong and Megachurch Practice," 296.

23. She was at the Weirs beach camp meeting. L.A.A. "New England Branch," *HWF*, October 1887: 97–98.

24. On Mrs. Dr. Hibbard of Clifton Springs, see Frances J. Decker, "New York Branch," *HWF*, October 1884, 86.

25. Edwards, *An Humble Attempt*, 17–18; Beaver, "The Concert for Prayer," 423–24; Chaney, *The Birth of Missions*, 68. See note 13.

26. Csordas, "Somatic Modes."

27. Italics and parentheses in original. Armin Gesswein, "Powerful Prayer Principles," February 1980, International Intercessors Mailing, n.p., WVIA. For more see Kaell, "Worshipping in Concert with the World," *Journal of Modern American History* 1, no. 2 (2018): 277–82.

28. They model it on the non-stop "prayer watch" that Moravians instituted in 1727 to unite their missionary outposts. It overlaps significantly with the concerts of prayers that developed shortly after. Sebastian Schüler, "Unmapped Territories: Discursive Networks and the Making of Transnational Religious Landscapes in Global Pentecostalism," *PentecoStudies* 7, no. 1 (2008): 55–60. N.A. "24–7 Prayer: Reviving the Church, Reviving the Culture," accessed November 11, 2018. https://www.24-7prayer.com/.

29. Detailed in David Bryant, *With Concerts of Prayer: Christians Join for Spiritual Awakening and World Evangelization*, Rev. ed. (Grand Rapids, MI: Baker, 1988) and replicated on numerous websites.

30. Sponsorship organizations did not normally tour children before the 1950s. A notable exception is the NER's fund-raising tours in the 1920s with Zadi Gannaway, an Armenian child adopted by missionaries. Today, Compassion organizes promotional tours featuring adults who were sponsored and now live in the United States. "Mediated spaces" from Elisha, "Saved by a Martyr," 1070–1071.

31. Documents in folder 9, box IIB5, CFA. On WV, see Woo, "Imagining Kin," 32, 36.

32. Bob Pierce, "A Child Worships," *WVM*, May 1960, 12; "Our God Is Different," *WVM*, June 1962, 9.

33. "All the Children of the World," *WVM*, August–September 1957, 3.

34. Woo, "Imagining Kin," 36. Woo views WV tours as "align[ing] the children with Christianity and in doing so further[ing] scripts of their Americanization." By contrast, I view these as *Christian*

scripts—first promoted by Korean Protestants (affiliated with churches and institutions that had arrived largely via U.S. missionaries)—that not surprisingly aligned with broader American scripts. Regarding the repertoires above, Old Black Joe was not a spiritual but mimicked the style.

35. She is writing a century before, which reminds us of the longevity of such techniques. Mrs. J. L. Hauser, "Missionary Music," *HWF*, April 1884, 235–37.

36. McAlister, "What Is Your Heart For?," 872–74. On a related STM experience, McAlister, *The Kingdom of God*, 244.

37. Buchanan quoted in *In Amazing Ways, Love Transcends Ocean Barriers*, Pamphlet, 1965: n.p., USA1965.01.05.05, folder 1965–76, box USA, CIA; Edith Wiebe, "Hear Orphan Choir" in "Letters From Our Readers," *WVM*, October 1962, 14.

38. *Korean Study Plan*, booklet, 1970, p. 6, folder 1970: Internal documents, box USA, CIA.

39. There were a number of reasons: the Korean government began to complain that the groups portrayed their country as underdeveloped; it became harder to secure visas for the underage singers; and the choirs no longer fit sponsorship organizations' new ethos that emphasized the role of families and communities.

40. Quote above from World Help, "Children of the World," accessed June 7, 2017, https://worldhelp .net/children-of-the-world/. "FAQS," *His Little Feet*. http://hislittlefeet.org/choir/faqs/

41. This and the quote above from International Children's Choir, "About the ICC," accessed June 6, 2017. http://internationalchildrenschoir.com/.

42. Watoto African Children's Choir, "About," accessed June 7, 2017. https://www.watoto.com/about /history/.

43. "31 Days of Prayer for Your Sponsored Child," *Compassion International*, accessed May 29, 2017. http://www.compassion.com/get-involved/31-days-of-prayer-for-children.htm.

44. Coleman, "Constructing the Globe," 197–98.

45. Berlant, *The Female Complaint*, viii.

46. Oosterbaan, "Virtually Global," 70. A similar feeling often pervades conferences or other events where Christians of many backgrounds come together, for example in O'Neill, *City of God*, 170–97; Coleman, "Only (Dis-)Connect," 375; Wuthnow, *Boundless Faith*, 205.

47. N.A. (likely Larry Ward), "He Watered the Seed," *WVM*, October 1959, back cover.

48. Hutchison (*Errand to the World*, 130) wryly noted that SVM missionary maps in this period showed arrows departing "seemingly from Des Moines" to the world.

49. From the Holy Childhood Association, through which Catholics supported infants abroad (without an exchange of letters). Rev. Wm. F. Stadelman, *The Association of the Holy Childhood History of the American Branch 1846–1922* (Pittsburgh, PA: The Colonial Press, c. 1923), 20, folder 73: 2544, Association of the Holy Childhood Annual Reports, Francis P. Clark: Collection PFCL, NDUA.

50. Hancock, "Short-Term Youth Mission," 165. Among charismatics/Pentecostals, maps are incorporated into "spiritual warfare." McAlister, "The Militarization of Prayer"; Holvast, *Spiritual Mapping*.

51. Appadurai's 1996 revision of Benedict Anderson's thesis is often seen as emblematic; it posited global scapes as the new "imagined worlds" that surpassed an older order of nation-states. Above I am referring to Jonathan Z. Smith, *Map Is Not Territory* (Chicago: Chicago University Press, 1978).

52. Laura Briggs, Gladys McCormick, and J. T. Way, "Transnationalism: A Category of Analysis," *American Quarterly* 60, no. 3 (2008): 627.

53. Morton, *Hyperobjects*, 32.

54. Viaene, "International History," 596; Tsing, *Friction*, 216.

55. Malkki, "Citizens of Humanity," 43.

56. Sponsors did talk about children in India or China and such, but mission stations (or regions) played a more prominent role in mapping. Dunch, "Beyond Cultural Imperialism," 320; Conroy-Krutz, *Christian Imperialism*, 48.

57. Frank Ineson to Intercessors, November 1974 and February 1975, folder "Ministries Int. Intercessors, January-December 74," WVIA. It was part of WV's MARC project. See McAlister, "The Global Conscience," 1205.

58. Referring to Mark 11:17. Norval Hadley, "Why Pray for a Country," February 1983, folder "Ministries Int. Intercessors, January-August 83," WVIA.

59. "Patchiness" in Inda and Rosaldo, "Tracking Global Flows," 30. Ferguson, *Global Shadows*, 379.
60. Hatje, "Revivalists Abroad," 68.
61. Csordas, "Mobility," 134, 141.
62. Coleman, "Charismatic Christianity," 254; O'Neill, *City of God*, 187–91; Frederick, "Neo-Pentecostalism" and *Colored Television*; Daswani, "The Globalization of Pentecostalism."
63. O'Neill, *City of God*, 176.
64. Not all sponsors addressed this issue, and I omit responses that were unique to one individual. On economy/trade (Catholics 15%; Evangelicals 21%); "have/have nots" (Catholics 23%; Evangelicals 12%); cultural affinity (Catholics 8%; Evangelicals 21%); environment (Catholics 0%; Evangelicals 17%). I am not convinced that the last category says anything about "Catholic" and "evangelical" differences. It may be a symptom of the fact that most Catholic sponsors were older.
65. Based on McAlister, "What Is Your Heart For?" 888.
66. Coleman, "Only (Dis-)Connect," 387; Kaplan, *Anarchy of Empire*, 211.
67. Bakker, *Sister Churches*, 51. In contrast to Unbound, only 10% of the Compassion sponsors I interviewed supported children in Latin America. Their sponsorships were more widespread globally, although mainly concentrated in Africa (nearly 40%, especially in Rwanda), and Haiti and the Philippines (about 12%, respectively). These patterns converge on evangelical networks and humanitarian hotspots.
68. Bialecki, "Angels and Grass," 704. Anthropological studies of global trends focus on evangelical or Pentecostal congregations; a few well-known examples studied by anthropologists include Word of Life (Sweden), El Shaddai (Guatemala and the Philippines, respectively), International Central Gospel Church (Ghana), Igreja Universal do Reino de Deus (Brazil), and Hillsong (Australia).
69. McAlister, *The Kingdom of God*, 144–58; Hancock, "Short-Term Youth Mission Practice," 162; McAlister, "Globalization and the Religious Production of Space," 252; Agnew, "Religion and Geopolitics," 183–91; Ju Hui Judy Han, "Reaching the Unreached in the 10/40 Window: The Missionary Geoscience of Race, Difference and Distance," in *Mapping the End Times: American Evangelical Geopolitics and Apocalyptic Visions*, ed. by T. Sturm (Burlington, VT: Ashgate, 2010); Michael A. Rynkiewich, "Corporate Metaphors and Strategic Thinking: The 10/40 Window in the American Evangelical Worldview," *Missiology* 25, no. 2 (2007): 217–41. On domestic/foreign as organizing metaphors and spheres of activity: Kaplan, *Anarchy of Empire*, 31.
70. Coleman, "Only (Dis-)Connect," 373.
71. This is certainly not the only way. For example, O'Neill (*City of God*, 170) describes El Shaddai's map room, which contains a wall map marking immensity (the world), the millennial (Israel), and the particular (Guatemalan church plants). By facing different directions as they pray, congregants move rapidly from immensity to the particular. Also Coleman, "Constructing the Globe," 192.
72. Italics in original. Barthes, *The Eiffel Tower*, 9–10. Although admittedly Barthes emphasized vision in this regard, he did not completely do away with sensation ("euphoria") or object materiality. He therefore called the view from on high a "concrete abstraction."
73. Ho, "Situating Global Capitalisms," 68–96. On pastors, see Frédéric Dejean, "Evangelical and Pentecostal Churches in Montreal and Paris: Between Local Territories and Global Networks," in *The Changing World Religion Map: Sacred Places, Identities, Practices and Politics*, ed. by Stanley D. Brunn, 1678–81 (New York: Springer, 2015); O'Neill, *City of God*, 179–81, 197; Oosterbaan, "Virtually Global," 66.
74. Coleman, "Only (Dis-)Connect," 375.
75. Amy DeRogatis, *Moral Geography: Maps, Missionaries, and the American Frontier* (New York: Columbia University Press, 2003), 33.
76. "Mapping Affect" in Bandak, "The Social Life of Prayers," 7. Webster, "Praying for Salvation"; Coleman, "Constructing the Globe." Although the point is a bit different, I am inspired by Massey, "Power-Geometry."
77. Rather than give my interlocutors a checkbox survey (e.g., with "travel" as an option), I asked them whether they viewed the world as interconnected and, if so, how. I then coded their responses thematically. The numbers listed are averages. "Cosmic" ties included the most variation: 72% of Catholics talked about "one body in Christ" and one Creator; 58% of mainline Protestants talked

about one Creator, as did 29% of evangelicals (always more pessimistic about human interconnections). In this last group, 17% also discussed connections to 'persecuted Christians.' For more on this trend among evangelicals, see Castelli, "Praying for the Persecuted Church," 1–31; McAlister, *The Kingdom of God*, 159–74; Elisha, "Saved by a Martyr," 1056–80; Wuthnow, *Boundless Faith*, 158–61.

78. Peggy Levitt, *Transnational Villagers* (Berkeley: University of California Press, 2001), 11.

79. Campbell, "Understanding the Relationship between Religion Online and Offline," 80.

80. Coleman, *The Globalisation of Charismatic Christianity*, 177.

81. Garbin, "Global Prayers in Global Cities."

82. "Does My Sponsored Child Know My Name?," posted July 30, 2014. https://www.youtube.com /watch?v=yF2DaXkG0_c; "How Many Children Will Be Sponsored Online Today?," Compassion website, https://www.compassion.com/become-a-sponsor-dashboard/; "Joyful Songs," Compassion, https://www.compassion.com/kids-magazine/joyful-noise-extras.htm. All accessed July 27, 2018.

83. Jenkins, *Convergence Culture*, 121–22.

84. Eisenlohr, "Introduction," 3.

85. Shaina Moats, "What Should I Do if My Sponsored Child Contacts Me Via Facebook?," June 7, 2010. Accessed July 27, 2018. https://blog.compassion.com/what-should-i-do-if-my-sponsored-child -contacts-me-via-facebook/.

CONCLUSION

1. This pattern by no means includes all Christian scholars, though there are a number of prominent examples. Among them, I mentioned historian Mark Noll in a previous footnote, who writes, "As a believer, I ascribe both the spread and vitality of Christianity around the world to forces intrinsic to the faith itself." Highly respected evangelical scholars in a similar vein include Andrew Walls and Lamin Sanneh. I am not the first one to point this out, but it deserves more recognition. See Oliver et al., "Special Issue," 1034.

2. Tsing, "The Global Situation," 332.

3. Appadurai, *Modernity at Large*, 36.

4. Fieldston, *Raising the World*; O'Neill, "Left Behind."

5. Tisa Wenger, "Global Evangelicalism Unbound," *The Immanent Frame*, September 13, 2018. https://tif .ssrc.org/2018/09/13/global-evangelicalism-unbound/; Halvorson, *Conversionary Sites*, 56–57.

6. Wuthnow, *Boundless Faith*, 7.

7. U.S. Americans gave an estimated $22.03 billion internationally in 2016. Although this includes corporate and "in-kind" giving, more than 72% of overall U.S. charitable giving is by individuals. "Giving USA 2017: Total Charitable Donations Rise to New High of $390.05 Billion," *Giving USA*, June 12, 2017. Accessed January 22, 2018. https://givingusa.org/giving-usa-2017-total-charitable -donations-rise-to-new-high-of-390-05-billion/.

8. "Capacity" alludes to Puar's "capacity for capacity" in chapter 4. Also see the discussion of the Compassion Experience in chapter 6.

9. Jenkins in Wuthnow, *Boundless Faith*, 27.

10. Coleman, "Only (Dis-) Connect," 368.

11. For example, in chapter 3. Also Curtis, "Popular Media," 1057.

12. Morton, *Hyperobjects*, 1–24.

SELECTED BIBLIOGRAPHY

Ahmed, Sara. "Collective Feelings. Or the Impression Left by Others." *Theory, Culture, Society* 20, no. 1 (2004): 25–42.

Andrew, Donna T. *Philanthropy and Police: London Charity in the Eighteenth Century.* Princeton, NJ: Princeton University Press, 1989.

Aoki, Shin. "Singing Exoticism: A Historical Anthropology of the G.I. Songs 'China Night' and 'Japanese Rumba.'" *Journal of American History* 103, no. 4 (2017): 943–55.

Appadurai, Arjun. *Modernity at Large: Cultural Dimensions of Globalization.* Minneapolis: Minnesota University Press, 1996.

———. "The Ghost in the Financial Machine." *Public Culture* 23, no. 3 (2011): 517–39.

———. *The Future as Cultural Fact: Essays on the Global Condition.* London/New York: Verso Books, 2013.

Appiah, Kwame Anthony. *My Father's House: Africa in the Philosophy of Culture.* Oxford: Oxford University Press, 1992.

Asad, Talal. "Ethnographic Representation, Statistics and Modern Power." *Social Research* 61, no. 1 (1994): 55–88.

Bakker, Janet Kragt. *Sister Churches: American Congregations and Their Partners Abroad.* New York: Oxford University Press, 2014.

Bandak, Andreas. "The Social Life of Prayers—Introduction." *Religion* 47, no. 1 (2017): 1–18.

Barber, Benjamin R. *Jihad vs. McWorld: How Globalism and Tribalism Are Reshaping the World.* New York: Ballantine Books, 1996.

Barnett, Michael. *Empire of Humanity: A History of Humanitarianism.* Ithaca, NY: Cornell University Press, 2011.

Barthes, Roland. *The Eiffel Tower and Other Mythologies.* Translated by Richard Howard. Berkeley: University of California Press, 1997.

———. *Camera Lucida: Reflections on Photography.* Translated by Richard Howard. New York: Hill and Wang, 1981.

———. *Mythologies.* Translated by Richard Howard and Annette Lavers. New York: Hill and Wang, 2013.

Baughan, Emily. "'Every Citizen of Empire Implored to Save the Children!' Empire, Internationalism and the Save the Children Fund in Inter-War Britain." *Historical Research* 86, no. 231 (2012): 116–37.

Bays, Daniel H., and Grant Wacker, eds. *The Foreign Missionary Enterprise at Home.* Tuscaloosa: University of Alabama Press, 2003.

Beaudrillard, Jean. *Le Système Des Objets.* London: Verso, 1996.

Beaver, R. Pierce. "The Concert for Prayer for Missions: An Early Venture in Ecumenical Action." *Ecumenical Review* (1958): 420–27.

———. *American Protestant Women in World Mission: History of the First Feminist Movement in North America* [1968]. Grand Rapids, MI: William B. Eerdmans, 1980.

Becker, Adam. *Revival and Awakening: American Evangelical Missionaries in Iran and the Origins of Assyrian Nationalism.* Chicago: University of Chicago Press, 2015.

Beliso de Jesus, Aisha. "Religious Cosmopolitanisms: Media, Transnational Santería, and Travel between the United States and Cuba." *American Ethnologist* 40, no. 4 (2013): 704–20.

Bennett, Jane. *Vibrant Matter: A Political Ecology of Things.* Durham, NC: Duke University Press, 2010.

Berger, John. "Photographs of Agony [1972]." In *Selected Essays.* New York: Vintage, 2001.

Berlant, Lauren. "Introduction: Compassion (and Withholding)." In *Compassion: The Culture and Politics of an Emotion,* edited by Lauren Berlant. New York: Routledge, 2004.

———. *The Female Complaint: The Unfinished Business of Sentimentality in American Culture.* Durham, NC: Duke University Press, 2008.

———. *Cruel Optimism.* Durham, NC: Duke University Press, 2011.
Bialecki, Jon. "Between Stewardship and Sacrifice: Agency and Economy in a Southern California Charismatic Church." *Journal of the Royal Anthropological Institute* 14, no. 2 (2008): 372–90
———. "Angels and Grass: Church, Revival, and the Neo-Pauline Truth." *South Atlantic Quarterly* 109, no. 4 (2010): 695–717.
Bielo, James. "'The Mind of Christ': Financial Success, Born-Again Personhood, and the Anthropology of Christianity." *Ethnos* 72, no. 3 (2007): 315–38.
———. "Replication as Religious Practice, Temporality as Religious Problem." *History and Anthropology* 28, no. 2 (2017): 131–48.
Blanton, Anderson. *Hittin' The Prayer Bones: Materiality of Spirit in the Pentecostal South.* Chapel Hill: University of North Carolina Press, 2015.
Boltanski, Luc. *Distant Suffering: Morality, Media and Politics.* Cambridge: Cambridge University Press, 1999.
Bornstein, Erica. "Child Sponsorship, Evangelism, and Belonging in the Work of World Vision Zimbabwe." *American Ethnologist* 28, no. 3 (2001): 595–622.
———. *The Spirit of Development: Protestant NGOs, Morality, and Economics in Zimbabwe.* New York: Routledge, 2003.
———. "Rituals Without Final Acts: Prayer and Success in World Vision Zimbabwe's Humanitarian Work." In *The Limits of Meaning: Case Studies in the Anthropology of Christianity*, edited by Matthew Engelke and Rodney Harrison, 85–104. New York: Berghahn Books, 2006.
Bourdieu, Pierre. *The Logic of Practice.* Stanford, CA: Stanford University Press, 1990.
Bramen, Carrie Tirado. *The Uses of Variety: Modern Americanism and the Quest for National Distinctiveness.* Cambridge, MA: Harvard University Press, 2000.
Brenneman, Todd M. *Homespun Gospel: The Triumph of Sentimentality in Contemporary American Evangelicalism.* New York: Oxford University Press, 2014.
Briggs, Laura. *Somebody's Children: The Politics of Transracial and Transnational Adoption.* Durham, NC: Duke University Press, 2012.
Brouwer, Steve, Paul Gifford, and Susan Rose. *Exporting the American Gospel: Global Christian Fundamentalism.* London: Routledge, 1996.
Brumberg, Joan Jacobs. "The Ethnological Mirror: American Evangelical Women and Their Heathen Sisters, 1870–1910." In *Women and the Structure of Society*, edited by Jo Ann McNamara and Barbara Harris, 109–28. Durham, NC: Duke University Press, 1984.
Bunge, Marcia J., ed. *The Child in Christian Thought.* Grand Rapids, MI: William B. Eerdmans, 2001.
Burman, Erica. "Innocents Abroad: Western Fantasies of Childhood and the Iconography of Emergencies." *Disasters* 18, no. 3 (1994): 238–53.
Caldwell, Melissa. *Living Faithfully in an Unjust World: Compassionate Care in Russia.* Berkeley: University of California Press, 2016.
Campbell, Colin. *The Romantic Ethic and the Spirit of Modern Consumerism* [1987]. Great Britain: Alcuin Academics, 2005.
Campbell, Heidi. "Understanding the Relationship between Religion Online and Offline in a Networked Society." *Journal of the American Academy of Religion* 80, no. 1 (2012): 64–93.
Carrier, James G. "Introduction." In *Ethical Consumption: Social Value and Economic Practice*, edited by James G. Carrier and Peter G. Luetchford. New York: Berghahn Books, 2012.
Carson, Penelope. *The East India Company and Religion, 1698–1858.* Woodbridge, UK: Boydell Press, 2012.
Carsten, Janet, ed. *Cultures of Relatedness: New Approaches to the Study of Kinship.* Cambridge: Cambridge University Press, 2000.
Cartwright, Lisa. *Moral Spectatorship: Technologies of Voice and Affect in Postwar Representations of the Child.* Durham, NC: University of North Carolina Press, 2008.
Castelli, Elizabeth. "Praying for the Persecuted Church: US Christian Activism in the Global Arena." *Journal of Human Rights* 4, no. 3 (2005): 321–51.
Ceniza Choy, Catherine. *Global Families: A History of Asian International Adoption in America.* New York: New York University Press, 2013.
Certeau, Michel de. *The Practice of Everyday Life.* Translated by Steven Randall. Berkeley: University of California Press, 1984.

Chaney, Charles L. *The Birth of Missions in America*. Pasadena, CA: William Carey Library, 1976.

Chang, Derek. "Marked in Body, Mind, and Spirit: Home Missionaries and the Remaking of Race and Nation." In *Race, Nation, and Religion in the Americas*, edited by Henry Goldschmidt and Elizabeth McAlister, 133–56. New York: Oxford University Press, 2004.

Chu, Julie Y. *Cosmologies of Credit: Transnational Mobility and the Politics of Destination in China*. Durham, NC: Duke University Press, 2010.

Clifford, James. *Routes: Travel and Translation in the Late Twentieth Century*. Cambridge, MA: Harvard University Press, 1997.

Coleman, Simon. "Charismatic Christianity and the Dilemmas of Globalization." *Religion* 28 (1998): 245–56.

———. *The Globalisation of Charismatic Christianity: Spreading the Gospel of Prosperity*. Cambridge: Cambridge University Press, 2000.

———. "Constructing the Globe: A Charismatic Sublime?" In *Traveling Spirits: Migrants, Markets and Mobilities*, edited by Gertrud Hüwelmeier and Kristina Krause, 186–202. London: Routledge, 2009.

———. "Only (Dis-)Connect: Pentecostal Global Networking as Revelation and Concealment." *Religions* 4 (2013): 367–390.

Comaroff, John, and Jean Comaroff. *Millennial Capitalism and the Culture of Neoliberalism*. Durham, NC: Duke University Press, 2001.

Conroy-Krutz, Emily. *Christian Imperialism: Converting the World in the Early American Republic*. Ithaca, NY: Cornell University Press, 2015.

Corrigan, John. *Business of the Heart: Religion and Emotion in the Nineteenth Century*. Berkeley: University of California Press, 2002.

Corsín Jiménez, Alberto. "Trust in Anthropology." *Anthropology* 1, no. 12 (2011): 177–96.

Crapanzano, Vincent. "Reflections on Hope as a Category of Social and Psychological Analysis." *Cultural Anthropology* 18 (2003): 3–32.

Crowley, John E. "The Sensibility of Comfort." *American Historical Review* 104, no. 3 (1999): 759–71.

Csordas, Thomas J. "Somatic Modes of Attention." *Cultural Anthropology* 8, no. 2 (1993): 135–56.

———. *Transnational Transcendence: Essays on Religion and Globalization*. Berkeley: University of California Press, 2009.

———. "Mobility: A Global Geography of the Spirit Among Catholic Charismatic Communities." In *The Anthropology of Global Pentecostalism and Evangelicals*, edited by Simon Coleman and Rosalind Hackett. New York: New York University Press, 2015.

Cunningham, Hugh. *Children of the Poor: Representations of Childhood since the Seventeenth Century*. Oxford: Blackwell, 991.

Curtis, Heather. "Depicting Distant Suffering: Evangelicals and the Politics of Pictorial Humanitarianism in the Age of American Empire." *Material Religion* 8, no. 2 (2012): 154–83.

———. "Popular Media and the Global Expansion of American Evangelicalism in an Imperial Age." *Journal of American Studies* 51 (2017): 1043–67.

———. *Holy Humanitarians: American Evangelicals and Global Aid*. Cambridge, MA: Harvard University Press, 2018.

Curtis, Susan. *A Consuming Faith: The Social Gospel and Modern American Culture*. Columbia: University of Missouri Press, 1992.

Da Silva, Denise Ferreira. *Toward a Global Idea of Race*. Minneapolis: University of Minnesota Press, 2007.

Daston, Lorraine. *Classical Probability in the Enlightenment*. Princeton, NJ: Princeton University Press, 1988.

Daswani, Girish. "The Globalization of Pentecostalism and the Limits of Globalization." In *The Globalization of Pentecostalism and the Limits of Globalization*, edited by Janice Boddy and Michael Lambek, 239–54. Hoboken, NJ: Wiley Blackwell, 2013.

Desrosières, Alain. *The Politics of Large Numbers: A History of Statistical Reasoning*. Translated by Camille Nash. Cambridge, MA: Harvard University Press, 1998.

Dunch, Ryan. "Beyond Cultural Imperialism: Cultural Theory, Christian Missions, and Global Modernity." *History and Theory* 41 (2002): 301–25.

Durkheim, Émile. *The Elementary Forms of Religious Life*. Translated by Joseph Ward Swain. London: George Allen and Unwin Limited, 1915.

Edwards, Mark. "'My God and My Good Mother': The Irony of Horace Bushnell's Gendered Republic." *Religion and American Culture* 13, no. 1 (2003): 111–37.

Eisenlohr, Patrick. "Introduction: What Is a Medium? Theologies, Technologies and Aspirations." *Social Anthropology* 19, no. 1 (2011): 1–5.

Elisha, Omri. "Moral Ambitions of Grace: The Paradox of Compassion and Accountability in Evangelical Faith-Based Activism." *Cultural Anthropology* 23, no. 1 (2008): 154–89.

———. "The Time and Place for Prayer: Evangelical Urbanism and Citywide Prayer Movements." *Religion* 43, no. 3 (2013): 312–30.

———. "Personhood: Sin, Sociality and the Unbuffered Self in US Evangelicalism." In *The Anthropology of Global Pentecostalism and Evangelicalism*, edited by Simon Coleman and Rosalind Hackett, 41–56. New York: New York University Press, Press, 2015.

———. "Saved by a Martyr: Evangelical Mediation, Sanctification, and the 'Persecuted Church.'" *Journal of the American Academy of Religion* 84, no. 4 (2016): 1056–80.

Elsbree, Oliver Wendell. *The Rise of the Missionary Spirit in America 1790–1815* [1928]. Philadelphia: Porcupine Press, 1980.

Emerson, Michael O., and Christian Smith. *Divided by Faith: Evangelical Religion and the Problem of Race in America*. New York: Oxford University Press, 2000.

Engelke, Matthew. "Number and the Imagination of Global Christianity; or, Mediation and Immediacy in the Work of Alain Badiou." *South Atlantic Quarterly* 109, no. 4 (2010): 811–29.

Engell, James. *The Creative Imagination: Enlightenment to Romanticism*. Cambridge: Cambridge University Press, 1981.

Englund, Harri. "Universal Africa," *CODESRIA Bulletin* 33 (2005): 2–15.

Erben, Patrick. *A Harmony of the Spirits: Translation and Language of Community in Early Pennsylvania*. Chapel Hill: University of North Carolina Press, 2012.

Eriksen, Thomas Hylland. *Overheating: An Anthropology of Accelerated Change*. London: Pluto Press, 2016.

Fassin, Didier. *Humanitarian Reason: A Moral History of the Present*. Berkeley: University of California Press, 2011.

Faubion, James D. "Introduction: Towards an Anthropology of the Ethics of Kinship." In *The Ethics of Kinship: Ethnographic Inquiries*, edited by James D. Faubion, 1–21. London: Rowman & Littlefield, 2001.

Ferguson, James. *The Anti-Politics Machine: "Development," Depoliticization, and Bureaucratic Power in Lesotho*. Minneapolis: University of Minnesota Press, 1994.

———. *Global Shadows: Africa in the Neoliberal Order*. Durham, NC: Duke University Press, 2006.

Fieldston, Sara. *Raising the World: Child Welfare in the American Century*. Cambridge, MA: Harvard University Press, 2015.

Foucault, Michel. "Nietzsche, Genealogy, History." In *Language, Counter-Memory, Practice: Selected Essays and Interviews*, edited and translated by Donald L. Bouchard, 139–64. Ithaca, NY: Cornell University Press, 1977.

———. *The Order of Things: An Archaeology of the Human Sciences* [1970]. New York: Vintage Books, 1994.

———. *Ethics: Subjectivity and Truth*. Edited by Paul Rabinow. Translated by Robert Hurley. New York: New Press, 1997.

Frederick, Marla. "Neo-Pentecostalism and Globalization." In *The Cambridge Companion to Religious Studies*, edited by Robert A. Orsi, 380–402. Cambridge: Cambridge University Press, 2012.

———. *Colored Television: American Religion Gone Global*. Stanford, CA: Stanford University Press, 2016.

Garbin, David. "Global Prayers in Global Cities: Notes on Afro-Christian Spatiality in Atlanta and London." In *Global Prayers, Contemporary Manifestations of the Religious in the City*, edited by Jochen Becker, Katrin Klingan, and Stephen Lanz, 258–273. Baden: Lars Muller, 2013.

Giddens, Anthony. *The Consequences of Modernity*. Stanford, CA: Stanford University Press, 1990.

———. *Modernity and Self-Identity*. Cambridge: Polity Press, 1991.

Goh, Robbie B. H. "Hillsong and 'Megachurch' Practice: Semiotics, Spatial Logic and the Embodiment of Contemporary Evangelical Protestantism." *Material Religion* 4, no. 3 (2008): 284–304.

Griffith, Marie. *Born Again Bodies: Flesh and Spirit in Christianity*. Berkeley: University of California Press, 2004.

Guyer, Jane. "Prophecy and the Near Future: Thoughts on Macroeconomic, Evangelical, and Punctuated Time." *American Ethnologist* 34, no. 3 (2007): 409–21.

Hacking, Ian. "Biopower and the Avalanche of Printed Numbers." *Humanities in Society* 5, (1983): 279–95.

Halttunen, Karen. "Humanitarianism and the Pornography of Pain in Anglo-American Culture." *American Historical Review* 100, no. 2 (1995): 303–34.

Halvorson, Britt. "Woven Worlds: Material Things, Bureaucratization, and Dilemmas of Caregiving in Lutheran Humanitarianism." *American Ethnologist* 39, no. 1 (2012): 122–37.

———. *Conversionary Sites: Transforming Medical Aid and Global Christianity from Madagascar to Minnesota*. Chicago: Chicago University Press, 2018.

Hancock, Mary. "Short-Term Youth Mission Practice and the Visualization of Global Christianity." *Material Religion* 10, no. 2 (2014): 154–80.

Hann, Chris, and Keith Hart. *Economic Anthropology: History, Ethnography, Critique*. Cambridge: Polity Press, 2011.

Hannerz, Ulf. "Notes on the Global Ecumene." *Public Culture* 1, no. 2 (1989): 66–75.

Harvey, David. *The Condition of Postmodernity: An Enquiry into the Origins of Cultural Change*. Cambridge: Blackwell, 1990.

———. *A Brief History of Neoliberalism*. Oxford: Oxford University Press, 2005.

Hasinoff, Erin L. *Faith in Objects: American Missionary Expositions in the Early Twentieth Century*. New York: Palgrave Macmillan, 2011.

Hatje, Frank. "Revivalists Abroad." In *Migration and Transfer from Germany to Britain, 1660–1914*, edited by Stefan Manz, 65–80. Munich: De Gruyter, 2007.

Herman, Ellen. *Kinship by Design: A History of Adoption in the Modern United States*. Chicago: Chicago University Press, 2008.

Herzog, Jonathan P. *The Spiritual-Industrial Complex: America's Religious Battle Against Communism in the Early Cold War*. New York: Oxford University Press, 2011.

Hill, Patricia R. *The World Their Household: The American Woman's Foreign Mission Movement and Cultural Transformation, 1870–1920*. Ann Arbor: University of Michigan Press, 1984.

Ho, Karen. "Situating Global Capitalisms: A View from Wall Street Investment Banks." *Cultural Anthropology* 20, no. 1 (2005): 68–96.

Hollinger, David A. *Protestants Abroad: How Missionaries Tried to Change the World But Changed America*. Princeton, NJ: Princeton University Press, 2017.

Holvast, René. *Spiritual Mapping in the United States and Argentina 1989–2005*. Leiden: Brill, 2009.

Hopkins, Dwight N., et al. *Religions/Globalizations: Theories and Cases*. Durham, NC: Duke University Press, 2001.

Howell, Brian M. "Practical Belief and the Localization of Christianity: Pentecostal and Denominational Christianity in Global/Local Perspective." *Religion* 33, no. 3 (2003): 233–48.

———. *Short-Term Mission: An Ethnography of Christian Travel Narrative and Experience*. Downers Grove, IL: IVP Academic, 2012.

Howell, Signe. *The Kinning of Foreigners: Transnational Adoption in a Global Perspective*. New York: Berghahn Books, 2006.

Hulsether, Lucia. "Buying into the Dream." *Public Culture* 30, no. 3 (2018): 483–508.

Hutchison, William. *Errand to the World: American Protestant Thought and Foreign Missions*. Chicago: Chicago University Press, 1987.

Inboden, William. *Religion and American Foreign Policy, 1945–1960: The Soul of Containment*. Cambridge: Cambridge University Press, 2008.

Irwin, Julia F. *Making the World Safe: The American Red Cross and the Nation's Humanitarian Awakening*. New York: Oxford University Press, 2013.

———. "Teaching 'Americanism with a World Perspective': The Junior Red Cross in the U.S. Schools from 1917 to the 1920s." *History of Education Quarterly* 53, no. 3 (2013): 255–79.

Jenkins, Henry. *Convergence Culture: Where Old and New Media Collide*. New York: New York University Press, 2006.

Jenkins, Philip. *The Next Christendom: The Coming of Global Christianity*. New York: Oxford University Press, 2002.

Kaell, Hillary. "Renamed: The Living, the Dead, and the Global in Nineteenth-Century U.S. Christianity." *American Historical Review*, forthcoming.

———. "Immobile Global: Christian Globalism at Home in the United States." *American Anthropologist*, forthcoming.

———. "How Distrust Begets Asking and Giving in Christian Child Sponsorship." In *The Request and the Gift in Religious and Humanitarian Endeavors*, edited by Frederick Klaits, 93–116. New York: Palgrave Macmillan. 2017.

———. "Evangelist of Fragments: Doing Mite-Box Capitalism in the Late Nineteenth Century." *Church History* 86, no. 1 (2017): 86–119.

Kaplan, Amy. *Anarchy of Empire in the Making of U.S. Culture*. Cambridge, MA: Harvard University Press, 2002.

Keane, Webb. *Christian Moderns: Freedom and Fetish in the Mission Encounter*. Berkeley: University of California Press, 2007.

———. *Ethical Life: Its Natural and Social Histories*. Princeton, NJ: Princeton University Press, 2015.

Kenny, Gale L. "The World Day of Prayer: Ecumenical Churchwomen and Christian Cosmopolitanism, 1920–1946." *Religion and American Culture* 27, no. 2 (2017): 129–58.

Kim, Eleana. *Adopted Territory: Transnational Adoptees and the Politics of Belonging*. Durham, NC: Duke University Press, 2010.

King, David P. "The New Internationalists: World Vision and the Revival of American Evangelical Humanitarianism, 1950–2010." *Religions* 3 (2012): 922–49.

———. "Heartbroken for God's World: The Story of Bob Pierce, Founder of World Vision and Samaritan's Purse." In *Philanthropic Organizations: Family, Friend, Foe?*, edited by Thomas J. Davis, 71–92. Bloomington: Indiana University Press, 2013.

Klassen, Pamela. *Spirits of Protestantism: Medicine, Healing, and Liberal Christianity*. Berkeley: University of California Press, 2011.

Klein, Christina. "Family Ties and Political Obligation: The Discourse of Adoption and the Cold War Commitment to Asia." In *Cold War Constructions: The Political Culture of United States Imperialism, 1945–1966*, edited by Christian Appy,143–90. Amherst: University of Massachusetts Press, 2000.

———. *Cold War Orientalism: Asia in the Middlebrow Imagination*. Berkeley: University of California Press, 2003.

Kleinman, Arthur, and Joan Kleinman. "The Appeal of Experience: The Dismay of Images: Cultural Appropriations of Suffering in Our Times." *Daedalus* 125, no. 1 (1996): 1–23.

Kollman, Paul. *The Evangelization of Slaves and Catholic Origins in Eastern Africa*. Maryknoll, NY: Orbis, 2005.

Laqueur, Thomas W. "Bodies, Details and the Humanitarian Narrative." In *New Cultural History*, edited by Lynn Hunt, 176–204. Berkeley: University of California Press, 1989.

Lears, T. J. Jackson. *No Place of Grace: Antimodernism and the Transformation of American Culture, 1880–1920*. Chicago: University of Chicago Press, 1981.

Lefebvre, Henri. *The Production of Space*. Translated by Donald Nicholson-Smith. Cambridge, MA: Blackwell, 1991.

Lindsey, Rachel McBride. *A Communion of Shadows: Religion and Photography in Nineteenth Century America*. Chapel Hill: University of North Carolina Press, 2017.

Lloyd, Sarah. *Charity and Poverty in England, c. 1680–1820: Wild and Visionary Schemes*. Manchester: Manchester University Press, 2009.

Lofton, Kathryn. *Oprah: The Gospel of an Icon*. Berkeley: University of California Press, 2011.

Lott, Eric. *Love & Theft: Blackface Minstrelsy and the American Working Class* [1993]. New York: Oxford University Press, 2013.

Luhrmann, Tanya M. *When God Talks Back: Understanding the American Evangelical Relationship with God*. New York: Alfred A. Knopf, 2012.

Lum, Kathryn Gin. *Damned Nation: Hell in America from the Revolution to Reconstruction*. New York: Oxford University Press, 2014.

MacKendrick, Karmen. *The Matter of Voice: Sensual Soundings*. New York: Fordham University Press, 2016.

Mahmood, Saba. *Politics of Piety: The Islamic Revival and the Feminist Subject*. Princeton, NJ: Princeton University Press, 2001.

Makdisi, Ussama S. *Artillery of Heaven: American Missionaries and the Failed Conversion of the Middle East*. Ithaca, NY: Cornell University Press, 2008.

Malkki, Liisa. "Citizens of Humanity: Internationalism and the Imagined Community of Nations." *Diaspora* 3, no. 1 (1994): 41–68.

———. "Speechless Emissaries: Refugees, Humanitarianism and Dehistoricization." *Cultural Anthropology* 1, no. 3 (1996): 377–404.

———. "Children, Humanity, and the Infantilization of Peace." In *The Name of Humanity: The Government of Threat and Care*, edited by Ilana Feldman and Miriam Ticktin, 58–85. Durham, NC: Duke University Press, 2010.

———. *The Need to Help: The Domestic Arts of International Humanitarianism*. Durham, NC: Duke University Press, 2015.

Massey, Doreen. "Power-Geometry and a Progressive Sense of Place." In *Mapping the Futures: Local Cultures, Global Change*, edited by John Bird, Barry Curtis, Tim Putnam, George Robertson, and Lisa Tickner, 59–69. New York: Routledge, 1993.

Mauss, Marcel. *The Gift: The Form and Reason for Exchange in Archaic Societies* [1925]. Translated by W. D. Halls. London: Norton, 2000.

———. "Techniques of the Body [1935]." In *Techniques, Technology, and Civilization*, edited by Nathan Schlanger, 77–96. New York/Oxford: Berghahn Books, 2009.

May, Elaine Tyler. *Homeward Bound: American Families in the Cold War Era*. New York: Basic Books, 1988.

Mayblin, Maya. *Gender, Catholicism, and Morality in Brazil: Virtuous Husbands, Powerful Wives*. New York: Palgrave Macmillan, 2010.

McAlister, Elizabeth. "Globalization and the Religious Production of Space." *Journal for the Scientific Study of Religion* 44, no. 3 (2005): 249–55.

———. "The Militarization of Prayer in America: White and Native American Spiritual Warfare." *Journal of Religious and Practical Practice* 2, no. 1 (2016): 114–30.

McAlister, Melani. "What Is Your Heart For?: Affect and Internationalism in the Evangelical Public Sphere." *American Literary History* 20, no. 4 (2008): 870–95.

———. "The Global Conscience of American Evangelicalism: Internationalism and Social Concern in the 1970s and Beyond." *Journal of American Studies* 51, no. 4 (2017): 1197–1220.

———. *The Kingdom of God Has No Borders: A Global History of American Evangelicals*. New York: Oxford University Press, 2018.

McLisky, Claire, Daniel Midena, and Karen Vallgarda, eds. *Emotions and Christian Missions: Historical Perspectives*. New York: Palgrave Macmillan, 2015.

Mehta, Uday. "Liberal Strategies of Exclusion." In *Tensions of Empire: Colonial Cultures in a Bourgeois World*, edited by Frederick Cooper and Ann Laura Stoler, 59–86. Berkeley: University of California Press, 1997.

Merish, Lori. *Sentimental Materialism: Gender, Commodity Culture, and Nineteenth-Century American Literature*. Durham, NC: Duke University Press, 2000.

Meyer, Birgit. "Make a Complete Break with the Past: Memory and Post-Colonial Modernity in Ghanaian Pentecostalist Discourse." *Journal of Religion in Africa* 28, no. 3 (1998): 316–49.

———. "Aesthetics of Persuasion: Global Christianity and Pentecostalism's Sensational Forms." *South Atlantic Quarterly* 109, no. 4 (2010): 741–63.

———. "How to Capture the 'Wow': R. R. Marett's Notion of Awe and the Study of Religion." *Journal of the Royal Anthropological Institute* 22, no. 1 (2016): 7–26.

Meyer, Birgit, and Jojada Verrips. "Aesthetics." In *Key Words in Religion, Media, and Culture*, edited by David Morgan, 20–30. London: Routledge, 2008.

Miller, Daniel. *A Theory of Shopping*. Ithaca, NY: Cornell University Press, 1998.

Miller, William Ian. *The Anatomy of Disgust*. Cambridge, MA: Harvard University Press, 1997.

Miller-Davenport, Sarah. "'Their Blood Shall Not Be Shed in Vain': American Evangelical Missionaries and the Search for God and Country in Post–World War II Asia." *Journal of American History* 9, no. 4 (2013): 1109–32.

Mislin, David. *Saving Faith: Making Religious Pluralism an American Value at the Dawn of the Secular Age*. Ithaca, NY: Cornell University Press, 2015.

Modern, John Lardas. *Secularism in Antebellum America*. Chicago: University of Chicago Press, 2011.

Moeller, Susan D. *Compassion Fatigue: How the Media Sell Disease, Famine, War and Death*. New York: Routledge, 1999.

Mollering, Guido. "The Nature of Trust: From Georg Simmel to a Theory of Expectation, Interpretation and Suspension." *Sociology* 35, no. 2 (2001): 403–20.

Morgan, David. "The Ecology of Images: Seeing and the Study of Religion." *Religion and Society* 5 (2014): 83–105.

Morton, Timothy. *Hyperobjects: Philosophy and Ecology After the End of the World*. Minneapolis: University of Minnesota Press, 2013.

Moyn, Samuel. *Christian Human Rights*. Philadelphia: University of Pennsylvania Press, 2015.

Muehlebach, Andrea. *The Moral Neoliberal: Welfare and Citizenship in Italy*. Chicago: University of Chicago Press, 2012.

———. "The Catholicization of Neoliberalism." In *A Companion to the Anthropology of Religion*, edited by Janice Boddy and Michael Lambek, 507–27. New York: Wiley Blackwell, 2013.

Napolitano, Valentina. *Migrant Hearts and the Atlantic Return: Transnationalism and the Roman Catholic Church*. New York: Fordham University Press, 2016.

Ngai, Sianne. *Ugly Feelings*. Cambridge, MA: Harvard University Press, 2005.

Noll, Mark. *America's God: From Jonathan Edwards to Abraham Lincoln*. New York: Oxford University Press, 2002.

———. *The New Shape of World Christianity: How American Experience Reflects Global Faith*. Downers Grove, IL: IVP Academic, 2009.

Nurser, John S. *For All Peoples and All Nations: The Ecumenical Church and Human Rights*. Washington, DC: Georgetown University Press, 2005.

Oh, Arissa. *To Save the Children of Korea: The Cold War Origins of International Adoption*. Stanford, CA: Stanford University Press, 2015.

Okazawa-Rey, Margo. "Amerasian Children of G.I. Town: A Legacy of U.S. Militarism in South Korea." *Asian Journal of Women's Studies* 3 (1997): 71–102.

Oliver, Kendrick et al. "Exploring the Global History of American Evangelicalism Introduction." *Journal of American Studies* 51, no. 4 (2017): 1019–42.

O'Neill, Kevin L. *City of God: Christian Citizenship in Postwar Guatemala*. Berkeley: University of California Press, 2009.

———. "Beyond Broken: Affective Spaces and the Study of American Religion." *Journal of the American Academy of Religion* 81, no. 4 (2013): 1093–1116.

———. "Left Behind: Security, Salvation, and the Subject of Prevention." *Cultural Anthropology* 28, no. 2 (2013): 217.

Oosterbaan, Martijn. "Virtually Global: Online Evangelical Cartography." *Social Anthropology* 19, no. 1 (2011): 56–73.

Orsi, Robert A. *History and Presence*. Cambridge, MA: Harvard University Press, 2016.

Pandey, Gyanendra. "The Prose of Otherness." In *Subaltern Studies: Essays in Honour of Ranajit Guha*, edited by David Arnold and David Hardiman, 188–221. Delhi: Oxford University Press, 1995.

Park, Eunjin. *"White" Americans in "Black" Africa: Black and White American Methodist Missionaries in Liberia, 1820–1875*. New York: Routledge, 2001.

Perry, Samuel L. *Growing God's Family: The Global Orphan Care Movement and the Limits of Evangelical Action*. New York: New York University Press, 2017.

Phillips, Clifton Jackson. *Protestant America and the Pagan World: The First Half Century of the American Board of Commissioner for Foreign Missions, 1810–1860*. Cambridge, MA: Harvard East Asian Monographs, 1969.

Poovey, Mary. *A History of Modern Fact: Problems of Knowledge in the Sciences of Wealth and Society*. Chicago: University of Chicago Press, 1998.

Porter, Theodore M. *Trust in Numbers: The Pursuit of Objectivity in Science and Public Life*. Princeton, NJ: Princeton University Press, 1995.

Pratt, Mary Louise. *Imperial Eyes: Travel Writing and Transculturation*. London: Routledge, 1992.

Pruitt, Lisa Joy. *A Looking-Glass for Ladies: American Protestant Women and the Orient in the Nineteenth Century*. Macon, GA: Mercer University Press, 2005.

Puar, Jasbir K. *Terrorist Assemblages: Homonationalism in Queer Times*. Durham, NC: Duke University Press, 2007.

Rabinowitz, Richard. *The Spiritual Self in Everyday Life: The Transformation of Personal Religious Experience in Nineteenth-Century England*. Boston: Northeastern University Press, 1989.

Rai, Amit. *The Rule of Sympathy: Sentiment, Race, and Power, 1750–1850*. New York: Palgrave Macmillan, 2002.

Redfield, Peter. "Doctors, Borders, and Life in Crisis." *Cultural Anthropology* 20, no. 3 (2005): 328–61.

Reinders, Eric. *Borrowed Gods and Foreign Bodies: Christian Missionaries Imagine Chinese Religion*. Berkeley: University of California Press, 2004.

Robbins, Joel. *Becoming Sinners: Christianity and Moral Torment in a Papua New Guinea Society*. Berkeley: University of California Press, 2004.

Robert, Dana L. *American Women in Mission: A Social History of Their Thought and Practice*. Macon, GA: Mercer University Press, 1997.

———. "The First Globalization: The Internationalization of the Protestant Missionary Movement Between the World Wars." *International Bulletin of Missionary Research* 26, no. 2 (2002): 50–66.

Robertson, Roland, and William R. Garrett, eds. *Religion and Global Order*. New York: Paragon House, 1991.

Roof, Wade Clark, ed. *World Order and Religion*. Albany: State University of New York Press, 1991.

Rose, Lena. "Geometries of 'Global' Evangelicalism." *Global Networks* 19, no. 1 (January 2019): 86–100.

Rosenberg, Emily S. "Rescuing Women and Children." *Journal of American History* 89, no. 2 (2002): 456–65.

Rowse, Tim, and Tiffany Shellam. "The Colonial Emergence of a Statistical Imaginary." *Comparative Studies in Society and History* 55, no. 4 (2013): 922–54.

Ruble, Sarah E. *The Gospel of Freedom and Power: Protestant Missionaries in American Culture after World War II*. Chapel Hill: University of North Carolina Press, 2012.

Rudnyckyj, Daromir, and Filippo Osella. "Introduction: Assembling Market and Religious Moralities." In *Religion and the Morality of the Market*, edited by Daromir Rudnyckyj and Filippo Osella, 1–28. Cambridge: Cambridge University Press, 2017.

Scherz, China. "Let Us Make God Our Banker: Ethics, Temporality, and Agency in a Ugandan Charity Home." *American Ethnologist* 40, no. 4 (2013): 624–36.

———. "Seeking the Wound of the Gift: Recipient Agency in Catholic Charity and Kiganda Patronage." In *The Request and the Gift in Religious and Humanitarian Endeavors*, edited by Frederick Klaits, 47–64. New York: Palgrave Macmillan, 2017.

Schuller, Kyla. *The Biopolitics of Feeling: Race, Sex, and Science in the Nineteenth Century*. Durham, NC: Duke University Press, 2018.

Settje, David E. *Faith and War: How Christians Debated the Cold and Vietnam Wars*. New York: New York University Press, 2011.

Simmel, Georg. *The Philosophy of Money* [1907]. Translated by Tom Bottomore and David Frisby. London: Routledge, 1978.

Slack, Paul. *From Reformation to Improvement: Public Welfare in Early Modern England*. New York: Oxford University Press, 1999.

Sontag, Susan. *On Photography*. New York: Picador, 1977.

———. *Regarding the Pain of Others*. New York: Picador, 2004.

Stephens, Sharon. "Introduction." In *Children and the Politics of Culture*, edited by Sharon Stephens. Princeton, NJ: Princeton University Press, 1995.

Stevens, Laura M. *The Poor Indians: British Missionaries, Native Americans, and Colonial Sensibility*. Philadelphia: University of Pennsylvania Press, 2004.

Stewart, Kathleen. "Still Life." In *Intimacy*, edited by Lauren Berlant. Chicago: University of Chicago Press, 2000.

Stewart, Susan. *On Longing: Narratives of the Miniature, the Gigantic, the Souvenir, the Collection*. Baltimore, MD: Johns Hopkins University Press, 1984.

Stoler, Ann Laura. *Carnal Knowledge and Imperial Power: Race and the Intimate in Colonial Rule*. Berkeley: University of California Press, 2002.

———. "Intimidations of Empire: Predicaments of the Tactile and Unseen." In *Haunted by Empire: Geographies of Intimacy in North American History*, edited by Ann Laura Stoler, 1–22. Durham, NC: Duke University Press, 2006.

Strathern, Marilyn. "Introduction: New Accountabilities." In *Audit Cultures: Anthropological Studies in Accountability, Ethics and the Academy*, edited by Marilyn Strathern, 1–18. London: Routledge, 2000.

Swartz, David R. "Embodying the Global Soul: Internationalism and the American Evangelical Left." *Religions* 3 (2012): 887–901.

Taithe, Bertrand. "Algerian Orphans and Colonial Christianity in Algeria, 1866–1939." *French History* 20, no. 3 (2006): 240–59.

Takaki, Ronald. "The Tempest in the Wilderness: The Racialization of Savagery." *Journal of American History* 79 (1992): 892–912.

Taussig, Michael. *Defacement: Public Secrecy and the Labor of the Negative*. Stanford, CA: Stanford University Press, 1999.

Ticktin, Miriam. "Transnational Humanitarianism." *Annual Review of Anthropology* 43 (2014): 273–89.

———. "A World Without Innocence." *American Ethnologist* 44, no. 4 (2017): 577–90.

Torchin, Leshu. "Ravished Armenia: Visual Media, Humanitarian Advocacy, and the Formation of Witnessing Publics." *American Anthropologist* 108 (2006): 214–20.

Tsing, Anna L. "The Global Situation." *Cultural Anthropology* 15, no. 3 (2000): 327–60.

———. *Friction: An Ethnography of Global Connection*. Princeton, NJ: Princeton University Press, 2005.

Tweed, Thomas A. *Crossing and Dwelling: A Theory of Religion*. Cambridge, MA: Harvard University Press, 2006.

Tyrrell, Ian. *Reforming the World: The Creation of America's Moral Empire*. Princeton, NJ: Princeton University Press, 2010.

Vàsquez, Manuel A. "Studying Religion in Motion: A Networks Approach." *Method and Theory in the Study of Religion* 20, no. 2 (2008): 151–84.

Viaene, Vincent. "International History, Religious History, Catholic History: Perspectives for Cross-Fertilization (1830–1914)." *European History Quarterly* 38 (2008): 587–607.

Webster, Joseph. "Praying for Salvation: A Map of Relatedness." *Religion* 47, no. 1 (2017): 19–34.

Willis, Laurie Denyer. "'It Smells Like a Thousand Angels Marching': The Salvific Sensorium in Rio de Janeiro's Western Subúrbios." *Cultural Anthropology* 33, no. 2 (2018): 324–48.

Woo, Susie. "Imagining Kin: Cold War Sentimentalism and Korean Children's Choir." *American Quarterly* 67, no. 1 (2015): 25–53.

Wuthnow, Robert. *Boundless Faith: The Global Outreach of American Churches*. Berkeley: University of California Press, 2009.

Wydick, Bruce, Paul Glewwe, and Laine Rutledge. "Does International Child Sponsorship Work? A Six-Country Study of Impacts on Adult Life Outcomes." *Journal of Political Economy* 121, no. 2 (2013): 393–436.

Zaloom, Caitlin. "Future Knowledge." *American Ethnologist* 34, no. 3 (2007): 444–46.

———. "The Evangelical Financial Ethic: Doubled Forms and the Search for God in the Economic World." *American Ethnologist* 43, no. 2 (2016): 325–38.

Zarzycka, Marta. "Save the Child: Photographed Faces and Affective Transactions in NGO Child Sponsoring Programs." *European Journal of Women's Studies* 23, no. 1 (2016): 28–42.

Zelizer, Vivian A. *Pricing the Priceless Child: The Changing Social Value of Children*. New York: Basic Books, 1985.

Zito, Angela. "Secularizing the Pain of Footbinding in China: Missionary and Medical Stagings of the Universal Body." *Journal of the American Academy of Religion* 75, no. 1 (2007): 1–24.

Zwissler, Laurel. "Markets of the Heart: Weighing Economic and Ethical Values at Ten Thousand Villages." In *Anthropological Considerations of Production, Exchange, Vending and Tourism*, edited by Donald C. Wood, 115–35. Bingley: Emerald Publishing Limited, 2017.

INDEX

Page numbers in italics indicate illustrations.

GPSR Authorized Representative: Easy Access System Europe - Mustamäe tee
50, 10621 Tallinn, Estonia, gpsr.requests@easproject.com

www.ingramcontent.com/pod-product-compliance
Lightning Source LLC
Chambersburg PA
CBHW031401270326
41929CB00010BA/1285